Quantitative Social Science

Quantitative Social Science

An Introduction

KOSUKE IMAI

PRINCETON UNIVERSITY PRESS
Princeton and Oxford

Epigraph on page 189 from Tukey, John W., 1977, *Exploratory data analysis*. Reading, Mass: Addison-Wesley Publishing, an imprint of Pearson Education, Inc.

In the United Kingdom: Princeton University Press, 6 Oxford Street, Woodstock, Oxfordshire OX20 1TR

press.princeton.edu

ISBN 978-0-691-16703-9
ISBN (pbk.) 978-0-691-17546-1

Library of Congress Control Number 2016962298

British Library Cataloging-in-Publication Data is available

This book has been composed in Minion Pro and Univers for display
Printed on acid-free paper ∞

Typeset by Nova Techset Pvt Ltd, Bangalore, India
Printed in the United States of America

10   9   8   7   6   5   4   2   1

To Christina, Keiji, and Misaki

Contents

List of Tables

List of Figures

Preface

I decided to write this book in order to convince the next generation of students and researchers that data analysis is a powerful tool for answering many important and interesting questions about societies and human behavior. Today's societies confront a number of challenging problems, including those in economics, politics, education, and public health. Data-driven approaches are useful for solving these problems, and we need more talented individuals to work in this area. I hope that this book will entice young students and researchers into the fast-growing field of quantitative social science.

This book grew out of the two undergraduate courses I have taught at Princeton over the last several years: POL 245: Visualizing Data and POL 345: Quantitative Analysis and Politics. While teaching these courses, I realized that students need to be exposed to exciting ideas from actual quantitative social science research as early in the course as possible. For this reason, unlike traditional introductory statistics textbooks, this book features data analysis from the very beginning, using examples directly taken from published social science research. The book provides readers with extensive data analysis experience before introducing probability and statistical theories. The idea is that by the time they reach those challenging chapters, readers will understand why those materials are necessary in order to conduct quantitative social science research.

The book starts with a discussion of causality in both experimental and observational studies using the examples of racial discrimination and get-out-the-vote campaigns. We then cover measurement and prediction as two other primary goals of data analysis in social science research. The book also includes a chapter on the analysis of textual, network, and spatial data, giving readers a glimpse of modern quantitative social science research. Probability and statistical theories are introduced after these data analysis chapters. The mathematical level of the book is kept to a minimum, and neither calculus nor linear algebra is used. However, the book introduces probability and statistical theories in a conceptually rigorous manner so that readers can understand the underlying logic.

This book would not exist without support from a number of individuals. I would like to thank my colleagues at Princeton, especially those in the Dean of the College's office and the McGraw Center for Teaching and Learning, for their generous support. I was one of the first beneficiaries of the 250th Anniversary Fund for Teaching Innovation in Undergraduate Education. I thank Liz Colagiuri, Khristina Gonzalez, Lisa Herschbach, Clayton Marsh, Diane McKay, and Nic Voge, who trusted my ambitious vision of how introductory data analysis and statistics should be taught.

They allowed me to design a course at the Freshman Scholars Institute (FSI), and many of the ideas in this book were born there. The FSI is a great diversity initiative for first-generation college students, and I am proud to be a part of it. I am also grateful to Princeton University administrators for their generous support for my teaching initiatives. They include Jill Dolan, Chris Eisgruber, Dave Lee, Nolan McCarty, Debbie Prentice, and Val Smith.

I especially thank my coinstructors who helped me develop the materials included in this book. James Lo, Jonathan Olmsted, and Will Lowe made significant contributions to POL 245 taught at FSI. I was fortunate to have an amazing group of graduate students who served as teaching assistants for my courses. They include Alex Acs, Jaquilyn Waddell Boie, Will Bullock, Munji Choi, Winston Chou, Elisha Cohen, Brandon de la Cuesta, Ted Enamorado, Matt Incantalupo, Tolya Levshin, Asya Magazinnik, Carlos Velasco Rivera, Alex Tarr, Bella Wang, and Teppei Yamamoto, several of whom won teaching awards for their incredible work. Evan Chow and Hubert Jin contributed to the creation of **swirl** exercises. Other students, including Alessia Azermadhi, Naoki Egami, Tyler Pratt, and Arisa Wada, helped me develop materials at various stages of this book project.

During the production phase of this book, the following individuals gave me detailed comments and suggestions that have significantly improved the presentation: Jaquilyn Waddell Boie, Lauren Konken, Katie McCabe, Grace Rehaut, Ruby Shao, and Tyler Simko. Without their contributions, this book would have looked quite different. I also thank at least several hundred students at Princeton and many other institutions who used an earlier version of this book. Their extensive feedback has helped me revise the manuscript. I also thank Neal Beck, Andy Hall, Ryan Moore, and Marc Ratkovic for their comments on earlier versions of the manuscript. I wish to thank Eric Crahan and Brigitte Pelner of Princeton University Press for guiding me through the publication process.

Several people had a significant impact on how this book is written. My graduate school adviser, Gary King, taught me everything, from how to conduct quantitative social science research to how to teach statistics to social scientists. Although more than a decade has passed since I left Harvard, Gary has always been someone to whom I can turn for advice and support. Three of my Princeton colleagues—Christina Davis, Amaney Jamal, and Evan Liebenman—formed the team "old dogs learning new tricks" and took the three-course graduate quantitative methods sequence. Their willingness to patiently sit through my lectures gave me new motivation. They also set a great example for young researchers that even senior scholars should continue learning. Interactions with them during those classes gave me new insights about how statistical methods should be taught.

My deepest gratitude goes to my family. My mother, Fumiko, my father, Takashi, and my brother, Mineki, have always encouraged me to pursue my dreams regardless of what they are. Although we now live on opposite sides of the globe, every day I feel lucky to have such a wonderful family. My parents-in-law, Al and Carole Davis, have been supportive of me since the mid-1990s when I first came to the United States without being able to speak or understand much English. They have always made me feel at home and part of their family. My two wonderful children, Keiji and Misaki, have been a source of joy and happiness. However difficult my work is, their beautiful smiles remind me what the most important things are in my life. Finally, I dedicate this book to my wife, Christina, who has been the best partner and a constant source of inspiration for more than two decades. Christina encouraged me to write this book, and as always I am glad to have followed her advice. Even though one never observes counterfactuals, I can say with confidence that I have lived and will continue to live life to the fullest because of our partnership.

Kosuke Imai
November 2016
Princeton, New Jersey

Quantitative Social Science

Introduction

Quantitative social science is an interdisciplinary field encompassing a large number of disciplines, including economics, education, political science, public policy, psychology, and sociology. In quantitative social science research, scholars analyze data to understand and solve problems about society and human behavior. For example, researchers examine racial discrimination in the labor market, evaluate the impact of new curricula on students' educational achievements, predict election outcomes, and analyze social media usage. Similar data-driven approaches have been taken up in other neighboring fields such as health, law, journalism, linguistics, and even literature. Because social scientists directly investigate a wide range of real-world issues, the results of their research have enormous potential to directly influence individual members of society, government policies, and business practices.

Over the last couple of decades, quantitative social science has flourished in a variety of areas at an astonishing speed. The number of academic journal articles that present empirical evidence from data analysis has soared. Outside academia, many organizations—including corporations, political campaigns, news media, and government agencies—increasingly rely on data analysis in their decision-making processes. Two transformative technological changes have driven this rapid growth of quantitative social science. First, the Internet has greatly facilitated the *data revolution*, leading to a spike in the amount and diversity of available data. Information sharing makes it possible for researchers and organizations to disseminate numerous data sets in digital form. Second, the *computational revolution*, in terms of both software and hardware, means that anyone can conduct data analysis using their personal computer and favorite data analysis software.

As a direct consequence of these technological changes, the sheer volume of data available to quantitative social scientists has rapidly grown. In the past, researchers largely relied upon data published by governmental agencies (e.g., censuses, election outcomes, and economic indicators) as well as a small number of data sets collected by research groups (e.g., survey data from national election studies and hand-coded data sets about war occurrence and democratic institutions). These data sets still play an important role in empirical analysis. However, the wide variety of new data has significantly expanded the horizon of quantitative social science research. Researchers are designing and conducting randomized experiments and surveys on their own. Under pressure to increase transparency and accountability, government agencies are making more data publicly available online. For example, in the United States, anyone can download detailed data on campaign contributions and lobbying activities to their personal computers. In Nordic countries like Sweden, a wide range of registers, including income, tax, education, health, and workplace, are available for academic research.

New data sets have emerged across diverse areas. Detailed data about consumer transactions are available through electronic purchasing records. International trade data are collected at the product level between many pairs of countries over several decades. Militaries have also contributed to the data revolution. During the Afghanistan war in the 2000s, the United States and international forces gathered data on the geo-location, timing, and types of insurgent attacks and conducted data analysis to guide counterinsurgency strategy. Similarly, governmental agencies and nongovernmental organizations collected data on civilian casualties from the war. Political campaigns use data analysis to devise voter mobilization strategies by targeting certain types of voters with carefully selected messages.

These data sets also come in varying forms. Quantitative social scientists are analyzing digitized texts as data, including legislative bills, newspaper articles, and the speeches of politicians. The availability of social media data through websites, blogs, tweets, SMS messaging, and Facebook has enabled social scientists to explore how people interact with one another in the online sphere. Geographical information system (GIS) data sets are also widespread. They enable researchers to analyze the legislative redistricting process or civil conflict with attention paid to spatial location. Others have used satellite imagery data to measure the level of electrification in rural areas of developing countries. While still rare, images, sounds, and even videos can be analyzed using quantitative methods for answering social science questions.

Together with the revolution of information technology, the availability of such abundant and diverse data means that anyone, from academics to practitioners, from business analysts to policy makers, and from students to faculty, can make data-driven discoveries. In the past, only statisticians and other specialized professionals conducted data analysis. Now, everyone can turn on their personal computer, download data from the Internet, and analyze them using their favorite software. This has led to increased demands for accountability to demonstrate policy effectiveness. In order to secure funding and increase legitimacy, for example, nongovernmental organizations and governmental agencies must now demonstrate the efficacy of their policies and programs through rigorous evaluation.

This shift towards greater transparency and data-driven discovery requires that students in the social sciences learn how to analyze data, interpret the results, and effectively communicate their empirical findings. Traditionally, introductory statistics courses have focused on teaching students basic statistical concepts by having them conduct straightforward calculations with paper and pencil or, at best, a scientific calculator. Although these concepts are still important and covered in this book, this traditional approach cannot meet the current demands of society. It is simply not sufficient to achieve "statistical literacy" by learning about common statistical concepts and methods. Instead, all students in the social sciences should acquire basic data analysis skills so that they can exploit the ample opportunities to learn from data and make contributions to society through data-driven discovery.

The belief that everyone should be able to analyze data is the main motivation for writing this book. The book introduces the three elements of data analysis required for quantitative social science research: research contexts, programming techniques, and statistical methods. Any of these elements in isolation is insufficient. Without research contexts, we cannot assess the credibility of assumptions required for data analysis and will not be able to understand what the empirical findings imply. Without programming techniques, we will not be able to analyze data and answer research questions. Without the guidance of statistical principles, we cannot distinguish systematic patterns, known as signals, from idiosyncratic ones, known as noise, possibly leading to invalid inference. (Here, inference refers to drawing conclusions about unknown quantities based on observed data.) This book demonstrates the power of data analysis by combining these three elements.

1.1 Overview of the Book

This book is written for anyone who wishes to learn data analysis and statistics for the first time. The target audience includes researchers, undergraduate and graduate students in social science and other fields, as well as practitioners and even ambitious high-school students. The book has no prerequisite other than some elementary algebra. In particular, readers do not have to possess knowledge of calculus or probability. No programming experience is necessary, though it can certainly be helpful. The book is also appropriate for those who have taken a traditional "paper-and-pencil" introductory statistics course where little data analysis is taught. Through this book, students will discover the excitement that data analysis brings. Those who want to learn R programming might also find this book useful, although here the emphasis is on how to use R to answer quantitative social science questions.

As mentioned above, the unique feature of this book is the presentation of programming techniques and statistical concepts simultaneously through analysis of data sets taken directly from published quantitative social science research. The goal is to demonstrate how social scientists use data analysis to answer important questions about societal problems and human behavior. At the same time, users of the book will learn fundamental statistical concepts and basic programming skills. Most importantly, readers will gain experience with data analysis by examining approximately forty data sets.

The book consists of eight chapters. The current introductory chapter explains how to best utilize the book and presents a brief introduction to R, a popular open-source statistical programming environment. R is freely available for download and runs on Macintosh, Windows, and Linux computers. Readers are strongly encouraged to use RStudio, another freely available software package that has numerous features to make data analysis easier. This chapter ends with two exercises that are designed to help readers practice elementary R functionalities using data sets from published social science research. All data sets used in this book are freely available for download via links from `http://press.princeton.edu/qss/`. Links to other useful materials, such as the review exercises for each chapter, can also be found on the website. With the exception of chapter 5, the book focuses on the most basic syntax of R and does not introduce the wide range of additional packages that are available. However, upon completion of this book, readers will have acquired enough R programming skills to be able to utilize these packages.

Chapter 2 introduces *causality*, which plays an essential role in social science research whenever we wish to find out whether a particular policy or program changes an outcome of interest. Causality is notoriously difficult to study because we must infer counterfactual outcomes that are not observable. For example, in order to understand the existence of racial discrimination in the labor market, we need to know whether an African-American candidate who did not receive a job offer would have done so if they were white. We will analyze the data from a well-known experimental study in which researchers sent the résumés of fictitious job applicants to potential employers after randomly choosing applicants' names to sound either African-American or Caucasian. Using this study as an application, the chapter will explain how the randomization of treatment assignment enables researchers to identify the average causal effect of the treatment.

Additionally, readers will learn about causal inference in observational studies where researchers do not have control over treatment assignment. The main application is a classic study whose goal was to figure out the impact of increasing the minimum wage on employment. Many economists argue that a minimum-wage increase can reduce employment because employers must pay higher wages to their workers and are therefore made to hire fewer workers. Unfortunately, the decision to increase the minimum wage is not random, but instead is subject to many factors, like economic growth, that are themselves associated with employment. Since these factors influence which companies find themselves in the treatment group, a simple comparison between those who received treatment and those who did not can lead to biased inference.

We introduce several strategies that attempt to reduce this type of selection bias in observational studies. Despite the risk that we will inaccurately estimate treatment effects in observational studies, the results of such studies are often easier to generalize than those obtained from randomized controlled trials. Other examples in chapter 2 include a field experiment concerning social pressure in get-out-the-vote mobilization. Exercises then include a randomized experiment that investigates the causal effect of small class size in early education as well as a natural experiment about political leader assassination and its effects. In terms of R programming, chapter 2 covers logical statements and subsetting.

Chapter 3 introduces the fundamental concept of *measurement*. Accurate measurement is important for any data-driven discovery because bias in measurement can lead to incorrect conclusions and misguided decisions. We begin by considering how to measure public opinion through sample surveys. We analyze the data from a study in which researchers attempted to measure the degree of support among Afghan citizens for international forces and the Taliban insurgency during the Afghanistan war. The chapter explains the power of randomization in survey sampling. Specifically, random sampling of respondents from a population allows us to obtain a representative sample. As a result, we can infer the opinion of an entire population by analyzing one small representative group. We also discuss the potential biases of survey sampling. Nonresponses can compromise the representativeness of a sample. Misreporting poses a serious threat to inference, especially when respondents are asked sensitive questions, such as whether they support the Taliban insurgency.

The second half of chapter 3 focuses on the measurement of latent or unobservable concepts that play a key role in quantitative social science. Prominent examples of such concepts include ability and ideology. In the chapter, we study political ideology. We first describe a model frequently used to infer the ideological positions of legislators from roll call votes, and examine how the US Congress has polarized over time. We then introduce a basic clustering algorithm, k-means, that makes it possible for us to find groups of similar observations. Applying this algorithm to the data, we find that in recent years, the ideological division within Congress has been mainly characterized by the party line. In contrast, we find some divisions within each party in earlier years. This chapter also introduces various measures of the spread of data, including quantiles, standard deviation, and the Gini coefficient. In terms of R programming, the chapter introduces various ways to visualize univariate and bivariate data. The exercises include the reanalysis of a controversial same-sex marriage experiment, which raises issues of academic integrity while illustrating methods covered in the chapter.

Chapter 4 considers *prediction*. Predicting the occurrence of certain events is an essential component of policy and decision-making processes. For example, the forecasting of economic performance is critical for fiscal planning, and early warnings of civil unrest allow foreign policy makers to act proactively. The main application of this chapter is the prediction of US presidential elections using preelection polls. We show that we can make a remarkably accurate prediction by combining multiple polls in a straightforward manner. In addition, we analyze the data from a psychological experiment in which subjects are shown the facial pictures of unknown political candidates and asked to rate their competence. The analysis yields the surprising result that a quick facial impression can predict election outcomes. Through this example, we introduce linear regression models, which are useful tools to predict the values of one variable based on another variable. We describe the relationship between linear regression and correlation, and examine the phenomenon called "regression towards the mean," which is the origin of the term "regression."

Chapter 4 also discusses when regression models can be used to estimate causal effects rather than simply make predictions. Causal inference differs from standard prediction in requiring the prediction of counterfactual, rather than observed, outcomes using the treatment variable as the predictor. We analyze the data from a randomized natural experiment in India where randomly selected villages reserved some of the seats in their village councils for women. Exploiting this randomization, we investigate whether or not having female politicians affects policy outcomes, especially concerning the policy issues female voters care about. The chapter also introduces the regression discontinuity design for making causal inference in observational studies. We investigate how much of British politicians' accumulated wealth is due to holding political office. We answer this question by comparing those who barely won an election with those who narrowly lost it. The chapter introduces powerful but challenging R programming concepts: loops and conditional statements. The exercises at the end of the chapter include an analysis of whether betting markets can precisely forecast election outcomes.

Chapter 5 is about the *discovery* of patterns from data of various types. When analyzing "big data," we need automated methods and visualization tools to identify consistent patterns in the data. First, we analyze texts as data. Our primary application here is authorship prediction of *The Federalist Papers*, which formed the basis of the US Constitution. Some of the papers have known authors while others do not. We show that by analyzing the frequencies of certain words in the papers with known authorship, we can predict whether Alexander Hamilton or James Madison authored each of the papers with unknown authorship. Second, we show how to analyze network data, focusing on explaining the relationships among units. Within marriage networks in Renaissance Florence, we quantify the key role played by the Medici family. As a more contemporary example, various measures of centrality are introduced and applied to social media data generated by US senators on Twitter.

Finally in chapter 5, we introduce geo-spatial data. We begin by discussing the classic spatial data analysis conducted by John Snow to examine the cause of the 1854 cholera outbreak in London. We then demonstrate how to visualize spatial data through the creation of maps, using US election data as an example. For spatial–temporal data, we create a series of maps as an animation in order to visually characterize changes in spatial patterns over time. Thus, the chapter applies various data visualization techniques using several specialized R packages.

Chapter 6 shifts the focus from data analysis to *probability*, a unified mathematical model of uncertainty. While earlier chapters examine how to estimate parameters and make predictions, they do not discuss the level of uncertainty in empirical findings, a topic that chapter 7 introduces. Probability is important because it lays a foundation for statistical inference, the goal of which is to quantify inferential uncertainty. We begin by discussing the question of how to interpret probability from two dominant perspectives, frequentist and Bayesian. We then provide mathematical definitions of probability and conditional probability, and introduce several fundamental rules of probability. One such rule is called Bayes' rule. We show how to use Bayes' rule and accurately predict individual ethnicity using surname and residence location when no survey data are available.

This chapter also introduces the important concepts of random variables and probability distributions. We use these tools to add a measure of uncertainty to election predictions that we produced in chapter 4 using preelection polls. Another exercise adds uncertainty to the forecasts of election outcomes based on betting market data. The chapter concludes by introducing two fundamental theorems of probability: the law of large numbers and the central limit theorem. These two theorems are widely applicable and help characterize how our estimates behave over repeated sampling as sample size increases. The final set of exercises then addresses two problems: the German cryptography machine from World War II (Enigma), and the detection of election fraud in Russia.

Chapter 7 discusses how to quantify the *uncertainty* of our estimates and predictions. In earlier chapters, we introduced various data analysis methods to find patterns in data. Building on the groundwork laid in chapter 6, chapter 7 thoroughly explains how certain we should be about such patterns. This chapter shows how to distinguish signals from noise through the computation of standard errors and confidence intervals as well as the use of hypothesis testing. In other words, the chapter concerns statistical inference. Our examples come from earlier chapters, and we focus on measuring the uncertainty of these previously computed estimates. They include the analysis of preelection polls, randomized experiments concerning the effects of class size in early education on students' performance, and an observational study assessing the effects of a minimum-wage increase on employment. When discussing statistical hypothesis tests, we also draw attention to the dangers of multiple testing and publication bias. Finally, we discuss how to quantify the level of uncertainty about the estimates derived from a linear regression model. To do this, we revisit the randomized natural experiment of female politicians in India and the regression discontinuity design for estimating the amount of wealth British politicians are able to accumulate by holding political office.

The final chapter concludes by briefly describing the next steps readers might take upon completion of this book. The chapter also discusses the role of data analysis in quantitative social science research.

1.2 How to Use this Book

In this section, we explain how to use this book, which is based on the following principle:

One can learn data analysis only by doing, not by reading.

This book is not just for reading. The emphasis must be placed on gaining experience in analyzing data. This is best accomplished by trying out the code in the book on one's own, playing with it, and working on various exercises that appear at the end of each chapter. All code and data sets used in the book are freely available for download via links from `http://press.princeton.edu/qss/`.

The book is cumulative. Later chapters assume that readers are already familiar with most of the materials covered in earlier parts. Hence, in general, it is not advisable to skip chapters. The exception is chapter 5, "Discovery," the contents of which are not used in subsequent chapters. Nevertheless, this chapter contains some of the most interesting data analysis examples of the book and readers are encouraged to study it.

The book can be used for course instruction in a variety of ways. In a traditional introductory statistics course, one can assign the book, or parts of it, as supplementary reading that provides data analysis exercises. The book is best utilized in a data analysis course where an instructor spends less time on lecturing to students and instead works interactively with students on data analysis exercises in the classroom. In such a course, the relevant portion of the book is assigned prior to each class. In the classroom, the instructor reviews new methodological and programming concepts and then applies them to one of the exercises from the book or any other similar application of their choice. Throughout this process, the instructor can discuss the exercises interactively with students, perhaps using the Socratic method, until the class collectively arrives at a solution. After such a classroom discussion, it would be ideal to follow up with a computer lab session, in which a small number of students, together with an instructor, work on another exercise.

This teaching format is consistent with the "particular general particular" principle.[1] This principle states that an instructor should first introduce a particular example to illustrate a new concept, then provide a general treatment of it, and finally apply it to another particular example. Reading assignments introduce a particular example and a general discussion of new concepts to students. Classroom discussion then allows the instructor to provide another general treatment of these concepts and then, together with students, apply them to another example. This is an effective teaching strategy that engages students with active learning and builds their ability to conduct data analysis in social science research. Finally, the instructor can assign another application as a problem set to assess whether students have mastered the materials. To facilitate this, for each chapter instructors can obtain, upon request, access to a private repository that contains additional exercises and their solutions.

In terms of the materials to cover, an example of the course outline for a 15-week-long semester is given below. We assume that there are approximately two hours of lectures and one hour of computer lab sessions each week. Having hands-on computer lab sessions with a small number of students, in which they learn how to analyze data, is essential.

Chapter title	Chapter number	Weeks
Introduction	1	1
Causality	2	2–3
Measurement	3	4–5
Prediction	4	6–7
Discovery	5	8–9
Probability	6	10–12
Uncertainty	7	13–15

For a shorter course, there are at least two ways to reduce the material. One option is to focus on aspects of data science and omit statistical inference. Specifically, from the above outline, we can remove chapter 6, "Probability," and chapter 7, "Uncertainty." An alternative approach is to skip chapter 5, "Discovery," which covers the analysis of textual, network, and spatial data, and include the chapters on probability and uncertainty.

Finally, to ensure mastery of the basic methodological and programming concepts introduced in each chapter, we recommend that users first read a chapter, practice all of the code it contains, and upon completion of each chapter, try the online review questions before attempting to solve the associated exercises. These review questions

---

[1] Frederick Mosteller (1980) "Classroom and platform performance." *American Statistician*, vol. 34, no. 1 (February), pp. 11–17.

Table 1.1. The **swirl** Review Exercises.

Chapter	*swirl* lesson	Sections covered
1: Introduction	INTRO1	1.3
	INTRO2	1.3
2: Causality	CAUSALITY1	2.1–2.4
	CAUSALITY2	2.5–2.6
3: Measurement	MEASUREMENT1	3.1–3.4
	MEASUREMENT2	3.5–3.7
4: Prediction	PREDICTION1	4.1
	PREDICTION2	4.2
	PREDICTION3	4.3
5: Discovery	DISCOVERY1	5.1
	DISCOVERY2	5.2
	DISCOVERY3	5.3
6: Probability	PROBABILITY1	6.1–6.3
	PROBABILITY2	6.4–6.5
7: Uncertainty	UNCERTAINTY1	7.1
	UNCERTAINTY2	7.2
	UNCERTAINTY3	7.3

Note: The table shows the correspondence between the chapters and sections of the book and each set of **swirl** review exercises.

are available as **swirl** lessons via links from `http://press.princeton.edu/ qss/`, and can be answered within R. Instructors are strongly encouraged to assign these **swirl** exercises prior to each class so that students learn the basics before moving on to more complicated data analysis exercises. To start the online review questions, users must first install the **swirl** package (see section 1.3.7) and then the lessons for this book using the following three lines of commands within R. Note that this installation needs to be done only once.

```r
install.packages("swirl") # install the package

library(swirl) # load the package

install_course_github("kosukeimai", "qss-swirl") # install the course
```

Table 1.1 lists the available set of **swirl** review exercises along with their corresponding chapters and sections. To start a **swirl** lesson for review questions, we can use the following command.

```r
library(swirl)
swirl()
```

More information about **swirl** is available at `http://swirlstats.com/`.

1.3   Introduction to R

This section provides a brief, self-contained introduction to R that is a prerequisite for the remainder of this book. R is an open-source statistical programming environment, which means that anyone can download it for free, examine source code, and make their own contributions. R is powerful and flexible, enabling us to handle a variety of data sets and create appealing graphics. For this reason, it is widely used in academia and industry. The *New York Times* described R as

> a popular programming language used by a growing number of data analysts inside corporations and academia. It is becoming their lingua franca...whether being used to set ad prices, find new drugs more quickly or fine-tune financial models. Companies as diverse as Google, Pfizer, Merck, Bank of America, the InterContinental Hotels Group and Shell use it.... "The great beauty of R is that you can modify it to do all sorts of things," said Hal Varian, chief economist at Google. "And you have a lot of prepackaged stuff that's already available, so you're standing on the shoulders of giants."[2]

To obtain R, visit `https://cran.r-project.org/` (The Comprehensive R Archive Network or CRAN), select the link that matches your operating system, and then follow the installation instructions.

While a powerful tool for data analysis, R's main cost from a practical viewpoint is that it must be learned as a programming language. This means that we must master various syntaxes and basic rules of computer programming. Learning computer programming is like becoming proficient in a foreign language. It requires a lot of practice and patience, and the learning process may be frustrating. Through numerous data analysis exercises, this book will teach you the basics of statistical programming, which then will allow you to conduct data analysis on your own. The core principle of the book is that we can learn data analysis only by analyzing data.

Unless you have prior programming experience (or have a preference for another text editor such as Emacs), we recommend that you use RStudio. RStudio is an open-source and free program that greatly facilitates the use of R. In one window, RStudio gives users a text editor to write programs, a graph viewer that displays the graphics we create, the R console where programs are executed, a help section, and many other features. It may look complicated at first, but RStudio can make learning how to use R much easier. To obtain RStudio, visit `http://www.rstudio.com/` and follow the download and installation instructions. Figure 1.1 shows a screenshot of RStudio.

In the remainder of this section, we cover three topics: (1) using R as a calculator, (2) creating and manipulating various objects in R, and (3) loading data sets into R.

1.3.1   ARITHMETIC OPERATIONS

We begin by using R as a calculator with standard arithmetic operators. In figure 1.1, the left-hand window of RStudio shows the R console where we can directly enter R

---

[2] Vance, Ashlee. 2009. "Data Analysts Captivated by R's Power." *New York Times*, January 6.

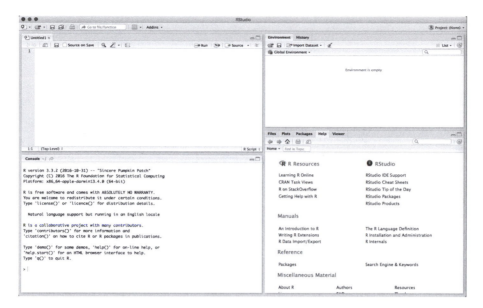

Figure 1.1. Screenshot of RStudio (version 1.0.44). The upper-left window displays a script that contains code. The lower-left window shows the console where R commands can be directly entered. The upper-right window lists R objects and a history of executed R commands. Finally, the lower-right window enables us to view plots, data sets, files and subdirectories in the working directory, R packages, and help pages.

commands. In this R console, we can type in, for example, 5 + 3, then hit Enter on our keyboard.

```
5 + 3
## [1] 8
```

R ignores spaces, and so 5+3 will return the same result. However, we added a space before and after the operator + to make it easier to read. As this example illustrates, this book displays R commands followed by the outputs they would produce if entered in the R console. These outputs begin with ## to distinguish them from the R commands that produced them, though this mark will not appear in the R console. Finally, in this example, [1] indicates that the output is the first element of a *vector* of length 1 (we will discuss vectors in section 1.3.3). It is important for readers to try these examples on their own. Remember that we can learn programming only by doing! Let's try other examples.

```
5 - 3
## [1] 2
5 / 3
## [1] 1.666667
5 ^ 3
```

```
## [1] 125
5 * (10 - 3)
## [1] 35
sqrt(4)
## [1] 2
```

The final expression is an example of a so-called *function*, which takes an input (or multiple inputs) and produces an output. Here, the function `sqrt()` takes a nonnegative number and returns its square root. As discussed in section 1.3.4, R has numerous other functions, and users can even make their own functions.

1.3.2   OBJECTS

R can store information as an *object* with a name of our choice. Once we have created an object, we just refer to it by name. That is, we are using objects as "shortcuts" to some piece of information or data. For this reason, it is important to use an intuitive and informative name. The name of our object must follow certain restrictions. For example, it cannot begin with a number (but it can contain numbers). Object names also should not contain spaces. We must avoid special characters such as `%` and `$`, which have specific meanings in R. In RStudio, in the upper-right window, called `Environment` (see figure 1.1), we will see the objects we created. We use the *assignment operator* `<-` to assign some value to an object.

For example, we can store the result of the above calculation as an object named `result`, and thereafter we can access the value by referring to the object's name. By default, R will print the value of the object to the console if we just enter the object name and hit Enter. Alternatively, we can explicitly print it by using the `print()` function.

```
result <- 5 + 3
result
## [1] 8
print(result)
## [1] 8
```

Note that if we assign a different value to the same object name, then the value of the object will be changed. As a result, we must be careful not to overwrite previously assigned information that we plan to use later.

```
result <- 5 - 3
result
## [1] 2
```

Another thing to be careful about is that object names are case sensitive. For example, `Hello` is not the same as either `hello` or `HELLO`. As a consequence, we receive an error in the R console when we type `Result` rather than `result`, which is defined above.

```
Result

## Error in eval(expr, envir, enclos): object 'Result' not found
```

Encountering programming errors or bugs is part of the learning process. The tricky part is figuring out how to fix them. Here, the error message tells us that the `Result` object does not exist. We can see the list of existing objects in the `Environment` tab in the upper-right window (see figure 1.1), where we will find that the correct object is `result`. It is also possible to obtain the same list by using the `ls()` function.

So far, we have assigned only numbers to an object. But R can represent various other types of values as objects. For example, we can store a string of characters by using quotation marks.

```
kosuke <- "instructor"
kosuke

## [1] "instructor"
```

In character strings, spacing is allowed.

```
kosuke <- "instructor and author"
kosuke

## [1] "instructor and author"
```

Notice that R treats numbers like characters when we tell it to do so.

```
Result <- "5"
Result

## [1] "5"
```

However, arithmetic operations like addition and subtraction cannot be used for character strings. For example, attempting to divide or take a square root of a character string will result in an error.

```
Result / 3

## Error in Result/3: non-numeric argument to binary operator
```

```
sqrt(Result)

## Error in sqrt(Result): non-numeric argument to mathematical function
```

R recognizes different types of objects by assigning each object to a *class*. Separating objects into classes allows R to perform appropriate operations depending on the objects' class. For example, a number is stored as a numeric object whereas a character string is recognized as a character object. In RStudio, the Environment window will show the class of an object as well as its name. The function (which by the way is another class) class() tells us to which class an object belongs.

```
result

## [1] 2

class(result)

## [1] "numeric"

Result

## [1] "5"

class(Result)

## [1] "character"

class(sqrt)

## [1] "function"
```

There are many other classes in R, some of which will be introduced throughout this book. In fact, it is even possible to create our own object classes.

1.3.3 VECTORS

We present the simplest (but most inefficient) way of entering data into R. Table 1.2 contains estimates of world population (in thousands) over the past several decades. We can enter these data into R as a numeric vector object. A *vector* or a one-dimensional array simply represents a collection of information stored in a specific order. We use the function c(), which stands for "concatenate," to enter a data vector containing multiple values with commas separating different elements of the vector we are creating. For example, we can enter the world population estimates as elements of a single vector.

```
world.pop <- c(2525779, 3026003, 3691173, 4449049, 5320817, 6127700,
    6916183)
world.pop

## [1] 2525779 3026003 3691173 4449049 5320817 6127700 6916183
```

Table 1.2. World Population Estimates.

Year	World population (thousands)
1950	2,525,779
1960	3,026,003
1970	3,691,173
1980	4,449,049
1990	5,320,817
2000	6,127,700
2010	6,916,183

Source: United Nations, Department of Economic and Social Affairs, Population Division (2013). *World Population Prospects: The 2012 Revision, DVD Edition.*

We also note that the `c()` function can be used to combine multiple vectors.

```
pop.first <- c(2525779, 3026003, 3691173)
pop.second <- c(4449049, 5320817, 6127700, 6916183)
pop.all <- c(pop.first, pop.second)
pop.all
## [1] 2525779 3026003 3691173 4449049 5320817 6127700 6916183
```

To access specific elements of a vector, we use square brackets [ ]. This is called *indexing*. Multiple elements can be extracted via a vector of indices within square brackets. Also within square brackets the dash, –, removes the corresponding element from a vector. Note that none of these operations change the original vector.

```
world.pop[2]
## [1] 3026003

world.pop[c(2, 4)]
## [1] 3026003 4449049

world.pop[c(4, 2)]
## [1] 4449049 3026003

world.pop[-3]
## [1] 2525779 3026003 4449049 5320817 6127700 6916183
```

Since each element of this vector is a numeric value, we can apply arithmetic operations to it. The operations will be repeated for each element of the vector. Let's give the population estimates in millions instead of thousands by dividing each element of the vector by 1000.

```
pop.million <- world.pop / 1000
pop.million

## [1] 2525.779 3026.003 3691.173 4449.049 5320.817 6127.700
## [7] 6916.183
```

We can also express each population estimate as a proportion of the 1950 population estimate. Recall that the 1950 estimate is the first element of the vector `world.pop`.

```
pop.rate <- world.pop / world.pop[1]
pop.rate

## [1] 1.000000 1.198047 1.461400 1.761456 2.106604 2.426063
## [7] 2.738238
```

In addition, arithmetic operations can be done using multiple vectors. For example, we can calculate the percentage increase in population for each decade, defined as the increase over the decade divided by its beginning population. For example, suppose that the population was 100 thousand in one year and increased to 120 thousand in the following year. In this case, we say, "the population increased by 20%." To compute the percentage increase for each decade, we first create two vectors, one without the first decade and the other without the last decade. We then subtract the second vector from the first vector. Each element of the resulting vector equals the population increase. For example, the first element is the difference between the 1960 population estimate and the 1950 estimate.

```
pop.increase <- world.pop[-1] - world.pop[-7]
percent.increase <- (pop.increase / world.pop[-7]) * 100
percent.increase

## [1] 19.80474 21.98180 20.53212 19.59448 15.16464 12.86752
```

Finally, we can also replace the values associated with particular indices by using the usual assignment operator (`<-`). Below, we replace the first two elements of the `percent.increase` vector with their rounded values.

```
percent.increase[c(1, 2)] <- c(20, 22)
percent.increase

## [1] 20.00000 22.00000 20.53212 19.59448 15.16464 12.86752
```

1.3.4 FUNCTIONS

Functions are important objects in R and perform a wide range of tasks. A function often takes multiple input objects and returns an output object. We have already seen several functions: `sqrt()`, `print()`, `class()`, and `c()`. In R, a function generally runs as `funcname(input)` where `funcname` is the function name and `input` is the input object. In programming (and in math), we call these inputs *arguments*. For example, in the syntax `sqrt(4)`, `sqrt` is the function name and 4 is the argument or the input object.

Some basic functions useful for summarizing data include `length()` for the length of a vector or equivalently the number of elements it has, `min()` for the *minimum* value, `max()` for the *maximum* value, `range()` for the *range* of data, `mean()` for the *mean*, and `sum()` for the *sum* of the data. Right now we are inputting only one object into these functions so we will not use argument names.

```
length(world.pop)
## [1] 7

min(world.pop)
## [1] 2525779

max(world.pop)
## [1] 6916183

range(world.pop)
## [1] 2525779 6916183

mean(world.pop)
## [1] 4579529

sum(world.pop) / length(world.pop)
## [1] 4579529
```

The last expression gives another way of calculating the mean as the sum of all the elements divided by the number of elements.

When multiple arguments are given, the syntax looks like `funcname(input1, input2)`. The order of inputs matters. That is, `funcname(input1, input2)` is different from `funcname(input2, input1)`. To avoid confusion and problems stemming from the order in which we list arguments, it is also a good idea to specify the name of the argument that each input corresponds to. This looks like `funcname(arg1 = input1, arg2 = input2)`.

For example, the `seq()` function can generate a vector composed of an increasing or decreasing sequence. The first argument `from` specifies the number to start from; the second argument `to` specifies the number at which to end the sequence; the last argument `by` indicates the interval to increase or decrease by. We can create an object for the `year` variable from table 1.2 using this function.

```
year <- seq(from = 1950, to = 2010, by = 10)
year

## [1] 1950 1960 1970 1980 1990 2000 2010
```

Notice how we can switch the order of the arguments without changing the output because we have named the input objects.

```
seq(to = 2010, by = 10, from = 1950)

## [1] 1950 1960 1970 1980 1990 2000 2010
```

Although not relevant in this particular example, we can also create a decreasing sequence using the `seq()` function. In addition, the colon operator `:` creates a simple sequence, beginning with the first number specified and increasing or decreasing by 1 to the last number specified.

```
seq(from = 2010, to = 1950, by = -10)
## [1] 2010 2000 1990 1980 1970 1960 1950

2008:2012
## [1] 2008 2009 2010 2011 2012

2012:2008
## [1] 2012 2011 2010 2009 2008
```

The `names()` function can access and assign names to elements of a vector. Element names are not part of the data themselves, but are helpful attributes of the R object. Below, we see that the object `world.pop` does not yet have the names attribute, with `names(world.pop)` returning the `NULL` value. However, once we assign the `year` as the labels for the object, each element of `world.pop` is printed with an informative label.

```
names(world.pop)
## NULL

names(world.pop) <- year
names(world.pop)
## [1] "1950" "1960" "1970" "1980" "1990" "2000" "2010"
```

```
world.pop

##    1950    1960    1970    1980    1990    2000    2010
## 2525779 3026003 3691173 4449049 5320817 6127700 6916183
```

In many situations, we want to create our own functions and use them repeatedly. This allows us to avoid duplicating identical (or nearly identical) sets of code chunks, making our code more efficient and easily interpretable. The `function()` function can create a new function. The syntax takes the following form.

```
myfunction <- function(input1, input2, ..., inputN) {

    DEFINE "output" USING INPUTS

    return(output)
}
```

In this example code, `myfunction` is the function name, `input1`, `input2`, `...`, `inputN` are the input arguments, and the commands within the braces { } define the actual function. Finally, the `return()` function returns the output of the function. We begin with a simple example, creating a function to compute a summary of a numeric vector.

```
my.summary <- function(x){ # function takes one input
  s.out <- sum(x)
  l.out <- length(x)
  m.out <- s.out / l.out
  out <- c(s.out, l.out, m.out) # define the output
  names(out) <- c("sum", "length", "mean") # add labels
  return(out) # end function by calling output
}
z <- 1:10
my.summary(z)

##    sum length   mean
##   55.0   10.0    5.5

my.summary(world.pop)

##       sum    length      mean
## 32056704         7   4579529
```

Note that objects (e.g., `x`, `s.out`, `l.out`, `m.out`, and `out` in the above example) can be defined within a function independently of the environment in which the function is being created. This means that we need not worry about using identical names for objects inside a function and those outside it.

1.3.5 DATA FILES

So far, the only data we have used has been manually entered into R. But, most of the time, we will load data from an external file. In this book, we will use the following two data file types:

- *CSV* or comma-separated values files represent tabular data. This is conceptually similar to a spreadsheet of data values like those generated by Microsoft Excel or Google Spreadsheet. Each observation is separated by line breaks and each field within the observation is separated by a comma, a tab, or some other character or string.
- *RData* files represent a collection of R objects including data sets. These can contain multiple R objects of different kinds. They are useful for saving intermediate results from our R code as well as data files.

Before interacting with data files, we must ensure they reside in the *working directory*, which R will by default load data from and save data to. There are different ways to change the working directory. In RStudio, the default working directory is shown in the bottom-right window under the `Files` tab (see figure 1.1). Oftentimes, however, the default directory is not the directory we want to use. To change the working directory, click on `More > Set As Working Directory` after choosing the folder we want to work from. Alternatively, we can use the RStudio pull-down menu `Session > Set Working Directory > Choose Directory...` and pick the folder we want to work from. Then, we will see our files and folders in the bottom-right window.

It is also possible to change the working directory using the `setwd()` function by specifying the full path to the folder of our choice as a character string. To display the current working directory, use the function `getwd()` without providing an input. For example, the following syntax sets the working directory to `qss/INTRO` and confirms the result (we suppress the output here).

```
setwd("qss/INTRO")
getwd()
```

Suppose that the United Nations population data in table 1.2 are saved as a CSV file `UNpop.csv`, which resembles that below:

```
year, world.pop
1950, 2525779
1960, 3026003
1970, 3691173
1980, 4449049
1990, 5320817
2000, 6127700
2010, 6916183
```

In RStudio, we can read in or load CSV files by going to the drop-down menu in the upper-right window (see figure 1.1) and clicking `Import Dataset > From Text`

File ....Alternatively, we can use the read.csv() function. The following syntax loads the data as a data frame object (more on this object below).

```
UNpop <- read.csv("UNpop.csv")
class(UNpop)
## [1] "data.frame"
```

On the other hand, if the same data set is saved as an object in an RData file named UNpop.RData, then we can use the load() function, which will load all the R objects saved in UNpop.RData into our R session. We do not need to use the assignment operator with the load() function when reading in an RData file because the R objects stored in the file already have object names.

```
load("UNpop.RData")
```

Note that R can access any file on our computer if the full location is specified. For example, we can use syntax such as read.csv("Documents/qss/INTRO/UNpop.csv") if the data file UNpop.csv is stored in the directory Documents/qss/INTRO/. However, setting the working directory as shown above allows us to avoid tedious typing.

A data frame object is a collection of vectors, but we can think of it like a spreadsheet. It is often useful to visually inspect data. We can view a spreadsheet-like representation of data frame objects in **RStudio** by double-clicking on the object name in the Environment tab in the upper-right window (see figure 1.1). This will open a new tab displaying the data. Alternatively, we can use the View() function, which as its main argument takes the name of a data frame to be examined. Useful functions for this object include names() to return a vector of variable names, nrow() to return the number of rows, ncol() to return the number of columns, dim() to combine the outputs of ncol() and nrow() into a vector, and summary() to produce a summary.

```
names(UNpop)
## [1] "year"      "world.pop"

nrow(UNpop)
## [1] 7

ncol(UNpop)
## [1] 2

dim(UNpop)
## [1] 7 2
```

```
summary(UNpop)

##       year          world.pop
##   Min.   :1950    Min.   :2525779
##   1st Qu.:1965    1st Qu.:3358588
##   Median :1980    Median :4449049
##   Mean   :1980    Mean   :4579529
##   3rd Qu.:1995    3rd Qu.:5724258
##   Max.   :2010    Max.   :6916183
```

Notice that the `summary()` function yields, for each variable in the data frame object, the minimum value, the first *quartile* (or 25th *percentile*), the *median* (or 50th percentile), the third quartile (or 75th percentile), and the maximum value. See section 2.6 for more discussion.

The $ operator is one way to access an individual variable from within a data frame object. It returns a vector containing the specified variable.

```
UNpop$world.pop

## [1] 2525779 3026003 3691173 4449049 5320817 6127700 6916183
```

Another way of retrieving individual variables is to use indexing inside square brackets `[ ]`, as done for a vector. Since a data frame object is a two-dimensional array, we need two indexes, one for rows and the other for columns. Using brackets with a comma `[rows, columns]` allows users to call specific rows and columns by either row/column numbers or row/column names. If we use row/column numbers, sequencing functions covered above, i.e., `:` and `c()`, will be useful. If we do not specify a row (column) index, then the syntax will return all rows (columns). Below are some examples, demonstrating the syntax of indexing.

```
UNpop[, "world.pop"] # extract the column called "world.pop"

## [1] 2525779 3026003 3691173 4449049 5320817 6127700 6916183

UNpop[c(1, 2, 3),]   # extract the first three rows (and all columns)

##   year world.pop
## 1 1950    2525779
## 2 1960    3026003
## 3 1970    3691173

UNpop[1:3, "year"]   # extract the first three rows of the "year" column

## [1] 1950 1960 1970
```

When extracting specific observations from a variable in a data frame object, we provide only one index since the variable is a vector.

```
## take elements 1, 3, 5, ... of the "world.pop" variable
UNpop$world.pop[seq(from = 1, to = nrow(UNpop), by = 2)]

## [1] 2525779 3691173 5320817 6916183
```

In R, missing values are represented by NA. When applied to an object with missing values, functions may or may not automatically remove those values before performing operations. We will discuss the details of handling missing values in section 3.2. Here, we note that for many functions, like mean(), the argument na.rm = TRUE will remove missing data before operations occur. In the example below, the eighth element of the vector is missing, and one cannot calculate the mean until R has been instructed to remove the missing data.

```
world.pop <- c(UNpop$world.pop, NA)
world.pop

## [1] 2525779 3026003 3691173 4449049 5320817 6127700  6916183
## [8]       NA

mean(world.pop)

## [1] NA

mean(world.pop, na.rm = TRUE)

## [1] 4579529
```

1.3.6 SAVING OBJECTS

The objects we create in an R session will be temporarily saved in the *workspace*, which is the current working environment. As mentioned earlier, the ls() function displays the names of all objects currently stored in the workspace. In RStudio, all objects in the workspace appear in the Environment tab in the upper-right corner. However, these objects will be lost once we terminate the current session. This can be avoided if we save the workspace at the end of each session as an RData file.

When we quit R, we will be asked whether we would like to save the workspace. We should answer no to this so that we get into the habit of explicitly saving only what we need. If we answer yes, then R will save the entire workspace as .RData in the working directory without an explicit file name and automatically load it next time we launch R. This is not recommended practice, because the .RData file is invisible to users of many operating systems and R will not tell us what objects are loaded unless we explicitly issue the ls() function.

In RStudio, we can save the workspace by clicking the Save icon in the upper-right Environment window (see figure 1.1). Alternatively, from the navigation bar, click on `Session > Save Workspace As...`, and then pick a location to save the file. Be sure to use the file extension `.RData`. To load the same workspace the next time we start **RStudio**, click the `Open File` icon in the upper-right `Environment` window, select `Session > Load Workspace...`, or use the `load()` function as before.

It is also possible to save the workspace using the `save.image()` function. The file extension `.RData` should always be used at the end of the file name. Unless the full path is specified, objects will be saved to the working directory. For example, the following syntax saves the workspace as `Chapter1.RData` in the `qss/INTRO` directory provided that this directory already exists.

```
save.image("qss/INTRO/Chapter1.RData")
```

Sometimes, we wish to save only a specific object (e.g., a data frame object) rather than the entire workspace. This can be done with the `save()` function as in `save(xxx, file = "yyy.RData")`, where `xxx` is the object name and `yyy.RData` is the file name. Multiple objects can be listed, and they will be stored as a single RData file. Here are some examples of syntax, in which we again assume the existence of the `qss/INTRO` directory.

```
save(UNpop, file = "Chapter1.RData")
save(world.pop, year, file = "qss/INTRO/Chapter1.RData")
```

In other cases, we may want to save a data frame object as a CSV file rather than an RData file. We can use the `write.csv()` function by specifying the object name and the file name, as the following example illustrates.

```
write.csv(UNpop, file = "UNpop.csv")
```

Finally, to access objects saved in the RData file, simply use the `load()` function as before.

```
load("Chapter1.RData")
```

1.3.7 PACKAGES

One of R's strengths is the existence of a large community of R users who contribute various functionalities as R packages. These packages are available through the Comprehensive R Archive Network (CRAN; `http://cran.r-project.org`). Throughout the book, we will employ various packages. For the purpose of illustration, suppose that we wish to load a data file produced by another statistical software package such as Stata or SPSS. The **foreign** package is useful when dealing with files from other statistical software.

To use the package, we must load it into the workspace using the `library()` function. In some cases, a package needs to be installed before being loaded. In RStudio, we can do this by clicking on `Packages` > `Install` in the bottom-right window (see figure 1.1), where all currently installed packages are listed, after choosing the desired packages to be installed. Alternatively, we can install from the R console using the `install.packages()` function (the output is suppressed below). Package installation needs only to occur once, though we can update the package later upon the release of a new version (by clicking `Update` or reinstalling it via the `install.packages()` function).

```r
install.packages("foreign") # install package
library("foreign") # load package
```

Once the package is loaded, we can use the appropriate functions to load the data file. For example, the `read.dta()` and `read.spss()` functions can read Stata and SPSS data files, respectively (the following syntax assumes the existence of the `UNpop.dta` and `UNpop.sav` files in the working directory).

```r
read.dta("UNpop.dta")
read.spss("UNpop.sav")
```

As before, it is also possible to save a data frame object as a data file that can be directly loaded into another statistical software package. For example, the `write.dta()` function will save a data frame object as a Stata data file.

```r
write.dta(UNpop, file = "UNpop.dta")
```

1.3.8 PROGRAMMING AND LEARNING TIPS

We conclude this brief introduction to R by providing several practical tips for learning how to program in the R language. First, we should use a text editor like the one that comes with RStudio to write our program rather than directly typing it into the R console. If we just want to see what a command does, or quickly calculate some quantity, we can go ahead and enter it directly into the R console. However, for more involved programming, it is always better to use the text editor and save our code as a text file with the `.R` file extension. This way, we can keep a record of our program and run it again whenever necessary.

In RStudio, use the pull-down menu `File` > `New File` > `R Script` or click the `New File` icon (a white square with a green circle enclosing a white plus sign) and choose `R Script`. Either approach will open a blank document for text editing in the upper-left window where we can start writing our code (see figure 1.2). To run our code from the RStudio text editor, simply highlight the code and press the `Run` icon. Alternatively, in Windows, Ctrl+Enter works as a shortcut. The equivalent shortcut for Mac is Command+Enter. Finally, we can also run the entire code in the background

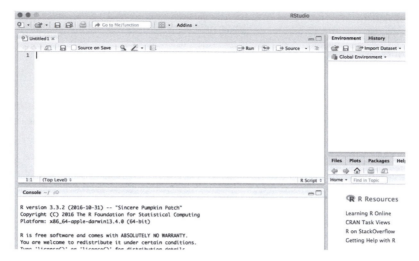

Figure 1.2. Screenshot of the RStudio Text Editor. Once we open an R script file in RStudio, the text editor will appear as one of the windows. It can then be used to write our code.

(so, the code will not appear in the console) by clicking the `Source` icon or using the `source()` function with the code file name (including a full path if it is not placed in the working directory) as the input.

```
source("UNpop.R")
```

Second, we can annotate our R code so that it can be easily understandable to ourselves and others. This is especially important as our code gets more complex. To do this, we use the comment character #, which tells R to ignore everything that follows it. It is customary to use a double comment character ## if a comment occupies an entire line and use a single comment character # if a comment is made within a line after an R command. An example is given here.

```
##
## File: UNpop.R
## Author: Kosuke Imai
## The code loads the UN population data and saves it as a Stata file
##

library(foreign)
UNpop <- read.csv("UNpop.csv")
UNpop$world.pop <- UNpop$world.pop / 1000   # population in millions
write.dta(UNpop, file = "UNpop.dta")
```

Third, for further clarity it is important to follow a certain set of coding rules. For example, we should use informative names for files, variables, and functions. Systematic spacing and indentation are essential too. In the above examples, we place spaces around all binary operators such as <-, =, +, and -, and always add a space after a comma. While comprehensive coverage of coding style is beyond the scope of this book, we encourage you to follow a useful R style guide published by Google at https://google.github.io/styleguide/Rguide.xml. In addition, it is possible to check our R code for potential errors and incorrect syntax. In computer science, this process is called *linting*. The lintr() function in the **lintr** package enables the linting of R code. The following syntax implements the linting of the UNpop.R file shown above, where we replace the assignment operator <- in line 8 with the equality sign = for the sake of illustration.

```
library(lintr)
lint("UNpop.R")

## UNpop.R:8:7: style: Use <-, not =, for assignment.
## UNpop = read.csv("UNpop.csv")
##       ^
```

Finally, R Markdown via the **rmarkdown** package is useful for quickly writing documents using R. R Markdown enables us to easily embed R code and its output within a document using straightforward syntax in a plain-text format. The resulting documents can be produced in the form of HTML, PDF, or even Microsoft Word. Because R Markdown embeds R code as well as its output, the results of data analysis presented in documents are reproducible. R Markdown is also integrated into RStudio, making it possible to produce documents with a single click. For a quick start, see http://rmarkdown.rstudio.com/.

1.4 Summary

This chapter began with a discussion of the important role that quantitative social science research can play in today's data-rich society. To make contributions to this society through data-driven discovery, we must learn how to analyze data, interpret the results, and communicate our findings to others. To start our journey, we presented a brief introduction to R, which is a powerful programming language for data analysis. The remaining pages of this chapter are dedicated to exercises, designed to ensure that you have mastered the contents of this section. Start with the **swirl** review questions that are available via links from http://press.princeton.edu/qss/. If you answer these questions incorrectly, be sure to go back to the relevant sections and review the materials before moving on to the exercises.

Table 1.3. US Election Turnout Data.

Variable	Description
year	election year
ANES	ANES estimated turnout rate
VEP	voting eligible population (in thousands)
VAP	voting age population (in thousands)
total	total ballots cast for highest office (in thousands)
felons	total ineligible felons (in thousands)
noncitizens	total noncitizens (in thousands)
overseas	total eligible overseas voters (in thousands)
osvoters	total ballots counted by overseas voters (in thousands)

1.5 Exercises

1.5.1 BIAS IN SELF-REPORTED TURNOUT

Surveys are frequently used to measure political behavior such as voter turnout, but some researchers are concerned about the accuracy of self-reports. In particular, they worry about possible *social desirability bias* where, in postelection surveys, respondents who did not vote in an election lie about not having voted because they may feel that they should have voted. Is such a bias present in the American National Election Studies (ANES)? ANES is a nationwide survey that has been conducted for every election since 1948. ANES is based on face-to-face interviews with a nationally representative sample of adults. Table 1.3 displays the names and descriptions of variables in the turnout.csv data file.

1. Load the data into R and check the dimensions of the data. Also, obtain a summary of the data. How many observations are there? What is the range of years covered in this data set?

2. Calculate the turnout rate based on the voting age population or VAP. Note that for this data set, we must add the total number of eligible overseas voters since the VAP variable does not include these individuals in the count. Next, calculate the turnout rate using the voting eligible population or VEP. What difference do you observe?

3. Compute the differences between the VAP and ANES estimates of turnout rate. How big is the difference on average? What is the range of the differences? Conduct the same comparison for the VEP and ANES estimates of voter turnout. Briefly comment on the results.

4. Compare the VEP turnout rate with the ANES turnout rate separately for presidential elections and midterm elections. Note that the data set excludes the year 2006. Does the bias of the ANES estimates vary across election types?

Table 1.4. Fertility and Mortality Estimate Data.

Variable	Description
country	abbreviated country name
period	period during which data are collected
age	age group
births	number of births (in thousands), i.e., the number of children born to women of the age group
deaths	number of deaths (in thousands)
py.men	person-years for men (in thousands)
py.women	person-years for women (in thousands)

Source: United Nations, Department of Economic and Social Affairs, Population Division (2013). *World Population Prospects: The 2012 Revision, DVD Edition.*

5. Divide the data into half by election years such that you subset the data into two periods. Calculate the difference between the VEP turnout rate and the ANES turnout rate separately for each year within each period. Has the bias of ANES increased over time?

6. ANES does not interview prisoners and overseas voters. Calculate an adjustment to the 2008 VAP turnout rate. Begin by subtracting the total number of ineligible felons and noncitizens from the VAP to calculate an adjusted VAP. Next, calculate an adjusted VAP turnout rate, taking care to subtract the number of overseas ballots counted from the total ballots in 2008. Compare the adjusted VAP turnout with the unadjusted VAP, VEP, and the ANES turnout rate. Briefly discuss the results.

1.5.2 UNDERSTANDING WORLD POPULATION DYNAMICS

Understanding population dynamics is important for many areas of social science. We will calculate some basic demographic quantities of births and deaths for the world's population from two time periods: 1950 to 1955 and 2005 to 2010. We will analyze the following CSV data files: Kenya.csv, Sweden.csv, and World.csv. The files contain population data for Kenya, Sweden, and the world, respectively. Table 1.4 presents the names and descriptions of the variables in each data set. The data are collected for a period of 5 years where *person-year* is a measure of the time contribution of each person during the period. For example, a person who lives through the entire 5-year period contributes 5 person-years, whereas someone who lives only through the first half of the period contributes 2.5 person-years. Before you begin this exercise, it would be a good idea to directly inspect each data set. In R, this can be done with the View() function, which takes as its argument the name of the data frame to be examined. Alternatively, in RStudio, double-clicking a data frame in the Environment tab will enable you to view the data in a spreadsheet-like form.

1. We begin by computing *crude birth rate* (CBR) for a given period. The CBR is defined as

$$CBR = \frac{\text{number of births}}{\text{number of person-years lived}}.$$

   Compute the CBR for each period, separately for Kenya, Sweden, and the world. Start by computing the total person-years, recorded as a new variable within each existing data frame via the $ operator, by summing the person-years for men and women. Then, store the results as a vector of length 2 (CBRs for two periods) for each region with appropriate labels. You may wish to create your own function for the purpose of efficient programming. Briefly describe patterns you observe in the resulting CBRs.

2. The CBR is easy to understand but contains both men and women of all ages in the denominator. We next calculate the *total fertility rate* (TFR). Unlike the CBR, the TFR adjusts for age compositions in the female population. To do this, we need to first calculate the *age-specific fertility rate* (ASFR), which represents the fertility rate for women of the reproductive age range $[15, 50)$. The ASFR for the age range $[x, x + \delta)$, where x is the starting age and δ is the width of the age range (measured in years), is defined as

$$ASFR_{[x, \ x+\delta)} = \frac{\text{number of births to women of age } [x, \ x + \delta)}{\text{number of person-years lived by women of age } [x, \ x + \delta)}.$$

   Note that square brackets, [and], include the limit whereas parentheses, (and), exclude it. For example, $[20, 25)$ represents the age range that is greater than or equal to 20 years old and less than 25 years old. In typical demographic data, the age range δ is set to 5 years. Compute the ASFR for Sweden and Kenya as well as the entire world for each of the two periods. Store the resulting ASFRs separately for each region. What does the pattern of these ASFRs say about reproduction among women in Sweden and Kenya?

3. Using the ASFR, we can define the TFR as the average number of children that women give birth to if they live through their entire reproductive age:

$$TFR = ASFR_{[15, \ 20)} \times 5 + ASFR_{[20, \ 25)} \times 5 + \cdots + ASFR_{[45, \ 50)} \times 5.$$

   We multiply each age-specific fertility rate by 5 because the age range is 5 years. Compute the TFR for Sweden and Kenya as well as the entire world for each of the two periods. As in the previous question, continue to assume that the reproductive age range of women is $[15, 50)$. Store the resulting two TFRs for each country or the world as vectors of length 2. In general, how has the number of women changed in the world from 1950 to 2000? What about the total number of births in the world?

4. Next, we will examine another important demographic process: death. Compute the *crude death rate* (CDR), which is a concept analogous to the CBR, for each

period and separately for each region. Store the resulting CDRs for each country and the world as vectors of length 2. The CDR is defined as

$$\text{CDR} = \frac{\text{number of deaths}}{\text{number of person-years lived}}.$$

Briefly describe the patterns you observe in the resulting CDRs.

5. One puzzling finding from the previous question is that the CDR for Kenya during the period 2005–2010 is about the same level as that for Sweden. We would expect people in developed countries like Sweden to have a lower death rate than those in developing countries like Kenya. While it is simple and easy to understand, the CDR does not take into account the age composition of a population. We therefore compute the *age-specific death rate* (ASDR). The ASDR for age range $[x, x + \delta)$ is defined as

$$\text{ASDR}_{[x,\ x+\delta)} = \frac{\text{number of deaths for people of age } [x,\ x+\delta)}{\text{number of person-years of people of age } [x,\ x+\delta)}.$$

Calculate the ASDR for each age group, separately for Kenya and Sweden, during the period 2005–2010. Briefly describe the pattern you observe.

6. One way to understand the difference in the CDR between Kenya and Sweden is to compute the counterfactual CDR for Kenya using Sweden's population distribution (or vice versa). This can be done by applying the following alternative formula for the CDR:

$$\text{CDR} = \text{ASDR}_{[0,5)} \times P_{[0,5)} + \text{ASDR}_{[5,10)} \times P_{[5,10)} + \cdots,$$

where $P_{[x,x+\delta)}$ is the proportion of the population in the age range $[x, x + \delta)$. We compute this as the ratio of person-years in that age range relative to the total person-years across all age ranges. To conduct this counterfactual analysis, we use $\text{ASDR}_{[x,x+\delta)}$ from Kenya and $P_{[x,x+\delta)}$ from Sweden during the period 2005–2010. That is, first calculate the age-specific population proportions for Sweden and then use them to compute the counterfactual CDR for Kenya. How does this counterfactual CDR compare with the original CDR of Kenya? Briefly interpret the result.

Chapter 2

Causality

Shallow men believe in luck, believe in circumstances.
Strong men believe in cause and effect.
— Ralph Waldo Emerson, *The Conduct of Life*

In this chapter, we consider causality, one of the most central concepts of quantitative social science. Much of social science research is concerned with the causal effects of various policies and other societal factors. Do small class sizes raise students' standardized test scores? Would universal health care improve the health and finances of the poor? What makes voters turn out in elections and determines their choice of candidates? To answer these causal questions, one must infer a counterfactual outcome and compare it with what actually happens (i.e., a factual outcome). We show how careful research design and data analysis can shed light on these causal questions that shape important academic and policy debates. We begin with a study of racial discrimination in the labor market. We then introduce various research designs useful for causal inference and apply them to additional studies concerning social pressure and voter turnout, as well as the impact of minimum-wage increases on employment. We also learn how to subset data in different ways and compute basic descriptive statistics in R.

2.1 Racial Discrimination in the Labor Market

Does racial discrimination exist in the labor market? Or, should racial disparities in the unemployment rate be attributed to other factors such as racial gaps in educational attainment? To answer this question, two social scientists conducted the following experiment.[1] In response to newspaper ads, the researchers sent out résumés of fictitious job candidates to potential employers. They varied only the names of job applicants, while leaving the other information in the résumés unchanged.

---

[1] This section is based on Marianne Bertrand and Sendhil Mullainathan (2004) "Are Emily and Greg more employable than Lakisha and Jamal? A field experiment on labor market discrimination." *American Economic Review*, vol. 94, no. 4, pp. 991–1013.

Table 2.1. Résumé Experiment Data.

Variable	Description
firstname	first name of the fictitious job applicant
sex	sex of applicant (female or male)
race	race of applicant (black or white)
call	whether a callback was made (1 = yes, 0 = no)

For some candidates, stereotypically African-American-sounding names such as Lakisha Washington or Jamal Jones were used, whereas other résumés contained stereotypically white-sounding names, such as Emily Walsh or Greg Baker. The researchers then compared the callback rates between these two groups and examined whether applicants with stereotypically black names received fewer callbacks than those with stereotypically white names. The positions to which the applications were sent were either in sales, administrative support, clerical, or customer services.

Let's examine the data from this experiment in detail. We begin by loading the CSV data file, resume.csv, into R as a data frame object called resume using the function read.csv(). Table 2.1 presents the names and descriptions of the variables in this data set.

```
resume <- read.csv("resume.csv")
```

Instead of using read.csv(), you can also import the data set using the pull-down menu Tools > Import Dataset > From Text File... in RStudio.

This data frame object resume is an example of *experimental data*. Experimental data are collected from an experimental research design, in which a *treatment variable*, or a causal variable of interest, is manipulated in order to examine its causal effects on an *outcome variable*. In this application, the treatment refers to the race of a fictitious applicant, implied by the name given on the résumé. The outcome variable is whether the applicant receives a callback. We are interested in examining whether or not the résumés with different names yield varying callback rates.

> **Experimental research** examines how a treatment causally affects an outcome by assigning varying values of the treatment variable to different observations, and measuring their corresponding values of the outcome variable.

```
dim(resume)

## [1] 4870    4
```

Using the dim() function, we can see that resume consists of 4870 observations and 4 variables. Each observation represents a fictitious job applicant. The outcome variable is whether the fictitious applicant received a callback from a prospective employer. The treatment variable is the race and gender of each applicant, though more precisely the researchers were manipulating how potential employers perceive the gender and race of applicants, rather than directly manipulating those attributes.

Once imported, the data set is displayed in a spreadsheet-like format in an RStudio window. Alternatively, we can look at the first several observations of the data set using the head() function.

```
head(resume)
##    firstname    sex  race call
## 1    Allison female white    0
## 2    Kristen female white    0
## 3    Lakisha female black    0
## 4    Latonya female black    0
## 5     Carrie female white    0
## 6        Jay   male white    0
```

For example, the second observation contains a résumé for Kristen, identified as a white female who did not receive a callback. In addition, we can also create a summary of the data frame via the summary() function.

```
summary(resume)
##     firstname            sex            race
##    Tamika : 256    female:3746    black:2435
##    Anne   : 242    male  :1124    white:2435
##    Allison: 232
##    Latonya: 230
##    Emily  : 227
##    Latoya : 226
##    (Other):3457
##        call
##    Min.   :0.00000
##    1st Qu.:0.00000
##    Median :0.00000
##    Mean   :0.08049
##    3rd Qu.:0.00000
##    Max.   :1.00000
##
```

The summary indicates the number of résumés for each name, gender, and race as well as the overall proportion of résumés that received a callback. For example, there were 230 résumés whose applicants had the first name of "Latonya." The summary also shows that the data set contains the same number of black and white names, while there are more female than male résumés.

We can now begin to answer whether or not the résumés with African-American-sounding names are less likely to receive callbacks. To do this, we first create a *contingency table* (also called a *cross tabulation*) summarizing the relationship between the race of each fictitious job applicant and whether a callback was received. A two-way contingency table contains the number of observations that fall within each category, defined by its corresponding row (race variable) and column (call variable). Recall that a variable in a data frame can be accessed using the $ operator (see section 1.3.5). For example, the syntax resume$race will extract the race variable in the resume data frame.

```
race.call.tab <- table(race = resume$race,  call = resume$call)
race.call.tab

##          call
## race        0    1
##    black 2278  157
##    white 2200  235
```

The table shows, for example, that among 2435 (= 2278 + 157) résumés with stereotypically black names, only 157 received a callback. It is convenient to add totals for each row and column by applying the addmargins() function to the output of the table() function.

```
addmargins(race.call.tab)

##          call
## race        0    1  Sum
##    black 2278  157 2435
##    white 2200  235 2435
##    Sum   4478  392 4870
```

Using this table, we can compute the callback rate, or the proportion of those who received a callback, for the entire sample and then separately for black and white applicants.

```
## overall callback rate: total callbacks divided by the sample size
sum(race.call.tab[, 2]) / nrow(resume)

## [1] 0.08049281

## callback rates for each race
race.call.tab[1, 2] / sum(race.call.tab[1, ]) # black

## [1] 0.06447639

race.call.tab[2, 2] / sum(race.call.tab[2, ]) # white

## [1] 0.09650924
```

Recall that the syntax `race.call.tab[1, ]`, which does not specify the column number, extracts all the elements of the first row of this matrix. Note that in the square brackets, the number before the comma identifies the row of the matrix whereas the number after the comma identifies the column (see section 1.3.5). This can be seen by simply typing the syntax into R.

```
race.call.tab[1, ]    # the first row

##    0     1
## 2278   157

race.call.tab[, 2]    # the second column

## black white
##   157   235
```

From this analysis, we observe that the callback rate for the résumés with African-American-sounding names is 0.032, or 3.2 percentage points, lower than those with white-sounding names. While we do not know whether this is the result of intentional discrimination, the lower callback rate for black applicants suggests the existence of racial discrimination in the labor market. Specifically, our analysis shows that the same résumé with a black-sounding name is substantially less likely to receive a callback than an identical résumé with a white-sounding name.

An easier way to compute callback rates is to exploit the fact that `call` is a *binary variable*, or *dummy variable*, that takes the value 1 if a potential employer makes a callback and 0 otherwise. In general, the sample mean of a binary variable equals the sample proportion of 1s. This means that the callback rate can be conveniently calculated as the *sample mean*, or *sample average*, of this variable using the `mean()` function rather than dividing the counts of 1s by the total number of observations. For example, instead of the slightly more complex syntax we used above, the overall callback rate can be calculated as follows.

```
mean(resume$call)

## [1] 0.08049281
```

What about the callback rate for each race? To compute this using the `mean()` function, we need to first subset the data for each race and then compute the mean of the `call` variable within this subset. The next section shows how to subset data in R.

2.2 Subsetting the Data in R

In this section, we learn how to subset a data set in various ways. We first introduce logical values and operators, which enable us to specify which observations and variables of a data set should be extracted. We also learn about factor variables, which represent categorical variables in R.

2.2.1   LOGICAL VALUES AND OPERATORS

To understand subsetting, we first note that R has a special representation of the two *logical values*, TRUE and FALSE, which belong to the object class logical (see section 1.3.2).

```
class(TRUE)

## [1] "logical"
```

These logical values can be converted to a binary variable in the integer class using the function as.integer(), where TRUE is recoded as 1 and FALSE becomes 0.

```
as.integer(TRUE)

## [1] 1

as.integer(FALSE)

## [1] 0
```

In many cases, R will coerce logical values into a binary variable so that performing numerical operations is straightforward. For example, in order to compute the proportion of TRUEs in a vector, one can simply use the mean() function to compute the sample mean of a logical vector. Similarly, we can use the sum() function to sum the elements of this vector in order to compute the total number of TRUEs.

```
x <- c(TRUE, FALSE, TRUE) # a vector with logical values
mean(x) # proportion of TRUEs

## [1] 0.6666667

sum(x) # number of TRUEs

## [1] 2
```

The logical values are often produced with the *logical operators* & and | corresponding to *logical conjunction* ("*AND*") and *logical disjunction* ("*OR*"), respectively. The value of "AND" (&) is TRUE only when both of the objects have a value of TRUE.

```
FALSE & TRUE

## [1] FALSE

TRUE & TRUE

## [1] TRUE
```

Table 2.2. Logical Conjunction "AND" and Disjunction "OR".

Statement a	Statement b	a AND b	a OR b
TRUE	TRUE	TRUE	TRUE
TRUE	FALSE	FALSE	TRUE
FALSE	TRUE	FALSE	TRUE
FALSE	FALSE	FALSE	FALSE

The table shows the value of a AND b and that of a OR b when statements a and b are either TRUE or FALSE.

"OR" (|) is used in a similar way. However, unlike "AND", "OR" is true when at least one of the objects has the value TRUE.

```
TRUE | FALSE

## [1] TRUE

FALSE | FALSE

## [1] FALSE
```

We summarize these relationships in table 2.2. For example, if one statement is FALSE and the other is TRUE, then the logical conjunction of the two statements is FALSE but their logical disjunction is TRUE (the second and third rows of the table).

With the same principle in mind, we can also chain multiple comparisons together where all elements must be TRUE in order for the syntax to return TRUE.

```
TRUE & FALSE & TRUE

## [1] FALSE
```

Furthermore, "AND" and "OR" can be used simultaneously, but parentheses should be used to avoid confusion.

```
(TRUE | FALSE) & FALSE # the parentheses evaluate to TRUE

## [1] FALSE

TRUE | (FALSE & FALSE) # the parentheses evaluate to FALSE

## [1] TRUE
```

We can perform the logical operations "AND" and "OR" on the entire vector all at once. In the following syntax example, each element of the TF1 logical vector is compared against the corresponding element of the logical TF2 vector.

```
TF1 <- c(TRUE, FALSE, FALSE)
TF2 <- c(TRUE, FALSE, TRUE)
TF1 | TF2

## [1]  TRUE FALSE  TRUE


TF1 & TF2

## [1]  TRUE FALSE FALSE
```

2.2.2   RELATIONAL OPERATORS

Relational operators evaluate the relationships between two values. They include "greater than" (>), "greater than or equal to" (>=), "less than" (<), "less than or equal to" (<=), "equal to" (==, which is different from =), and "not equal to" (!=). These operators return logical values.

```
4 > 3
## [1] TRUE


"Hello" == "hello"   # R is case sensitive
## [1] FALSE


"Hello" != "hello"
## [1] TRUE
```

Like the logical operators, the relational operators may be applied to vectors all at once. When applied to a vector, the operators evaluate each element of the vector.

```
x <- c(3, 2, 1, -2, -1)
x >= 2

## [1]  TRUE  TRUE FALSE FALSE FALSE


x != 1

## [1]  TRUE  TRUE FALSE  TRUE  TRUE
```

Since the relational operators produce logical values, we can combine their outputs with "AND" (&) and "OR" (|). When there are multiple instances of evaluation, it is good practice to put each evaluation within parentheses for ease of interpretation.

```
## logical conjunction of two vectors with logical values
(x > 0) & (x <= 2)

## [1] FALSE  TRUE  TRUE FALSE FALSE
```

```
## logical disjunction of two vectors with logical values
(x > 2) | (x <= -1)

## [1]  TRUE FALSE FALSE   TRUE   TRUE
```

As we saw earlier, the logical values, TRUE and FALSE, can be coerced into integers (1 and 0 representing TRUE and FALSE, respectively). We can therefore compute the number and proportion of TRUE elements in a vector very easily.

```
x.int <- (x > 0) & (x <= 2) # logical vector
x.int

## [1] FALSE  TRUE   TRUE FALSE FALSE

mean(x.int) # proportion of TRUEs

## [1] 0.4

sum(x.int)   # number of TRUEs

## [1] 2
```

2.2.3 SUBSETTING

In sections 1.3.3 and 1.3.5, we learned how to subset vectors and data frames using indexing. Here, we show how to subset them using logical values, introduced above. At the end of section 2.1, we saw how to calculate the callback rate for the entire sample by applying the mean() function to the binary call variable. To compute the callback rate among the résumés with black-sounding names, we use the following syntax.

```
## callback rate for black-sounding names
mean(resume$call[resume$race == "black"])

## [1] 0.06447639
```

This command syntax subsets the call variable in the resume data frame for the observations whose values for the race variable are equal to black. That is, we can utilize square brackets [ ] to index the values in a vector by placing the logical value of each element into a vector of the same length within the square brackets. The elements whose indexing value is TRUE are extracted. The syntax then calculates the sample mean of this subsetted vector using the mean() function, which is equal to the proportion of subsetted observations whose values for the call variable are equal to 1. It is instructive to print out the logical vector used inside the square brackets for subsetting. We observe that if the value of the `race` variable equals `black` (`white`) for an observation then its corresponding element of the resulting logical vector is `TRUE` (`FALSE`).

```
## race of first 5 observations
resume$race[1:5]

## [1] white white black black white
## Levels: black white

## comparison of first 5 observations
(resume$race == "black")[1:5]

## [1] FALSE FALSE  TRUE  TRUE FALSE
```

Note that `Levels` in the above output represent the values of a *factor* or categorical variable, which will later be explained in detail (see section 2.2.5). The calculation of callback rate for black-sounding names can also be done in two steps. We first subset a data frame object so that it contains only the résumés with black-sounding names and then compute the callback rate.

```
dim(resume) # dimension of original data frame

## [1] 4870    4

## subset blacks only
resumeB <- resume[resume$race == "black", ]
dim(resumeB) # this data.frame has fewer rows than the original data.frame

## [1] 2435    4

mean(resumeB$call) # callback rate for blacks

## [1] 0.06447639
```

Here, the data frame `resumeB` contains only the information about the résumés with black-sounding names. Notice that we used square brackets `[ , ]` to index the rows of this original data frame. Unlike in the case of indexing vectors, we use a comma to separate row and column indexes. This comma is important and forgetting to include it will lead to an error.

Instead of indexing through the square brackets, we can alternatively use the `subset()` function to construct a data frame that contains just some of the original observations and just some of the original variables. The function's two primary arguments, other than the original data frame object, are the `subset` and `select` arguments. The `subset` argument takes a logical vector that indicates whether each individual row should be kept for the new data frame. The `select` argument takes a character vector that specifies the names of variables to be retained. For example, the following syntax will extract the `call` and `firstname` variables for the résumés which contain female black-sounding names.

```
## keep "call" and "firstname" variables
## also keep observations with female black-sounding names
resumeBf <- subset(resume, select = c("call", "firstname"),
                   subset = (race == "black" & sex == "female"))
head(resumeBf)

##      call firstname
## 3       0   Lakisha
## 4       0   Latonya
## 8       0     Kenya
## 9       0   Latonya
## 11      0     Aisha
## 13      0     Aisha
```

When using the `subset()` function, we can eliminate the `subset` argument label. For example, `subset(resume, subset = (race == "black" & sex == "female"))` shortens to `subset(resume, race == "black" & sex == "female")`. Note that one could specify the data frame name to which the `race` and `sex` variables belong, i.e., `subset(resume, (resume$race == "black" & resume$sex == "female"))`, but this is unnecessary. By default, the variable names in this argument are assumed to come from the data frame specified in the first argument (`resume` in this case). So we can use simpler syntax: `subset(resume, (race == "black" & sex == "female"))`. It is important to pay close attention to parentheses so that each logical statement is contained within a pair of parentheses.

An identical subsetting result can be obtained using `[ , ]` rather than the `subset()` function, where the first element of the square brackets specifies the rows to be retained (using a logical vector) and the second element specifies the columns to be kept (using a character or integer vector).

```
## alternative syntax with the same results
resumeBf <- resume[resume$race == "black" & resume$sex == "female",
                   c("call", "firstname")]
```

We can now separately compute the racial gap in callback rate among female and male job applicants. Notice that we do not include a `select` argument to specify which variables to keep. Consequently, all variables will be retained.

```
## black male
resumeBm <- subset(resume, subset = (race == "black") & (sex == "male"))
```

```
## white female
resumeWf <- subset(resume, subset = (race == "white") & (sex == "female"))
## white male
resumeWm <- subset(resume, subset = (race == "white") & (sex == "male"))
## racial gaps
mean(resumeWf$call) - mean(resumeBf$call) # among females

## [1] 0.03264689

mean(resumeWm$call) - mean(resumeBm$call) # among males

## [1] 0.03040786
```

It appears that the racial gap exists but does not vary across gender groups. For both female and male job applicants, the callback rate is higher for whites than blacks by roughly 3 percentage points.

2.2.4 SIMPLE CONDITIONAL STATEMENTS

In many situations, we would like to perform different actions depending on whether a statement is true or false. These "actions" can be as complex or as simple as you need them to be. For example, we may wish to create a new variable based on the values of other variables in a data set. In chapter 4, we will learn more about *conditional statements*, but here we cover simple conditional statements that involve the ifelse() function.

The function ifelse(X, Y, Z) contains three elements. For each element in X that is TRUE, the corresponding element in Y is returned. In contrast, for each element in X that is FALSE, the corresponding element in Z is returned. For example, suppose that we want to create a new binary variable called BlackFemale in the resume data frame that equals 1 if the job applicant's name sounds black and female, and 0 otherwise. The following syntax achieves this goal.

```
resume$BlackFemale <- ifelse(resume$race == "black" &
                             resume$sex == "female", 1, 0)
```

We then use a three-way *contingency table* obtained by the table() function to confirm the result. As expected, the BlackFemale variable equals 1 only when a résumé belongs to a female African-American.

```
table(race = resume$race, sex = resume$sex,
      BlackFemale = resume$BlackFemale)

## , , BlackFemale = 0
##
##        sex
## race    female male
##   black      0  549
##   white   1860  575
```

```
##
## , , BlackFemale = 1
##
##         sex
## race     female male
##    black   1886    0
##    white      0    0
```

In the above output, the `, , BlackFemale = 0` and `, , BlackFemale = 1` headers indicate that the first two dimensions of the three-dimensional table are shown with the third variable, `BlackFemale`, equal to `0` and `1` for the first and second tables, respectively.

2.2.5 FACTOR VARIABLES

Next we show how to create a *factor variable* (or *factorial variable*) in R. A factor variable is another name for a *categorical variable* that takes a finite number of distinct values or levels. Here, we wish to create a factor variable that takes one of the four values, i.e., `BlackFemale`, `BlackMale`, `WhiteFemale`, and `WhiteMale`. To do this, we first create a new variable, `type`, which is filled with missing values `NA`. We then specify each type using the characteristics of the applicants.

```
resume$type <- NA
resume$type[resume$race == "black" & resume$sex == "female"] <- "BlackFemale"
resume$type[resume$race == "black" & resume$sex == "male"] <- "BlackMale"
resume$type[resume$race == "white" & resume$sex == "female"] <- "WhiteFemale"
resume$type[resume$race == "white" & resume$sex == "male"] <- "WhiteMale"
```

It turns out that this new variable is a character vector, and so we use the `as.factor()` function to turn this vector into a factor variable. While a factor variable looks like a character variable, the former actually has numeric values called *levels*, each of which has a character label. By default, the levels are sorted into alphabetical order based on their character labels. The levels of a factor variable can be obtained using the `levels()` function. Moreover, the `table()` function can be applied to obtain the number of observations that fall into each level.

```
## check object class
class(resume$type)

## [1] "character"

## coerce new character variable into a factor variable
resume$type <- as.factor(resume$type)
## list all levels of a factor variable
levels(resume$type)

## [1] "BlackFemale" "BlackMale" "WhiteFemale" "WhiteMale"
```

```
## obtain the number of observations for each level
table(resume$type)

##
## BlackFemale   BlackMale WhiteFemale   WhiteMale
##        1886         549        1860         575
```

The main advantage of factor objects is that R has a number of useful functionalities for them. One such example is the tapply() function, which applies a function repeatedly within each level of the factor variable. Suppose, for example, we want to calculate the callback rate for each of the four categories we just created. If we use the tapply() function this can be done in one line, rather than computing them one by one. Specifically, we use the function as in tapply(X, INDEX, FUN), which applies the function indicated by argument FUN to the object X for each of the groups defined by unique values of the vector INDEX. Here, we apply the mean() function to the call variable separately for each category of the type variable using the resume data frame.

```
tapply(resume$call, resume$type, mean)

## BlackFemale   BlackMale WhiteFemale   WhiteMale
##  0.06627784  0.05828780  0.09892473  0.08869565
```

Recall that the order of arguments in a function matters unless the name of the argument is explicitly specified. The result indicates that black males have the lowest callback rate followed by black females, white males, and white females. We can even go one step further and compute the callback rate for each first name. Using the sort() function, we can sort the result into increasing order for ease of presentation.

```
## turn first name into a factor variable
resume$firstname <- as.factor(resume$firstname)
## compute callback rate for each first name
callback.name <- tapply(resume$call, resume$firstname, mean)
## sort the result into increasing order
sort(callback.name)

##       Aisha     Rasheed      Keisha    Tremayne      Kareem
##  0.02222222  0.02985075  0.03825137  0.04347826  0.04687500
##      Darnell      Tyrone       Hakim      Tamika     Lakisha
##  0.04761905  0.05333333  0.05454545  0.05468750  0.05500000
##      Tanisha        Todd       Jamal        Neil       Brett
##  0.05797101  0.05882353  0.06557377  0.06578947  0.06779661
##      Geoffrey     Brendan        Greg       Emily        Anne
##  0.06779661  0.07692308  0.07843137  0.07929515  0.08264463
```

```
##        Jill      Latoya      Kenya     Matthew     Latonya
## 0.08374384 0.08407080 0.08673469 0.08955224 0.09130435
##       Leroy     Allison       Ebony    Jermaine      Laurie
## 0.09375000 0.09482759 0.09615385 0.09615385 0.09743590
##       Sarah     Meredith     Carrie     Kristen         Jay
## 0.09844560 0.10160428 0.13095238 0.13145540 0.13432836
##        Brad
## 0.15873016
```

As expected from the above aggregate result, we find that many typical names for black males and females have low callback rates.

2.3 Causal Effects and the Counterfactual

In the résumé experiment, we are trying to quantify the *causal effects* of applicants' names on their likelihood of receiving a callback from a potential employer. What do we exactly mean by causal effects? How should we think about causality in general? In this section, we discuss a commonly used framework for *causal inference* in quantitative social science research.

The key to understanding causality is to think about the *counterfactual*. Causal inference is a comparison between the factual (i.e., what actually happened) and the counterfactual (i.e., what would have happened if a key condition were different). The very first observation of the résumé experiment data shows that a potential employer received a résumé with a stereotypically white female first name Allison but decided not to call back (the value of the call variable is 0 for this observation).

```
resume[1, ]

##   firstname    sex   race call BlackFemale        type
## 1   Allison female white    0           0 WhiteFemale
```

The key causal question here is whether the same employer would have called back if the applicant's name were instead a stereotypically African-American name such as Lakisha. Unfortunately, we would never observe this counterfactual outcome, because the researchers who conducted this experiment did not send out the same résumé to the same employer using Lakisha as the first name (perhaps out of fear that sending two identical résumés with different names would raise suspicion among potential employers).

Consider another example where researchers are interested in figuring out whether raising the minimum wage increases the unemployment rate. Some argue that increasing the minimum wage may not be helpful for the poor, because employers would hire fewer workers if they have to pay higher wages (or hire higher-skilled instead of low-skilled workers). Suppose that one state in a country decided to raise the minimum wage and in this state the unemployment rate increased afterwards. This does not

Table 2.3. Potential Outcome Framework of Causal Inference.

Résumé i	Black-sounding name T_i	Callback		Age	Education
		$Y_i(1)$	$Y_i(0)$		
1	1	1	?	20	college
2	0	?	0	55	high school
3	0	?	1	40	graduate school
⋮	⋮	⋮	⋮	⋮	⋮
n	1	0	?	62	college

Note: The table illustrates the potential outcome framework of causal inference using the example of the résumé experiment. For each résumé of fictitious job applicant i, either the black-sounding, $T_i = 1$, or white-sounding, $T_i = 0$, name is used. The résumé contains other characteristics such as age and education, which are neither subject to nor affected by the manipulation. For a résumé with a black-sounding name, we can observe whether or not it receives a callback from the potential employer who received it, $Y_i(1)$, but will not be able to know the callback outcome if a white-sounding name was used, $Y_i(0)$. For every résumé, only one of the two potential outcomes is observed and the other is missing (indicated by "?").

necessarily imply that a higher minimum wage led to the increase in the unemployment rate. In order to know the causal effect of increasing the minimum wage, we would need to observe the unemployment rate that would have resulted if this state had not raised the minimum wage. Clearly, we would never be able to directly survey this counterfactual unemployment rate. Another example concerns the question of whether a job training program increases one's prospect of employment. Even if someone who actually had received job training secured a job afterwards, it does not necessarily follow that it was the job training program which led to the employment. The person may have become employed even in the absence of such a training program.

These examples illustrate the *fundamental problem of causal inference*, which arises because we cannot observe the counterfactual outcomes. We refer to a key causal variable of interest as a *treatment variable*, even though the variable may have nothing to do with a medical treatment. To determine whether a *treatment* variable of interest T, causes a change in an outcome variable Y, we must consider two *potential outcomes*, i.e., the potential values of Y that would be realized in the presence and absence of the treatment, denoted by $Y(1)$ and $Y(0)$, respectively. In the résumé experiment, T may represent the race of a fictitious applicant ($T = 1$ is a black-sounding name and $T = 0$ is a white-sounding name) while Y denotes whether a potential employer who received the résumé called back. Then, $Y(1)$ and $Y(0)$ represent whether a potential employer calls back when receiving a résumé with stereotypically black and white names, respectively.

All of these variables can be defined for each observation and marked by a corresponding subscript. For example, $Y_i(1)$ represents the potential outcome under the treatment condition for the ith observation, and T_i is the treatment variable for the same observation. Table 2.3 illustrates the potential outcome framework in the context of the résumé experiment. Each row represents an observation for which only one of the two potential outcomes is observed (the missing potential outcome is indicated by "?"). The treatment status T_i determines which potential outcome is observed. Variables such as age and education are neither subject to nor affected by the manipulation of treatment.

We can now define, for each observation, the causal effect of T_i on Y_i as the difference between these two potential outcomes, $Y_i(1) - Y_i(0)$. The race of the applicant has a causal effect if a potential employer's decision to callback depends on it. As stated earlier, the fundamental problem of causal inference is that we are only able to observe one of the two potential outcomes even though causal inference requires comparison of both. An important implication is that for estimation of causal effects, we must find a credible way to infer these unobserved counterfactual outcomes. This requires making certain assumptions. The credibility of any causal inference, therefore, rests upon the plausibility of these identification assumptions.

> For each observation i, we can define the **causal effect** of a binary treatment T_i as the difference between two potential outcomes, $Y_i(1) - Y_i(0)$, where $Y_i(1)$ represents the outcome that would be realized under the treatment condition ($T_i = 1$) and $Y_i(0)$ denotes the outcome that would be realized under the control condition ($T_i = 0$).
>
> The **fundamental problem of causal inference** is that we observe only one of the two potential outcomes, and which potential outcome is observed depends on the treatment status. Formally, the observed outcome Y_i is equal to $Y_i(T_i)$.

This simple framework of causal inference also clarifies what is and is not an appropriate causal question. For example, consider a question of whether one's race causally affects one's employment prospects. In order to answer this question directly, it would be necessary to consider the counterfactual employment status if the applicant were to belong to a different racial group. However, this is a difficult proposition to address because one's race is not something that can be manipulated. Characteristics like gender and race are called *immutable characteristics*, and many scholars believe that causal questions about these characteristics are not answerable. In fact, there exists a mantra which states, "No causation without manipulation." It may be difficult to think about causality if the treatment variable of interest cannot be easily manipulated.

The résumé experiment, however, provides a clever way of addressing an important social science question about racial discrimination. Instead of tackling the difficult task of directly estimating the causal effect of race, the researchers of this study manipulated potential employers' *perception* of job applicants' race by changing the names on identical résumés. This research design strategy enables one to study racial discrimination in the causal inference framework by circumventing the difficulty of manipulating one's race itself. Many social scientists use similar research design strategies to study discrimination due to factors such as race, gender, and religion in various environments.

2.4 Randomized Controlled Trials

Now that we have provided the general definition of causal effects, how should we go about estimating them? We first consider *randomized experiments*, also referred to as *randomized controlled trials* (RCTs), in which researchers randomly assign the receipt of treatment. An RCT is often regarded as the gold standard for establishing causality in many scientific disciplines because it enables researchers to isolate the effects of a treatment variable and quantify uncertainty. In this section, we discuss how randomization identifies the average causal effects. A discussion of how to quantify uncertainty will be given in chapter 7.

2.4.1 THE ROLE OF RANDOMIZATION

As explained in the previous section, the fundamental problem of causal inference states that for the estimation of causal effects, we must infer counterfactual outcomes. This problem prevents us from obtaining a valid estimate of the causal effect of treatment for each individual. However, it turns out that the randomization of treatment assignment enables the estimation of *average treatment effect*, which averages the treatment effect over a group of individuals.

Suppose that we are interested in estimating the *sample average treatment effect* (SATE), which is defined as the average of individual-level treatment effects in the sample.

The **sample average treatment effect** (SATE) is defined as the sample average of individual-level causal effects (i.e., $Y_i(1) - Y_i(0)$):

$$\text{SATE} = \frac{1}{n} \sum_{i=1}^{n} \{Y_i(1) - Y_i(0)\}, \tag{2.1}$$

where n is the sample size, and $\sum_{i=1}^{n}$ denotes the summation operator from the first observation, $i = 1$, to the last, $i = n$.

The SATE is not directly observable. For the *treatment group* that received the treatment, we observe the average outcome under the treatment but do not know what their average outcome would have been in the absence of the treatment. The same problem exists for the *control group* because this group does not receive the treatment and as a result we do not observe the average outcome that would occur under the treatment condition.

In order to estimate the average counterfactual outcome for the treatment group, we may use the observed average outcome of the control group. Similarly, we can use the observed average outcome of the treatment group as an estimate of the average counterfactual outcome for the control group. This suggests that the SATE can be estimated by calculating the difference in the average outcome between the treatment and control groups or the *difference-in-means estimator*. The critical question is whether we can interpret this difference as a valid estimate of the average causal effect. In the résumé experiment, the treatment group consists of the potential employers who were sent résumés with black-sounding names. In contrast, the control group comprises other potential employers who received the résumés with stereotypically white names. Does the difference in callback rate between these two groups represent the average causal effect of the applicant's race?

Randomization of treatment assignment plays an essential role in enabling the interpretation of this *association* as a causal relationship. By randomly assigning each subject to either the treatment or control group, we ensure that these two groups are similar to each other in every aspect. In fact, even though they consist of different individuals, the treatment and control groups are *on average* identical to each other in terms of *all* pretreatment characteristics, both observed and unobserved. Since the only systematic difference between the two groups is the receipt of treatment, we can interpret the difference in the outcome variable as the estimated average causal effect of the treatment. In this way, the randomization of treatment assignment separates the causal effect of treatment from other possible factors that may influence the outcome. As we will see in section 2.5, we cannot guarantee that the treatment and control groups are comparable across all unobserved characteristics in the absence of random assignment.

> In a **randomized controlled trial (RCT)**, each unit is randomly assigned either to the treatment or control group. The randomization of treatment assignment guarantees that the average difference in outcome between the treatment and control groups can be attributed solely to the treatment, because the two groups are on average identical to each other in all pretreatment characteristics.

RCTs, when successfully implemented, can yield valid estimates of causal effects. For this reason, RCTs are said to have a significant advantage for *internal validity*, which refers to whether the causal assumptions are satisfied in the study. However, RCTs are not without weaknesses. In particular, their strong internal validity often comes with a compromise in *external validity*. External validity is defined as the extent to which the conclusions can be generalized beyond a particular study. One common reason for a lack of external validity is that the study sample may not be representative of a population of interest. For ethical and logistical reasons, RCTs are often done using a convenient sample of subjects who are willing to be study subjects. This is an example of *sample selection bias*, making the experimental sample nonrepresentative of a target population. Another potential problem of external validity is that RCTs are often conducted in an environment (e.g., laboratory) quite different from real-world situations. In addition, RCTs may use interventions that are unrealistic in nature. As we saw in the résumé experiment, however, researchers have attempted to overcome these problems by conducting RCTs in the field and making their interventions as realistic as possible.

> The main advantage of randomized controlled trials (RCTs) is their improved **internal validity**—the extent to which causal assumptions are satisfied in the study. One weakness of RCTs, however, is the potential lack of **external validity**— the extent to which the conclusions can be generalized beyond a particular study.

Dear Registered Voter:

WHAT IF YOUR NEIGHBORS KNEW WHETHER YOU VOTED?

Why do so many people fail to vote? We've been talking about the problem for years, but
it only seems to get worse. This year, we're taking a new approach.
We're sending this mailing to you and your neighbors to publicize who does and does not
vote.

The chart shows the names of some of your neighbors, showing which have voted in the
past. After the August 8 election, we intend to mail an updated chart. You and your
neighbors will all know who voted and who did not.

DO YOUR CIVIC DUTY – VOTE!
- -

MAPLE DR	Aug 04	Nov 04	Aug 06
9995 JOSEPH JAMES SMITH	Voted	Voted	_____
995 JENNIFER KAY SMITH		Voted	_____
9997 RICHARD B JACKSON		Voted	_____
9999 KATHY MARIE JACKSON		Voted	_____

Figure 2.1. Naming-and-Shaming Get-out-the-Vote Message. Reprinted from Gerber,
Green, and Larimer (2008).

2.4.2   SOCIAL PRESSURE AND VOTER TURNOUT

We consider a study of peer pressure and voter turnout,[2] another example of an
RCT. Three social scientists conducted an RCT in which they investigated whether
social pressure within neighborhoods increases participation. Specifically, during a
primary election in the state of Michigan, they randomly assigned registered voters
to receive different *get-out-the-vote* (GOTV) messages and examined whether sending
postcards with these messages increased turnout. The researchers exploited the fact
that the turnout of individual voters is public information in the United States.

The GOTV message of particular interest was designed to induce social pressure by
telling voters that after the election their neighbors would be informed about whether
they voted in the election or not. The researchers hypothesized that such a naming-
and-shaming GOTV strategy would increase participation. An example of the actual
naming-and-shaming message is shown in figure 2.1. In addition to the control group,
which did not receive any mailing, the study also included other GOTV messages.
For example, a standard "civic duty" message began with the same first two sentences
of the naming-and-shaming message, but did not contain the additional information
about neighbors learning about a person's electoral participation. Instead, the message
continued to read as follows:

The whole point of democracy is that citizens are active participants in
government; that we have a voice in government. Your voice starts with your
vote. On August 8, remember your rights and responsibilities as a citizen.
Remember to vote. DO YOUR CIVIC DUTY – VOTE!

[2] This section is based on Alan S. Gerber, Donald P. Green, and Christopher W. Larimer (2008) "Social
pressure and voter turnout: Evidence from a large-scale field experiment." *American Political Science Review*,
vol. 102, no. 1, pp. 33–48.

Another important feature of this RCT is that the researchers attempted to separate the effect of naming-and-shaming from that of being observed. In many RCTs, there is a concern that study subjects may behave differently if they are aware of being observed by researchers. This phenomenon is called the *Hawthorne effect*, named after the factory where researchers observed an increase in workers' productivity simply because they knew that they were being monitored as part of a study. To address this issue, the study included another GOTV message, which starts with "YOU ARE BEING STUDIED!" followed by the same first two sentences as the naming-and-shaming message. The rest of the message reads,

> This year, we're trying to figure out why people do or do not vote. We'll be studying voter turnout in the August 8 primary election. Our analysis will be based on public records, so you will not be contacted again or disturbed in any way. Anything we learn about your voting or not voting will remain confidential and will not be disclosed to anyone else. DO YOUR CIVIC DUTY – VOTE!

The **Hawthorne effect** refers to the phenomenon where study subjects behave differently because they know they are being observed by researchers.

In this experiment, therefore, there are three treatment groups: voters who receive either the social pressure message, the civic duty message, or the Hawthorne effect message. The experiment also has a control group which consists of those voters receiving no message. The researchers randomly assigned each voter to one of the four groups and examined whether the voter turnout was different across the groups.

Now that we understand the design of this experiment, let us analyze the data. The data file, which is in CSV format, is named `social.csv` and can be loaded into R via the `read.csv()` function. Table 2.4 displays the names and descriptions of the variables in the social pressure experiment data.

```
social <- read.csv("social.csv") # load the data
summary(social) # summarize the data
##      sex           yearofbirth      primary2004
##  female:152702   Min.   :1900    Min.   :0.0000
##  male  :153164   1st Qu.:1947    1st Qu.:0.0000
##                  Median :1956    Median :0.0000
##                  Mean   :1956    Mean   :0.4014
##                  3rd Qu.:1965    3rd Qu.:1.0000
##                  Max.   :1986    Max.   :1.0000
##       messages        primary2006         hhsize
##  Civic Duty: 38218   Min.   :0.0000    Min.   :1.000
##  Control   :191243   1st Qu.:0.0000    1st Qu.:2.000
##  Hawthorne : 38204   Median :0.0000    Median :2.000
##  Neighbors : 38201   Mean   :0.3122    Mean   :2.184
##                      3rd Qu.:1.0000    3rd Qu.:2.000
##                      Max.   :1.0000    Max.   :8.000
```

Table 2.4. Social Pressure Experiment Data.

Variable	Description
hhsize	household size of the voter
messages	GOTV messages the voter received (Civic Duty, Control, Neighbors, Hawthorne)
sex	sex of the voter (female or male)
yearofbirth	year of birth of the voter
primary2004	whether the voter voted in the 2004 primary election (1=voted, 0=abstained)
primary2006	whether the voter turned out in the 2006 primary election (1=voted, 0=abstained)

As shown in section 2.2.5, we can use the `tapply()` function to compute the turnout for each treatment group. Subtracting the baseline turnout from the control group gives the average causal effect of each message. Note that the outcome variable of interest is the turnout in the 2006 primary election, which is coded as a binary variable `primary2006` where 1 represents turnout and 0 is abstention.

```
## turnout for each group
tapply(social$primary2006, social$messages, mean)

## Civic Duty    Control   Hawthorne   Neighbors
##   0.3145377  0.2966383  0.3223746   0.3779482

## turnout for control group
mean(social$primary2006[social$messages == "Control"])

## [1] 0.2966383

## subtract control group turnout from each group
tapply(social$primary2006, social$messages, mean) -
    mean(social$primary2006[social$messages == "Control"])

## Civic Duty    Control   Hawthorne   Neighbors
## 0.01789934 0.00000000 0.02573631 0.08130991
```

We find that the naming-and-shaming GOTV message substantially increases turnout. Compared to the control group turnout, the naming-and-shaming message increases turnout by 8.1 percentage points, whereas the civic duty message has a much smaller effect of 1.8 percentage points. It is interesting to see that the *Hawthorne effect* of being observed is somewhat greater than the effect of the civic duty message, though it is far smaller than the effect of the naming-and-shaming message.

Finally, if the randomization of treatment assignment is successful, we should not observe large differences across groups in the *pretreatment variables* such as age (indicated by `yearofbirth`), turnout in the previous primary election (`primary2004`), and household size (`hhsize`). We examine these using the same syntax.

```
social$age <- 2006 - social$yearofbirth # create age variable
tapply(social$age, social$messages, mean)

## Civic Duty    Control  Hawthorne  Neighbors
##    49.65904   49.81355   49.70480   49.85294


tapply(social$primary2004, social$messages, mean)

## Civic Duty    Control  Hawthorne  Neighbors
##  0.3994453  0.4003388  0.4032300  0.4066647


tapply(social$hhsize, social$messages, mean)

## Civic Duty    Control  Hawthorne  Neighbors
##    2.189126   2.183667   2.180138   2.187770
```

We see that the differences in these pretreatment variables are negligible across groups, confirming that the randomization of treatment assignment makes the four groups essentially identical to one another on average.

2.5 Observational Studies

Although RCTs can provide an internally valid estimate of causal effects, in many cases social scientists are unable to randomize treatment assignment in the real world for ethical and logistical reasons. We next consider *observational studies* in which researchers do not conduct an intervention. Instead, in observational studies, researchers simply observe naturally occurring events and collect and analyze the data. In such studies, *internal validity* is likely to be compromised because of possible selection bias, but *external validity* is often stronger than that of RCTs. The findings from observational studies are typically more generalizable because researchers can examine the treatments that are implemented among a relevant population in a real-world environment.

2.5.1 MINIMUM WAGE AND UNEMPLOYMENT

Our discussion of observational studies is based on the aforementioned minimum-wage debate. Two social science researchers examined the impact of raising the minimum wage on employment in the fast-food industry.[3] In 1992, the state of New Jersey (NJ) in the United States raised the minimum wage from $4.25 to $5.05 per hour. Did such an increase in the minimum wage reduce employment as economic theory predicts? As discussed above, answering this question requires inference about the NJ employment rate in the absence of such a raise in the minimum wage. Since this

---

[3] This section is based on David Card and Alan Krueger (1994) "Minimum wages and employment: A case study of the fast-food industry in New Jersey and Pennsylvania." *American Economic Review*, vol. 84, no. 4, pp. 772–793.

Table 2.5. Minimum-Wage Study Data.

Variable	Description
chain	name of the fast-food restaurant chain
location	location of the restaurants (centralNJ, northNJ, PA, shoreNJ, southNJ)
wageBefore	wage before the minimum-wage increase
wageAfter	wage after the minimum-wage increase
fullBefore	number of full-time employees before the minimum-wage increase
fullAfter	number of full-time employees after the minimum-wage increase
partBefore	number of part-time employees before the minimum-wage increase
partAfter	number of part-time employees after the minimum-wage increase

counterfactual outcome is not observable, we must somehow estimate it using observed data.

One possible strategy is to look at another state in which the minimum wage did not increase. For example, the researchers of this study chose the neighboring state, Pennsylvania (PA), on the grounds that NJ's economy resembles that of Pennsylvania, and hence the fast-food restaurants in the two states are comparable. Under this *cross-section comparison design*, therefore, the fast-food restaurants in NJ serve as the *treatment group* receiving the treatment (i.e., the increase in the minimum wage), whereas those in PA represent the *control group*, which did not receive such a treatment. To collect pretreatment and outcome measures, the researchers surveyed the fast-food restaurants before and after the minimum wage increase. Specifically, they gathered information about the number of full-time employees, the number of part-time employees, and their hourly wages, for each restaurant.

The CSV file `minwage.csv` contains this data set. As usual, the `read.csv()` function loads the data set, the `dim()` function gives the number of observations and the number of variables, and the `summary()` function provides a summary of each variable. Table 2.5 displays the names and descriptions of the variables in the minimum-wage study data.

```
minwage <- read.csv("minwage.csv") # load the data
dim(minwage) # dimension of data

## [1] 358    8

summary(minwage) # summary of data

##         chain          location      wageBefore
##   burgerking:149   centralNJ: 45   Min.   :4.250
##   kfc       : 75   northNJ  :146   1st Qu.:4.250
```

```
##   roys      : 88   PA       : 67   Median :4.500
##   wendys    : 46   shoreNJ  : 33   Mean   :4.618
##                    southNJ  : 67   3rd Qu.:4.987
##                                    Max.   :5.750
##    wageAfter        fullBefore        fullAfter
##   Min.   :4.250   Min.   : 0.000   Min.   : 0.000
##   1st Qu.:5.050   1st Qu.: 2.125   1st Qu.: 2.000
##   Median :5.050   Median : 6.000   Median : 6.000
##   Mean   :4.994   Mean   : 8.475   Mean   : 8.362
##   3rd Qu.:5.050   3rd Qu.:12.000   3rd Qu.:12.000
##   Max.   :6.250   Max.   :60.000   Max.   :40.000
##    partBefore       partAfter
##   Min.   : 0.00   Min.   : 0.00
##   1st Qu.:11.00   1st Qu.:11.00
##   Median :16.25   Median :17.00
##   Mean   :18.75   Mean   :18.69
##   3rd Qu.:25.00   3rd Qu.:25.00
##   Max.   :60.00   Max.   :60.00
```

To make sure that the restaurants followed the law, we first examine whether the minimum-wage actually increased in NJ after the law was enacted. We first subset the data based on location and then calculate the proportion of restaurants in each state with hourly wages less than the new minimum wage in NJ, i.e., \$5.05. This analysis can be done using the `wageBefore` and `wageAfter` variables, which represent the wage before and after the NJ law went into effect. The `subset()` function can be used to conduct this analysis.

```
## subsetting the data into two states
minwageNJ <- subset(minwage, subset = (location != "PA"))
minwagePA <- subset(minwage, subset = (location == "PA"))
## proportion of restaurants whose wage is less than $5.05
mean(minwageNJ$wageBefore < 5.05) # NJ before

## [1] 0.9106529

mean(minwageNJ$wageAfter < 5.05)  # NJ after

## [1] 0.003436426

mean(minwagePA$wageBefore < 5.05) # PA before

## [1] 0.9402985

mean(minwagePA$wageAfter < 5.05)  # PA after

## [1] 0.9552239
```

We observe that more than 91% of NJ restaurants were paying less than $5.05 before the minimum wage was raised and yet afterwards the proportion of such restaurants dramatically declined to less than 1%. In contrast, this proportion is essentially unchanged in PA, suggesting that the NJ law had minimal impact on the wages in PA restaurants. The analysis shows that the NJ restaurants followed the law by increasing their wage above the new minimum wage $5.05 while the PA restaurants did not have to make a similar change.

We now use the PA restaurants as the control group and estimate the average causal effect of increasing the minimum wage on employment among the NJ restaurants. An economic theory would predict that raising the minimum wage will encourage employers to replace full-time employees with part-time ones to recoup the increased cost in wages. To test this theory, we examine the proportion of full-time employees as a key outcome variable by simply comparing the *sample mean* of this variable between the NJ and PA restaurants after the NJ law went into effect. Let's compute this difference-in-means estimator.

```
## create a variable for proportion of full-time employees in NJ and PA
minwageNJ$fullPropAfter <- minwageNJ$fullAfter /
     (minwageNJ$fullAfter + minwageNJ$partAfter)
minwagePA$fullPropAfter <- minwagePA$fullAfter /
    (minwagePA$fullAfter + minwagePA$partAfter)
## compute the difference-in-means
mean(minwageNJ$fullPropAfter) - mean(minwagePA$fullPropAfter)

## [1] 0.04811886
```

The result of this analysis suggests that the increase in the minimum wage had no negative impact on employment. If anything, it appears to have slightly increased the proportion of full-time employment in NJ fast-food restaurants.

2.5.2 CONFOUNDING BIAS

The important assumption of observational studies is that the treatment and control groups must be comparable with respect to everything related to the outcome other than the treatment. In the current example, we cannot attribute the above difference in the full-time employment rate between NJ and PA restaurants to the minimum-wage increase in NJ if, for example, there is a competing industry for low-skilled workers in NJ but such an industry does not exist in PA. If that is the case, then the restaurants in the two states are not comparable and PA restaurants cannot serve as a valid control group for NJ restaurants. Indeed, NJ restaurants may have had a relatively high full-time employment rate, even in the absence of the increased minimum wage, in order to attract low-skilled workers. More generally, any other differences that exist between the fast-food restaurants in the two states before the administration of the NJ law would bias our inference if they are also related to outcomes.

The *pretreatment variables* that are associated with both the treatment and outcome variables are known as *confounders*. They are the variables that are realized prior to the administration of treatment and hence are not causally affected by the treatment.

However, they may determine who is likely to receive the treatment and influence the outcome. The existence of such variables is said to confound the causal relationship between the treatment and outcome, making it impossible to draw causal inferences from observational data. *Confounding bias* of this type is often a serious concern for social science research because in many cases human beings self-select into treatments. The aforementioned possibility that there exists a competing industry in NJ but not in PA is an example of confounding.

> A pretreatment variable that is associated with both the treatment and the outcome variables is called a **confounder** and is a source of **confounding bias** in the estimation of the treatment effect.

Confounding bias due to self-selection into the treatment group is called *selection bias*. Selection bias often arises in observational studies because researchers have no control over who receives the treatment. In the minimum-wage study, NJ politicians decided to increase the minimum wage at this particular moment in time whereas politicians in PA did not. One might suspect that there were reasons, related to the economy and employment in particular, why the minimum wage was raised in NJ but not in PA. If that is the case, then the cross-sectional comparison of NJ and PA after the minimum-wage increase in NJ is likely to yield selection bias. The lack of control over treatment assignment means that those who self-select themselves into the treatment group may differ significantly from those who do not in terms of observed and unobserved characteristics. This makes it difficult to determine whether the observed difference in outcome between the treatment and control groups is due to the difference in the treatment condition or the differences in confounders. The possible existence of confounding bias is the reason behind the existence of the popular mantra, "Association does not necessarily imply causation."

In observational studies, the possibility of confounding bias can never be ruled out. However, researchers can try to address it by means of *statistical control*, whereby the researcher adjusts for confounders using statistical procedures. We describe some basic strategies in this section. One simple way is the statistical method called *subclassification*. The idea is to make the treatment and control groups as similar to each other as possible by comparing them within a subset of observations defined by shared values in pretreatment variables or a subclass. For example, we notice that the PA sample has a larger proportion of Burger Kings than the NJ sample. This difference between the two states could confound the relationship between minimum-wage increase and employment if, for example, Burger King has an employment policy that is different from that of other fast-food chains. To address this possibility, we could conduct a comparison only among Burger King restaurants. This analysis enables us to eliminate the confounding bias due to different fast-food chains through statistical control.

To begin our analysis, we first check the proportions of different fast-food chains for each of the two samples. We use the `prop.table()` function, which takes as its main input the output from the `table()` function, i.e., a table of counts, and converts it to proportions.

```
prop.table(table(minwageNJ$chain))
##
## burgerking          kfc         roys       wendys
##   0.4054983    0.2233677    0.2508591    0.1202749

prop.table(table(minwagePA$chain))
##
## burgerking          kfc         roys       wendys
##   0.4626866    0.1492537    0.2238806    0.1641791
```

The result shows that PA has a higher proportion of Burger King restaurants than NJ. We compare the full-time employment rate between NJ and PA Burger King restaurants after the increase in the minimum wage. Though not shown here, a similar analysis can be conducted for other fast-food chain restaurants as well.

```
## subset Burger King only
minwageNJ.bk <- subset(minwageNJ, subset = (chain == "burgerking"))
minwagePA.bk <- subset(minwagePA, subset = (chain == "burgerking"))
## comparison of full-time employment rates
mean(minwageNJ.bk$fullPropAfter) - mean(minwagePA.bk$fullPropAfter)

## [1] 0.03643934
```

This finding is quite similar to the overall result presented earlier, suggesting that the fast-food chain may not be a confounding factor.

Another possible confounder is the location of restaurants. In particular, it may be the case that the NJ Burger King restaurants closer to PA yield a more credible comparison to those in PA, perhaps because their local economies share similar characteristics. To address this possible confounding bias, we may further subclassify the data on the basis of restaurant location. Specifically, we focus on the Burger King restaurants located in northern and southern NJ that are near PA, while excluding those in the Jersey shore and central New Jersey, and repeat the analysis. This analysis adjusts for both the type of restaurants and their locations through statistical control.

```
minwageNJ.bk.subset <-
    subset(minwageNJ.bk, subset = ((location != "shoreNJ") &
                                   (location != "centralNJ")))
mean(minwageNJ.bk.subset$fullPropAfter) - mean(minwagePA.bk$fullPropAfter)

## [1] 0.03149853
```

The result shows that even within this smaller subset of the original data, the estimated impact of the minimum-wage increase remains similar to the overall estimate. This finding further improves our confidence in the claim that the increase in the minimum wage had little effect on full-time employment.

> Confounding bias can be reduced through **statistical control**. For example, we can use the method of **subclassification** by comparing treated and control units which have an identical value of a confounding variable.

2.5.3 BEFORE-AND-AFTER AND DIFFERENCE-IN-DIFFERENCES DESIGNS

In observational studies, the data collected over time are a valuable source of information. Multiple measurements taken over time on the same units are called *longitudinal data* or *panel data*. Longitudinal data often yield a more credible comparison of the treatment and control groups than *cross-section data* because the former contain additional information about changes over time. In the minimum-wage study, the researchers had collected the employment and wage information from the same set of restaurants before the minimum wage was increased in NJ. This pretreatment information allows several alternative designs for estimating causal effects in observational studies.

The first possibility is comparison between pre- and posttreatment measurements, which is called the *before-and-after design*. Instead of comparing the fast-food restaurants in NJ with those in PA after the increase in the NJ minimum wage, this design compares the same set of fast-food restaurants in NJ before and after the minimum wage was raised. We compute the estimate under this design as follows.

```
## full-time employment proportion in the previous period for NJ
minwageNJ$fullPropBefore <- minwageNJ$fullBefore /
    (minwageNJ$fullBefore + minwageNJ$partBefore)
## mean difference between before and after the minimum wage increase
NJdiff <- mean(minwageNJ$fullPropAfter) - mean(minwageNJ$fullPropBefore)
NJdiff

## [1] 0.02387474
```

The before-and-after analysis gives an estimate that is similar to those obtained earlier. The advantage of this design is that any confounding factor that is specific to each state is held constant because the comparison is done within NJ. The disadvantage of the before-and-after design, however, is that time-varying confounding factors can bias the resulting inference. For example, suppose that there is an upwards *time trend* in the local economy and wages and employment are improving. If this trend is not caused by the minimum-wage increase, then we may incorrectly attribute the outcome difference between the two time periods to the raise in the minimum

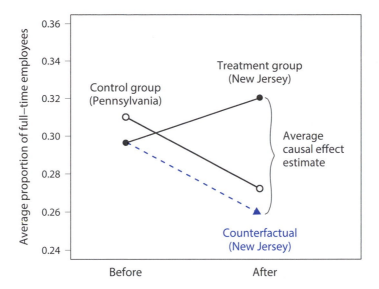

Figure 2.2. The Difference-in-Differences Design in the Minimum-Wage Study. The observed outcomes, i.e., the average proportion of full-time employees, are shown before and after the increase in the minimum wage for both the treatment group (fast-food restaurants in New Jersey; solid black circles) and the control group (restaurants in Pennsylvania; open black circles). Under the difference-in-differences design, the counterfactual outcome for the treatment group (solid blue triangle) is estimated by assuming that the time trend for the treatment group is parallel to the observed trend for the control group. The estimated average causal effect for New Jersey restaurants is indicated by the curly brace.

wage. The before-and-after design critically rests upon the nonexistence of such time trends.

> The **before-and-after design** examines how the outcome variable changed from the pretreatment period to the posttreatment period for the same set of units. The design is able to adjust for any confounding factor that is specific to each unit but does not change over time. However, the design does not address possible bias due to time-varying confounders.

The *difference-in-differences* (DiD) design extends the before-and-after design to address the confounding bias due to time trends. The key assumption behind the DiD design is that the outcome variable follows a parallel trend in the absence of treatment. Figure 2.2 graphically illustrates this assumption using the minimum-wage study data. The figure shows the outcome of interest, i.e., the average proportion of full-time employees, before and after the increase in the minimum wage for both the treatment group (fast-food restaurants in NJ, indicated by the solid black circles) and the control group (restaurants in PA, represented by the open black circles). In this setting, we can estimate the counterfactual outcome for the treatment group by assuming that the time trend for the treatment group is parallel to the observed trend for the control group. This estimate is indicated by the solid blue triangle.

Here, the counterfactual outcome of interest is the average proportion of full-time employees that we would have observed if NJ did not raise the minimum wage. We estimate this counterfactual outcome by supposing that NJ would have experienced the same economic trend as PA in the absence of the minimum-wage increase. In the figure, the blue dashed line is drawn to obtain the estimate of this counterfactual outcome and runs parallel to the observed time trend for the control group (indicated by the black solid line).

Under the DiD design, the sample average causal effect estimate for the NJ restaurants is the difference between the observed outcome after the minimum-wage increase and the counterfactual outcome derived under the parallel time trend assumption. The quantity of interest under the DiD design is called the *sample average treatment effect for the treated* (SATT). SATT differs from SATE, which is defined in equation (2.1), because it applies only to the treatment group, which consists of NJ restaurants in the current example.[4] In the figure, this estimate is indicated by the curly brace. To compute this estimate, we first calculate the difference in the outcome for the restaurants in PA after and before the minimum wage was raised in NJ. We then subtract this difference from the estimate obtained under the before-and-after design, which equals the difference in NJ after and before the minimum-wage increase. The average causal effect estimate is, therefore, given by the difference in the before-and-after differences between the treatment and control groups.

In this way, the DiD design uses the pretreatment and posttreatment measurements obtained for both the treatment and control groups. In contrast, the cross-section comparison requires only the posttreatment measurements from the two groups, and the before-and-after design utilizes the pretreatment and posttreatment measurements for the treatment group alone.

The **difference-in-differences** (DiD) design uses the following estimate of the sample average treatment effect for the treated (SATT):

$$\text{DiD estimate} = \underbrace{\left(\overline{Y}_{\text{treated}}^{\text{after}} - \overline{Y}_{\text{treated}}^{\text{before}}\right)}_{\text{difference for the treatment group}} - \underbrace{\left(\overline{Y}_{\text{control}}^{\text{after}} - \overline{Y}_{\text{control}}^{\text{before}}\right)}_{\text{difference for the control group}} .$$

The assumption is that the counterfactual outcome for the treatment group has a time trend parallel to that of the control group.

In the case of the minimum-wage study, we can compute the DiD estimate as follows.

---

[4] Formally, the sample average treatment effect for the treated (SATT) is the sample average of individual-level causal effect among the treated units, $\text{SATT} = \frac{1}{n_1}\sum_{i=1}^{n} T_i\{Y_i(1) - Y_i(0)\}$, where T_i is the binary treatment indicator variable and $n_1 = \sum_{i=1}^{n} T_i$ is the size of the treatment group.

```
## full-time employment proportion in the previous period for PA
minwagePA$fullPropBefore <- minwagePA$fullBefore /
    (minwagePA$fullBefore + minwagePA$partBefore)
## mean difference between before and after for PA
PAdiff <- mean(minwagePA$fullPropAfter) - mean(minwagePA$fullPropBefore)
## difference-in-differences
NJdiff - PAdiff

## [1] 0.06155831
```

The result is inconsistent with the prediction of some economists that raising the minimum wage has a negative impact on employment. To the contrary, our DiD analysis suggests that, if anything, the increase in the minimum wage may have led to a small rise in the proportion of full-time employees in NJ fast-food restaurants. The DiD estimate is greater than the before-and-after estimate, which reflected a negative trend in PA.

When does the DiD design fail? The DiD design yields an invalid estimate of causal effect if the time trend of the counterfactual outcome for the treatment group is not parallel to the observed time trend for the control group. We cannot verify this assumption because the counterfactual time trend for the treatment group is unobserved. However, in some cases, we can increase the credibility of this assumption. For example, if researchers had collected employment information from the restaurants in earlier time periods, then they could have examined whether the proportion of full-time employees in NJ restaurants had changed parallel to that of PA restaurants when the minimum wage had not been raised.

2.6 Descriptive Statistics for a Single Variable

So far, we have been examining the average outcome as the quantity of interest, but it is also possible to consider some other statistics of outcome. As the final topic of this chapter, we discuss how to numerically summarize the distribution of a single variable using *descriptive statistics*. We have already seen some examples of descriptive statistics, including the range (i.e., minimum and maximum values), median, and mean. In this section, we introduce other commonly used univariate statistics to describe the distribution of a single variable.

2.6.1 QUANTILES

We begin by introducing *quantiles*, which divide a set of observations into groups based on the magnitude of the variable. An example of quantiles is the *median*, which divides the data into two groups, one with lower data values and the other with higher values. That is, the median of a variable equals the middle value if the total number of observations is odd, whereas the median is the average of two middle values if the total number of observations is even (because there is no single middle value in this case). For example, the median of {1, 3, 4, 10} is 3.5, which is the average of the middle values 3 and 4, because this example has an even number of values. Meanwhile, the mean of this vector is 4.5.

While both the mean and median measure the center of the distribution, the mean is more sensitive to *outliers*. For example, a single observation of extreme value can dramatically change the mean but it will not affect the median as much. The median of {1, 3, 4, 10, 82} is 4, but the mean now increases to 20. In the minimum-wage data, the mean and median wages are similar. For example, the median wage before the minimum-wage increase is \$4.50, which is close to its mean of \$4.62.

The **median** of a variable x is defined as:

$$\text{median} = \begin{cases} x_{((n+1)/2)} & \text{if } n \text{ is odd,} \\ \dfrac{1}{2}\left(x_{(n/2)} + x_{(n/2+1)}\right) & \text{if } n \text{ is even,} \end{cases} \tag{2.2}$$

where $x_{(i)}$ denotes the value of the ith smallest observation for variable x and n is the sample size. The median is less sensitive to outliers than the **mean** and hence is a more robust measure of the center of a distribution.

To examine the robustness of previous findings, we examine how the increase in the minimum wage influenced the proportion of full-time employees in terms of the median rather than the mean. The median of a variable can be computed by using the `median()` function.

```
## cross-section comparison between NJ and PA
median(minwageNJ$fullPropAfter) - median(minwagePA$fullPropAfter)

## [1] 0.07291667


## before and after comparison
NJdiff.med <- median(minwageNJ$fullPropAfter) -
    median(minwageNJ$fullPropBefore)
NJdiff.med

## [1] 0.025


## median difference-in-differences
PAdiff.med <- median(minwagePA$fullPropAfter) -
    median(minwagePA$fullPropBefore)
NJdiff.med - PAdiff.med

## [1] 0.03701923
```

These results are largely consistent with those of the previous analysis, though the DiD estimate is smaller than before. Again, there is little evidence for the hypothesis that increasing the minimum wage decreases full-time employment. If anything, it may have instead slightly increased full-time employment.

To obtain a more complete description of the distribution, we can use *quartiles*, which divide the data into four groups. The *first quartile* (or *lower quartile*) is the value under which 25% of the observations fall, while the proportion of observations below the *third quartile* (or *upper quartile*) is 75%. The *second quartile* is equal to the median. The quartiles are a part of the output from the `summary()` function along with the minimum, mean, and maximum values. In addition, the difference between the upper and lower quartiles (i.e., 75th percentile and the 25th percentile) is called the *interquartile range* or *IQR*. That is, the IQR represents the range that contains 50% of the data, thereby measuring the spread of a distribution. This statistic can be computed by the `IQR()` function.

```
## summary shows quartiles as well as minimum, maximum, and mean
summary(minwageNJ$wageBefore)

##    Min. 1st Qu.  Median    Mean 3rd Qu.    Max.
##    4.25    4.25    4.50    4.61    4.87    5.75


summary(minwageNJ$wageAfter)

##    Min. 1st Qu.  Median    Mean 3rd Qu.    Max.
##   5.000   5.050   5.050   5.081   5.050   5.750


## interquartile range
IQR(minwageNJ$wageBefore)

## [1] 0.62


IQR(minwageNJ$wageAfter)

## [1] 0
```

This analysis shows that before the minimum-wage increase, the distribution of wages ranged from \$4.25 to \$5.75 with 75% of the fast-food restaurants in NJ having wages of \$4.87 per hour or less. However, after the minimum wage was raised to \$5.05, many restaurants raised their wages just to the new minimum wage but not any higher. As a result, both the lower and upper quartiles are equal to \$5.05, reducing the IQR from \$0.62 to \$0.

Finally, quartiles belong to a class of general statistics called *quantiles*, which divide the observations into a certain number of equally sized groups. Other quantiles include *terciles* (which divide the data into 3 groups), *quintiles* (5 groups), *deciles* (10 groups), and *percentiles* (100 groups). The `quantile()` function can generate any quantiles by specifying the `probs` argument. This argument takes a sequence of probabilities, indicating how the data should be divided up. For example, the deciles of the wage variable are obtained using the `seq()` function to create a sequence of numbers 0, 0.1, ..., 0.9, 1.

```
## deciles (10 groups)
quantile(minwageNJ$wageBefore, probs = seq(from = 0, to = 1, by = 0.1))

##    0%   10%   20%   30%   40%   50%   60%   70%   80%   90%  100%
## 4.25  4.25  4.25  4.25  4.50  4.50  4.65  4.75  5.00  5.00  5.75
```

```
quantile(minwageNJ$wageAfter, probs = seq(from = 0, to = 1, by = 0.1))

##    0%   10%   20%   30%   40%   50%   60%   70%   80%   90% 100%
## 5.00 5.05 5.05 5.05 5.05 5.05 5.05 5.05 5.05 5.15 5.75
```

We find that at least 90% of the fast-food restaurants in NJ set their wages to $5.05 or higher after the law was enacted. In contrast, before the increase in the minimum wage, there were few restaurants that offered wages of $5.05 or higher. Thus, the law had a dramatic effect on raising the wage to the new minimum wage, but no higher than that. In fact, the highest wage stayed unchanged at $5.75 even after the minimum wage was increased.

> **Quantiles** represent a set of data values that divide observations into a certain number of equally sized groups. They include quartiles (dividing the observations into 4 groups) and percentiles (100 groups):
>
> - 25th percentile = lower quartile;
> - 50th percentile = median;
> - 75th percentile = upper quartile.
>
> The difference between the upper and lower quartiles is called the **interquartile range** and measures the spread of a distribution.

2.6.2   STANDARD DEVIATION

We have used the range and quantiles (including the IQR) to describe the spread of a distribution. Another commonly used measure is *standard deviation*. Before introducing standard deviation, we first describe a statistic called the *root mean square* or *RMS*. The RMS describes the magnitude of a variable and is defined as

$$\text{RMS} = \sqrt{\text{mean of squared entries}}$$

$$= \sqrt{\frac{\text{entry}1^2 + \text{entry}2^2 + \cdots}{\text{number of entries}}}$$

$$= \sqrt{\frac{1}{n} \sum_{i=1}^{n} x_i^2}. \tag{2.3}$$

Equation (2.3) gives the formal mathematical definition. The equation exactly follows its name—square each entry, compute the mean, and then take the square root.

While the mean describes the center of the distribution, the RMS represents the average absolute magnitude of each data entry, ignoring the sign of the entry (e.g., the absolute magnitude or *absolute value* of -2 is 2 and is written as $|-2|$). For example, the mean of $\{-2, -1, 0, 1, 2\}$ is 0 but its RMS is $\sqrt{2}$. In the minimum-wage data, we can compute the RMS of the change in the proportion of full-time employees before and after the increase in the minimum wage, which is quite different from its mean.

```
sqrt(mean((minwageNJ$fullPropAfter - minwageNJ$fullPropBefore)^2))

## [1] 0.3014669

mean(minwageNJ$fullPropAfter - minwageNJ$fullPropBefore)

## [1] 0.02387474
```

Thus, on average, the absolute magnitude of change in the proportion of full-time employees, after the minimum wage was raised, is about 0.3. This represents a relatively large change even though the average difference is close to zero.

Using the RMS, we can define the sample *standard deviation* as the average deviation of each data entry from its mean. Therefore, the standard deviation measures the spread of a distribution by quantifying how far away data points are, on average, from their mean. Specifically, the standard deviation is defined as the RMS of deviation from the average:

$$\text{standard deviation} = \text{RMS of deviation from average}$$

$$= \sqrt{\frac{(\text{entry1} - \text{mean})^2 + (\text{entry2} - \text{mean})^2 + \cdots}{\text{number of entries}}}$$

$$= \sqrt{\frac{1}{n} \sum_{i=1}^{n} (x_i - \bar{x})^2}. \tag{2.4}$$

In some cases, one uses $n - 1$ instead of n in the denominator of equation (2.4) for a reason that will become clear in chapter 7, but this results in only a minor difference so long as one has enough data. We note that few data points are more than 2 or 3 standard deviations away from the mean. Hence, knowing the standard deviation helps researchers understand the approximate range of the data as well. Finally, the square of the standard deviation is called the *variance* and represents the average squared deviation from the mean. We will study variance more closely in later chapters. Variance is more difficult to interpret than standard deviation, but it has useful analytical properties, as shown in chapter 6.

> The sample **standard deviation** measures the average deviation from the mean and is defined as
>
> $$\text{standard deviation} = \sqrt{\frac{1}{n}\sum_{i=1}^{n}(x_i - \bar{x})^2} \quad \text{or} \quad \sqrt{\frac{1}{n-1}\sum_{i=1}^{n}(x_i - \bar{x})^2},$$
>
> where $\bar{x}$ represents the sample mean, i.e., $\bar{x} = \frac{1}{n}\sum_{i=1}^{n} x_i$ and n is the sample size. Few data points lie outside 2 or 3 standard deviations away from the mean. The square of the standard deviation is called the **variance**.

In R, we can easily compute the standard deviation using the `sd()` function (this function uses $n-1$ in its denominator). The `var()` function returns the sample variance. The examples from the minimum-wage data are given here.

```
## standard deviation
sd(minwageNJ$fullPropBefore)

## [1] 0.2304592

sd(minwageNJ$fullPropAfter)

## [1] 0.2510016

## variance
var(minwageNJ$fullPropBefore)

## [1] 0.05311145

var(minwageNJ$fullPropAfter)

## [1] 0.0630018
```

The results indicate that, on average, the proportion of full-time employees for a NJ fast-food restaurant is approximately 0.2 away from its mean. We find that for this variable the standard deviation did not change much after the minimum wage had been increased.

2.7 Summary

We began this chapter with the analysis of an experimental study concerning racial discrimination in the labor market. The **fundamental problem of causal inference** is the fact that we observe only one of two potential outcomes and yet the estimation of causal effect involves comparison between counterfactual and factual outcomes. This chapter also introduced various research design strategies to infer counterfactual outcomes from observed data. It is important to understand the assumptions that underlie each research design as well as their strengths and weaknesses.

In **randomized controlled experiments (RCTs)**, a simple comparison of the treatment and control groups enables researchers to estimate the causal effects of treatment. By randomizing the treatment assignment, we can ensure that the treatment and control groups are, on average, identical to each other in all observed and unobserved characteristics except for the receipt of treatment. Consequently, any average difference between the treatment and control groups can be attributed to the treatment. While RCTs tend to yield internally valid estimates of causal effects, they often suffer from a lack of external validity, which makes it difficult to generalize empirical conclusions to a relevant population in real-world settings.

In **observational studies**, researchers do not directly conduct interventions. Since some subjects may self-select into the treatment group, the difference in outcome between the treatment and control groups can be attributed to factors other than the receipt of treatment. Thus, while observational studies often have stronger external validity, this advantage typically comes with compromises in internal validity. When the treatment assignment is not randomized, we must confront the possibility of confounding bias in observational studies using statistical control. The existence of confounders that are associated with both the treatment and outcome means that a simple comparison of the two groups yields misleading inference. We introduced various research design strategies to reduce such bias, including subclassification, before-and-after design, and difference-in-differences design.

Finally, we learned how to subset data in various ways using R. Subsetting can be done using logical values, relational operators, and conditional statements. We also introduced a number of descriptive statistics that are useful for summarizing each variable in a data set. They include the mean, median, quantiles, and standard deviation. R provides a set of functions that enable researchers to compute these and other descriptive statistics from their data sets.

2.8 Exercises

2.8.1 EFFICACY OF SMALL CLASS SIZE IN EARLY EDUCATION

The STAR (Student–Teacher Achievement Ratio) Project is a four-year *longitudinal study* examining the effect of class size in early grade levels on educational performance and personal development.[5] A longitudinal study is one in which the same participants are followed over time. This particular study lasted from 1985 to 1989 and involved 11,601 students. During the four years of the study, students were randomly assigned to small classes, regular-sized classes, or regular-sized classes with an aid. In all, the experiment cost around $12 million. Even though the program stopped in 1989 after the first kindergarten class in the program finished third grade, the collection of various measurements (e.g., performance on tests in eighth grade, overall high-school GPA) continued through to the end of participants' high-school attendance.

We will analyze just a portion of this data to investigate whether the small class sizes improved educational performance or not. The data file name is STAR.csv, which is

---

[5] This exercise is in part based on Frederick Mosteller (1995) "The Tennessee study of class size in the early school grades." *The Future of Children*, vol. 5, no. 2, pp. 113–127.

Table 2.6. STAR Project Data.

Variable	Description
race	student's race (white = 1, black = 2, Asian = 3, Hispanic = 4, Native American = 5, others = 6)
classtype	type of kindergarten class (small = 1, regular = 2, regular with aid = 3)
g4math	total scaled score for the math portion of the fourth-grade standardized test
g4reading	total scaled score for the reading portion of the fourth-grade standardized test
yearssmall	number of years in small classes
hsgrad	high-school graduation (did graduate = 1, did not graduate = 0)

in CSV format. The names and descriptions of variables in this data set are displayed in table 2.6. Note that there are a fair amount of missing values in this data set, which arise, for example, because some students left a STAR school before third grade, or did not enter a STAR school until first grade.

1. Create a new factor variable called `kinder` in the data frame. This variable should recode `classtype` by changing integer values to their corresponding informative labels (e.g., change 1 to `small` etc.). Similarly, recode the `race` variable into a factor variable with four levels (`white`, `black`, `hispanic`, `others`) by combining the Asian and Native American categories with the others category. For the `race` variable, overwrite the original variable in the data frame rather than creating a new one. Recall that `na.rm = TRUE` can be added to functions in order to remove missing data (see section 1.3.5).

2. How does performance on fourth-grade reading and math tests for those students assigned to a small class in kindergarten compare with those assigned to a regular-sized class? Do students in the smaller classes perform better? Use means to make this comparison while removing missing values. Give a brief substantive interpretation of the results. To understand the size of the estimated effects, compare them with the standard deviation of the test scores.

3. Instead of just comparing average scores of reading and math tests between those students assigned to small classes and those assigned to regular-sized classes, look at the entire range of possible scores. To do so, compare a high score, defined as the 66th percentile, and a low score (the 33rd percentile) for small classes with the corresponding score for regular classes. These are examples of *quantile treatment effects*. Does this analysis add anything to the analysis based on mean in the previous question?

4. Some students were in small classes for all four years that the STAR program ran. Others were assigned to small classes for only one year and had either regular-sized classes or regular-sized classes with an aid for the rest. How many students

Table 2.7. Gay Marriage Data.

Variable	Description
study	source of the data (1 = study 1, 2 = study 2)
treatment	five possible treatment assignment options
wave	survey wave (a total of seven waves)
ssm	five-point scale on same-sex marriage, higher scores indicate support.

of each type are in the data set? Create a contingency table of proportions using the `kinder` and `yearssmall` variables. Does participation in more years of small classes make a greater difference in test scores? Compare the average and median reading and math test scores across students who spent different numbers of years in small classes.

5. Examine whether the STAR program reduced achievement gaps across different racial groups. Begin by comparing the average reading and math test scores between white and minority students (i.e., blacks and Hispanics) among those students who were assigned to regular-sized classes with no aid. Conduct the same comparison among those students who were assigned to small classes. Give a brief substantive interpretation of the results of your analysis.

6. Consider the long-term effects of kindergarten class size. Compare high-school graduation rates across students assigned to different class types. Also, examine whether graduation rates differ depending on the number of years spent in small classes. Finally, as in the previous question, investigate whether the STAR program has reduced the racial gap between white and minority students' graduation rates. Briefly discuss the results.

2.8.2 CHANGING MINDS ON GAY MARRIAGE

In this exercise, we analyze the data from two experiments in which households were canvassed for support on gay marriage.[6] Note that the original study was later retracted due to allegations of fabricated data; we will revisit this issue in a follow-up exercise (see section 3.9.1). In this exercise, however, we analyze the original data while ignoring the allegations.

Canvassers were given a script leading to conversations that averaged about twenty minutes. A distinctive feature of this study is that gay and straight canvassers were randomly assigned to households, and canvassers revealed whether they were straight or gay in the course of the conversation. The experiment aims to test the "contact hypothesis," which contends that out-group hostility (towards gay people in this case) diminishes when people from different groups interact with one another. The data file is `gay.csv`, which is a CSV file. Table 2.7 presents the names and descriptions

---

[6] This exercise is based on the following article: Michael J. LaCour and Donald P. Green (2015) "When contact changes minds: An experiment on transmission of support for gay equality." *Science*, vol. 346, no. 6215, pp. 1366–1369.

of the variables in this data set. Each observation of this data set is a respondent giving a response to a four-point survey item on same-sex marriage. There are two different studies in this data set, involving interviews during seven different time periods (i.e., seven waves). In both studies, the first wave consists of the interview before the canvassing treatment occurs.

1. Using the baseline interview wave before the treatment is administered, examine whether randomization was properly conducted. Base your analysis on the three groups of study 1: "same-sex marriage script by gay canvasser," "same-sex marriage script by straight canvasser" and "no contact." Briefly comment on the results.

2. The second wave of the survey was implemented two months after canvassing. Using study 1, estimate the average treatment effects of gay and straight canvassers on support for same-sex marriage, separately. Give a brief interpretation of the results.

3. The study contained another treatment that involves contact, but does not involve using the gay marriage script. Specifically, the authors used a script to encourage people to recycle. What is the purpose of this treatment? Using study 1 and wave 2, compare outcomes from the treatment "same-sex marriage script by gay canvasser" to "recycling script by gay canvasser." Repeat the same for straight canvassers, comparing the treatment "same-sex marriage script by straight canvasser" to "recycling script by straight canvasser." What do these comparisons reveal? Give a substantive interpretation of the results.

4. In study 1, the authors reinterviewed the respondents six different times (in waves 2 to 7) after treatment, at two-month intervals. The last interview, in wave 7, occurs one year after treatment. Do the effects of canvassing last? If so, under what conditions? Answer these questions by separately computing the average effects of straight and gay canvassers with the same-sex marriage script for each of the subsequent waves (relative to the control condition).

5. The researchers conducted a second study to replicate the core results of the first study. In this study, same-sex marriage scripts are given only by gay canvassers. For study 2, use the treatments "same-sex marriage script by gay canvasser" and "no contact" to examine whether randomization was appropriately conducted. Use the baseline support from wave 1 for this analysis.

6. For study 2, estimate the treatment effects of gay canvassing using data from wave 2. Are the results consistent with those of study 1?

7. Using study 2, estimate the average effect of gay canvassing at each subsequent wave and observe how it changes over time. Note that study 2 did not have a fifth or sixth wave, but the seventh wave occurred one year after treatment, as in study 1. Draw an overall conclusion from both study 1 and study 2.

Table 2.8. Leader Assassination Data.

Variable	Description
country	country
year	year
leadername	name of the leader who was targeted
age	age of the targeted leader
politybefore	average polity score of the country during the three-year period prior to the attempt
polityafter	average polity score of the country during the three-year period after the attempt
civilwarbefore	1 if the country was in civil war during the three-year period prior to the attempt, 0 otherwise
civilwarafter	1 if the country was in civil war during the three-year period after the attempt, 0 otherwise
interwarbefore	1 if the country was in international war during the three-year period prior to the attempt, 0 otherwise
interwarafter	1 if the country was in international war during the three-year period after the attempt, 0 otherwise
result	result of the assassination attempt

2.8.3 SUCCESS OF LEADER ASSASSINATION AS A NATURAL EXPERIMENT

One longstanding debate in the study of international relations concerns the question of whether individual political leaders can make a difference. Some emphasize that leaders with different ideologies and personalities can significantly affect the course of a nation. Others argue that political leaders are severely constrained by historical and institutional forces. Did individuals like Hitler, Mao, Roosevelt, and Churchill make a big difference? The difficulty of empirically testing these arguments stems from the fact that the change of leadership is not random and there are many confounding factors to be adjusted for.

In this exercise, we consider a *natural experiment* in which the success or failure of assassination attempts is assumed to be essentially random.[7] Each observation of the CSV data set leaders.csv contains information about an assassination attempt. Table 2.8 presents the names and descriptions of variables in this leader assassination data set. The polity variable represents the so-called *polity score* from the Polity Project. The Polity Project systematically documents and quantifies the regime types of all countries in the world from 1800. The polity score is a 21-point scale ranging from −10 (hereditary monarchy) to 10 (consolidated democracy). The result variable is a 10-category factor variable describing the result of each assassination attempt.

1. How many assassination attempts are recorded in the data? How many countries experience at least one leader assassination attempt? (The unique() function,

---

[7] This exercise is based on the following article: Benjamin F. Jones and Benjamin A. Olken (2009) "Hit or miss? The effect of assassinations on institutions and war." *American Economic Journal: Macroeconomics*, vol. 1, no. 2, pp. 55–87.

which returns a set of unique values from the input vector, may be useful here.) What is the average number of such attempts (per year) among these countries?

2. Create a new binary variable named `success` that is equal to 1 if a leader dies from the attack and 0 if the leader survives. Store this new variable as part of the original data frame. What is the overall success rate of leader assassination? Does the result speak to the validity of the assumption that the success of assassination attempts is randomly determined?

3. Investigate whether the average polity score over three years prior to an assassination attempt differs on average between successful and failed attempts. Also, examine whether there is any difference in the age of targeted leaders between successful and failed attempts. Briefly interpret the results in light of the validity of the aforementioned assumption.

4. Repeat the same analysis as in the previous question, but this time using the country's experience of civil and international war. Create a new binary variable in the data frame called `warbefore`. Code the variable such that it is equal to 1 if a country is in either civil or international war during the three years prior to an assassination attempt. Provide a brief interpretation of the result.

5. Does successful leader assassination cause democratization? Does successful leader assassination lead countries to war? When analyzing these data, be sure to state your assumptions and provide a brief interpretation of the results.

Chapter 3

Measurement

Not everything that can be counted counts, and not
everything that counts can be counted.
— William Bruce Cameron, *Informal Sociology*

Measurement plays a central role in social science research. In this chapter, we
first discuss survey methodology, which is perhaps the most common mode of data
collection. For example, the minimum-wage study discussed in chapter 2 used a survey
to measure information about employment at each fast-food restaurant. Surveys are
also effective tools for making inferences about a large target population of interest
from a relatively small sample of randomly selected units. In addition to surveys,
we also discuss the use of latent concepts, such as ideology, that are essential for
social science research. These concepts are fundamentally unobservable and must be
measured using a theoretical model. Thus, issues of measurement often occupy the
intersection of theoretical and empirical analyses in the study of human behavior.
Finally, we introduce a basic clustering method, which enables researchers to conduct
an exploratory analysis of data by discovering interesting patterns. We also learn how
to plot data in various ways and compute relevant descriptive statistics in R.

3.1 Measuring Civilian Victimization during Wartime

After the September 11 attacks, the United States and its allies invaded Afghanistan
with the goal of dismantling al-Qaeda, which had been operating there under the
protection of the Taliban government. In 2003, the North Atlantic Treaty Organization
(NATO) became involved in the conflict, sending in a coalition of international troops
organized under the name of the International Security Assistance Force (ISAF). To
wage this war against the Taliban insurgency, the ISAF engaged in a "hearts and
minds" campaign, combining economic assistance, service delivery, and protection in
order to win the support of civilians. To evaluate the success of such a campaign, it
is essential to measure and understand civilians' experiences and sentiments during
the war. However, measuring the experiences and opinions of civilians during wartime
is a challenging task because of harsh security conditions, posing potential threats to

Table 3.1. Afghanistan Survey Data.

Variable	Description
province	province where the respondent lives
district	district where the respondent lives
village.id	ID of the village where the respondent lives
age	age of the respondent
educ.years	years of education of the respondent
employed	whether the respondent is employed
income	monthly income of the respondent (five levels)
violent.exp.ISAF	whether the respondent experienced violence by ISAF
violent.exp.taliban	whether the respondent experienced violence by the Taliban
list.group	randomly assigned group for the list experiment (control, ISAF, taliban)
list.response	response to the list experiment question (0–4)

interviewers and respondents. This means that respondents may inaccurately answer survey questions in order to avoid giving socially undesirable responses.

A group of social scientists conducted a public opinion *survey* in southern Afghanistan, the heartland of the insurgency.[1] The survey was administered to a sample of 2754 respondents between January and February 2011. The researchers note that the participation rate was 89%. That is, they originally contacted 3097 males and 343 of them refused to take the survey. Because local culture prohibited interviewers from talking to female citizens, the respondents were all males.

We begin by summarizing the characteristics of respondents in terms of age, years of education, employment, and monthly income in Afghani (the local currency). The CSV file `afghan.csv` contains the survey data and can be loaded via the `read.csv()` function. The names and descriptions of the variables are given in table 3.1. We use the `summary()` function to provide numerical summaries of several variables.

```
## load data
afghan <- read.csv("afghan.csv")
## summarize variables of interest
summary(afghan$age)

##    Min. 1st Qu.  Median    Mean 3rd Qu.    Max.
##   15.00   22.00   30.00   32.39   40.00   80.00
```

[1] This section is based on the following two articles: Jason Lyall, Graeme Blair, and Kosuke Imai (2013) "Explaining support for combatants during wartime: A survey experiment in Afghanistan." *American Political Science Review*, vol. 107, no. 4 (November), pp. 679–705 and Graeme Blair, Kosuke Imai, and Jason Lyall (2014) "Comparing and combining list and endorsement experiments: Evidence from Afghanistan." *American Journal of Political Science*, vol. 58, no. 4 (October), pp. 1043–1063.

```
summary(afghan$educ.years)

##    Min. 1st Qu.  Median    Mean 3rd Qu.    Max.
##   0.000   0.000   1.000   4.002   8.000  18.000


summary(afghan$employed)

##    Min. 1st Qu.  Median    Mean 3rd Qu.    Max.
##  0.0000  0.0000  1.0000  0.5828  1.0000  1.0000


summary(afghan$income)

##    10,001-20,000     2,001-10,000   20,001-30,000
##             616            1420              93
## less than 2,000     over 30,000            NA's
##             457              14             154
```

We observe that the average age of the respondents is 32, a large fraction of them have very little education, and approximately 60% of the respondents are employed. Most respondents have a monthly income of less than 10,000 Afghani, which is about 200 dollars.

While civilians are often victimized during war, it is difficult to systematically measure the extent to which attacks against civilians occur. A survey measure, though it is based on self-reporting, is one possible way to quantify civilian victimization. In this survey, the interviewers asked the following question: "Over the past year, have you or anyone in your family suffered harm due to the actions of the Foreign Forces / the Taliban?" They explained to the respondents that the phrase "harm" refers to physical injury, as well as property damage. We analyze the violent.exp.ISAF and violent.exp.taliban variables, which represent whether the respondents were harmed by the ISAF and the Taliban, respectively.

```
prop.table(table(ISAF = afghan$violent.exp.ISAF,
                 Taliban = afghan$violent.exp.taliban))

##      Taliban
## ISAF           0           1
##    0 0.4953445 0.1318436
##    1 0.1769088 0.1959032
```

Using the table() and prop.table() functions, which were introduced in chapter 2, the analysis shows that over the past year, 37% (= 17.7% + 19.6%) and 33% (= 13.2% + 19.6%) of the respondents were victimized by the ISAF (second row) and the Taliban (second column), respectively. Approximately 20% of the respondents suffered from physical or property damage caused by both parties. This finding suggests that Afghan civilians were victimized (or at least they perceived that they were being victimized) by both the ISAF and the Taliban to a similar extent, rather than one warring party disproportionately harming civilians.

3.2 Handling Missing Data in R

In many surveys, researchers may encounter nonresponse because either respondents refuse to answer some questions or they simply do not know the answer. Such missing values are also common in other types of data. For example, many developing countries lack certain official statistics such as the gross domestic product (GDP) or unemployment rate. In R, missing data are coded as NA. For example, in the Afghanistan survey, we saw in the above analysis that 154 respondents did not provide their income. Since NA is a special value reserved for missing data, we can count the number of missing observations using the is.na() function. This function returns a logical value of TRUE if its argument is NA and yields FALSE otherwise.

```
## print income data for first 10 respondents
head(afghan$income, n = 10)

##  [1] 2,001-10,000  2,001-10,000  2,001-10,000  2,001-10,000
##  [5] 2,001-10,000  <NA>          10,001-20,000 2,001-10,000
##  [9] 2,001-10,000  <NA>
## 5 Levels: 10,001-20,000 2,001-10,000 ... over 30,000


## indicate whether respondents' income is missing
head(is.na(afghan$income), n = 10)

##  [1] FALSE FALSE FALSE FALSE FALSE  TRUE FALSE FALSE FALSE
## [10]  TRUE
```

Here, we see that the sixth and tenth respondents are not reporting their monthly income and hence are coded as NA. The syntax is.na(afghan$income) returns a vector of logical values, each indicating whether the corresponding respondent provided an answer to the income question. Thus, the sixth and tenth elements of the output from this syntax are TRUE. Given this function, it is now straightforward to count the total number and proportion of missing data for this variable.

```
sum(is.na(afghan$income)) # count of missing values

## [1] 154


mean(is.na(afghan$income)) # proportion missing

## [1] 0.05591866
```

Some R functions treat missing data differently from other data. For example, the mean() function returns NA when a variable contains at least one missing value. Fortunately, the mean() function takes an additional argument na.rm, which can be set to TRUE so that missing data are removed before the function is applied. Many other functions, including max(), min(), and median(), take this argument as well.

```
x <- c(1, 2, 3, NA)
mean(x)

## [1] NA

mean(x, na.rm = TRUE)

## [1] 2
```

In our data, the application of the `table()` function above ignored missing data, as if observations with missing values were not part of the data set. We can tell these functions to explicitly account for missing data. This can be done by setting the additional argument `exclude` to `NULL` so that no data including a missing value is excluded.

```
prop.table(table(ISAF = afghan$violent.exp.ISAF,
                 Taliban = afghan$violent.exp.taliban, exclude = NULL))

##         Taliban
## ISAF              0            1          <NA>
##    0      0.482933914  0.128540305  0.007988381
##    1      0.172476398  0.190994916  0.007988381
##    <NA>   0.002541757  0.002904866  0.003631082
```

We find that almost all respondents answered the victimization questions. Indeed, the nonresponse rates for these questions are less than 2%. The nonresponse rates for the Taliban and ISAF victimization questions can be obtained by adding the entries of the final column and those of the final row of the above generated table, respectively. It appears that the Afghan civilians are willing to answer questions about their experiences of violence.

Finally, the `na.omit()` function provides a straightforward way to remove all observations with at least one missing value from a data frame. The function then returns another data frame without these observations. However, we should note that this operation will result in *listwise deletion*, which eliminates an entire observation if at least one of its variables has a missing value. For example, if a respondent answers every question asked of him except for the question about income, listwise deletion would completely remove all of his information from the data, including the responses to the questions that he did answer. In our Afghanistan survey data, other variables that we have not yet discussed also have missing data. As a result, applying the `na.omit()` function to the `afghan` data frame returns a subset of the data with far fewer observations than applying the same function to the `income` variable alone.

```
afghan.sub <- na.omit(afghan) # listwise deletion
nrow(afghan.sub)

## [1] 2554
```

```
length(na.omit(afghan$income))

## [1] 2600
```

We find that the procedure of listwise deletion yields a data set of 2554 observations, whereas a total of 2600 respondents answered the income question. The difference represents the number of respondents who did answer the income question but refused to answer at least one other question in the survey.

3.3 Visualizing the Univariate Distribution

Up until now, we have been summarizing the distribution of each variable in a data set using descriptive statistics such as the mean, median, and quantiles. However, it is often helpful to visualize the distribution itself. In this section, we introduce several ways to visualize the distribution of a single variable in R. When making a figure in RStudio, you may occasionally encounter the error message "figure margins too large." We can solve this problem by increasing the size of the plots pane.

3.3.1 BAR PLOT

To summarize the distribution of a *factor variable* or *factorial variable* with several categories (see section 2.2.5), a simple table with counts or proportions, as produced above using the `table()` and `prop.table()` functions, is often sufficient. However, it is also possible to use a *bar plot* to visualize the distribution. In R, the `barplot()` function takes a vector of height and displays a bar plot in a separate graphical window. In this example, the vector of height represents the proportion of respondents in each response category.

```
## a vector of proportions to plot
ISAF.ptable <- prop.table(table(ISAF = afghan$violent.exp.ISAF,
                                 exclude = NULL))
ISAF.ptable

## ISAF
##            0            1         <NA>
## 0.619462600 0.371459695 0.009077705


## make bar plots by specifying a certain range for y-axis
barplot(ISAF.ptable,
        names.arg = c("No harm", "Harm", "Nonresponse"),
        main = "Civilian victimization by the ISAF",
        xlab = "Response category",
        ylab = "Proportion of the respondents", ylim = c(0, 0.7))
## repeat the same for victimization by the Taliban
Taliban.ptable <- prop.table(table(Taliban = afghan$violent.exp.taliban,
                                    exclude = NULL))
```

```
barplot(Taliban.ptable,
        names.arg = c("No harm", "Harm", "Nonresponse"),
        main = "Civilian victimization by the Taliban",
        xlab = "Response category",
        ylab = "Proportion of the respondents", ylim = c(0, 0.7))
```

The plots in this book, including these below, may appear different from those produced by running the corresponding code in R.

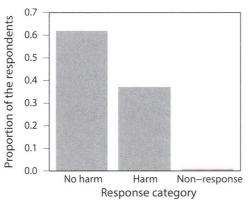

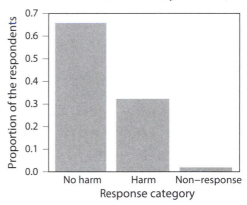

We immediately see that the distributions for civilian victimization by the ISAF and the Taliban are quite similar. In addition, the nonresponse rate is equally low for both variables. Note that `names.arg` is an optional argument unique to the `barplot()` function and takes a vector of characters specifying the label for each bar. The above syntax also illustrates the use of several arguments that are common to other plot functions and are summarized here:

- `main`: a character string, i.e., a series of characters in double quotes, for the main title of the plot
- `ylab`, `xlab`: character strings for labeling the vertical axis (i.e., *y*-axis) and the horizontal axis (i.e., *x*-axis), respectively (R will automatically set these arguments to the default labels if left unspecified)
- `ylim`, `xlim`: numeric vectors of length 2 specifying the interval for the *y*-axis and *x*-axis, respectively (R will automatically set these arguments if left unspecified)

3.3.2 HISTOGRAM

The *histogram* is a common method for visualizing the distribution of a *numeric variable* rather than a factor variable. Suppose that we would like to plot the histogram for the `age` variable in our Afghanistan survey data. To do this, we first discretize the variable by creating *bin*s or intervals along the variable of interest. For example, we may use 5 years as the size of each bin for the `age` variable, which results in the intervals [15, 20), [20, 25), [25, 30), and so on. Recall from an exercise of chapter 1 (see section 1.5.2) that in mathematics square brackets, [and], include the limit, whereas parentheses, (and), exclude it. For example, [20, 25) represents the age range that is greater than or equal to 20 years old and less than 25 years old. We then count the number of observations that fall within each bin. Finally, we compute the *density* for each bin, which is the height of the bin and is defined as

$$\text{density} = \frac{\text{proportion of observations in the bin}}{\text{width of the bin}}.$$

We often care about not the exact value of each density, but rather the variable's distribution as shown by the relationship of the different bins' densities to one another within a histogram. We can therefore think of histograms as rectangular approximations of the distribution.

To create histograms in R, we use the `hist()` function and set the argument `freq` to `FALSE`. The default for this argument is `TRUE`, which plots the frequency, i.e., counts, instead of using density as the height of each bin. Using density rather than frequency is useful for comparing two distributions, because the density scale is comparable across distributions even when the number of observations is different. Below, we create histograms for the `age` variable from the Afghanistan survey data.

```r
hist(afghan$age, freq = FALSE, ylim = c(0, 0.04), xlab = "Age",
     main = "Distribution of respondent's age")
```

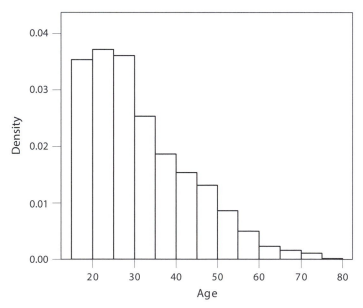

Importantly, the area of each bin in a histogram equals the proportion of observations that fall in that bin. Therefore, in general, we interpret the density scale, the unit of the vertical axis, as percentage per horizontal unit. In the age example, the density is measured as percentage per year. This implies that density is not a proportion and hence the height of each bin can exceed 1. On the other hand, the area of each bin represents the percentage of observations it contains, so the areas of all bins sum to 1. In this way, histograms visualize how observations are distributed across the different values of the variable of interest. The age distribution for the survey respondents is skewed towards the left, suggesting that a larger number of young males were interviewed.

> **A histogram** divides the data into bins where the area of each bin represents the proportion of observations that fall within the bin. The height of each bin represents **density**, which is equal to the proportion of observations within each bin divided by the width of the bin. A histogram approximates the distribution of a variable.

Our next histogram features the years of education variable, `educ.years`. Instead of letting R automatically choose the width of bins, as we did for the age variable, we now specify exactly how the bins are created using $[-0.5, 0.5), [0.5, 1.5), [1.5, 2.5), \ldots$, to center each bin around each of the integer values, i.e., $0, 1, 2, \ldots$, corresponding to the observed values. The height of each bin then represents the proportion of observations that received the corresponding number of years of education. We implement this by specifying a vector of the breakpoints between histogram bins with the `breaks` argument. In this case, the default specification, which we will get by leaving the argument unspecified, is $[0, 1), [1, 2), [2, 3), \ldots$ where it is centered around $0.5, 1.5, 2.5, \ldots$, failing to correspond to the observed values. Note that the `breaks` argument can take other forms of input to manipulate the histogram. For example, it also accepts a single integer specifying the number of bins for the histogram.

```
## histogram of education.  use "breaks" to choose bins
hist(afghan$educ.years, freq = FALSE,
     breaks = seq(from = -0.5, to = 18.5, by = 1),
     xlab = "Years of education",
     main = "Distribution of respondent's education")
## add a text label at (x, y) = (3, 0.5)
text(x = 3, y = 0.5, "median")
## add a vertical line representing median
abline(v = median(afghan$educ.years))
```

The histogram for the years of education variable clearly shows that the education level of these respondents is extremely low. Indeed, almost half of them have never attended school. We also add a vertical line and a text label indicating the *median* value, using the `abline()` and `text()` functions, respectively. Both of these functions add a layer to any existing plot, and this is why they are used after the `hist()` function in the above example. The `text(x,y,z)` function adds character text z centered at

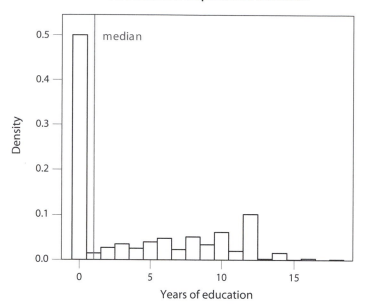

Distribution of respondent's education

the points specified by the coordinate vectors, (x, y). The `abline()` function can add a straight line to an existing plot in the following three ways:

- `abline(h = x)` to place a horizontal line at height x
- `abline(v = x)` to place a vertical line at point x
- `abline(a = y, b = s)` to place a line with intercept y and slope s

A more general function to plot a line is `lines()`. This function takes two arguments, x and y. These two arguments must be vectors with the same number of x-coordinates and y-coordinates respectively. The function will then draw line segments connecting the point denoted by the first coordinate in argument x and the first coordinate in argument y, to the point denoted by the second coordinates in each argument, to the point denoted by the third coordinates in each argument, and so on. For example, we can draw the median line as done above using this function instead.

```
## adding a vertical line representing the median
lines(x = rep(median(afghan$educ.years), 2), y = c(0,0.5))
```

In this example, we want to create a vertical line at the x value for the median of `afghan$educ.years`. We use y values, 0 and 0.5, so that the line will extend between the bottom and top limits of the histogram respectively. We then need x-coordinates equal to the median of `afghan$educ.years` to correspond with each y-coordinate. To do this easily, we can use the `rep()` function, whose first argument takes the value we want to repeat and whose second argument takes the number of repetitions, which is the length of the resulting vector. The above `rep()` function creates a vector of length 2 with the median of `afghan$educ.years` as each element in that vector. Thus, a line goes from point $(x, y) = (1, 0)$ to point $(x, y) = (1, 0.5)$, since the median year of education is 1.

It is also possible to add points to any existing plot using the `points()` function. Specifically, in `points(x, y)`, two vectors—x and y—specify the coordinates of points to be plotted. Finally, R has various functionalities that enable users to choose different colors, line types, and other aesthetic choices. Some commonly used arguments are given below, but the details about each function can be obtained on their manual pages:

- `col` specifies the color to use, such as `"blue"` and `"red"`. This argument can be used in many functions including `text()`, `abline()`, `lines()`, and `points()`. Type `colors()` to see all the built-in color names R has (see section 5.3.3 for more details).
- `lty` specifies the type of line to be drawn, using either a character or a numeric value, including `"solid"` or 1 (default) for solid lines, `"dashed"` or 2 for dashed lines, `"dotted"` or 3 for dotted lines, `"dotdash"` or 4 for dotted and dashed lines, and `"longdash"` or 5 for long dashed lines. This argument can be used in many functions that produce lines, including `abline()` and `lines()`.
- `lwd` specifies the thickness of lines where `lwd = 1` is the default value. This argument can be used in many functions that produce lines, including `abline()` and `lines()`.

3.3.3 BOX PLOT

The *box plot* represents another way to visualize the distributions of a numeric variable. It is particularly useful when comparing the distribution of several variables by placing them side by side. A box plot visualizes the median, the quartiles, and the IQR all together as a single object. To make box plots in R, we use the `boxplot()` function by simply giving a variable of interest as an input. Again, we use the `age` variable as an example.

```
## commands for plotting curly braces and text in blue are omitted
boxplot(afghan$age, main = "Distribution of age", ylab = "Age",
        ylim = c(10, 80))
```

As illustrated below, the box contains 50% of the data ranging from the lower quartile (25th percentile) to the upper quartile (75th percentile) with the solid horizontal line indicating the median value (50th percentile). Then, dotted vertical lines, each of which has its end indicated by a short horizontal line called a "whisker," extend below and above the box. These two dotted lines represent the data that are contained within 1.5 IQR below the lower quartile and above the upper quartile, respectively. Furthermore, the observations that fall outside 1.5 IQR from the upper

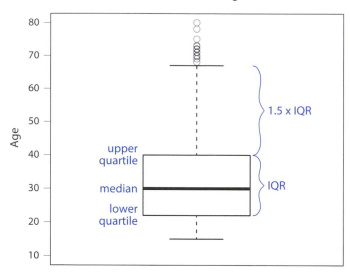

Distribution of age

and lower quartiles are indicated by open circles. In this plot, the section of the dotted line extending from the top of the box to the horizontal line represents 1.5 IQR. If the minimum (maximum) value is contained within 1.5 IQR below the lower quartile (above the upper quartile), the dotted line will end at the minimum (maximum) value. The absence of open circles below the horizontal line implies that the minimum value of this variable is indeed within the 1.5 IQR of the lower quantile.

If we wish to visualize the distribution of a single variable, then a histogram is often more informative than a box plot because the former shows the full shape of the distribution. One of the main advantages of a box plot is that it allows us to compare multiple distributions in a more compact manner than histograms, as the next example shows. Using the `boxplot()` function, we can create a box plot for a different group of observations where the groups are defined by a factor variable. This is done by using the formula in R, which takes the form y ˜ x. In the current context, `boxplot(y ˜ x, data = d)` creates box plots for variable y for different groups defined by a factor x where the variables, x and y, are taken from the data frame `d`. As an illustration, we plot the distribution of the years of education variable by province.

```
boxplot(educ.years ~ province, data = afghan,
        main = "Education by province", ylab = "Years of education")
```

We find that the education level in Helmand and Uruzgan provinces is much lower than that of the other three provinces. It also turns out that civilians in these two provinces report harm inflicted by both parties more than those who live in the other provinces. This is shown below by computing the proportion of affirmative answers to the corresponding question, for each province.

Education by province

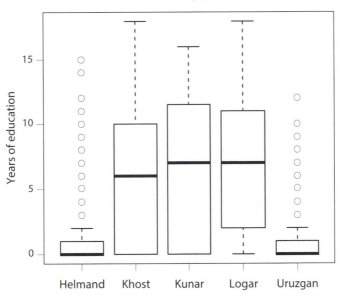

```
tapply(afghan$violent.exp.taliban, afghan$province, mean, na.rm = TRUE)

##    Helmand       Khost       Kunar       Logar     Uruzgan
## 0.50422195 0.23322684 0.30303030 0.08024691 0.45454545


tapply(afghan$violent.exp.ISAF, afghan$province, mean, na.rm = TRUE)

##    Helmand       Khost       Kunar       Logar     Uruzgan
## 0.5410226 0.2424242 0.3989899 0.1440329 0.4960422
```

Note that the syntax, na.rm = TRUE, is passed to the mean() function within the tapply() function so that missing observations are deleted when computing the mean for each province (see section 3.2).

> A **box plot** visualizes the distribution of a variable by indicating its median, lower and upper quartiles, and the points outside the 1.5 interquartile range from the lower and upper quartiles. It enables the comparison of distributions across multiple variables in a compact manner.

3.3.4   PRINTING AND SAVING GRAPHS

There are a few ways to print and save the graphs you create in R. The easiest way is to use the menus in RStudio. In RStudio, each time you create a graph using any of the R plotting functions, a new tab will open in the bottom-right window. To save an image of the plot, click Export and then either Save Plot as Image or Save Plot as PDF.

You can also save or print a graph with a command by using the `pdf()` function to open the PDF device before your plotting commands and then the `dev.off()` function afterwards to close the device. For example, the following syntax saves the box plots we just created above as a PDF file `educ.pdf` in the working directory. The `pdf()` function can specify the height and width of the graphics region in inches.

```
pdf(file = "educ.pdf", height = 5, width = 5)
boxplot(educ.years ~ province, data = afghan,
        main = "Education by province", ylab = "Years of education")
dev.off()
```

In many cases, we want to compare multiple plots by printing them next to each other in a single figure file. To do this, we use the function `par()` as `par(mfrow = c(X, Y))` before we start making plots. This will create an `X` by `Y` grid of "subplots" (`mfrow` stands for multiple figures in rows). Our multiple plots will fill in this grid, row by row. To fill the grid column by column, you can, instead, use the syntax `par(mfcol = c(X, Y))`. Note that the `par()` function also takes many other arguments that allow users to control graphics in R. For example, the `cex` argument changes the size of a character or symbol, with `cex = 1` as the default value. We can set the `cex` argument to a value greater than 1 (e.g., `par(cex = 1.2)`) in order to enlarge the fonts in displayed graphics. Note that it is also possible to separately specify the size for different parts of a plot using `cex.main` (main plot title), `cex.lab` (axis title labels), and `cex.axis` (axis value labels). Executing the following code chunk all at once creates the two histograms we made earlier in this chapter and saves them side by side in a single PDF file.

```
pdf(file = "hist.pdf", height = 4, width = 8)
## one row with 2 plots with font size 0.8
par(mfrow = c(1, 2), cex = 0.8)
## for simplicity omit the text and lines from the earlier example
hist(afghan$age, freq = FALSE,
     xlab = "Age", ylim = c(0, 0.04),
     main = "Distribution of respondent's age")
hist(afghan$educ.years, freq = FALSE,
     breaks = seq(from = -0.5, to = 18.5, by = 1),
     xlab = "Years of education", xlim = c(0, 20),
     main = "Distribution of respondent's education")
dev.off()
```

3.4 Survey Sampling

Survey sampling is one of the main data collection methods in quantitative social science research. It is often used to study public opinion and behavior when such information is not available from other sources such as administrative records. Survey sampling is a process in which researchers select a subset of the population, called a sample, to understand the features of a target population. It should be distinguished from a *census*, for which the goal is to enumerate all members of the population.

What makes survey sampling remarkable is that one can learn about a fairly large population by interviewing a small fraction of it. In the Afghanistan data, a sample of 2754 respondents was used to infer the experiences and attitudes of approximately 15 million civilians. In the United States, a sample of just about 1000 respondents is typically used to infer the public opinion of more than 200 million adult citizens. In this section, we explain what makes this seemingly impossible task possible and discuss important methodological issues when collecting and analyzing survey data.

3.4.1 THE ROLE OF RANDOMIZATION

As in the randomized control trials (RCTs) discussed in chapter 2, randomization plays an essential role in survey sampling. We focus on a class of sampling procedures called *probability sampling* in which every unit of a target population has a known nonzero probability of being selected. Consider the most basic probability sampling procedure, called *simple random sampling* (SRS), which selects the predetermined number of respondents to be interviewed from a target population, with each potential respondent having an equal chance of being selected. The sampling is done *without replacement* rather than *with replacement* so that once individuals are selected for interview they are taken out of the *sampling frame*, which represents the complete list of potential respondents. Therefore, sampling without replacement assigns at most one interview per individual.

SRS produces a sample of respondents that are *representative* of the population. By "representative," we mean that if we repeat the procedure many times, the features of each resulting sample would not be exactly the same as those of the population, but on average (across all the samples) would be identical. For example, while one may happen to obtain, due to random chance, a sample of individuals who are slightly older than those of the population, the age distribution over repeated samples would resemble that of the population. Moreover, as in RCTs, probability sampling guarantees that the characteristics of the sample, whether observed or unobserved, are on average identical to the corresponding characteristics of the population. For this reason, we can infer population characteristics using those of a representative sample obtained through probability sampling procedures (see chapter 7 for more details).

Before probability sampling was invented, researchers often used a procedure called *quota sampling*. Under this alternative sampling strategy, we specify fixed quotas of certain respondents to be interviewed such that the resulting sample characteristics resemble those of the population. For example, if 20% of the population has a college degree, then researchers will set the maximum number of college graduates who will be selected for interview to be 20% of the sample size. They will stop interviewing those with college degrees once they reach that quota. The quota can be defined using multiple variables. Often, the basic demographics such as age, gender, education, and race are used to construct the categories for which the quota is specified. For example, we may interview black females with a college degree and between 30 and 40 years old, up to 5% of the sample size.

The problem of quota sampling is similar to that of the observational studies discussed in chapter 2. Even if a sample is representative of the population in terms of some observed characteristics, which are used to define quotas, its unobserved features may be quite different from those of the population. Just as individuals may self-select to receive a treatment in an observational study, researchers may inadvertently interview individuals who have characteristics systematically different from those who are not interviewed. Probability sampling eliminates this potential *sample selection bias* by making sure that the resulting sample is representative of the target population.

> **Simple random sampling** (SRS) is the most basic form of **probability sampling**, which avoids **sample selection bias** by randomly choosing units from a population. Under SRS, the predetermined number of units is randomly selected from a target population without replacement, where each unit has an equal probability of being selected. The resulting sample is representative of the population in terms of any observed and unobserved characteristics.

Quota sampling is believed to have caused one of the most well-known errors in the history of newspapers. In the 1948 US presidential election, most major preelection polls, including those conducted by Gallup and Roper, used quota sampling and predicted that Thomas Dewey, then the governor of New York, would decisively defeat Harry Truman, the incumbent, on Election Day. On election night, the *Chicago Tribune* went ahead and sent the next morning's newspaper to press, with the erroneous headline "Dewey defeats Truman," even before many East Coast states reported their polling results. The election result, however, was the exact opposite. Truman won by a margin of 5 percentage points in the national vote. Figure 3.1 shows a well-known picture of Truman happily holding a copy of the *Chicago Tribune* with the erroneous headline.

In order to apply SRS, we need a list of all individuals in the population to sample from. As noted earlier, such a list is called a *sampling frame*. In practice, given a target population, obtaining a sampling frame that enumerates all members of the population is not necessarily straightforward. Lists of phone numbers, residential addresses, and email addresses are often incomplete, missing a certain subset of the population who have different characteristics. *Random digit dialing* is a popular technique for phone surveys. However, the procedure may suffer from sample selection bias since some people may not have a phone number and others may have multiple phone numbers.

Most in-person surveys employ a complex sampling procedure due to logistical challenges. While an in-depth study of various survey sampling strategies is beyond the scope of this book, we briefly discuss how the Afghanistan survey was conducted in order to illustrate how survey sampling is done in practice. For the Afghanistan survey, the researchers used a *multistage cluster sampling* procedure. In countries like Afghanistan, it is difficult to obtain a sampling frame that contains most, let alone all, of their citizens. However, comprehensive lists of administrative units such as districts and villages are often readily available. In addition, since sending interviewers across a large number of distant areas may be too costly, it is often necessary to sample respondents within a reasonable number of subregions.

Figure 3.1. Harry Truman, the Winner of the 1948 US Presidential Election, Holding a Copy of the *Chicago Tribune* with the Erroneous Headline. Source: Copyright unknown, Courtesy of Harry S. Truman Library.

Table 3.2. Afghanistan Village Data.

Variable	Description
village.surveyed	whether a village is sampled for survey
altitude	altitude of the village
population	population of the village

   The multistage cluster sampling method proceeds in multiple stages by sampling larger units first and then randomly selecting smaller units within each of the selected larger units. In the Afghanistan survey, within each of the five provinces of interest, the researchers sampled districts and then villages within each selected district. Within each sampled village, interviewers selected a household in an approximately random manner based on their location within the village, and finally administered a survey to a male respondent aged 16 years or older, who was sampled using the *Kish grid* method. While the probability of selecting each individual in the population is known only approximately, the method in theory should provide a roughly representative sample of the target population.

   We examine the representativeness of the randomly sampled villages in the Afghanistan data. The data file `afghan-village.csv` contains the altitude and population of each village (see table 3.2 for the names and descriptions of the variables). For the population variable, it is customary to take the *logarithmic transformation* so that the distribution does not look too skewed with a small number of extremely large or small values. The logarithm of a positive number x is defined as the exponent of a base value b, i.e., $y = \log_b x \iff x = b^y$. For example, if the base value is 10, then the

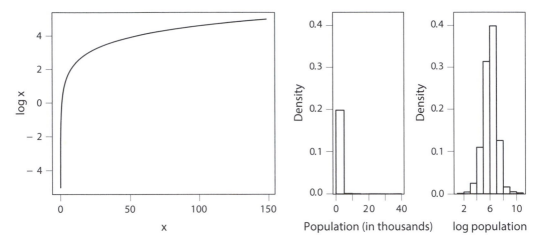

Figure 3.2. The Natural Logarithm. The left plot shows the natural logarithm $\log_e x$ where x is a positive number and $e = 2.7182\ldots$ is Euler's number. The remaining plots display the histograms for the population of Afghan villages on the original scale (in thousands) and the natural logarithmic scale. The population distribution is skewed without the logarithmic transformation.

logarithm of 1000 is $3 = \log_{10} 1000$. Similarly, the logarithm of 0.01 is $-2 = \log_{10} 0.01$. The *natural logarithm* uses as its base value an important mathematical constant $e = 2.7182\ldots$, which is defined as the limit of $(1 + 1/n)^n$ as n approaches infinity and is sometimes called Euler's number, so that $y = \log_e x \iff x = e^y$. The left-hand plot of figure 3.2 depicts the natural logarithm function graphically. The figure also shows that in the Afghanistan data, without the logarithmic transformation, the distribution of the population is quite skewed because there exist a large number of small villages and a small number of large villages.

> The **natural logarithmic transformation** is often used to correct the skewness of variables such as income and population that have a small number of observations with extremely large or small positive values. The natural logarithm is the logarithm with base e, which is a mathematical constant approximately equal to 2.7182, and defined as $y = \log_e x$. It is the inverse function of the exponential function, so $x = e^y$.

We use box plots to compare the distribution of these variables across sampled and nonsampled villages. The variable `village.surveyed` indicates whether each village in the data is (randomly) sampled and surveyed; `1` indicates yes and `0` no. As explained above, we take the natural logarithmic transformation for the population variable using the `log()` function. By default R uses e as its base, though it is possible to specify a different base using the `base` argument in this function. Note that the exponential function in R is given by `exp()`. In the `boxplot()` function, we can use the `names` argument to specify a character vector of labels for each group.

```
## load village data
afghan.village <- read.csv("afghan-village.csv")
## box plots for altitude
boxplot(altitude ~ village.surveyed, data = afghan.village,
        ylab = "Altitude (meters)", names = c("Nonsampled", "Sampled"))
## box plots for log population
boxplot(log(population) ~ village.surveyed, data = afghan.village,
        ylab = "log population", names = c("Nonsampled", "Sampled"))
```

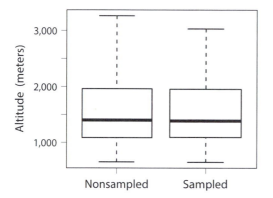 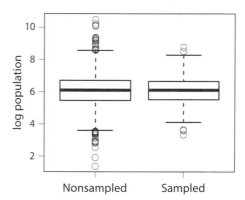

The result shows that although there are some outliers, the distribution of these two variables is largely similar between the sampled and nonsampled villages. So, at least for these variables the sample appears to be representative of the population.

3.4.2 NONRESPONSE AND OTHER SOURCES OF BIAS

While probability sampling has attractive theoretical properties, in practice conducting a survey faces many obstacles. As mentioned earlier, a *sampling frame*, which enumerates all members of a target population, is difficult to obtain. In many cases, we end up sampling from a list that may systematically diverge from the target population in terms of some important characteristics. Even if a representative sampling frame is available, interviewing randomly selected individuals may not be straightforward. Failure to reach selected units is called *unit nonresponse*. For example, many individuals refuse to participate in phone surveys. In the Afghanistan survey, the authors report that 2754 out of 3097 potential respondents agreed to participate in the survey, resulting in an 11% refusal rate. If those to whom researchers fail to administer the survey are systematically different from those who participate in the survey, then bias due to unit nonresponse arises.

In addition to unit nonresponse, most surveys also encounter the *item nonresponse* problem when respondents refuse to answer certain survey questions. For example, we saw in section 3.2 that in the Afghanistan survey, the income variable had a nonresponse rate of approximately 5%. If those who refuse to answer are systematically different from those who answer, then the resulting inference based only on the observed responses may be biased. In the Afghanistan data, for example, the item nonresponse rates for the questions about civilian victimization by the Taliban and the ISAF appear to vary across provinces.

```
tapply(is.na(afghan$violent.exp.taliban), afghan$province, mean)

##     Helmand       Khost       Kunar       Logar     Uruzgan
## 0.030409357 0.006349206 0.000000000 0.000000000 0.062015504

tapply(is.na(afghan$violent.exp.ISAF), afghan$province, mean)

##     Helmand       Khost       Kunar       Logar     Uruzgan
## 0.016374269 0.004761905 0.000000000 0.000000000 0.020671835
```

We observe that in Helmand and Uruzgan, which are known to be the most violent provinces (see section 3.3.3), the item nonresponse rates are the highest. These differences are especially large for the question about civilian victimization by the Taliban. The evidence presented here suggests that although the item nonresponse rate in this survey is relatively low, certain systematic factors appear to affect its magnitude. While they are beyond the scope of this book, there exist many statistical methods of reducing the bias due to unit and item nonresponse.

> There are two types of nonresponse in survey research. **Unit nonresponse** refers to a case in which a potential respondent refuses to participate in a survey. **Item nonresponse** occurs when a respondent who agreed to participate refuses to answer a particular question. Both nonresponses can result in biased inferences if those who respond to a question are systematically different from those who do not.

Beyond item and unit nonresponse, another potential source of bias is *misreporting*. Respondents may simply lie because they may not want interviewers to find out their true answers. In particular, *social desirability bias* refers to the problem where respondents choose an answer that is seen as socially desirable regardless of what their truthful answer is. For example, it is well known that in advanced democracies voters tend to report they participated in an election even when they actually did not, because abstention is socially undesirable. Similarly, social desirability bias makes it difficult to accurately measure sensitive behavior and opinions such as corruption, illegal behavior, racial prejudice, and sexual activity. For this reason, some scholars remain skeptical of self-reports as measurement for social science research.

One main goal of the Afghanistan study was to measure the extent to which Afghan citizens support foreign forces. To defeat local insurgent forces and win the wars in Afghanistan and Iraq, many Western policy makers believed that "winning the hearts and minds" of a civilian population was essential. Unfortunately, directly asking whether citizens are supportive of foreign forces and insurgents in rural Afghan villages can put interviewers and respondents at risk because interviews are often conducted in public. The *Institutional Review Board*, which evaluates the ethical issues and potential risks of research projects involving human subjects, may not approve direct questioning of sensitive questions in a civil war setting. Even if possible, direct questioning may lead to nonresponse and misreporting.

To address this problem, the authors of the original study implemented a survey methodology called *item count technique* or *list experiment*. The idea is to use aggregation to provide a certain level of anonymity to respondents. The method first randomly divides the sample into two comparable groups. In the "control" group, the following question was asked.

> I'm going to read you a list with the names of different groups and individuals on it. After I read the entire list, I'd like you to tell me how many of these groups and individuals you broadly support, meaning that you generally agree with the goals and policies of the group or individual. Please don't tell me which ones you generally agree with; only tell me how many groups or individuals you broadly support.

> Karzai Government; National Solidarity Program; Local Farmers

The "treatment" group received the same question except with an additional sensitive item:

> Karzai Government; National Solidarity Program; Local Farmers; Foreign Forces

Here, the last item, Foreign Forces, which refers to the ISAF, is the sensitive item. The item count technique does not require respondents to answer each item separately. Instead, they give an aggregate count of items. Since the two conditions are comparable apart from the sensitive item, the difference in the average number of items a respondent reports will be an estimate of the proportion of those who support the ISAF. The `list.group` variable indicates which group each respondent is randomly assigned to, where for the two relevant groups the variable equals `ISAF` and `control`. The outcome variable is `list.response`, which represents the item count reported by each respondent.

```
mean(afghan$list.response[afghan$list.group == "ISAF"])-
    mean(afghan$list.response[afghan$list.group == "control"])

## [1] 0.04901961
```

The item count technique estimates that approximately 5% of Afghan citizens support the ISAF, implying that the ISAF is unpopular among Afghans.

The weakness of the item count technique, however, is that in the "treatment" group, answering either "0" or "4" in this case reveals one's honest answer. These potential problems are called *floor effects* and *ceiling effects*, respectively. In the Afghan data, we see clear evidence of this problem when the Taliban, instead of the ISAF, is added to the list as the sensitive item.

```
table(response = afghan$list.response, group = afghan$list.group)

##          group
## response control ISAF taliban
##        0     188  174       0
##        1     265  278     433
##        2     265  260     287
##        3     200  182     198
##        4       0   24       0
```

Remarkably, no respondents in the `taliban` group answered either "0" or "4," perhaps because they do not want to be identified as either supportive or critical of the Taliban.

As we can see, measuring the truthful responses to sensitive questions is a challenging task. In addition to the item count technique, social scientists have used a variety of survey methodologies in an effort to overcome this problem. Another popular methodology is called the *randomized response technique* in which researchers use randomization to provide anonymity to respondents. For example, respondents are asked to roll a six-sided die in private without revealing the outcome. They are then asked to answer yes if the outcome of rolling the die was 1, no if 6, and give an honest answer if the outcome was between 2 and 5. Therefore, unlike the item count technique, the secrecy of individual responses is completely protected. Since the probability of each outcome is known, the researchers can estimate the aggregate proportion of honest responses out of those who responded with a yes answer even though they have no way of knowing the truthfulness of individual answers with certainty.

3.5 Measuring Political Polarization

Social scientists often devise *measurement models* to summarize and understand the behaviors, attitudes, and unobservable characteristics of human beings. A prominent example is the question of how to quantitatively characterize the *ideology* of political actors such as legislators and judges from their behavior. Of course, we do not directly observe the extent to which an individual is liberal or conservative. While ideology is perhaps a purely artificial concept, it is nonetheless a useful way to describe the political orientation of various individuals. Over the past several decades, social scientists have attempted to infer the ideology of politicians from their roll call votes. In each year, for example, legislators in the US Congress vote on hundreds of bills. Using this voting record, which is publicly available, researchers have tried to characterize the political ideology of each member of Congress and how the overall ideological orientation in the US Congress has changed over time.[2]

A simple measurement model of *spatial voting* can relate a legislator's ideology to their votes. Figure 3.3 illustrates this model, which characterizes the ideology

---

[2] This section is based on Nolan McCarty, Keith T. Poole, and Howard Rosenthal (2006) *Polarized America: The Dance of Ideology and Unequal Riches*. MIT Press.

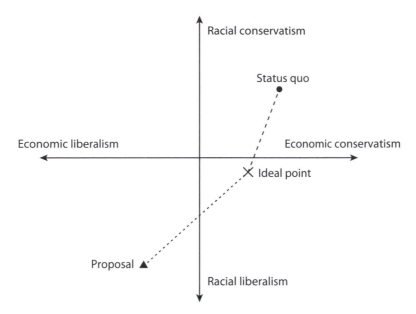

Figure 3.3. An Illustration for the Spatial Voting Model of Legislative Ideology.

or "ideal point" of legislators by two dimensions—economic and racial liberalism/ conservatism—identified by researchers as the main ideological characteristics of postwar congressional politics. Researchers have found that much of congressional roll call voting can be explained by the economic liberalism/conservatism dimension while the racial liberalism/conservatism dimension is less pronounced. Under this model, the legislator, whose ideal point is indicated by a cross mark in the figure, is more likely to vote against the proposal (solid triangle) whenever their ideal point is closer to the status quo (solid circle) than to the proposal location. The outcomes of congressional votes on controversial proposals reveal much about legislators' ideologies. On the other hand, a unanimously accepted or rejected proposal provides no information about legislators' ideological orientations.

A similar model is used in educational testing literature. Scholars have developed a class of statistical methods called *item response theory* for standardized tests such as the SAT and Graduate Record Examination (GRE). In this context, legislators and legislative proposals are replaced with student examinees and exam questions. Instead of ideal points, the goal is to measure students' abilities. The model also estimates the difficulty of each question. This helps the researchers choose good exam questions, which are neither too difficult nor too easy, so that only competent students will be able to provide a correct answer. These examples illustrate the importance of latent (i.e., unobserved) measurements in social science research.

3.6 Summarizing Bivariate Relationships

In this section, we introduce several ways to summarize the relationship between two variables. We analyze the estimates of legislators' ideal points, known as *DW-NOMINATE scores*, where more negative (positive) scores are increasingly liberal

Table 3.3. Legislative Ideal Points Data.

Variable	Description
name	name of the congressional representative
state	state of the congressional representative
district	district number of the congressional representative
party	party of the congressional representative
congress	congressional session number
dwnom1	DW-NOMINATE score (first dimension)
dwnom2	DW-NOMINATE score (second dimension)

(conservative). The CSV file `congress.csv` contains the estimated ideal points of all legislators who served in the House of Representatives from the 80th (1947–1948) to the 112th (2011–2012) Congresses. Table 3.3 presents the names and descriptions of the variables in the data set.

3.6.1 SCATTER PLOT

Using the `plot()` function, we create a *scatter plot*, which plots one variable against another in order to visualize their relationship. The syntax for this function is `plot(x, y)`, where `x` and `y` are vectors of horizontal and vertical coordinates, respectively. Here, we plot the DW-NOMINATE first dimension score (`dwnom1` variable) on the horizontal axis, which represents economic liberalism/conservatism, against its second dimension score on the vertical axis (`dwnom2` variable), which represents racial liberalism/conservatism. We will start by creating scatter plots for the 80th and 112th Congresses. We begin by subsetting the relevant part of the data.

```r
congress <- read.csv("congress.csv")
## subset the data by party
rep <- subset(congress, subset = (party == "Republican"))
dem <- congress[congress$party == "Democrat", ] # another way to subset
## 80th and 112th Congress
rep80 <- subset(rep, subset = (congress == 80))
dem80 <- subset(dem, subset = (congress == 80))
rep112 <- subset(rep, subset = (congress == 112))
dem112 <- subset(dem, subset = (congress == 112))
```

We will be creating multiple scatter plots with the same set of axis labels and axis limits. To avoid repetition, we store them as objects for later use.

```r
## preparing the labels and axis limits to avoid repetition
xlab <- "Economic liberalism/conservatism"
ylab <- "Racial liberalism/conservatism"
lim <- c(-1.5, 1.5)
```

Finally, using this axis information, we create scatter plots of ideal points for the 80th and 112th Congresses. Note that the `pch` argument in the `plot()` and `points()` functions can be used to specify different plotting symbols for the two parties. In the current example, `pch = 16` graphs solid triangles for Republicans while `pch = 17` graphs solid circles for Democrats. More options are available and can be viewed by typing `example(points)` into R console.

```
## scatter plot for the 80th Congress
plot(dem80$dwnom1, dem80$dwnom2, pch = 16, col = "blue",
     xlim = lim, ylim = lim, xlab = xlab, ylab = ylab,
     main = "80th Congress") # Democrats
points(rep80$dwnom1, rep80$dwnom2, pch = 17, col = "red") # Republicans
text(-0.75, 1, "Democrats")
text(1, -1, "Republicans")
## scatter plot for the 112th Congress
plot(dem112$dwnom1, dem112$dwnom2, pch = 16, col = "blue",
     xlim = lim, ylim = lim, xlab = xlab, ylab = ylab,
     main = "112th Congress")
points(rep112$dwnom1, rep112$dwnom2, pch = 17, col = "red")
```

The plots below use solid gray triangles instead of red triangles for Republicans. See page C1 for the full-color version.

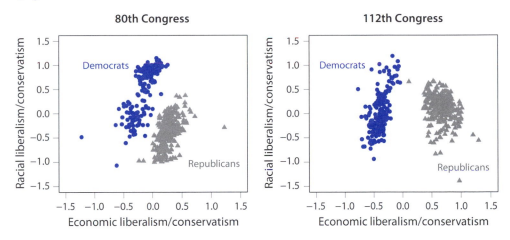

The plots show that in the 112th Congress (as opposed to the 80th Congress), the racial liberalism/conservatism dimension is no longer important in explaining the ideological difference between Democrats and Republicans. Instead, the economic dimension appears to be a dominant explanation for the partisan difference, and the difference between Democrats and Republicans in the racial dimension is much less pronounced.

Next, we compute the median legislator, based on the DW-NOMINATE first dimension score, separately for the Democratic and Republican Parties and for each Congress. These party median ideal points represent the center of each party in the economic liberalism/conservatism dimension. We can do this easily by using the `tapply()` function.

```
## party median for each congress
dem.median <- tapply(dem$dwnom1, dem$congress, median)
rep.median <- tapply(rep$dwnom1, rep$congress, median)
```

Finally, using the `plot()` function, we create a *time-series plot* where each party median is displayed for each Congress. We set the `type` argument to `"l"` in order to draw a line connecting the median points over time. This plot enables us to visualize how the party medians have changed over time. We will use the term of Congress as the horizontal axis. This information is available as the `name` of the `dem.median` vector.

```
## Democrats
plot(names(dem.median), dem.median, col = "blue", type = "l",
     xlim = c(80, 115), ylim = c(-1, 1), xlab = "Congress",
     ylab = "DW-NOMINATE score (first dimension)")
## add Republicans
lines(names(rep.median), rep.median, col = "red")
text(110, -0.6, "Democratic\n Party")
text(110, 0.85, "Republican\n Party")
```

The plot below uses a gray line instead of a red line for Republicans. See page C1 for the full-color version.

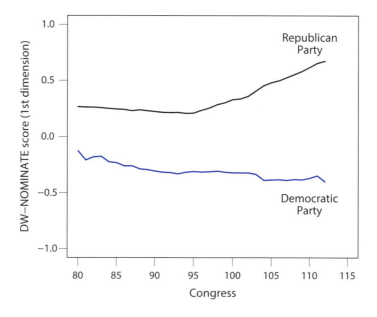

Note that the syntax `\n` used in the `text()` function indicates a change to a new line. The plot clearly shows that the ideological centers of the two parties diverge over

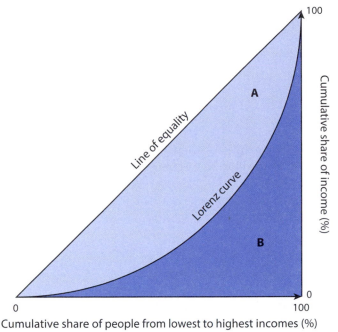

Figure 3.4. Gini Coefficient and Lorenz Curve.

time. The Democratic Party has become more liberal while the Republican Party has increasingly moved in a conservative direction in recent years. Many scholars refer to this phenomenon as *political polarization*.

> A **scatter plot** graphically compares two variables measured on the same set of units by plotting the value of one variable against that of the other for each unit.

3.6.2   CORRELATION

What is the cause of political polarization? This is a difficult question to answer, and is the subject of much scholarly debate. However, it has been pointed out that rising income inequality may be responsible for the widening partisan gap. To measure income inequality, we use the *Gini coefficient* (*Gini index*), which is best understood graphically. Figure 3.4 illustrates the idea. The horizontal axis represents the cumulative share of people sorted from the lowest to highest income. The vertical axis, on the other hand, plots the cumulative share of income held by those whose income is equal to or less than that of a person at a given income percentile. The *Lorenz curve* connects these two statistics. If everyone earns exactly the same income, then the Lorenz curve will be the same as the 45-degree line because x% of the population will hold exactly x% of national income regardless of the value of x. Let's call this the line of equality. However, if low income people earn a lot less than high income people, the Lorenz curve will become flatter at the beginning and then sharply increase at the end.

Table 3.4. US Gini Coefficient Data.

Variable	Description
year	year
gini	US Gini coefficient

Now, we can define the Gini coefficient as the area between the line of equality and the Lorenz curve divided by the area under the line of equality. In terms of figure 3.4,

$$\text{Gini coefficient} = \frac{\text{area between the line of equality and the Lorenz curve}}{\text{area under the line of equality}}$$

$$= \frac{\text{area A in figure 3.4}}{\text{area A + area B in figure 3.4}}.$$

The formula implies that the larger (smaller) area A is, the higher (lower) the Gini coefficient, meaning more (less) inequality. In a perfectly equal society, the Gini coefficient is 0. In contrast, a society where one person possesses all the wealth has a Gini coefficient of 1.

> The **Gini coefficient** (Gini index) measures the degree of income equality and inequality in a given society. It ranges from 0 (everyone has the same amount of wealth) to 1 (one person possesses all the wealth).

To examine the relationship between political polarization and income inequality, we create two time-series plots side by side. The first plot shows the partisan gap, i.e., the difference between the two party medians, over time. The second time-series plot displays the Gini coefficient during the same time period. The CSV data file, USGini.csv, contains the Gini coefficient from 1947 to 2013 (see table 3.4). We notice that both political polarization and income inequality have been steadily increasing in the United States.

```
## Gini coefficient data
gini <- read.csv("USGini.csv")
## time-series plot for partisan difference
plot(seq(from = 1947.5, to = 2011.5, by = 2),
     rep.median - dem.median, xlab = "Year",
     ylab = "Republican median -\n Democratic median",
     main = "Political polarization")
## time-series plot for Gini coefficient
plot(gini$year, gini$gini, ylim = c(0.35, 0.45), xlab = "Year",
     ylab = "Gini coefficient", main = "Income inequality")
```

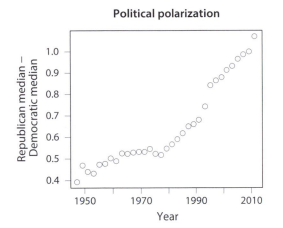

However, in chapter 2, we learned that *association does not necessarily imply causation* and hence we should not necessarily interpret this upwards trend as evidence for income inequality causing polarization. For example, life expectancy has also constantly increased during this time period, and yet this does not imply that longer life expectancy caused political polarization or vice versa.

Correlation (also referred to as a *correlation coefficient*) is one of the most frequently used statistics to summarize bivariate relationships. The measure represents how, on average, two variables move together relative to their respective means. Before defining correlation, we need to introduce the *z-score*, which represents the number of standard deviations an observation is above or below the mean. Specifically, the *z*-score of the *i*th observation of variable x is defined as

$$z\text{-score of } x_i = \frac{x_i - \text{mean of } x}{\text{standard deviation of } x}. \tag{3.1}$$

For example, if the *z*-score of a particular observation equals 1.5, the observation is 1.5 standard deviations above the mean. The *z*-score standardizes a variable so its unit of measurement no longer matters. More formally, the *z*-score of $ax_i + b$, where a and b are constants (a is non-zero), is identical to the *z*-score of x_i. Simple algebra can show this property:

$$z\text{-score of } (ax_i + b) = \frac{(ax_i + b) - \text{mean of } (ax + b)}{\text{standard deviation of } (ax + b)}$$

$$= \frac{a \times (x_i - \text{mean of } x)}{a \times \text{standard deviation of } x}$$

$$= z\text{-score of } x_i,$$

where the first equality follows from the definition of z-score in equation (3.1) and the second equality is based on the definitions of mean and standard deviation (see equation (2.4)). The constant b can be dropped in the above equations because its mean equals b itself.

> The z-**score** of the ith observation of a variable x measures the number of standard deviations an observation is above or below the mean. It is defined as
>
> $$z\text{-score of } x_i = \frac{x_i - \bar{x}}{S_x},$$
>
> where $\bar{x}$ and S_x are the mean and standard deviation of x, respectively. The z-score, as a measure of deviation from the mean, is not sensitive to how the variable is scaled and/or shifted.

Now, we can define the correlation between two variables x and y, measured for the same set of n observations, as the average products of z-scores for the two variables:

$$\text{correlation}(x, y) = \frac{1}{n} \sum_{i=1}^{n} (z\text{-score of } x_i \times z\text{-score of } y_i). \qquad (3.2)$$

As in the case of standard deviation (see section 2.6.2), the denominator of the correlation is often $n - 1$ rather than n. However, this difference should not affect one's conclusion so long as the sample size is sufficiently large. Within the summation, each z-score measures the deviation of the corresponding observation from its mean in terms of standard deviation. Suppose that when one variable is above its mean, the other variable is also likely to be greater than its own mean. Then, the correlation is likely to be positive because the signs of the standardized units tend to agree with each other. On the other hand, suppose that when one variable is above its mean, the other variable is likely to be less than its own mean. Then, the correlation is likely to be negative. In the current example, a positive correlation means that in years when income inequality is above its over-time mean, political polarization is also likely to be higher than its over-time mean.

Recall that z-scores are not sensitive to what units are used to measure a variable. Because it is based on z-scores, correlation also remains identical even if different units are used for measurement. For example, the correlation does not change even if one measures income in thousands of dollars instead of dollars. Indeed, one can even use a different currency. This is convenient because, for example, the relationship between income and education should not change depending on what scales we use to measure income. As another consequence of standardization, correlation varies only between -1 and 1. This allows us to compare the strengths and weaknesses of association between different pairs of variables.

Correlation (correlation coefficient) measures the degree to which two variables are associated with each other. It is defined as

$$\text{correlation of } x \text{ and } y = \frac{1}{n} \sum_{i=1}^{n} \left(\frac{x_i - \bar{x}}{S_x} \times \frac{y_i - \bar{y}}{S_y} \right)$$

$$\text{or} \quad \frac{1}{n-1} \sum_{i=1}^{n} \left(\frac{x_i - \bar{x}}{S_x} \times \frac{y_i - \bar{y}}{S_y} \right),$$

where $\bar{x}$ and $\bar{y}$ are the means and S_x and S_y are the standard deviations for variables x and y, respectively. Correlation ranges from -1 to 1 and is not sensitive to how a variable is scaled and/or shifted.

In R, the correlation can be calculated using the `cor()` function. For example, we can now calculate the correlation between the Gini coefficient and the measure of political polarization. To do this, since each US congressional session lasts two years, we take the Gini coefficient for the second year of each session.

```
cor(gini$gini[seq(from = 2, to = nrow(gini), by = 2)],
    rep.median - dem.median)

## [1] 0.9418128
```

We find that the correlation is positive and quite high, indicating that political polarization and income inequality move in a similar direction. As we have already emphasized, this correlation alone does not imply causality. Many variables have an upwards trend during this time, leading to a high positive correlation among them.

3.6.3 QUANTILE–QUANTILE PLOT

Finally, in some cases, we are interested in comparing the entire distributions of two variables rather than just the mean or median. One way to conduct such a comparison is to simply plot two histograms side-by-side. As an example, we compare the distribution of ideal points on the racial liberalism/conservatism dimension in the 112th Congress. When comparing across multiple plots, it is important to use the same scales for the horizontal and vertical axes for all plots to facilitate the comparison.

```
hist(dem112$dwnom2, freq = FALSE, main = "Democrats",
     xlim = c(-1.5, 1.5), ylim = c(0, 1.75),
     xlab = "Racial liberalism/conservatism dimension")
hist(rep112$dwnom2, freq = FALSE, main = "Republicans",
     xlim = c(-1.5, 1.5), ylim = c(0, 1.75),
     xlab = "Racial liberalism/conservatism dimension")
```

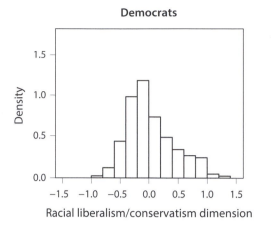

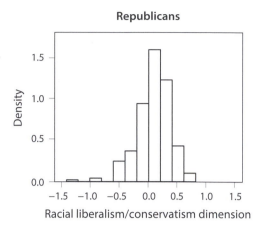

We observe that the two distributions are similar, though the distribution for Democrats appears to have a longer upper tail (i.e., the distribution extends further to the right) than that for Republicans. In addition, the Republicans' ideological positions seem to have a greater concentration towards the center than those of the Democrats.

A more direct way of comparing two distributions is a *quantile–quantile plot* or *Q–Q plot*. The Q–Q plot is based on *quantiles*, defined in section 2.6.1. It is a scatter plot of quantiles where each point represents the same quantile. For example, the median, upper quartile, and lower quartile of one sample will be plotted against the corresponding quantiles of the other sample. If two distributions are identical, then all quantiles have the same values. In this case, the Q–Q plot will result in the 45-degree line. Points above the 45-degree line indicate that a variable plotted on the vertical axis has a greater value at the corresponding quantile than a variable on the horizontal axis. In contrast, points below a 45-degree line imply the opposite relationship. This implies, for example, that if all points are above the 45-degree line, the variable on the vertical axis takes a greater value in every quantile than the variable on the horizontal axis.

Another useful feature of the Q–Q plot is that we can check the relative dispersion of two distributions. If the points in a Q–Q plot form a flatter line than the 45-degree line, they indicate that the distribution plotted on the horizontal axis is more dispersed than that on the vertical axis. In contrast, if the line has a steeper slope than 45 degrees, then the distribution plotted on the vertical line has a greater spread. The `qqplot()` function generates this plot by specifying the arguments `x` and `y`.

```r
qqplot(dem112$dwnom2, rep112$dwnom2, xlab = "Democrats",
       ylab = "Republicans", xlim = c(-1.5, 1.5), ylim = c(-1.5, 1.5),
       main = "Racial liberalism/conservatism dimension")
abline(0, 1) # 45-degree line
```

Racial liberalism/conservatism dimension

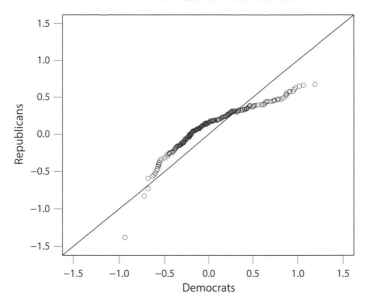

In this Q–Q plot, the horizontal and vertical axes represent the racial dimension for Democrats and Republicans, respectively. The fact that the points representing lower quantiles appear above the 45-degree line indicate that liberal Republicans are more conservative than liberal Democrats. This is because these quantiles have greater values (i.e., more conservative) for Republicans than the corresponding quantiles for Democrats. In contrast, the points representing upper quantiles are located below the 45-degree line. That is, at the highest quantiles, i.e., the conservative ones, the Democrats score higher and so more conservatively than the Republicans. Thus, conservative Democrats are more conservative than conservative Republicans. Conservative Republicans would be more conservative than conservative Democrats if all the points for the upper quantiles were above the 45-degree line. Finally, the line connecting the points is flatter than the 45-degree line, indicating that the distribution of ideological positions is more dispersed for Democrats than for Republicans.

The **quantile–quantile plot** or Q–Q plot is a scatter plot of quantiles. It plots the value of each quantile for one variable against the value of the corresponding quantile for another variable. If the distributions of the two variables are identical, all points of the Q–Q plot lie on the 45-degree line. If the points form a line whose slope is steeper than 45 degrees, the distribution plotted on the vertical axis is more dispersed than the distribution on the horizontal axis. If the slope is less than 45 degrees, then the distribution on the vertical axis has less dispersion.

3.7 Clustering

In the previous analysis, the scatter plot made it visually clear that the 112th Congress had two ideologically distinct groups, Democrats and Republicans. But, are there any *clusters* of ideologically similar legislators within each party? Is there a well-defined procedure that can uncover groups of similar observations? We consider one of the most basic *clustering algorithms*, called *k-means*. Before we describe the *k*-means algorithm, we briefly introduce two new important R objects: *matrix* and *list*. These objects will be used when we implement the *k*-means algorithm in R.

3.7.1 MATRIX IN R

Although both the matrix and data frame objects are rectangular arrays and have many similarities, there are critical differences. Most importantly, a data frame can take different types of variables (e.g., numeric, factor, character) whereas a matrix in principle takes only numeric values (though it also can accommodate logical and other special values under certain circumstances). While one can extract variables from a data frame object using the $ operator, in general the entries of a matrix need to be extracted by using square brackets [,] whose first and second elements, separated by a comma, indicate the rows and columns of interest, respectively. Although we do not exploit it in this book, a matrix is useful for *linear algebra* operations and is generally more computationally efficient than a data frame.

To create a matrix object, we can use the `matrix()` function by specifying the size of the matrix via the `nrow` (number of rows) and `ncol` (number of columns) arguments and indicating whether the matrix should be filled with the input data by row (`byrow = TRUE`) or column (`byrow = FALSE`). Moreover, adding labels to rows and columns can be done by the `rownames()` and `colnames()` functions.

```r
## 3x4 matrix filled by row; first argument takes actual entries
x <- matrix(1:12, nrow = 3, ncol = 4, byrow = TRUE)
rownames(x) <- c("a", "b", "c")
colnames(x) <- c("d", "e", "f", "g")
dim(x) # dimension

## [1] 3 4

x

##   d  e  f  g
## a 1  2  3  4
## b 5  6  7  8
## c 9 10 11 12
```

If one coerces a data frame object into a matrix using the `as.matrix()` function, some features of the data frame object, such as variable types, will get lost. In the following example, we illustrate the fact that a data frame can take different data types such as character and numeric, but a matrix cannot accommodate them. Instead, the `as.matrix()` function converts variables of different types to a single type, `character` in this case.

```
## data frame can take different data types
y <- data.frame(y1 = as.factor(c("a", "b", "c")), y2 = c(0.1, 0.2, 0.3))
class(y$y1)

## [1] "factor"

class(y$y2)

## [1] "numeric"

## as.matrix() converts both variables to character
z <- as.matrix(y)
z

##      y1  y2
## [1,] "a" "0.1"
## [2,] "b" "0.2"
## [3,] "c" "0.3"
```

Finally, some useful operations on a matrix include `colSums()` and `colMeans()`, which calculate the column sums and means, respectively. The same operations can be applied to rows via the `rowSums()` and `rowMeans()` functions.

```
## column sums
colSums(x)

##  d  e  f  g
## 15 18 21 24

## row means
rowMeans(x)

##    a    b    c
##  2.5  6.5 10.5
```

More generally, we can use the `apply()` function to apply any function to a margin, meaning a row or a column, of a matrix. This function takes three main arguments: the first or X argument is a matrix, the second or `MARGIN` argument specifies a dimension over which we wish to apply a function (1 represents rows while 2 represents columns), and the third or `FUN` argument names a function. We provide three examples. The first two examples are equivalent to the `colSums()` and `rowMeans()` shown above. The last example computes the standard deviation of each row.

```
## column sums
apply(x, 2, sum)

##  d  e  f  g
## 15 18 21 24


## row means
apply(x, 1, mean)

##    a    b    c
##  2.5  6.5 10.5


## standard deviation for each row
apply(x, 1, sd)

##        a        b        c
## 1.290994 1.290994 1.290994
```

3.7.2   LIST IN R

We now turn to another important object class in R, called a list. The list object is useful because it can store different types of objects as its elements. For example, a list can take numeric and character vectors of different lengths. In contrast, a data frame assumes those vectors to be of the same length. In fact, a list can even contain multiple data frames of different sizes as its elements. Therefore, a list is a very general class of objects.

Each element of a list comes with a name and can be extracted using the $ operator (just like a variable in a data frame). It is also possible to extract an element using double square brackets, [[ ]], with an integer or its element name indicating the element to be extracted. Below is a simple illustrative example of a list, which contains an integer vector of length 10 (y1), a character vector of length 3 (y2), and a data frame with two variables and three observations (y3). To create a list, we use the list() function and specify its elements by using their names as arguments.

```
## create a list
x <- list(y1 = 1:10, y2 = c("hi", "hello", "hey"),
          y3 = data.frame(z1 = 1:3, z2 = c("good", "bad", "ugly")))
## three ways of extracting elements from a list
x$y1 # first element

## [1]  1  2  3  4  5  6  7  8  9 10


x[[2]] # second element

## [1] "hi"    "hello" "hey"
```

```
x[["y3"]] # third element
##   z1   z2
## 1  1  good
## 2  2  bad
## 3  3  ugly
```

Some of the functions we introduced can be applied to the list object. They include the `names()` (to extract the names of elements) and `length()` (to obtain the number of elements) functions.

```
names(x) # names of all elements
## [1] "y1" "y2" "y3"

length(x) # number of elements
## [1] 3
```

3.7.3 THE *k*-MEANS ALGORITHM

Now that we are familiar with matrices and lists, we can use them to apply the k-means algorithm. The k-means algorithm is an *iterative algorithm* in which a set of operations are repeatedly performed until a noticeable difference in results is no longer produced. The goal of the algorithm is to split the data into k similar groups where each group is associated with its *centroid*, which is equal to the within-group mean. This is done by first assigning each observation to its closest cluster and then computing the centroid of each cluster based on this new cluster assignment. These two steps are iterated until the cluster assignment no longer changes. The algorithm is defined as follows.

The *k*-**means algorithm** produces the prespecified number of clusters k and consists of the following steps:

Step 1: Choose the initial centroids of k clusters.

Step 2: Given the centroids, assign each observation to a cluster whose centroid is the closest (in terms of Euclidean distance) to that observation.

Step 3: Choose the new centroid of each cluster whose coordinate equals the within-cluster mean of the corresponding variable.

Step 4: Repeat Step 2 and 3 until cluster assignments no longer change.

Note that the researchers must choose the number of clusters k and the initial centroid of each cluster. In R, the initial locations of centroids are randomly selected, unless otherwise specified.

It is typically a good idea to *standardize* the inputs before applying the k-means algorithm. Doing so brings all variables to the same scale so that the clustering result does not depend on how each variable is measured. This is done by computing the *z-score* introduced earlier (see equation (3.1)). Recall that we compute the z-score of a variable by subtracting the mean from it (called *centering*) and then dividing it by the standard deviation (called *scaling*). In R, we can standardize a variable or a set of variables using the `scale()` function, which takes either a vector of a single variable or a matrix of multiple variables.

Going back to our study of partisanship, we apply the k-means clustering algorithm separately to the DW-NOMINATE scores for the 80th and 112th Congresses. We choose $k = 2$ and $k = 4$, producing 2 and 4 clusters, respectively. The function `kmeans()` implements the k-means algorithm in R. The function has various arguments, but the first argument x takes a *matrix* of observations to which one applies the k-means algorithm. For our application, this matrix has two columns, representing the first and second dimensions of DW-NOMINATE scores, and the number of rows equals the number of legislators in each Congress. We use the `cbind()` (or "column bind") function to combine two variables by columns in order to create this matrix. As a side note, the `rbind()` (or "row bind") function allows one to bind two vectors or matrices by rows. We do not standardize the input variables in this application since the DW-NOMINATE scores are already scaled in a substantively meaningful manner.

```
dwnom80 <- cbind(congress$dwnom1[congress$congress == 80],
                 congress$dwnom2[congress$congress == 80])
dwnom112 <- cbind(congress$dwnom1[congress$congress == 112],
                  congress$dwnom2[congress$congress == 112])
```

The main arguments of the `kmeans()` function include `centers` (the number of clusters), `iter.max` (the maximum number of iterations), and `nstart` (the number of randomly chosen initial centroids). It is recommended that the `nstart` argument is specified so that the algorithm is run several times with different starting values (the `kmeans()` function reports the best results). We begin by fitting the k-means algorithm with two clusters and five randomly selected starting values.

```
## k-means with 2 clusters
k80two.out <- kmeans(dwnom80, centers = 2, nstart = 5)
k112two.out <- kmeans(dwnom112, centers = 2, nstart = 5)
```

The output objects, `k80two.out` and `k112two.out`, are *lists*, which contain various elements regarding the results of the application of the k-means algorithm. They include `iter` (an integer representing the number of iterations until convergence, which is achieved when the cluster assignments no longer change), `cluster` (a vector of the resulting cluster membership), and `centers` (a matrix of cluster centroids).

```
## elements of a list
names(k80two.out)

## [1] "cluster"      "centers"      "totss"
```

```
## [4] "withinss"     "tot.withinss" "betweenss"
## [7] "size"         "iter"         "ifault"
```

As explained in section 3.7.2, the elements within each list can be accessed using $ like we access a variable in a data frame object. In both cases, the algorithm converged in just 1 iteration, which can be checked by examining the `iter` element of the output list object. The default maximum number of iterations is 10. If convergence is not achieved, the `iter.max` argument needs to be specified as a number greater than 10.

We now examine the final centroids of the resulting clusters using a 2-cluster model. Each output row shows a cluster with the horizontal and vertical coordinates of its centroid in the first and second columns, respectively.

```
## final centroids
k80two.out$centers

##            [,1]        [,2]
## 1   0.14681029 -0.3389293
## 2  -0.04843704  0.7827259


k112two.out$centers

##            [,1]        [,2]
## 1  -0.3912687 0.03260696
## 2   0.6776736 0.09061157
```

We next compute the numbers of Democratic and Republican legislators who belong to each cluster by creating a cross tabulation of party and cluster label variables.

```
## number of observations for each cluster by party
table(party = congress$party[congress$congress == 80],
      cluster = k80two.out$cluster)

##              cluster
## party           1    2
##    Democrat    62  132
##    Other        2    0
##    Republican 247    3


table(party = congress$party[congress$congress == 112],
      cluster = k112two.out$cluster)

##              cluster
## party           1    2
##    Democrat    200    0
##    Other         0    0
##    Republican    1  242
```

We find that for the 112th Congress, the k-means algorithm with 2 clusters produces 1 cluster containing only Democrats and the other consisting only of Republicans. While we chose the number of clusters to be 2 in this case, the algorithm discovers that these 2 clusters perfectly align on partisanship. In contrast, for the 80th Congress, one of the clusters contains a significant number of Democrats as well as Republicans. This is consistent with the fact that political polarization has worsened over time.

Next, we apply the k-means algorithm with 4 clusters and visualize the results. We begin by fitting the 4-cluster model to the 80th and 112th Congresses.

```
## k-means with 4 clusters
k80four.out <- kmeans(dwnom80, centers = 4, nstart = 5)
k112four.out <- kmeans(dwnom112, centers = 4, nstart = 5)
```

To visualize the results, we use the `plot()` function to create a scatter plot. The following syntax assigns different colors to observations that belong to different clusters. The centroid of each cluster is indicated by an asterisk.

```
## plotting the results using the labels and limits defined earlier
plot(dwnom80, col = k80four.out$cluster + 1, xlab = xlab, ylab = ylab,
     xlim = lim, ylim = lim, main = "80th Congress")
## plotting the centroids
points(k80four.out$centers, pch = 8, cex = 2)
## 112th Congress
plot(dwnom112, col = k112four.out$cluster + 1, xlab = xlab, ylab = ylab,
     xlim = lim, ylim = lim, main = "112th Congress")
points(k112four.out$centers, pch = 8, cex = 2)
```

For the full-color version of the plots, see page C2.

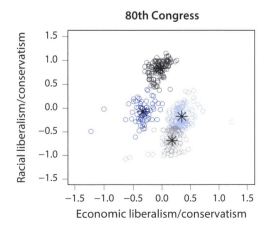

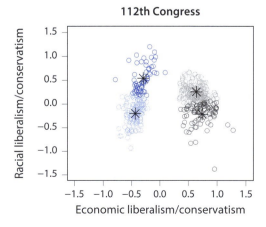

The `cex` argument given in the `points()` function controls the font size so that the centroid of each cluster is clearly visible. In addition, the `pch` argument specifies a certain symbol for plotting. Finally, we specify a vector of integer values, rather than actual color names, for the `col` argument so that each integer value is used for the corresponding cluster. We add 1 to the cluster labels so that we do not use black, the color of the cluster centroids, for the observations belonging to one of the clusters. The `palette()` function displays the exact correspondence between the color names and integer values (see section 5.3.3 for more details on the use of color in R).

```
palette()

## [1] "black"   "red"     "green3"  "blue"    "cyan"
## [6] "magenta" "yellow"  "gray"
```

The results show that the 4-cluster model splits the Democrats into 2 clusters and the Republicans into 2 clusters. Within each party, the division between the 2 clusters is clearest among the Democrats in the 80th Congress. For both parties, the within-party division is along the racial dimension. In contrast, the economic dimension dominates the difference between the two parties.

Clustering algorithms such as the *k*-means algorithm represent examples of *unsupervised learning* methods. Unlike in *supervised learning*, there is no outcome variable. Instead, the goal of unsupervised learning is to discover the hidden structures in data. The difficulty of unsupervised learning is that there is no clear measure of success and failure. In the absence of outcome data, it is difficult to know whether these clustering algorithms are producing the "correct" results. For this reason, human judgment is often required to make sure that the findings produced by clustering algorithms are reasonable.

3.8 Summary

This chapter focused on the issue of measurement. We discussed **survey sampling** as a principled and efficient way to infer the characteristics of a potentially large population from a small number of randomly sampled units without enumerating all units in the population. In chapter 2, we learned about the randomization of treatment assignment, which ensures that the treatment and control groups are equal on average in all aspects but the receipt of treatment. In survey sampling, we used the random sampling of units to make the sample representative of a target population. This allows researchers to infer population characteristics from the sample obtained from random sampling.

While random sampling is an effective technique, there are several complications in practice. First, while random sampling requires a complete list of potential units to be sampled, it is often difficult to obtain such a sampling frame. Second, due to cost and logistical constraints, researchers are forced to use complex random sampling techniques. Third, surveys typically lead to both **unit and item nonresponses**, which, if occurring nonrandomly, threaten the validity of inference. In recent years, the nonresponse rate of phone surveys has dramatically increased. As a result, many polling firms are starting to use cheap Internet surveys through platforms like Qualtrics, even though many such surveys are not based on probability sampling. Beyond nonresponse problems, sensitive questions in surveys often result in **social desirability bias** in which respondents may falsify their answers and provide socially acceptable answers.

Furthermore, social scientists often face the question of how to measure latent concepts such as ideology and ability. We discussed an application of item response theory to political polarization in the US Congress. The idea is to infer legislators' ideological positions from their roll call votes. The same method was also applied to measure students' abilities from standardized tests. Using the estimated ideal points as an example, we also learned how to apply a basic **clustering algorithm** called the k-means algorithm in order to discover latent groups of observations with similar characteristics in data.

In addition to these concepts and methods, the chapter also introduced various numerical and visual summaries of data. While a **bar plot** summarizes the distribution of a factor variable, **box plots** and **histograms** are useful tools for depicting the distribution of continuous variables. The **correlation coefficient** numerically characterizes the association between two variables, whereas a **scatter plot** plots one variable against the other. Finally, unlike scatter plots, **quantile–quantile plots** (Q–Q plots) enable comparison of the distributions of two variables even when they are not measured in the same units.

3.9 Exercises

3.9.1 CHANGING MINDS ON GAY MARRIAGE: REVISITED

In this exercise, we revisit the gay marriage study we analyzed in section 2.8.2. It is important to work on that exercise before answering the following questions. In May 2015, three scholars reported several irregularities in the data set used to produce the results in the study.[3] They found that the gay marriage experimental data were statistically indistinguishable from data in the Cooperative Campaign Analysis Project (CCAP), which interviewed voters throughout the 2012 US presidential campaign. The scholars suggested that the CCAP survey data—and not the original data alleged to have been collected in the experiment—were used to produce the results reported in the gay marriage study. The release of a report on these irregularities ultimately led to the retraction of the original article. In this exercise, we will use several measurement strategies to reproduce the irregularities observed in the gay marriage data set.

To do so, we will use two CSV data files: a reshaped version of the original data set in which every observation corresponds to a unique respondent, `gayreshaped.csv` (see table 3.5), and the 2012 CCAP data set alleged to have been used as the basis for the gay marriage study results, `ccap2012.csv` (see table 3.6). Note that the feeling

---

[3] This exercise is based on the unpublished report "Irregularities in LaCour (2014)" by David Broockman, Joshua Kalla, and Peter Aronow.

Table 3.5. Gay Marriage Reshaped Data.

Variable	Description
study	which study the data set is from (1 = study 1, 2 = study 2)
treatment	five possible treatment assignment options
therm1	survey thermometer rating of feeling towards gay couples in wave 1 (0-100)
therm2	survey thermometer rating of feeling towards gay couples in wave 2 (0-100)
therm3	survey thermometer rating of feeling towards gay couples in wave 3 (0-100)
therm4	survey thermometer rating of feeling towards gay couples in wave 4 (0-100)

Note: See table 2.7 for the original data.

Table 3.6. 2012 Cooperative Campaign Analysis Project (CCAP) Survey Data.

Variable	Description
caseid	unique respondent ID
gaytherm	survey thermometer rating of feeling towards gay couples (0-100)

thermometer measures how warmly respondents feel towards gay couples on a 0–100 scale.

1. In the gay marriage study, researchers used seven waves of a survey to assess how lasting the persuasion effects were over time. One irregularity the scholars found is that responses across survey waves in the control group (where no canvassing occurred) had unusually high correlation over time. What is the correlation between respondents' feeling thermometer ratings in waves 1 and 2 for the control group in study 1? To handle missing data, we should set the use argument of the cor() function to "complete.obs" so that the correlation is computed using only observations that have no missing data. Provide a brief substantive interpretation of the results.

2. Repeat the previous question using study 2 and comparing all waves within the control group. Note that the cor() function can take a single data frame with multiple variables. To handle missing data in this case, we can set the use argument to "pairwise.complete.obs". This means that the cor() function uses all observations that have no missing values for a given pair of waves even if some of them have missing values in other waves. Briefly interpret the results.

3. Most surveys find at least some *outliers* or individuals whose responses are substantially different from the rest of the data. In addition, some respondents may change their responses erratically over time. Create a scatter plot to visualize the relationships between wave 1 and each of the subsequent waves in study 2. Use only the control group. Interpret the results.

4. The researchers found that the data of the gay marriage study appeared unusually similar to the 2012 CCAP data set even though they were supposed to be samples of completely different respondents. We use the data contained in `ccap2012.csv` and `gayreshaped.csv` to compare the two samples. Create a histogram of the 2012 CCAP feeling thermometer, the wave-1 feeling thermometer from study 1, and the wave-1 feeling thermometer from study 2. There are a large number of missing values in the CCAP data. Consider how the missing data might have been recoded in the gay marriage study. To facilitate the comparison across histograms, use the `breaks` argument in the `hist()` function to keep the bin sizes equal across histograms. Briefly comment on the results.

5. A more direct way to compare the distributions of two samples is through a *quantile–quantile plot*. Use this visualization method to conduct the same comparison as in the previous question. Briefly interpret the plots.

3.9.2 POLITICAL EFFICACY IN CHINA AND MEXICO

In 2002, the World Health Organization conducted a survey of two provinces in China and three provinces in Mexico.[4] One issue of interest, which we analyze in this exercise, concerns political efficacy. First, the following self-assessment question was asked.

How much say do you have in getting the government to address issues that interest you?

(5) Unlimited say, (4) A lot of say, (3) Some say, (2) Little say, (1) No say at all.

After the self-assessment question, three vignette questions were asked.

[Alison] lacks clean drinking water. She and her neighbors are supporting an opposition candidate in the forthcoming elections that has promised to address the issue. It appears that so many people in her area feel the same way that the opposition candidate will defeat the incumbent representative.

[Jane] lacks clean drinking water because the government is pursuing an industrial development plan. In the campaign for an upcoming election, an opposition party has promised to address the issue, but she feels it would be futile to vote for the opposition since the government is certain to win.

[Moses] lacks clean drinking water. He would like to change this, but he can't vote, and feels that no one in the government cares about this issue. So he suffers in silence, hoping something will be done in the future.

The respondent was asked to assess each vignette in the same manner as the self-assessment question.

---

[4] This exercise is based on Gary King, Christopher J.L. Murray, Joshua A. Salomon, and Ajay Tandon (2004) "Enhancing the validity and cross-cultural comparability of measurement in survey research." *American Political Science Review*, vol. 98, no. 1 (February), pp. 191–207.

Table 3.7. Vignette Survey Data.

Variable	Description
self	self-assessment response
alison	response to the Alison vignette
jane	response to the Jane vignette
moses	response to the Moses vignette
china	1 for China and 0 for Mexico
age	age of respondent in years

How much say does ["name"] have in getting the government to address issues that interest [him/her]?

(5) Unlimited say, (4) A lot of say, (3) Some say, (2) Little say, (1) No say at all.

["name"] is replaced by either Alison, Jane, or Moses.

The data set we analyze `vignettes.csv` contains the variables whose names and descriptions are given in table 3.7. In the analysis that follows, we assume that these survey responses can be treated as numerical values. For example, "Unlimited say" = 5, and "Little say" = 2. This approach is not appropriate if, for example, the difference between "Unlimited say" and "A lot of say" is not the same as the difference between "Little say" and "No say at all." However, relaxing this assumption is beyond the scope of this chapter.

1. We begin by analyzing the self-assessment question. Plot the distribution of responses separately for China and Mexico using bar plots, where the vertical axis is the proportion of respondents. In addition, compute the mean response for each country. According to this analysis, which country appears to have a higher degree of political efficacy? How does this evidence match with the fact that in the 2000 election, Mexican citizens voted out of office the ruling Institutional Revolutionary Party (PRI) who had governed the country for more than 80 years, while Chinese citizens have not been able to vote in a fair election to date?

2. We examine the possibility that any difference in the levels of efficacy between Mexican and Chinese respondents is due to the difference in their age distributions. Create histograms for the age variable separately for Mexican and Chinese respondents. Add a vertical line representing the median age of the respondents for each country. In addition, use a quantile–quantile plot to compare the two age distributions. What differences in age distribution do you observe between the two countries? Answer this question by interpreting each plot.

3. One problem with the self-assessment question is that survey respondents may interpret the question differently. For example, two respondents who choose the same answer may be facing quite different political situations and hence may interpret "A lot of say" differently. To address this problem, we rank a respondent's answer to the self-assessment question relative to the same respondent's answer

to a vignette question. Compute the proportion of respondents, again separately for China and Mexico, who rank themselves (according to the self-assessment question) as having less say in the government's decisions than Moses (the last vignette). How does the result of this analysis differ from that of the previous analysis? Give a brief interpretation of the result.

4. We focus on survey respondents who ranked these three vignettes in the expected order (i.e., Alison $\geq$ Jane $\geq$ Moses). Create a variable that represents how respondents rank themselves relative to these vignettes. This variable should be equal to 1 if respondents rank themselves less than Moses, 2 if ranked the same as Moses or between Moses and Jane, 3 if ranked the same as Jane or between Jane and Alison, and 4 if ranked the same as Alison or higher. Create the bar plots of this new variable as done in question 1. The vertical axis should represent the proportion of respondents for each response category. Also, compute the mean value of this new variable separately for China and Mexico. Give a brief interpretation of the result by comparing these results with those obtained in question 1.

5. Is the problem identified above more or less severe among older respondents when compared to younger ones? Answer the previous question separately for those who are 40 years or older and those who are younger than 40 years. Does your conclusion for the previous question differ between these two groups of respondents? Relate your discussion to your finding for question 2.

3.9.3   VOTING IN THE UNITED NATIONS GENERAL ASSEMBLY

Like legislators in the US Congress, the member states of the United Nations (UN) are politically divided on many issues such as trade, nuclear disarmament, and human rights. During the Cold War, countries in the UN General Assembly tended to split into two factions: one led by the capitalist United States and the other by the communist Soviet Union. In this exercise, we will analyze how states' ideological positions, as captured by their votes on UN resolutions, have changed since the fall of communism.[5] Table 3.8 presents the names and descriptions of the variables in the data set contained in the CSV file `unvoting.csv`.

In the analysis that follows, we measure state preferences in two ways. First, we can use the proportion of votes by each country that coincide with votes on the same issue cast by the two major Cold War powers: the United States and the Soviet Union. For example, if a country voted for 10 resolutions in 1992, and if its vote matched the United States's vote on exactly 6 of these resolutions, the variable `PctAgreeUS` in 1992 would equal 60 for this country. Second, we can also measure state preferences in terms of numerical ideal points as explained in section 3.5. These ideal points capture what international relations scholars have called countries' *liberalism* on issues such as political freedom, democratization, and financial liberalization. The two measures

---

[5] This exercise is based on Michael A. Bailey, Anton Strezhnev, and Erik Voeten (2015) "Estimating dynamic state preferences from United Nations voting data." *Journal of Conflict Resolution*, doi = 10.1177/0022002715595700.

Table 3.8. United Nations Ideal Points Data.

Variable	Description
CountryName	name of the country
CountryAbb	abbreviated name of the country
idealpoint	its estimated ideal point
Year	year for which the ideal point is estimated
PctAgreeUS	proportion of votes that match with votes cast by the United States on the same issue
PctAgreeRUSSIA	proportion of votes that match with votes cast by Russia/the Soviet Union on the same issue

are highly correlated, with larger (more liberal) ideal points corresponding to a higher proportion of votes that agree with the United States.

1. We begin by examining how the distribution of state ideal points has changed since the end of communism. Plot the distribution of ideal points separately for 1980 and 2000—about 10 years before and 10 years after the fall of the Berlin Wall, respectively. Add the median to each plot as a vertical line. How do the two distributions differ? Pay attention to the degree of polarization and give a brief substantive interpretation of the results. Use the `quantile()` function to quantify the patterns you identified.

2. Next, examine how the number of countries voting with the United States has changed over time. Plot the average percentage agreement with the United States across all countries over time. Also, add the average percentage agreement with Russia as another line for comparison. Using the `tapply()` function may help with this analysis. Does the United States appear to be getting more or less isolated over time, as compared to Russia? Identify some countries that are consistently pro-US. What are the most pro-Russian countries? Give a brief substantive interpretation of the results.

3. One problem with using the proportion of votes that agree with the United States or Russia as a measure of state preferences is that the ideological positions, and consequently the voting patterns, of the two countries might themselves have changed over time. This makes it difficult to know which countries' ideological positions have changed. Investigate this issue by plotting the evolution of the two countries' ideal points over time. Add the yearly median ideal point of all countries. How might the results of this analysis modify (or not) your interpretation of the previous analysis?

4. Let's examine how countries that were formerly part of the Soviet Union differ in terms of their ideology and UN voting compared to countries that were not part of the Soviet Union. The former Soviet Union countries are Estonia, Latvia, Lithuania, Belarus, Moldova, Ukraine, Armenia, Azerbaijan, Georgia,

Kazakhstan, Kyrgyzstan, Tajikistan, Turkmenistan, Uzbekistan, and Russia. The `%in%` operator, which is used as `x %in% y`, may be useful. This operator returns a logical vector whose elements are `TRUE` if the corresponding element of vector `x` is equal to a value contained in vector `y` and otherwise `FALSE`. Focus on the most recently available UN data from 2012 and plot each post-Soviet Union state's ideal point against the proportion of its votes that agree with the United States. Compare the post-Soviet Union states, within the same plot, against the other countries. Briefly comment on what you observe.

5. We have just seen that while some post-Soviet countries have retained nonliberal ideologies, other post-Soviet countries were much more liberal in 2012. Let's examine how the median ideal points of Soviet/post-Soviet countries and all other countries have varied over all the years in the data. Plot these median ideal points by year. Be sure to indicate 1989, the year of the fall of the Berlin Wall, on the graph. Briefly comment on what you observe.

6. Following the end of communism, countries that were formerly part of the Soviet Union have become much more ideologically diverse. Is this also true of the world as a whole? In other words, do countries still divide into two ideological factions? Let's assess this question by applying the k-means clustering algorithm to ideal points and the proportion of votes agreeing with the United States. Initiate the algorithm with just two centroids and visualize the results separately for 1989 and 2012. Briefly comment on the results.

Chapter 4

Prediction

Prophecy is a good line of business, but it is full of risks.
— Mark Twain, *Following the Equator*

In this chapter, we discuss prediction. Prediction is another important goal of data analysis in quantitative social science research. Our first example concerns the prediction of election outcomes using public opinion polls. We also show how to predict outcomes of interest using a linear regression model, which is one of the most basic statistical models. While many social scientists see causal inference as the ultimate goal of scholarly inquiry, prediction is often the first step towards understanding complex causal relationships that underlie human behavior. Indeed, valid causal inference requires the accurate prediction of counterfactual outcomes. Later in the chapter we discuss the connections between prediction and causal inference.

4.1 Predicting Election Outcomes

The 2008 US presidential election was historic. For the first time in American history, an African-American candidate, Barack Obama, was elected. This election was also important for the statistics community because a number of pundits accurately predicted the election outcome.

The United States's unique *Electoral College* system makes predicting election outcomes challenging. A candidate is elected to office by winning an absolute majority of electoral votes. Each of the 538 electors casts a single electoral vote. As of 2016, 535 of these votes are allocated among 50 states, corresponding to the 435 members of the House of Representatives and the 100 members of the Senate. The remaining 3 votes are given to the District of Columbia. In most cases, the electors vote for the candidate who won the plurality of votes in the state they represent, leading to a "winner-take-all" system in these states. In fact, some states have criminal penalties for voting for the candidate who did not win the plurality of votes. A winning presidential candidate must obtain at least 270 electoral votes.

Figure 4.1 shows the map of Electoral College votes for the 2008 election. See page C2 for the full-color version. Obama won 365 electoral votes (blue states), whereas

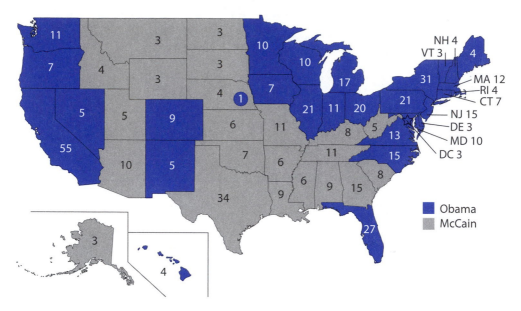

Figure 4.1. Electoral College Map of the 2008 US Presidential Election. The figure uses gray rather than red for the states won by McCain. See page C2 for the full-color version.

the Republican candidate John McCain received 173 votes (red states).[1] The Electoral College system implies that to successfully forecast the outcome of the US presidential election, we may need to accurately predict the winner of each state. Indeed, George W. Bush won the 2000 election by taking 25 electoral votes from Florida, where he defeated Al Gore by a slim margin of 537 votes after a controversial recount. As a result, Gore lost the election by the narrow margin of 5 electoral votes, even though he actually received a half million more popular votes than Bush at the national level. More recently, Donald Trump won the 2016 election even though Hillary Clinton received more votes nationally than Trump. Below, we show how to predict the election outcome using public opinion polls conducted within each state. Before we present the details of how this is done, we introduce two new programming concepts: loops and conditional statements.

4.1.1   LOOPS IN R

In many situations, we want to repeat the same operations multiple times where only small changes occur to the operations each time. For example, in order to forecast the result of the US presidential election, we must predict the election outcome within each state. This means that a similar set of computations will be performed a number of times. We would like to avoid writing nearly identical code chunks over and over again. A *loop* is a programming construct that allows us to repeatedly execute similar code chunks in a compact manner. The R syntax `for (i in X)` will create a loop, where `i` (or any other object name of your choice) is a *loop counter* that controls the

---

[1] Interestingly, Nebraska allocates two of its five electoral votes to the statewide winner while giving one electoral vote to the winner of each congressional district (Maine follows the same system). As a result, although McCain won a plurality of the popular vote in Nebraska, Obama received one electoral vote because he won the majority of votes in the second congressional district.

iterations of the loop, and X is the vector of values that the loop counter will successively take on. Consider the following pseudo-code.

```
for (i in X) {
    expression1
    expression2
    ...
    expressionN
}
```

Here, the collection of expressions from `expression1` through `expressionN` is repeated for each value `i` of the vector X. During each of these *iterations*, `i` takes on the corresponding value from the vector X, starting with the first element of X and ending with its last. Below is a simple example, which multiplies each number in a vector by 2. It is often useful to create an empty "container" vector whose elements are all NAs in order to store the results from computing all iterations. We use the `rep()` function to do this. Comments can be written into the loop as with any other code chunk in R. Braces { and } are used to denote the beginning and end of the body of the loop. When we start a loop (or related functions) in the **RStudio** text editor, the spacing will automatically indent and the closing bracket will align vertically with the `for` function. This makes the code easier to interpret and debug (i.e., identify and remove errors from the code).

```
values <- c(2, 4, 6)
n <- length(values) # number of elements in "values"
results <- rep(NA, n) # empty container vector for storing the results
## loop counter "i" will take values 1, 2, ..., n in that order
for (i in 1:n) {
    ## store the result of multiplication as the ith element of
    ## "results" vector
    results[i] <- values[i] * 2
    cat(values[i], "times 2 is equal to", results[i], "\n")
}

## 2 times 2 is equal to 4
## 4 times 2 is equal to 8
## 6 times 2 is equal to 12

results

## [1]  4  8 12
```

In each iteration of the above loop, the loop counter `i` takes an integer value, starting with 1 and ending with n with an increment of 1. Note that the `cat()` function, like `print()`, prints out an object on the screen. The `cat()` function combines multiple objects (character or other) into a character string, as inputs separated by commas. Without either the `cat()` or `print()` function, a loop will not print out the `results[i]` value on the screen. Finally, recall that `\n` indicates the addition of a new line. Of course, in the above example, the loop is not strictly necessary because one can simply execute `values * 2`, which multiplies each element of the `values` vector by 2. Indeed, while loops may be conceptually easier, they are computationally intensive and so should be avoided whenever possible.

One important process is debugging code that involves a loop. Several strategies can reveal why a loop is not running properly. Since a loop simply executes the same command chunks many times, one could check whether the commands that go inside the loop can be executed without any error given a specific value of the loop counter. In the above example, one may simply try the following command before constructing the loop.

```
## check if the code runs when i = 1
i <- 1
x <- values[i] * 2
cat(values[i], "times 2 is equal to", x, "\n")

## 2 times 2 is equal to 4
```

Then, to make sure it behaves as we expect, we can change the first line to `i <- 2` or any other value that we want the loop counter `i` to take on. Another useful tip is to use the `print()` or `cat()` functions to print out the current value of the loop counter. This way, when there is an error, you always know how much of the loop succeeded. For example, if you cannot even run one iteration, there is likely something wrong with the code in the body of the loop. Alternatively, if the loop works for several iterations and then fails, perhaps something specific about the iteration that failed is causing the problem. The following example prints the iteration number to help identify the coding error. We use the `data.frame()` function to create an artificial data set with three variables, one of which is a character variable, and then attempt to compute the median of each variable using a loop.

```
## a toy data frame
data <- data.frame("a" = 1:2, "b" = c("hi", "hey"), "c" = 3:4)
## we see an error occurring at iteration 2
results <- rep(NA, 3)
for (i in 1:3) {
    cat("iteration", i, "\n")
    results[i] <- median(data[, i])
}

## iteration 1
## iteration 2

## Error in median.default(data[, i]): need numeric data

results

## [1]  1 NA NA
```

The loop was successfully executed in the first iteration but failed in the second iteration. This can be seen from the fact that an error message was printed before the printout of the `iteration 3` message. The reason for the failure is that the `median()` function takes numeric data only. As a result, the function produced an error in the second iteration, making the loop halt without computing the median for the second and third variables. This is indicated by NAs in the second and third elements of the `results` vector.

4.1.2 GENERAL CONDITIONAL STATEMENTS IN R

In section 2.2.4, we introduced simple conditional statements. We used the `ifelse()` function to create a vector of values where the elements of the resulting vector depend on an input object of the logical class. The general syntax is `ifelse(X, Y, Z)`. If an element `X` in the input is evaluated as `TRUE`, the value `Y` would be returned. If `X` is evaluated as `FALSE`, then the other value, `Z`, would be returned. This function is useful when recoding variables. Now, we will consider a more powerful form of conditional statements that can implement (or not) arbitrary chunks of R code depending on a logical expression. These take the form of `if(){}` and `if(){}else{}`. The first basic syntax is as follows.

```
if (X) {
    expression1
    expression2
    ...
    expressionN
}
```

If the value of `X` is `TRUE`, the code chunk `expression1` through `expressionN` will be executed. If the value of `X` is `FALSE`, then it will skip that code chunk entirely. The following simple example illustrates this.

```
## define the operation to be executed
operation <- "add"
if (operation == "add") {
    cat("I will perform addition 4 + 4\n")
    4 + 4
}

## I will perform addition 4 + 4
## [1] 8

if (operation == "multiply") {
    cat("I will perform multiplication 4 * 4\n")
    4 * 4
}
```

In the above code, the second portion of code on multiplication was not executed because the `operation` object was set to "add" rather than "multiply". Thus, the expression `operation == "multiply"` returned a logical value of FALSE, indicating that the code chunk contained in the brackets is not performed. However, if `operation` is set to "multiply", then 4 * 4, rather than 4 + 4, will be evaluated.

The `if(){}else{}` statements allow for greater flexibility by incorporating a set of R expressions to be evaluated if the argument in the `if()` function is FALSE. They contrast with the `if(){}` statements, which specify only the expressions to be evaluated when the argument in the `if()` function is TRUE. The following code will execute the code chunk `expression1a` through `expressionNa` if X is TRUE and the code chunk `expression1b` through `expressionNb` if X is FALSE.

```
if (X) {
    expression1a
    ...
    expressionNa
} else {
    expression1b
    ...
    expressionNb
}
```

Building on the earlier example, the following code illustrates how `if(){}else{}` statements work, implementing a different operation depending on the value of an object. Specifically, if the `operation` object is set to "add", then the addition is performed, but otherwise, the multiplication is executed.

```
## note that "operation" is redefined
operation <- "multiply"
if (operation == "add") {
    cat("I will perform addition 4 + 4")
    4 + 4
} else {
    cat("I will perform multiplication 4 * 4")
    4 * 4
}

## I will perform multiplication 4 * 4
## [1] 16
```

One can construct even more complicated conditional statements using the `else if(){}` statement in the following manner.

```
if (X) {
    expression1a
    ...
    expressionNa
} else if (Y) {
    expression1b
    ...
    expressionNb
} else {
    expression1c
    ...
    expressionNc
}
```

The above syntax will execute the code chunk `expression1a` through `expressionNa` if condition `X` is met. If `X` is not met, but another condition `Y` is met, then the code chunk `expression1b` through `expressionNb` will be executed. Finally, if both `X` and `Y` are not satisfied, then the code chunk `expression1c` through `expressionNc` will be executed. Note that `else if()` can be repeated many times. In addition, the order of expressions matters. For example, if condition `Y` rather than `X` is evaluated first, then the code may produce a different result. Using `else if(){}`, we can modify the above example as follows.

```
## note that "operation" is redefined
operation <- "subtract"
if (operation == "add") {
    cat("I will perform addition 4 + 4\n")
    4 + 4
} else if (operation == "multiply") {
    cat("I will perform multiplication 4 * 4\n")
    4 * 4
} else {
    cat("", operation, "" is invalid. Use either "add" or "multiply."\n",
        sep = "")
}
## "subtract" is invalid. Use either "add" or "multiply."
```

Note that the `sep` argument specifies how each object should be separated. In the above example, `sep = ""` means that no character separates these objects. A separator can be any character string, commonly a comma and space (`sep = ", "`) or a semicolon and space (`sep = "; "`). The default is `sep = " "`, which will insert a space between objects.

Finally, conditional statements can be used effectively within a loop. Suppose, for example, that we want to perform a different arithmetic operation depending on whether an integer is even or odd. The following code first checks whether the input integer value is even or not. If it is even, R adds it to itself. If it is odd, R multiplies it. A message summarizing this operation is printed out for each iteration. In R, the %% operator computes the remainder of a division. For example, 5 %% 2 will return 1, which is the remainder for the division of 5 by 2. If dividing an input integer value by 2 returns the remainder of 0 rather than 1, we conclude that it is an even number.

```r
values <- 1:5
n <-length(values)
results <- rep(NA, n)
for (i in 1:n) {
    ## x and r get overwritten in each iteration
    x <- values[i]
    r <- x %% 2  # remainder when divided by 2 to check whether even or odd
    if (r == 0) { # remainder is zero
        cat(x, "is even and I will perform addition",
            x, "+", x, "\n")
        results[i] <- x + x
    } else { # remainder is not zero
        cat(x, "is odd and I will perform multiplication",
            x, "*", x, "\n")
        results[i] <- x * x
    }
}
## 1 is odd and I will perform multiplication 1 * 1
## 2 is even and I will perform addition 2 + 2
## 3 is odd and I will perform multiplication 3 * 3
## 4 is even and I will perform addition 4 + 4
## 5 is odd and I will perform multiplication 5 * 5

results

## [1]  1  4  9  8 25
```

Here, the code indentation, which is done automatically in RStudio, is important, making it clear that conditional statements are nested within a loop. The use of appropriate indentation is essential for writing computer code that contains loops and conditional statements.

4.1.3 POLL PREDICTIONS

Given that we now know how to use loops and conditional statements, we undertake the task of predicting the outcome of the 2008 US presidential election. Our forecast is based on a number of public opinion polls conducted before the election. The CSV data file pres08.csv contains the election results by state. In addition, we have the

Table 4.1. 2008 US Presidential Election Data.

Variable	Description
state	abbreviated name of the state
state.name	unabbreviated name of the state
Obama	Obama's vote share (percentage)
McCain	McCain's vote share (percentage)
EV	number of Electoral College votes for the state

Table 4.2. 2008 US Presidential Election Polling Data.

Variable	Description
state	abbreviated name of the state in which the poll was conducted
Obama	predicted support for Obama (percentage)
McCain	predicted support for McCain (percentage)
Pollster	name of the organization conducting the poll
middate	middate of the period when the poll was conducted

CSV file `polls08.csv`, which contains many polls within each state leading up to the election.[2] The names and descriptions of the variables in these data sets are given in tables 4.1 and 4.2, respectively. We begin by creating a variable, called `margin`, in both data frames, which represents Obama's vote margin over McCain in percentage points.

```
## load election results, by state
pres08 <- read.csv("pres08.csv")
## load polling data
polls08 <- read.csv("polls08.csv")
## compute Obama's margin
polls08$margin <- polls08$Obama - polls08$McCain
pres08$margin <- pres08$Obama - pres08$McCain
```

For each state, we generate a poll prediction for Obama's margin of victory using only the latest polls from the state. That is, we compute the mean prediction of all polls taken in the state on the day closest to the election. Note that this day may differ among states and there may be multiple polls conducted on the same day (more accurately, the same middate). To do this, we first initialize or create an empty vector of length 51, called `poll.pred`, which will contain the poll prediction for each of the 50 states and the District of Columbia. In the loop, we subset the data so that each iteration contains only the polls from one state.

[2] The polling data were obtained from http://electoral-vote.com.

We then further subset to extract the polls that were conducted within the state on the day closest to Election Day. This last step requires the conversion of the `middate` variable into the `Date` class using the `as.Date()` function. The `Date` class is useful because it can easily compute the number of days between the two specific dates. Input to the `as.Date()` function is a character string of the form `year-month-date` or `year/month/date`.

```r
x <- as.Date("2008-11-04")
y <- as.Date("2008/9/1")
x - y # number of days between 2008/9/1 and 11/4

## Time difference of 64 days
```

Using this operation, we create the variable, called `DaysToElection`, which represents the number of days to the election. We compute this as the difference in days between the middate and Election Day (November 4). Finally, we compute the mean of poll predictions and store it as the corresponding element of `poll.pred`. Note that we use the `unique()` function to extract the unique state names in the code chunk below.

```r
## convert to a Date object
polls08$middate <- as.Date(polls08$middate)
## compute the number of days to Election Day
polls08$DaysToElection <- as.Date("2008-11-04") - polls08$middate
poll.pred <- rep(NA, 51) # initialize a vector place holder
## extract unique state names which the loop will iterate through
st.names <- unique(polls08$state)
## add state names as labels for easy interpretation later on
names(poll.pred) <- as.character(st.names)
## loop across 50 states plus DC
for (i in 1:51){
    ## subset the ith state
    state.data <- subset(polls08, subset = (state == st.names[i]))
    ## further subset the latest polls within the state
    latest <- subset(state.data, DaysToElection == min(DaysToElection))
    ## compute the mean of latest polls and store it
    poll.pred[i] <- mean(latest$margin)
}
```

To set up the loop, we use the `unique()` function to extract the set of unique state names. Within the loop, we first subset the data for the `i`th state and store it as `state.data`. For example, if `i` equals 1, it is Alabama and hence `st.names[i]` yields `AL`. We then further subset the data by extracting only the polls taken on the day closest to Election Day, which is indicated by the minimum value of the

`DaysToElection` variable. Finally, the resulting data `latest` is used to compute the average of the predicted margins from the latest polls.

We investigate the accuracy of our poll prediction by subtracting it from the actual election result of each state. The difference between the actual and predicted outcome is called the *prediction error*. We compute the prediction error by comparing the actual margin of victory with the predicted margin. We then compute the mean of poll prediction errors across states. This represents the average prediction error, which we call *bias*.

```
## error of latest polls
errors <- pres08$margin - poll.pred
names(errors) <- st.names # add state names
mean(errors) # mean prediction error

## [1] 1.062092
```

The result shows that on average across all states the poll predictions are approximately *unbiased*. More precisely, the mean of poll prediction errors across states is 1.1 percentage points, representing a bias of small magnitude. The poll predictions are for some states above and for other states below the actual election results, but on average these errors appear to roughly cancel out. While the poll predictions are approximately unbiased across states, the prediction for each state may not be accurate. For some states, the poll predictions may be well above the actual margins of victory, and these positive prediction errors are offset by large negative prediction errors for other states. To investigate this possibility, we compute the *root mean square* (RMS) of prediction error (see equation (2.3) introduced in section 2.6.2) or *root-mean-squared error* (RMSE), which represents the average magnitude of prediction error.

```
sqrt(mean(errors^2))

## [1] 5.90894
```

The result indicates that the average magnitude of each poll prediction error is about 6 percentage points.

The **prediction error** is defined as

$$\text{prediction error} = \text{actual outcome} - \text{predicted outcome}.$$

The average prediction error is called **bias**, and prediction is said to be unbiased when its bias is zero. Finally, the root mean square of prediction error is called **root-mean-squared error**, representing the average magnitude of prediction error.

To obtain a more complete picture of prediction errors, we create a *histogram* using the `hist()` function (see section 3.3.2).

```
## histogram
hist(errors, freq = FALSE, ylim = c(0, 0.08),
     main = "Poll prediction error",
     xlab = "Error in predicted margin for Obama (percentage points)")
## add mean
abline(v = mean(errors), lty = "dashed", col = "blue")
text(x = -7, y = 0.08, "average error", col = "blue")
```

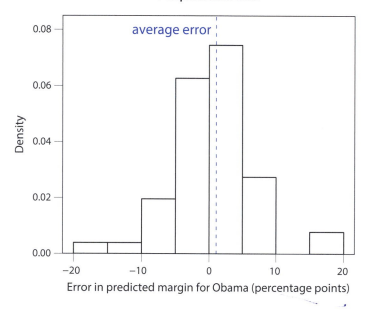

The histogram shows that the poll prediction error varies widely from one state to another. However, most errors are relatively small and larger errors are less likely to occur, yielding a *bell-shaped* distribution around zero.

We further examine the accuracy of poll predictions for each state by plotting them (horizontal axis) against the corresponding actual election results (vertical axis) using the two-letter state-name variable `state`. The states below (above) the 45-degree line indicate that the poll predictions were too favorable towards Obama (McCain). To plot text, we first create an "empty" plot by setting the `type` argument in the `plot()` function to `"n"` and then use the `text()` function to add state labels. As its first two arguments, the `text()` function takes the x and y coordinates for the location where the character string is to be plotted. The third argument of this function, `labels`, is a character vector of text labels to be plotted. In the current example, the *x*-coordinates and *y*-coordinates represent the poll predictions and Obama's actual margins.

```
## type = "n" generates "empty" plot
plot(poll.pred, pres08$margin, type = "n", main = "", xlab = "Poll results",
    xlim = c(-40, 90), ylim = c(-40, 90), ylab = "Actual election results")
## add state abbreviations
text(x = poll.pred, y = pres08$margin, labels = pres08$state, col = "blue")
## lines
abline(a = 0, b = 1, lty = "dashed") # 45-degree line
abline(v = 0)   # vertical line at 0
abline(h = 0)   # horizontal line at 0
```

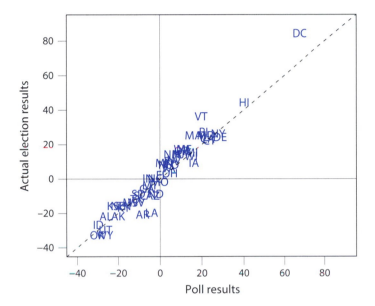

Although for some states like the District of Columbia (DC) and Vermont (VT) the poll prediction is grossly inaccurate, this may not matter given that the US presidential election is essentially based on the winner-take-all system for each state. On the other hand, even when poll predictions are close to the actual election results in terms of percentage points, polls may predict the wrong candidate as the winner of a state. There are two types of prediction errors where the poll predictions chose the wrong winner. In the above plot, for the states that are plotted in the upper-left quadrant, Obama was predicted to lose (because the poll results are negative) but he actually won the states (because the actual election results are positive). Conversely, for the states in the lower-right quadrant, Obama was predicted to win but actually lost the states. The plot suggests that the poll predictions accurately chose the winner for most states. However, three states, which the poll predictions called wrongly, had a close race with the margin of victory approximately equal to 1 percentage point. We can use the sign() function to determine the sign of poll.pred and pres08$margin for each state. The function returns 1 if positive (Obama wins) and –1 if negative (McCain wins) (0 if zero, a tie).

Table 4.3. Confusion Matrix.

| | Actual outcome | |
	Positive	Negative
Predicted outcome		
Positive	true positive	false positive
Negative	false negative	true negative

Note: There are two types of correct classification, true positive and true negative. Similarly, false positive and false negative are two kinds of misclassification.

```
## which state polls called wrong?
pres08$state[sign(poll.pred) != sign(pres08$margin)]

## [1] IN MO NC
## 51 Levels: AK AL AR AZ CA CO CT DC DE FL GA HI IA ID ... WY

## what was the actual margin for these states?
pres08$margin[sign(poll.pred) != sign(pres08$margin)]

## [1]  1 -1  1
```

The problem of predicting the outcome category or class is called *classification*. In the current context, for each state, we would like to predict whether Obama wins or not. In a classification problem, prediction is either exactly correct or incorrect, and an incorrect prediction is called *misclassification*. In our analysis, the misclassification rate is 3/51, which is about 6 percent.

In a binary classification problem, there are two types of misclassification. We may predict Obama to be the winner for a state where he actually lost the election. Conversely, Obama may be predicted to lose a state and yet in the actual election win it. If we regard Obama's victory (rather than his loss) as the "positive" outcome, then the former type of misclassification is called *false positive* whereas the latter is *false negative*. In the current example, Missouri (MO) is a false positive while Illinois (IN) and North Carolina (NC) are false negatives. Table 4.3 presents a *confusion matrix* where the two types of misclassification and correct classification are shown.

> **Classification** refers to the problem of predicting a categorical outcome. Classification is either correct or incorrect. In a binary classification problem, there are two types of **misclassification**: false positive and false negative, representing incorrectly predicted positive and negative outcomes, respectively.

Finally, we can compute the number of Electoral College votes for Obama based on the poll predictions and compare it against the actual result, which was 364 votes. Since 270 votes was the winning threshold, the results show that the polls correctly called Obama the elected president. The predicted total number of Electoral College votes was 15 fewer than the actual election result.[3]

```
## actual results: total number of electoral votes won by Obama
sum(pres08$EV[pres08$margin > 0])

## [1] 364

## poll prediction
sum(pres08$EV[poll.pred > 0])

## [1] 349
```

While the popular vote does not determine the election outcome, we can also examine the accuracy of national polls and how public opinion changed over the course of the campaign. To do this, we analyze the national polls contained in the CSV file `pollsUS08.csv`. The names and descriptions of the variables in this data set are identical to those of the last four variables in table 4.2. For each of the last 90 days of the campaign, we compute the average of support for each candidate using all polls taken within the past week and examine how it changes as Election Day nears. This can be done with a loop, where for a given day we take all polls that were conducted within the previous 7 days and on the corresponding day. We then compare these poll-based predictions against the actual vote shares in the election, which were 52.9% and 45.7% for Obama and McCain, respectively. Using the code for state polls above as a template, we construct the following code chunk.

```
## load the data
pollsUS08 <- read.csv("pollsUS08.csv")
## compute number of days to the election as before
pollsUS08$middate <- as.Date(pollsUS08$middate)
pollsUS08$DaysToElection <- as.Date("2008-11-04") - pollsUS08$middate
## empty vectors to store predictions
Obama.pred <- McCain.pred <- rep(NA, 90)
for (i in 1:90) {
    ## take all polls conducted within the past 7 days
    week.data <- subset(pollsUS08, subset = ((DaysToElection <= (90 - i + 7))
                                    & (DaysToElection > (90 - i))))
    ## compute support for each candidate using the average
    Obama.pred[i] <- mean(week.data$Obama)
    McCain.pred[i] <- mean(week.data$McCain)
}
```

Note that in the above code we utilize shortcut syntax to assign the same value to multiple objects. Specifically, we use the single expression `x <- y <- z` rather than

---

[3] As noted earlier, Obama received one vote from Nebraska even though he lost the statewide vote.

two separate expressions, x <- z and y <- z, in order to assign the same value z to two objects, x and y. Furthermore, within the loop, we subset the data pollsUS08 so that the resulting data contain only the polls conducted within the past 7 days and the day itself. For example, when the loop starts (i.e., i is equal to 1), we subset the polls for which the DaysToElection variable is less than or equal to 96 (= 90 − 1 + 7) and greater than 89 (= 90 − 1). In the final iteration (i.e., i is equal to 90), this variable for the subsetted data takes a value less than or equal to 7 (= 90 − 90 + 7) and greater than 0 (= 90 − 90).

We now display the results using a *time-series plot*. We define the horizontal axis such that its leftmost value is 90 days prior to Election Day and its rightmost value is Election Day. This can be done by specifying the xlim argument to be c(90, 0) instead of c(0, 90). The plot at the bottom uses gray circles rather than red for the states won by McCain. See page C3 for the full-color version.

```r
## plot going from 90 days to 1 day before the election
plot(90:1, Obama.pred, type = "b", xlim = c(90, 0), ylim = c(40, 60),
     col = "blue", xlab = "Days to the election",
     ylab = "Support for candidate (percentage points)")
## type = "b" gives plot that includes both points and lines
lines(90:1, McCain.pred, type = "b", col = "red")
## actual election results: pch = 19 gives solid circles
points(0, 52.93, pch = 19, col = "blue")
points(0, 45.65, pch = 19, col = "red")
## line indicating Election Day
abline(v = 0)
## labeling candidates
text(80, 48, "Obama", col = "blue")
text(80, 41, "McCain", col = "red")
```

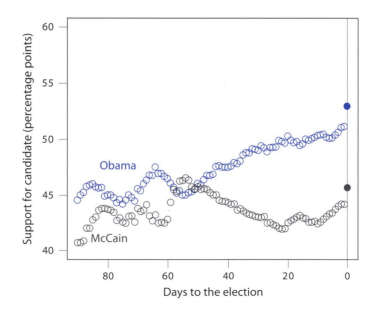

Which person is the most competent?

Figure 4.2. Example Pictures of Candidates Used in the Experiment. Source: A. Todorov et al. (2005) *Science*, vol. 308, no. 10 (June), pp. 1623–1626.

The resulting figure demonstrates the reasonable accuracy of preelection polls in terms of margin. Indeed, the Election Day margin (the difference between two solid circles) almost coincides with the predicted margin based on the polls taken within a week prior to the election. It is also interesting that public opinion shifts quite a bit during the course of campaign. Two months before the election, support for Obama was roughly tied with that for McCain. However, as Election Day approached, Obama's margin over McCain gradually increased. On Election Day, it was more than 7 percentage points. It is also worth noting that the proportion of other voters who were either undecided or supported third-party candidates declined.

4.2 Linear Regression

In the previous section, we used polling data to predict election outcomes. When doing so, we simply used the average of poll predictions. An alternative method of prediction is based on a statistical model. In this section, we introduce one of the most basic statistical models, called *linear regression*.

4.2.1 FACIAL APPEARANCE AND ELECTION OUTCOMES

Several psychologists have reported the intriguing result of an experiment showing that facial appearance predicts election outcomes better than chance.[4] In their experiment, the researchers briefly showed student subjects the black-and-white head shots of two candidates from a US congressional election (winner and runner-up). Figure 4.2 shows example pictures of the candidates from the 2004 Wisconsin Senate race. Russ Feingold of the Democratic Party (left) was the actual winner, and Tim Michels of the Republican Party (right) was the runner-up. The exposure of subjects to facial pictures lasted less than a second, and the subjects were then asked to evaluate the two candidates in terms of their perceived competence.

---

[4] This section is based on Alexander Todorov, Anesu N. Mandisodza, Amir Goren, and Crystal C. Hall (2005) "Inferences of competence from faces predict election outcomes." *Science*, vol. 308, no. 10 (June), pp. 1623–1626.

Table 4.4. Facial Appearance Experiment Data.

Variable	Description
congress	session of Congress
year	year of the election
state	state of the election
winner	name of the winner
loser	name of the runner-up
w.party	party of the winner
l.party	party of the loser
d.votes	number of votes for the Democratic candidate
r.votes	number of votes for the Republican candidate
d.comp	competence measure for the Democratic candidate
r.comp	competence measure for the Republican candidate

The researchers used these competence measures to predict election outcomes. The key hypothesis is whether or not a within-a-second evaluation of facial appearance can predict election outcomes. The CSV data set, face.csv, contains the data from the experiment. Table 4.4 presents the names and descriptions of the variables in this data set. Note that we include data only from subjects who did not know the candidates' political parties, their policies, or even which candidate was the incumbent or challenger. They were simply making snap judgments about which candidate appeared more competent based on their facial expression alone.

We begin our analysis of the facial appearance experiment data by creating a *scatter plot* of the competence measure against election outcomes. To do this, we create the win margins for Democratic candidates as the difference in two-party vote shares for Democratic and Republican candidates. Positive win margins favor Democrats. A two-party vote share is the number of votes each candidate receives out of just those votes cast for a major party candidate (not out of all votes cast).

```
## load the data
face <- read.csv("face.csv")
## two-party vote share for Democrats and Republicans
face$d.share <- face$d.votes / (face$d.votes + face$r.votes)
face$r.share <- face$r.votes / (face$d.votes + face$r.votes)
face$diff.share <- face$d.share - face$r.share
```

Next, we use the plot() function to generate a scatter plot. To make the symbols more informative, we can change them based on variables in our data set. The argument pch for the plot() function can specify the type of points to be plotted (see section 3.6). We use the ifelse() function when specifying the col argument so that red dots are used for the races with Republican winners and blue dots are used for those with Democratic winners. The plot shows a mild upward trend in the Democratic margin as the competence score for Democrats increases.

```
plot(face$d.comp, face$diff.share, pch = 16,
    col = ifelse(face$w.party == "R", "red", "blue"),
    xlim = c(0, 1), ylim = c(-1, 1),
    xlab = "Competence scores for Democrats",
    ylab = "Democratic margin in vote share",
    main = "Facial competence and vote share")
```

The plot below uses gray circles instead of red circles for Republican winners. See page C3 for the full-color version.

Facial competence and vote share

4.2.2   CORRELATION AND SCATTER PLOTS

We learned in section 3.6.2 that correlation represents the degree to which one variable is associated with another. A positive (negative) value of correlation means that one variable is more (less) likely to be above (below) its mean when the other variable is above its own mean. The upwards-sloping data cloud in the above scatter plot shows a positive *correlation* between perceived competence and vote share differential. To compute the correlation coefficient, we use the function `cor()`.

```
cor(face$d.comp, face$diff.share)
## [1] 0.4327743
```

This correlation of about 0.4 tells us that there is a moderately positive relationship between a candidate's perceived competence and his or her actual margin of victory on Election Day. That is, candidates who appear more competent than their

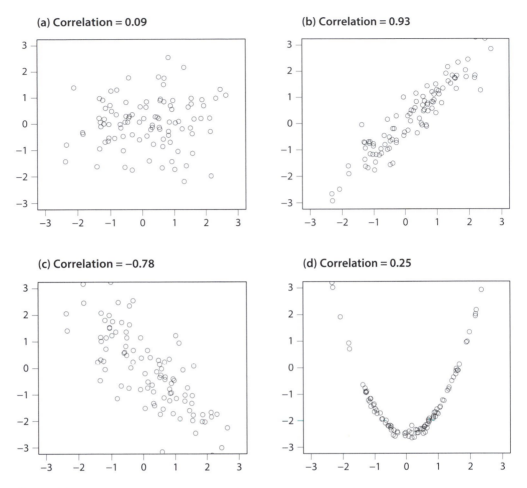

Figure 4.3. Correlation Coefficients and Patterns of the Data Cloud in Scatter Plots.

opponents—as rapidly judged by uninformed voters who don't recognize the candidates—are likely to win a higher share of the votes cast.

To get a better sense of the relationship between correlation coefficients and data cloud shapes, figure 4.3 presents four artificial data sets with various degrees of correlation. We observe that a positive (negative) correlation corresponds to an upwards (downwards) trend in the data cloud, and a greater magnitude of the correlation coefficient indicates a stronger linear relationship. Indeed, correlation represents a *linear relationship* between two variables. Perfect positive (negative) correlation, i.e., correlation of 1 (-1), would mean the two variables have a perfect linear relationship with data points located on a single line.

Thus, it is important for us to note that a lack of correlation does not necessarily imply a lack of a relationship. In panel (d), the correlation between the two variables is low but there is a clear *nonlinear relationship*, which in this case is a quadratic function.

> The **correlation coefficient** quantifies the linear relationship between two variables. An upwards trend in the data cloud in a scatter plot implies a positive correlation, whereas a downwards trend in the data cloud represents a negative correlation. Correlation is often not suitable for representing a nonlinear relationship.

4.2.3　LEAST SQUARES

As shown above, correlation describes a linear relationship between two variables. However, such a relationship is best characterized using the following *linear model*:

$$Y = \underbrace{\alpha}_{\text{intercept}} + \underbrace{\beta}_{\text{slope}} X + \underbrace{\epsilon}_{\text{error term}} . \tag{4.1}$$

In the model, Y is the outcome or response variable and X is the predictor or independent (explanatory) variable. In the current application, we will use the perceived competence measure as the predictor and the difference in two-party vote share as the outcome. Recall that any line can be defined by the *intercept* α and the *slope* parameter β. The intercept α represents the average value of Y when X is zero. The slope β measures the average increase in Y when X increases by one unit. The intercept and slope parameters are together called *coefficients*. The *error* (or *disturbance*) term, ϵ, allows an observation to deviate from a perfect linear relationship.

We use a model like this under the assumption that it approximates the *data-generating process* well. However, as well-known statistician George Box has stated, we must recognize that "all models are wrong, but some are useful." Even if the data are not generated according to the linear model specified in equation (4.1), the model can be a useful tool to predict the outcome of interest.

Since the values of α and β in equation (4.1) are unknown to researchers, they must be estimated from the data. In statistics, the estimates of parameters are indicated by "hats," where $\hat{\alpha}$ and $\hat{\beta}$ represent the estimates of α and β, respectively. Once we obtain the estimated values of coefficients α and β, then we have the so-called *regression line*. We can use this line to predict the value of the outcome variable given that of a predictor. Specifically, given a particular value of the predictor, $X = x$, we compute the *predicted value* (or *fitted value*) of the outcome variable, denoted by $\widehat{Y}$, using the regression function

$$\widehat{Y} = \hat{\alpha} + \hat{\beta}x. \tag{4.2}$$

Most likely, the predicted value will not equal the observed value. The difference between the observed outcome and its predicted value is called the *residual* or *prediction error*. Formally, we can write the residual as

$$\hat{\epsilon} = Y - \widehat{Y}. \tag{4.3}$$

Notice that the residual is represented by ϵ with a hat. Since the error term ϵ in equation (4.1) is unobserved, the residual represents an estimate of this error term.

> The **linear regression model** is defined as
>
> $$Y = \alpha + \beta X + \epsilon,$$
>
> where Y is the outcome (or response) variable, X is the predictor or the inde-
> pendent (or explanatory) variable, ϵ is the error (or disturbance) term, and (α, β)
> are the coefficients. The slope parameter β represents the increase in the average
> outcome associated with a one-unit increase in the predictor. Once the estimates
> of the coefficients $(\hat{\alpha}, \hat{\beta})$ are obtained from the data, we can predict the outcome,
> using a given value of the predictor $X = x$, as $\widehat{Y} = \hat{\alpha} + \hat{\beta}x$. The difference between
> the observed outcome and this fitted or predicted value $\widehat{Y}$ is called the residual and
> is denoted by $\hat{\epsilon} = Y - \widehat{Y}$.

To fit a linear regression model in R, we use the `lm()` function. This function takes
a formula of the form `Y ~ X` as the main argument where the outcome variable is `Y`
and the predictor is `X`, taken from a data frame specified as the `data` argument. Note
that an intercept will be automatically added to the regression model.

We now obtain the regression line for the facial appearance experiment data. We
use the Democratic margin in the two-party vote share as the response variable and the
perceived competence for Democratic candidates as the predictor.

```
fit <- lm(diff.share ~ d.comp, data = face) # fit the model
fit

##
## Call:
## lm(formula = diff.share ~ d.comp, data = face)
##
## Coefficients:
## (Intercept)        d.comp
##     -0.3122        0.6604
```

The output shows that the estimated intercept is -0.3122 whereas the estimated
slope is 0.6604. That is, when no experimental subject thinks a Democratic candidate
is more competent than a Republican counterpart, the predicted Democratic margin
of two-party vote share is approximately -31.2 percentage points. If the perceived
competence score increases by 10 percentage points, then the outcome variable is
predicted to increase on average by $6.6 (= 0.6604 \times 10)$ percentage points.

There is an alternative way of fitting the same model without the `data` argument.
This requires specifying the entire names of objects for the outcome variable and the
predictor as follows.

```
lm(face$diff.share ~ face$d.comp)
```

In general, this is not recommended because it unnecessarily complicates the syntax and may cause confusion. However, it may be useful when the variables we wish to use for regression exist as separate objects in the workspace.

In addition, to directly obtain the estimated coefficients $(\hat{\alpha}, \hat{\beta})$ and the predicted or fitted values $\widehat{Y}$, we can use the `coef()` and `fitted()` functions, respectively.

```r
coef(fit)  # get estimated coefficients

## (Intercept)      d.comp
##  -0.3122259   0.6603815

head(fitted(fit))  # get fitted or predicted values

##           1           2           3           4           5
##  0.06060411 -0.08643340  0.09217061  0.04539236 0.13698690
##           6
##  -0.10057206
```

It is straightforward to add the regression line to the scatter plot using the `abline()` function which takes the output object from the `lm()` function as its input. The plot also shows the estimated intercept $\hat{\alpha}$ as well as the observed outcome Y, the predicted or fitted value $\hat{Y}$, and the residual $\hat{\epsilon}$ for one of the observations.

```r
plot(face$d.comp, face$diff.share, xlim = c(0, 1.05), ylim = c(-1,1),
     xlab = "Competence scores for Democrats",
     ylab = "Democratic margin in vote share",
     main = "Facial competence and vote share")
abline(fit) # add regression line
abline(v = 0, lty = "dashed")
```

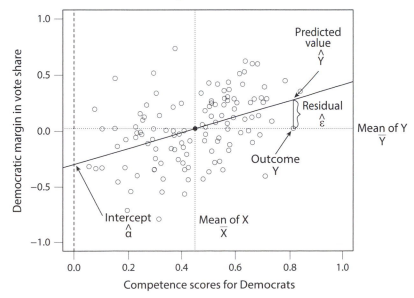

This regression line is the "line of best fit" because it minimizes the magnitude of prediction error. To estimate the line's intercept and slope parameters, a commonly used method is that of *least squares*. The idea is to choose $\hat{\alpha}$ and $\hat{\beta}$ such that together they minimize the *sum of squared residuals* (SSR), which is defined as

$$\text{SSR} = \sum_{i=1}^{n} \hat{\epsilon}_i^2 = \sum_{i=1}^{n} (Y_i - \hat{Y}_i)^2 = \sum_{i=1}^{n} (Y_i - \hat{\alpha} - \hat{\beta} X_i)^2. \tag{4.4}$$

In the equation, Y_i, X_i, and $\hat{\epsilon}_i$ represent the outcome variable, the predictor, and the residual, respectively, for the ith observation, and n is the sample size. The second and third equalities follow from the definition of the residual given in equations (4.3) and (4.2), respectively. The value of SSR is difficult to interpret. However, we can use the idea of *root mean square* (RMS) introduced in section 2.6.2 and applied earlier. Specifically, we can compute the *root-mean-squared error* (RMSE) as

$$\text{RMSE} = \sqrt{\frac{1}{n} \text{SSR}} = \sqrt{\frac{1}{n} \sum_{i=1}^{n} \hat{\epsilon}_i^2}. \tag{4.5}$$

Therefore, RMSE represents the average magnitude of the prediction error for the regression, and this is what the method of least squares minimizes.

In R, RMSE can be easily calculated by first obtaining the residuals from the `resid()` function.

```
epsilon.hat <- resid(fit)   # residuals
sqrt(mean(epsilon.hat^2))   # RMSE

## [1] 0.2642361
```

The result implies that while the perceived competence score does predict the election outcome, the prediction is not very accurate, yielding on average a prediction error of 26 percentage points.

The least squares estimates of intercept and slope parameters are given by

$$\hat{\alpha} = \overline{Y} - \hat{\beta}\overline{X}, \tag{4.6}$$

$$\hat{\beta} = \frac{\sum_{i=1}^{n} (Y_i - \overline{Y})(X_i - \overline{X})}{\sum_{i=1}^{n} (X_i - \overline{X})^2}. \tag{4.7}$$

Recall that the sample means of Y and X are given by $\overline{Y} = \frac{1}{n} \sum_{i=1}^{n} Y_i$ and $\overline{X} = \frac{1}{n} \sum_{i=1}^{n} X_i$, respectively. The results imply that the regression line always goes through the center of the data $(\overline{X}, \overline{Y})$. This is so because substituting $x = \overline{X}$ into equation (4.2) and using the expression for $\hat{\alpha}$ in equation (4.6) yields $\hat{Y} = \overline{Y}$:

$$\hat{Y} = \underbrace{(\overline{Y} - \hat{\beta}\overline{X})}_{\hat{\alpha}} + \hat{\beta}\overline{X} = \overline{Y}.$$

In the above plot, we observe that this is indeed the case. The regression line runs through the intersection of the vertical and horizontal dotted lines, which represent the means of X and Y, respectively.

In addition, when the method of least squares is used to estimate the coefficients, the predictions based on the fitted regression line are accurate on average. More precisely, the mean of residual $\hat{\epsilon}$ is zero, as the following algebraic manipulation shows:

$$\text{mean of } \hat{\epsilon} = \frac{1}{n} \sum_{i=1}^{n} (Y_i - \hat{\alpha} - \hat{\beta} X_i) = \overline{Y} - \hat{\alpha} - \hat{\beta} \overline{X} = 0.$$

In this equation, the first equality is due to the definition of the residual, the next equality is obtained by applying the summation for each term in the parentheses, and the final equality follows from equation (4.6). We emphasize that this is an algebraic equality and holds for *any* data set. In other words, a linear regression model always has zero average prediction error across all data points in the sample, but this does not necessarily mean that the linear regression model accurately represents the actual data-generating process.

> A common method of estimating the coefficients of the linear regression model is the method of **least squares**, which minimizes the sum of squared residuals,
>
> $$\text{SSR} = \sum_{i=1}^{n} \hat{\epsilon}_i^2 = \sum_{i=1}^{n} (Y_i - \hat{\alpha} - \hat{\beta} X_i)^2.$$
>
> The mean of residuals is always zero, and the regression line always goes through the center of data $(\overline{X}, \overline{Y})$ where $\overline{X}$ and $\overline{Y}$ are the sample means of X and Y, respectively.

It is also important to understand the relationship between the estimated slope of the regression and the correlation coefficient introduced in section 3.6.2:

$$\hat{\beta} = \frac{1}{n} \sum_{i=1}^{n} \frac{(Y_i - \overline{Y})(X_i - \overline{X})}{\sqrt{\frac{1}{n}\sum_{i=1}^{n}(Y_i - \overline{Y})^2}\sqrt{\frac{1}{n}\sum_{i=1}^{n}(X_i - \overline{X})^2}} \times \frac{\sqrt{\frac{1}{n}\sum_{i=1}^{n}(Y_i - \overline{Y})^2}}{\sqrt{\frac{1}{n}\sum_{i=1}^{n}(X_i - \overline{X})^2}}$$

$$= \text{correlation of } X \text{ and } Y \times \frac{\text{standard deviation of } Y}{\text{standard deviation of } X}. \tag{4.8}$$

The first equality holds because we divide and multiply the right hand side of equation (4.7) by the standard deviation of Y, i.e., $\sqrt{\frac{1}{n}\sum_{i=1}^{n}(Y_i - \overline{Y})^2}$, whereas the second equality follows from the definitions of correlation and standard deviation (see equations (3.2) and (2.4), respectively).

The expression for the estimated slope parameter in equation (4.8) has two important implications. First, a positive (negative) correlation corresponds to a positive (negative) slope because standard deviations never take a negative value. Second, each increase of 1 standard deviation in X is associated with an average increase of ρ standard deviations in Y, where ρ is the correlation between X and Y. For example, if the correlation is 0.5, then a 1 standard deviation increase in X would result in a 0.5 standard deviation increase in Y. In the current example, the correlation between the

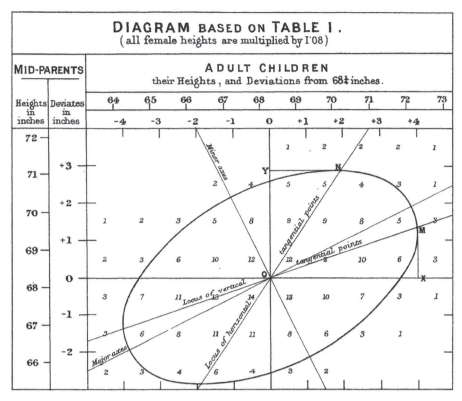

Figure 4.4. Galton's Regression Towards Mediocrity. Source: Francis Galton (1886) "Regression towards mediocrity in hereditary stature." *Journal of the Anthropological Institute of Great Britain and Ireland*, vol. 15, pp. 246–263.

perceived competence score and the two-party vote share differential is 0.43, whereas the standard deviations of X and Y are 0.19 and 0.29, respectively. Thus, an increase in the perceived competence score of 0.19 is associated with an average increase in the two-party vote share differential of roughly 13 percentage points ($\approx 0.43 \times 0.29$).

> The estimated **slope coefficient** from a linear regression model equals the ρ standard deviation unit increase in the outcome variable that is associated with an increase of 1 standard deviation in the predictor, where ρ is the correlation between the two variables.

4.2.4 REGRESSION TOWARDS THE MEAN

In his 1886 paper entitled "Regression towards mediocrity in hereditary stature," a British scholar, Sir Francis Galton, conducted one of the first regression analyses. He studied human hereditary stature by examining the relationship between the height of adult children and the average of their parents' heights, which Galton called the "mid-parents' height." Galton was the first to present an example of the phenomenon called *regression towards the mean*. He summarized this as "When Mid Parents are shorter (taller) than mediocrity, their Children tend to be taller (shorter) than they."

Figure 4.4 is taken from the original paper. In this figure, the values indicate the number of observations and the ellipse represents the data cloud. The "locus of vertical tangential points" represents a regression line where the outcome variable is adult children's height (horizontal axis) and the predictor is their mid-parents' height (vertical axis). Note that the outcome variable is measured on the horizontal axis while the predictor is on the vertical axis, which is the exact opposite of the current practice of plotting the outcome variable on the vertical axis. Galton also regressed mid-parents' heights on the heights of adult children. This regression line is denoted by the "locus of horizontal tangential points." The angle of the slope of this regression line, which Galton calculated to be 2/3, represents the rate of regression from mid-parents to children.

To demonstrate the regression effect numerically, consider the observations that have mid-parents' heights of approximately 71 inches. As we can see from figure 4.4, there are 24 such observations, represented by those in the second row from the top. Out of these observations, only 8, or 33% of them, have children who are at least as tall as their mid-parents. In contrast, focus on the observations whose mid-parents are about 67 inches and hence shorter than the average height (they are in the second row from the bottom). Out of 57 such observations, 40 observations, or 70%, have children whose heights are at least their mid-parents' height. Galton called this pattern the "regression towards mediocrity." Note, however, that as indicated by the positive slope of the regression line, children whose parents are taller also tend to be taller on average. We emphasize that as shown in chapter 6 this empirical phenomenon can be explained by chance alone. Thus, regression towards the mean does not imply that human heights are converging and everyone will have an identical height in the future!

Regression towards the mean is observed in other contexts as well. Below, we show another example of this phenomenon, demonstrating that Obama tended to gain fewer votes in 2012 than in 2008 for the states in which he did well in 2008. Other examples include test scores where students who perform well in the midterm exam tend not to do as well in the final exam. An important point is that this decline in performance may have arisen due to chance rather than to a lack of Obama's or the students' efforts.

> **Regression towards the mean** represents an empirical phenomenon where an observation with a value of the predictor further away from the distribution's mean tends to have a value of an outcome variable closer to that mean. This tendency can be explained by chance alone.

4.2.5 MERGING DATA SETS IN R

We will examine whether or not the US presidential election data exhibit the regression towards the mean phenomenon. To do this, we use Obama's vote share in the 2008 election to predict his vote share in his 2012 reelection. We *merge* the 2012 election result data set, `pres12.csv`, into the 2008 election data set. The variable names and descriptions of the 2012 election result data set are given in table 4.5.

Merging two data sets can be done in R using the `merge()` function. The function takes three main arguments, x, y, and by, where the x and y arguments represent two data frames to be merged and the by argument indicates the variable name(s) used for merging. Let's first look at two data sets we would like to merge.

Table 4.5. 2012 US Presidential Election Data.

Variable	Description
state	abbreviated name of the state
Obama	Obama's vote share (percentage)
Romney	Romney's vote share (percentage)
EV	number of Electoral College votes for the state

```
pres12 <- read.csv("pres12.csv")   # load 2012 data
## quick look at two data sets
head(pres08)

##    state.name state Obama McCain EV margin
## 1     Alabama    AL    39     60  9    -21
## 2      Alaska    AK    38     59  3    -21
## 3     Arizona    AZ    45     54 10     -9
## 4    Arkansas    AR    39     59  6    -20
## 5  California    CA    61     37 55     24
## 6    Colorado    CO    54     45  9      9

head(pres12)

##   state Obama Romney EV
## 1    AL    38     61  9
## 2    AK    41     55  3
## 3    AZ    45     54 11
## 4    AR    37     61  6
## 5    CA    60     37 55
## 6    CO    51     46  9
```

We will use the state name variable state, which is contained in both data sets, to merge the two data frames.

```
## merge two data frames
pres <- merge(pres08, pres12, by = "state")
## summarize the merged data frame
summary(pres)

##      state            state.name     Obama.x
## AK     : 1   Alabama    : 1   Min.   :33.00
## AL     : 1   Alaska     : 1   1st Qu.:43.00
## AR     : 1   Arizona    : 1   Median :51.00
## AZ     : 1   Arkansas   : 1   Mean   :51.37
## CA     : 1   California : 1   3rd Qu.:57.50
```

```
##   CO      : 1    Colorado  : 1    Max.      :92.00
##   (Other):45    (Other)   :45
##       McCain               EV.x              margin
##   Min.   : 7.00    Min.   : 3.00    Min.      :-32.000
##   1st Qu.:40.00    1st Qu.: 4.50    1st Qu.:-13.000
##   Median :47.00    Median : 8.00    Median :  4.000
##   Mean   :47.06    Mean   :10.55    Mean   :  4.314
##   3rd Qu.:56.00    3rd Qu.:11.50    3rd Qu.: 17.500
##   Max.   :66.00    Max.   :55.00    Max.   : 85.000
##
##       Obama.y              Romney               EV.y
##   Min.   :25.00    Min.   : 7.00    Min.   : 3.00
##   1st Qu.:40.50    1st Qu.:41.00    1st Qu.: 4.50
##   Median :51.00    Median :48.00    Median : 8.00
##   Mean   :49.06    Mean   :49.04    Mean   :10.55
##   3rd Qu.:56.00    3rd Qu.:58.00    3rd Qu.:11.50
##   Max.   :91.00    Max.   :73.00    Max.   :55.00
##
```

Note that if the data frames have variables with identical names, i.e., Obama and EV, then the merged data frame will append .x and .y to each name, thereby attributing each variable to its original data frame. The variable used for merging must exist in both data frames. This variable may have the same name in both data frames, as in the above code chunk, but if the variable happens to have different names, then we can use the by.x and by.y arguments to specify the exact variable names used in each data frame. By default, the merged data frame keeps the name of the variable from data frame x, which is specified by the by.x argument. An example code chunk is given here.

```
## change the variable name for illustration
names(pres12)[1] <- "state.abb"
## merging data sets using the variables of different names
pres <- merge(pres08, pres12, by.x = "state", by.y = "state.abb")
summary(pres)
##       state           state.name      Obama.x
##   AK      : 1    Alabama   : 1    Min.   :33.00
##   AL      : 1    Alaska    : 1    1st Qu.:43.00
##   AR      : 1    Arizona   : 1    Median :51.00
##   AZ      : 1    Arkansas  : 1    Mean   :51.37
##   CA      : 1    California: 1    3rd Qu.:57.50
##   CO      : 1    Colorado  : 1    Max.   :92.00
##   (Other):45    (Other)   :45
##       McCain               EV.x              margin
##   Min.   : 7.00    Min.   : 3.00    Min.      :-32.000
```

```
##   1st Qu.:40.00    1st Qu.: 4.50    1st Qu.:-13.000
##   Median :47.00    Median : 8.00    Median :   4.000
##   Mean   :47.06    Mean   :10.55    Mean   :   4.314
##   3rd Qu.:56.00    3rd Qu.:11.50    3rd Qu.:  17.500
##   Max.   :66.00    Max.   :55.00    Max.   :  85.000
##
##      Obama.y            Romney            EV.y
##   Min.   :25.00    Min.   : 7.00    Min.   : 3.00
##   1st Qu.:40.50    1st Qu.:41.00    1st Qu.: 4.50
##   Median :51.00    Median :48.00    Median : 8.00
##   Mean   :49.06    Mean   :49.04    Mean   :10.55
##   3rd Qu.:56.00    3rd Qu.:58.00    3rd Qu.:11.50
##   Max.   :91.00    Max.   :73.00    Max.   :55.00
##
```

An alternative way of combining two data frames is the cbind() function, which enables column-binding of multiple data frames. (As a side note, the rbind() function performs row-binding of multiple data frames by stacking one below another.) But sometimes problematically, the cbind() function assumes the proper sorting of data frames such that corresponding observations appear in the same row of the data frames. In our current application, each state must appear in the same row of the two data frames. The merge() function, on the other hand, appropriately sorts the data frames according to the variable used for merging. Another disadvantage of the cbind() function is that it preserves all columns in both data frames even when they represent the same variable, containing identical information.

The code chunk below illustrates these two problems. The resulting merged data frame keeps all variables from both data frames, and more importantly, the merged data frame has incorrect information for the District of Columbia (DC) and Delaware (DE) because their order is different in the two original data frames. In contrast, the merge() function will sort the second data frame, pres12, appropriately to match with the first data frame, pres08.

```
## cbinding two data frames
pres1 <- cbind(pres08, pres12)
## this shows all variables are kept
summary(pres1)

##     state.name       state         Obama
##   Alabama    : 1    AK    : 1    Min.   :33.00
##   Alaska     : 1    AL    : 1    1st Qu.:43.00
##   Arizona    : 1    AR    : 1    Median :51.00
##   Arkansas   : 1    AZ    : 1    Mean   :51.37
##   California : 1    CA    : 1    3rd Qu.:57.50
##   Colorado   : 1    CO    : 1    Max.   :92.00
##   (Other)    :45    (Other):45
```

```
##      McCain              EV              margin
##   Min.   : 7.00    Min.   : 3.00    Min.    :-32.000
##   1st Qu.:40.00    1st Qu.: 4.50    1st Qu.:-13.000
##   Median :47.00    Median : 8.00    Median :  4.000
##   Mean   :47.06    Mean   :10.55    Mean   :  4.314
##   3rd Qu.:56.00    3rd Qu.:11.50    3rd Qu.: 17.500
##   Max.   :66.00    Max.   :55.00    Max.   : 85.000
##
##     state.abb      Obama              Romney
##   AK     : 1    Min.   :25.00    Min.   : 7.00
##   AL     : 1    1st Qu.:40.50    1st Qu.:41.00
##   AR     : 1    Median :51.00    Median :48.00
##   AZ     : 1    Mean   :49.06    Mean   :49.04
##   CA     : 1    3rd Qu.:56.00    3rd Qu.:58.00
##   CO     : 1    Max.   :91.00    Max.   :73.00
##   (Other):45
##        EV
##   Min.   : 3.00
##   1st Qu.: 4.50
##   Median : 8.00
##   Mean   :10.55
##   3rd Qu.:11.50
##   Max.   :55.00
##

## DC and DE are flipped in this alternative approach
pres1[8:9, ]

##    state.name state Obama McCain EV margin state.abb Obama
## 8        D.C.    DC    92      7  3     85        DE    59
## 9    Delaware    DE    62     37  3     25        DC    91
##    Romney EV
## 8     40  3
## 9      7  3

## merge() does not have this problem
pres[8:9, ]

##    state state.name Obama.x McCain EV.x margin Obama.y
## 8    DC        D.C.      92      7    3     85      91
## 9    DE    Delaware      62     37    3     25      59
##    Romney EV.y
## 8       7    3
## 9      40    3
```

Using the merged data frame, we investigate whether or not the regression towards the mean phenomenon exists in the US presidential election data. Given the recent trend of increasing polarization in American politics (see section 3.5), we standardize vote shares across elections by computing their *z-scores* so that we can measure Obama's electoral performance in each state relative to his average performance of that year (see section 3.6.2). That is, we subtract the mean from Obama's vote share in each election and then divide it by the standard deviation. This can be done easily by using the `scale()` function. We perform this transformation because technically, the regression towards the mean phenomenon holds when both the outcome and explanatory variables are standardized.

```
pres$Obama2008.z <- scale(pres$Obama.x)
pres$Obama2012.z <- scale(pres$Obama.y)
```

We regress Obama's 2012 standardized vote share on his 2008 standardized vote share. As expected, we observe a strong positive linear relationship between the two. Obama tended to receive more votes in 2012 from states that gave him more votes in 2008. Note that when we standardize both the outcome variable and the predictor, the estimated intercept becomes zero. This is because the estimated intercept is given by $\hat{\alpha} = \overline{Y} - \hat{\beta}\overline{X}$ (see equation (4.6)) and after standardizing, the sample means of both variables, $\overline{Y}$ and $\overline{X}$, are zero. As shown below, in this case, R estimates the intercept to be essentially zero. It is also possible to fit the model without an intercept by including `-1` in the formula.

```
## intercept is estimated as essentially zero
fit1 <- lm(Obama2012.z ~ Obama2008.z, data = pres)
fit1

##
## Call:
## lm(formula = Obama2012.z ~ Obama2008.z, data = pres)
##
## Coefficients:
## (Intercept)   Obama2008.z
##   -3.521e-17    9.834e-01

## regression without an intercept; estimated slope is identical
fit1 <- lm(Obama2012.z ~ -1 + Obama2008.z, data = pres)
fit1

##
## Call:
## lm(formula = Obama2012.z ~ -1 + Obama2008.z, data = pres)
##
## Coefficients:
## Obama2008.z
##      0.9834
```

Here, we plot the fitted regression line as well as the data points where we observe a strong linear relationship.

```
plot(pres$Obama2008.z, pres$Obama2012.z, xlim = c(-4, 4), ylim = c(-4, 4),
     xlab = "Obama's standardized vote share in 2008",
     ylab = "Obama's standardized vote share in 2012")
abline(fit1) # draw a regression line
```

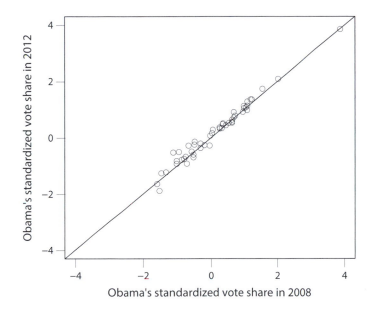

Now we compute the proportion of states where Obama received a greater share of standardized votes in 2012 than he did in 2008. We do so using first the bottom quartile of Obama's 2008 (standardized) vote share, then the top quartile. If the regression towards the mean phenomenon exists, then this proportion should be greater for the states in the bottom quartile than those in the top quartile.

```
## bottom quartile
mean((pres$Obama2012.z >
        pres$Obama2008.z)[pres$Obama2008.z
                            <= quantile(pres$Obama2008.z, 0.25)])

## [1] 0.5714286

## top quartile
mean((pres$Obama2012.z >
        pres$Obama2008.z)[pres$Obama2008.z
                            >= quantile(pres$Obama2008.z, 0.75)])

## [1] 0.4615385
```

In the above code, we use the `quantile()` function to compute the top and bottom quartiles. Then, a logical vector where `TRUE` (`FALSE`) indicates Obama's 2012 vote share being greater than (less than or equal to) his 2008 vote share is subsetted by another logical vector. This second logical vector, inside the square brackets, indicates whether Obama's 2008 vote share for a state is in the bottom or top quartile. The result clearly shows the regression towards the mean phenomenon. Obama fared better in 2012 than in 2008 in 57% of bottom quartile states, where he failed most in 2008. In contrast, Obama fared better in 2012 only among 46% of the top quartile states, where he succeeded most in 2008.

4.2.6 MODEL FIT

Model fit measures how well the model fits the data, i.e., how accurately the model predicts observations. We can assess model fit by looking at the *coefficient of determination*, or R^2, which represents the proportion of total variation in the outcome variable explained by the model. To define R^2, we first introduce the *total sum of squares* or TSS, which is defined as

$$\text{TSS} = \sum_{i=1}^{n} (Y_i - \overline{Y})^2.$$

The TSS represents the total variation of the outcome variable based on the square distance from its mean. Now, we can define R^2 as the proportion of TSS explained by the predictor X:

$$R^2 = \frac{\text{TSS} - \text{SSR}}{\text{TSS}} = 1 - \frac{\text{SSR}}{\text{TSS}}.$$

The SSR or sum of squared residuals is defined in equation (4.4) and represents the residual variation of Y left unexplained by X. The value of R^2 ranges from 0 (when the correlation between the outcome and the predictor is 0) to 1 (when the correlation is 1), indicating how well the linear model fits the data at hand.

> The **coefficient of determination** is a measure of model fit and represents the proportion of variation in the outcome variable explained by the predictor. It is defined as one minus the ratio of the sum of squared residuals (SSR) to the total sum of squares (TSS).

As an illustrative example, consider the problem of predicting the 2000 US election results in Florida using the 1996 US election results from the same state at the county level. In Florida, there are 68 counties, and the CSV file `florida.csv` contains the number of votes cast for each candidate in those two elections. Table 4.6 displays the names and descriptions of variables in this data file. We focus on libertarian candidates

Table 4.6. 1996 and 2000 US Presidential Election Data for Florida Counties.

Variable	Description
county	county name
Clinton96	Clinton's votes in 1996
Dole96	Dole's votes in 1996
Perot96	Perot's votes in 1996
Bush00	Bush's votes in 2000
Gore00	Gore's votes in 2000
Buchanan00	Buchanan's votes in 2000

Ross Perot in 1996 and Pat Buchanan in 2000, using the votes for the former to predict the votes for the latter. We then compute R^2 from this regression model by first computing TSS and then SSR. Recall that the resid() function extracts the vector of residuals from the regression output.

```
florida <- read.csv("florida.csv")
## regress Buchanan's 2000 votes on Perot's 1996 votes
fit2 <- lm(Buchanan00 ~ Perot96, data = florida)
fit2

##
## Call:
## lm(formula = Buchanan00 ~ Perot96, data = florida)
##
## Coefficients:
## (Intercept)        Perot96
##     1.34575        0.03592

## compute TSS (total sum of squares) and SSR (sum of squared residuals)
TSS2 <- sum((florida$Buchanan00 - mean(florida$Buchanan00))^2)
SSR2 <- sum(resid(fit2)^2)
## coefficient of determination
(TSS2 - SSR2) / TSS2

## [1] 0.5130333
```

The result shows that 51% of the variation of Buchanan's 2000 votes can be explained by Perot's 1996 votes.

We turn this calculation into a function so that we can easily compute the coefficient of determination for different regression models (see section 1.3.4). The function takes as input the output from the lm() function, which is a list object containing various elements (see section 3.7.2). The value of the outcome variable can be recomputed from the regression output object by summing the fitted value, which can be obtained using the `fitted()` function, and the residual for each observation.

```r
R2 <- function(fit) {
    resid <- resid(fit) # residuals
    y <- fitted(fit) + resid # outcome variable
    TSS <- sum((y - mean(y))^2)
    SSR <- sum(resid^2)
    R2 <- (TSS - SSR) / TSS
    return(R2)
}
R2(fit2)

## [1] 0.5130333
```

Alternatively, we can obtain the value of R^2 by applying the `summary()` function to the output from the `lm()` function (see also section 7.3).

```r
## built-in R function
fit2summary <- summary(fit2)
fit2summary$r.squared

## [1] 0.5130333
```

The resulting coefficient of determination appears relatively low given that we are predicting votes for a candidate from the same party using the previous election result. Earlier, we saw that Obama's vote shares at the state level are strongly correlated between the 2008 and 2012 elections. We can compute R^2 for that regression where the corresponding output object is `fit1`, which represents the output of the state-level regression. The coefficient of determination for the Florida regression proves to be much lower than that for the state-level regression.

```r
R2(fit1)

## [1] 0.9671579
```

Given this unusually poor performance, it is useful to more closely inspect the residuals from the Florida regression. To do this, we create a *residual plot* where residuals are plotted against fitted values.

```r
plot(fitted(fit2), resid(fit2), xlim = c(0, 1500), ylim = c(-750, 2500),
     xlab = "Fitted values", ylab = "Residuals")
abline(h = 0)
```

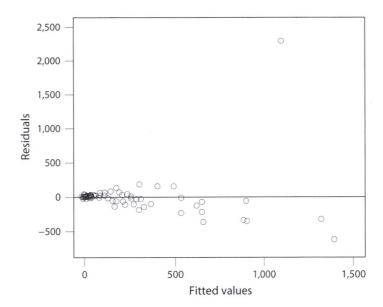

We observe an extremely large residual or *outlier*, where in the 2000 election, Buchanan received 2000 votes, substantially more than expected. The next line of code shows that this observation represents Palm Beach county. This can be seen by extracting the county name whose residual equals the maximum value of residuals.

```
florida$county[resid(fit2) == max(resid(fit2))]

## [1] PalmBeach
## 67 Levels: Alachua Baker Bay Bradford Brevard ... Washington
```

It turns out that in Palm Beach county, the so-called *butterfly ballot* was used for this election. A picture of this ballot is shown in figure 4.5. Voters are supposed to punch a hole that corresponds to the candidate they would like to vote for. However, as can be seen in the picture, the ballot is quite confusing. It appears that many supporters of Al Gore in this county mistakenly voted for Buchanan by punching the second hole from the top instead of the third hole. As mentioned at the beginning of the chapter, in the 2000 election, George Bush was elected to office by winning Florida with a razor-thin margin of 537 votes even though Gore won over half a million votes more than Bush in the entire country. It is widely believed that voting irregularities in Palm Beach county, as evident in the residual plot, cost Gore the presidency.

We now fit the same model without Palm Beach county. Later, we will see whether this removal improves the model fit, by comparing residual plots and regression lines with Palm Beach against those without it. We begin by computing the coefficient of determination without Palm Beach.

```
## data without Palm Beach
florida.pb <- subset(florida, subset = (county != "PalmBeach"))
```

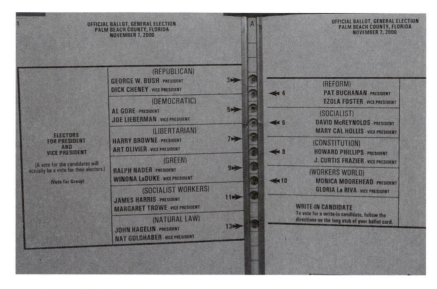

Figure 4.5. Butterfly Ballot in Palm Beach County.

```
fit3 <- lm(Buchanan00 ~ Perot96, data = florida.pb)
fit3

##
## Call:
## lm(formula = Buchanan00 ~ Perot96, data = florida.pb)
##
## Coefficients:
## (Intercept)        Perot96
##    45.84193        0.02435

## R-squared or coefficient of determination
R2(fit3)

## [1] 0.8511675
```

Without Palm Beach, the coefficient of determination dramatically increases from 0.51 to 0.85. The improvement in model fit can also be easily seen through the residual plot as well as the scatter plot with regression lines. We find that the regression line is influenced by Palm Beach—removing it shifts the regression line considerably. The new regression line fits the remaining observations better.

```
## residual plot
plot(fitted(fit3), resid(fit3), xlim = c(0, 1500), ylim = c(-750, 2500),
     xlab = "Fitted values", ylab = "Residuals",
     main = "Residual plot without Palm Beach")
abline(h = 0) # horizontal line at 0
```

```
plot(florida$Perot96, florida$Buchanan00, xlab = "Perot's votes in 1996",
    ylab = "Buchanan's votes in 2000")
abline(fit2, lty = "dashed") # regression with Palm Beach
abline(fit3) # regression without Palm Beach
text(30000, 3250, "Palm Beach")
text(30000, 1500, "regression\n with Palm Beach")
text(30000, 400, "regression\n without Palm Beach")
```

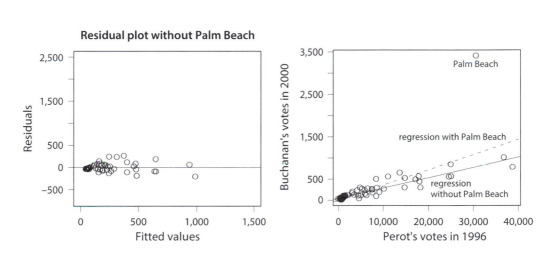

Finally, it is important to emphasize that the model fit considered in this section is based on *in-sample predictions* rather than *out-of-sample predictions*. That is, model fit statistics, such as the coefficient of determination, describe how well one's model fits the sample at hand. If tailored too closely to a particular sample, which is called *overfitting*, the model may make less accurate predictions in another sample. In cases where we seek a general model that can be applied to other data, we need to be careful to avoid overfitting the model to a particular sample. In section 4.3.2, we will describe one way to adjust R^2 in order to reduce the possibility of overfitting.

4.3 Regression and Causation

Regression is a primary tool for making predictions in social science research. How can regression be used to draw causal inference? As we discussed in chapter 2, causal inference requires the prediction of counterfactual outcomes. For example, for units who received a treatment, we wish to predict the values of the outcome variable that would result without the treatment. Under certain assumptions, regression models can be used to predict counterfactual outcomes. We must be careful, however, because association, which can be quantified through regression, does not necessarily imply causation.

Table 4.7. Women as Policy Makers Data.

Variable	Description
GP	identifier for the Gram Panchayat (GP)
village	identifier for each village
reserved	binary variable indicating whether the GP was reserved for women leaders or not
female	binary variable indicating whether the GP had a female leader or not
irrigation	variable measuring the number of new or repaired irrigation facilities in the village since the reserve policy started
water	variable measuring the number of new or repaired drinking water facilities in the village since the reservation policy started

4.3.1 RANDOMIZED EXPERIMENTS

Our running example is a study that examines the causal effects of having female politicians in government on policy outcomes.[5] Do women promote different policies than men? To answer this question, it is not sufficient to simply compare policy outcomes between districts that elect some female politicians and those that elect only male politicians. This is because these two types of districts may differ in terms of many factors other than having female politicians. For example, if liberal districts may be more likely to elect female politicians, it is not clear whether policy differences can be attributed to ideology or politician's gender.

To overcome this potential confounding problem, the authors of the study took advantage of a randomized policy experiment in India where, since the mid-1990s, one-third of village council heads have been randomly reserved for female politicians. The CSV data set women.csv contains a subset of this data from West Bengal. The policy was implemented at the level of government called Gram Panchayat or GP. Each GP contains many villages. For this study, two villages were selected at random within each GP for detailed data collection. Table 4.7 shows the names and descriptions of the variables in this data set. Each observation in the data set represents a village and there are two villages associated with each GP.

We first check whether or not the reservation policy was properly implemented by computing the proportions of female politicians elected for the reserved seats as well as the unreserved ones. Since each GP has the same number of villages, we can simply compute the average across villages without creating a new data set at the GP level. For the reserved seats, this proportion should be equal to 1.

---

[5] This section is based on Raghabendra Chattopadhyay and Esther Duflo (2004) "Women as policy makers: Evidence from a randomized policy experiment in India." *Econometrica*, vol. 72, no. 5, pp. 1409–1443.

```
women <- read.csv("women.csv")
## proportion of female politicians in reserved GP vs. unreserved GP
mean(women$female[women$reserved == 1])

## [1] 1

mean(women$female[women$reserved == 0])

## [1] 0.07476636
```

It appears that the reservation policy has been followed. Every GP that was supposed to reserve a council position for women actually elected at least one female politician. In contrast, 93% of the GPs to which the reservation policy was not applicable had no female representative. Following what we learned in chapter 2, we can compare the mean policy outcomes between the villages in the reserved GPs and those in the unreserved GPs. We hypothesize that female politicians are more likely to support policies that female voters want. The researchers found that more women complain about the quality of drinking water than men, who more frequently complain about irrigation. We estimate the average causal effects of the reservation policy on the number of new or repaired irrigation systems and drinking water facilities in the villages since the policy was implemented. We use the difference-in-means estimator as in section 2.4.

```
## drinking water facilities
mean(women$water[women$reserved == 1]) -
    mean(women$water[women$reserved == 0])

## [1] 9.252423

## irrigation facilities
mean(women$irrigation[women$reserved == 1]) -
    mean(women$irrigation[women$reserved == 0])

## [1] -0.3693319
```

We find that the reservation policy increased the number of drinking water facilities in a GP on average by about 9 (new or repaired), whereas the policy had little effect on irrigation systems. This finding is consistent with the aforementioned hypothesis that female politicians tend to represent the interests of female voters.

How can we use regression to analyze the data from randomized experiments like this one? It turns out that regressing an outcome variable on a treatment variable yields a slope coefficient identical to the difference in average outcomes between the two groups. In addition, the resulting intercept corresponds to the average outcome among the control units. More generally, when the predictor X is binary, taking a value of either 0 or 1, the linear model defined in equation (4.1) yields the estimated coefficients of the following expressions:

$$\hat{\alpha} = \underbrace{\frac{1}{n_0} \sum_{i=1}^{n}(1 - X_i)Y_i}_{\text{mean outcome among the control}} ,$$

$$\hat{\beta} = \underbrace{\frac{1}{n_1} \sum_{i=1}^{n} X_i Y_i}_{\text{mean outcome among the treated}} - \underbrace{\frac{1}{n_0} \sum_{i=1}^{n}(1 - X_i)Y_i}_{\text{mean outcome among the control}} .$$

In this equation, $n_1 = \sum_{i=1}^{n} X_i$ is the size of the treatment group and $n_0 = n - n_1$ is the size of the control group. Thus, $\hat{\beta}$ can be interpreted as the estimated average treatment effect.

Using our experimental data, we confirm this numerical equivalence between regression coefficients and average outcomes. That is, we observe that the estimated slope coefficient is equal to the corresponding *difference-in-means estimator*.

```
lm(water ~ reserved, data = women)

##
## Call:
## lm(formula = water ~ reserved, data = women)
##
## Coefficients:
## (Intercept)        reserved
##      14.738           9.252

lm(irrigation ~ reserved, data = women)

##
## Call:
## lm(formula = irrigation ~ reserved, data = women)
##
## Coefficients:
## (Intercept)        reserved
##       3.3879         -0.3693
```

We can directly connect the potential outcomes covered in chapter 2 to the regression model:

$$Y(X) = \alpha + \beta X + \epsilon.$$

Since the regression model predicts the average outcome given a value of the predictor, the estimated average treatment effect equals the estimated slope coefficient when X is binary. Recall that $\hat{\beta}$ represents the estimated change in Y when X is increased by one unit. Then, we have $\widehat{Y(1)} - \widehat{Y(0)} = (\hat{\alpha} + \hat{\beta}) - \hat{\alpha} = \hat{\beta}$, while the estimated average outcome for the control group is equal to the estimated intercept, i.e., $\widehat{Y(0)} = \hat{\alpha}$. Thus, the linear regression model provides an alternative, but numerically equivalent, way to analyze experimental data in this setting.

> When applied to experimental data with a single, binary treatment, the estimated slope coefficient of the linear regression model can be interpreted as an estimate of average treatment effect and is numerically equivalent to the **difference-in-means estimator**. The estimated intercept, on the other hand, is equal to the estimated average outcome under the control condition. The randomization of treatment assignment permits this **causal interpretation** of association identified under a linear regression model.

4.3.2   REGRESSION WITH MULTIPLE PREDICTORS

So far, we have included only one predictor in the linear regression model. However, a regression model can have more than one predictor. In general, a linear regression model with multiple predictors is defined as

$$Y = \alpha + \beta_1 X_1 + \beta_2 X_2 + \cdots + \beta_p X_p + \epsilon.$$

In this model, α is the intercept, β_j is the coefficient for predictor X_j, ϵ is an error term, and p is the number of predictors and can be greater than 1. The interpretation of each coefficient β_j is the amount of change in the outcome variable associated with a one-unit increase in the corresponding predictor X_j *when all other predictors are held constant* or so-called *ceteris paribus*. Therefore, linear regression with multiple predictors enables researchers to assess the impact of each predictor.

The least squares method, as described in section 4.2.3, can be used to estimate the model parameters. That is, we choose the values of $(\hat{\alpha}, \hat{\beta}_1, \ldots, \hat{\beta}_p)$ such that the *sum of squared residuals* (SSR) is minimized. The SSR is defined as

$$\text{SSR} = \sum_{i=1}^{n} \hat{\epsilon}_i^2 = \sum_{i=1}^{n} (Y_i - \hat{\alpha} - \hat{\beta}_1 X_{i1} - \hat{\beta}_2 X_{i2} - \cdots - \hat{\beta}_p X_{ip})^2.$$

In the equation, $\hat{\epsilon}_i$ is the *residual* and X_{ij} is the value of the jth predictor for the ith observation. Recall that the residual is defined as the difference between the observed response Y and its predicted or fitted value $\widehat{Y} = \hat{\alpha} + \hat{\beta}_1 X_1 + \hat{\beta}_2 X_2 + \cdots + \hat{\beta} X_p$.

The validity of predictions based on a linear regression model critically rests on the assumption of linearity. The method of least squares always gives us the line that "best fits" the data in the sense of minimizing the SSR. However, this does not necessarily mean that the linear model is appropriate. While a comprehensive treatment of testing and relaxing this assumption is beyond the scope of this book, we must not forget that any model or method requires an assumption, and linear regression is no exception.

As an example of linear regression models with multiple predictors, we consider the randomized experiment on social pressure and turnout introduced in section 2.4.2. In that study, registered voters were randomly assigned to one of the four groups. We can fit a linear regression model, in which group assignment is used to predict turnout. Fitting the linear regression model is done via the `lm()` function as before.

One can add more than one predictor by simply using the + operator, for example, `lm(y ~ x1 + x2 + x3)`. In this example, since the `messages` variable is a factor, the `lm()` function automatically creates a set of *indicator* or dummy variables, each of which is equal to `1` if a voter is assigned to the corresponding group. These indicator variables will be used for computation but will not be saved in the data frame. The model includes all but the variable corresponding to the base level. The base level of a factor variable is the level displayed first when we apply the `levels()` function, which lists levels in alphabetical order. The other values of a factor variable are defined in relation to this base level value.

```
social <- read.csv("social.csv")
levels(social$messages) # base level is "Civic Duty"

## [1] "Civic Duty" "Control"    "Hawthorne"    "Neighbors"
```

Now we fit the linear regression model using this factor variable.

```
fit <- lm(primary2008 ~ messages, data = social)
fit

##
## Call:
## lm(formula = primary2008 ~ messages, data = social)
##
## Coefficients:
##       (Intercept)    messagesControl      messagesHawthorne
##          0.314538          -0.017899               0.007837
## messagesNeighbors
##          0.063411
```

Alternatively, one can create an indicator variable for each group and then specify the regression model using them. The results are identical to those given above.

```
## create indicator variables
social$Control <- ifelse(social$messages == "Control", 1, 0)
social$Hawthorne <- ifelse(social$messages == "Hawthorne", 1, 0)
social$Neighbors <- ifelse(social$messages == "Neighbors", 1, 0)
## fit the same regression as above by directly using indicator variables
lm(primary2008 ~ Control + Hawthorne + Neighbors, data = social)
```

Mathematically, the linear regression model we just fit is given by

$$Y = \alpha + \beta_1\, \text{Control} + \beta_2\, \text{Hawthorne} + \beta_3\, \text{Neighbors} + \epsilon.$$

In this model, each predictor is an indicator variable for the corresponding group. Since the base level of the `messages` variable is `"Civic Duty"`, the `lm()` function excludes the corresponding indicator variable. Using the fitted model, we can predict the average outcome, which in this case is the average proportion of voters who turned out. For example, under the `Control` condition, the average outcome is predicted to be $\hat{\alpha} + \hat{\beta}_1 = 0.315 + (-0.018) = 0.297$ or 29.7%. Similarly, for the `Neighbors` group, the predicted average outcome is $\hat{\alpha} + \hat{\beta}_3 = 0.315 + 0.063 = 0.378$.

The predicted average outcome can be obtained using the `predict()` function. This function, like the `fitted()` function, takes the output from the `lm()` function and computes predicted values. However, unlike the `fitted()` function, which computes predicted values for the sample used to fit the model, the `predict()` function can take a new data frame as the `newdata` argument and make predictions for each observation in this data frame. The new data frame's variables must match the predictors of the fitted linear model, though they can have different values. In the current application, we create a new data frame using the `data.frame()` function. The resulting data frame contains the same variable `messages` as the predictor of the model but only four observations, each of which has one of the unique values of the original `messages` variable. We use the `unique()` function to extract these unique values and return them in the order of their first occurrence.

```
## create a data frame with unique values of "messages"
unique.messages <- data.frame(messages = unique(social$messages))
unique.messages

##       messages
## 1 Civic Duty
## 2   Hawthorne
## 3     Control
## 4   Neighbors

## make prediction for each observation from this new data frame
predict(fit, newdata = unique.messages)

##         1         2         3         4
## 0.3145377 0.3223746 0.2966383 0.3779482
```

As we saw in the case of a linear regression model with a single, binary predictor (see section 4.3.1), the predicted average outcome for each treatment condition equals the sample average within the corresponding subset of the data.

```
## sample average
tapply(social$primary2008, social$messages, mean)

## Civic Duty    Control   Hawthorne   Neighbors
##  0.3145377  0.2966383   0.3223746   0.3779482
```

To make the output of linear regression more interpretable, we can remove an intercept and use all four indicator variables (rather than removing the indicator variable for the base level in order to include a common intercept). This alternative specification enables us to directly obtain the average outcome within each group as a coefficient for the corresponding indicator variable. To omit the intercept in linear regression, we simply use `-1` in the formula. The following code chunk illustrates this.

```
## linear regression without intercept
fit.noint <- lm(primary2008 ~ -1 + messages, data = social)
fit.noint

##
## Call:
## lm(formula = primary2008 ~ -1 + messages, data = social)
##
## Coefficients:
## messagesCivic Duty      messagesControl    messagesHawthorne
##            0.3145               0.2966               0.3224
##   messagesNeighbors
##            0.3779
```

Each coefficient above represents the average outcome for a given group. As a result, we can estimate an average treatment effect relative to the control for each treatment condition (`Civic Duty`, `Hawthorne`, or `Neighbors`) by calculating that treatment condition's coefficient minus the coefficient for the control group, which is the baseline group under this model with no intercept. The difference in the estimated causal effects between any two groups equals the difference between the corresponding coefficients, whether one uses the model with no intercept or the original model. Therefore, the average effect of the `Neighbors` treatment (relative to the `Control` condition) equals $0.378 - 0.297$ in the model with no intercept, or $0.063 - (-0.018)$ in the original model, either of which equals 0.081 or 8.1 percentage points. As was the case before, the same estimate of average causal effect can be obtained in two ways—through linear regression with a factor treatment variable or the difference-in-means estimator.

```
## estimated average effect of "Neighbors" condition
coef(fit)["messagesNeighbors"] - coef(fit)["messagesControl"]

## messagesNeighbors
##        0.08130991

## difference-in-means
mean(social$primary2008[social$messages == "Neighbors"]) -
    mean(social$primary2008[social$messages == "Control"])

## [1] 0.08130991
```

Finally, we can compute the *coefficient of determination* or R^2 as in section 4.2.6. When there are multiple predictors, however, we often compute the *adjusted R^2* with the so-called *degrees of freedom* correction that accounts for the number of predictors.

Roughly speaking, the degrees of freedom refers to the number of observations that are "free to vary," which is often represented by the total number of observations minus the number of parameters to be estimated. In the current setting, the degrees of freedom equals $n - p - 1 = n - (p + 1)$ because n is the number of observations and $p + 1$ is the number of coefficients to be estimated, i.e., a coefficient for each of p predictors plus an intercept.

Since one can always increase the (unadjusted) R^2 by including an additional predictor (which always decreases SSR), the degrees of freedom correction adjusts R^2 downwards as more predictors are included in the model. The formula of the adjusted R^2 is given by

$$\text{adjusted } R^2 = 1 - \frac{\text{SSR}/(n - p - 1)}{\text{TSS}/(n - 1)}.$$

SSR is divided by the number of observations n minus the number of coefficients to be estimated $(p + 1)$. TSS is divided by $(n - 1)$ since TSS estimates only one parameter, the mean of the outcome variable or $\overline{Y}$. As in section 4.2.6, we create a function that computes the adjusted R^2.

```
## adjusted R-squared
adjR2 <- function(fit) {
    resid <- resid(fit) # residuals
    y <- fitted(fit) + resid # outcome
    n <- length(y)
    TSS.adj <- sum((y - mean(y))^2) / (n - 1)
    SSR.adj <- sum(resid^2) / (n - length(coef(fit)))
    R2.adj <- 1 - SSR.adj / TSS.adj
    return(R2.adj)
}
adjR2(fit)

## [1] 0.003272788

R2(fit) # unadjusted R-squared calculation

## [1] 0.003282564
```

In this case, the difference between unadjusted and adjusted R^2 is small because the number of observations is large relative to the number of coefficients. Alternatively, we can obtain both adjusted and unadjusted R^2 by applying the summary() function to output from the lm() function (see also section 7.3).

```
fitsummary <- summary(fit)
fitsummary$adj.r.squared

## [1] 0.003272788
```

> The **linear regression model with multiple predictors** is defined as
>
> $$Y = \alpha + \beta_1 X_1 + \beta_2 X_2 + \cdots + \beta_p X_p + \epsilon,$$
>
> where the coefficient β_j represents the increase in the average outcome associated with a one-unit increase in X_j while holding the other variables constant. The coefficients are estimated by minimizing the sum of squared residuals. The **degrees of freedom** adjustment is often made when computing the coefficient of determination.

4.3.3 HETEROGENOUS TREATMENT EFFECTS

When applied to randomized experiments, linear regression with multiple predictors can also be helpful for exploring *heterogenous treatment effects*. Even if the average treatment effect is positive, for example, the same treatment may affect some individuals in a negative way. Identifying the characteristics associated with the direction and magnitude of the treatment effect is essential in determining who should receive the treatment. In the current application, we might hypothesize that the social pressure treatment would barely affect those who vote infrequently. In contrast, they may be the ones who would be most affected by such treatment. To illustrate the analysis of heterogenous treatment effects, we examine the difference in the estimated average causal effect of the `Neighbors` message between those who voted in the 2004 primary election and those who did not. We can do this by subsetting the data and then estimating the average treatment effect within each subset. Finally, we compare these two estimated average treatment effects.

```r
## average treatment effect (ATE) among those who voted in 2004 primary
social.voter <- subset(social, primary2004 == 1)
ate.voter <-
    mean(social.voter$primary2008[social.voter$messages == "Neighbors"]) -
        mean(social.voter$primary2008[social.voter$messages == "Control"])
ate.voter

## [1] 0.09652525

## average effect among those who did not vote
social.nonvoter <- subset(social, primary2004 == 0)
ate.nonvoter <-
    mean(social.nonvoter$primary2008[social.nonvoter$messages == "Neighbors"]) -
        mean(social.nonvoter$primary2008[social.nonvoter$messages == "Control"])
ate.nonvoter

## [1] 0.06929617
```

```
## difference
ate.voter - ate.nonvoter

## [1] 0.02722908
```

We find that those who voted in the 2004 primary election have the estimated average effect of 9.7 percentage points, which is approximately 2.7 percentage points greater than those who did not vote in the election. This implies that the `Neighbors` message affects those who voted in the 2004 primary election more than those who did not.

The same analysis can be carried out through the use of linear regression with an *interaction effect* between the treatment variable `Neighbors` and the covariate of interest `primary2004`. In our application, the model is given by

$$Y = \alpha + \beta_1 \, \text{primary2004} + \beta_2 \, \text{Neighbors} + \beta_3 \, (\text{primary2004} \times \text{Neighbors}) + \epsilon.$$

$$(4.9)$$

The final predictor is the product of two indicator variables, primary2004 × Neighbors, which is equal to 1 if and only if an individual voted in the 2004 primary election (`primary2004 = 1`) and received the `Neighbors` treatment (`Neighbors = 1`).

Thus, according to the model, among the voters who turned out in the 2004 primary election (`primary2004 = 1`), the average effect of the `Neighbors` message equals $\beta_2 + \beta_3$, whereas the same effect for those who did not vote in the 2004 election (`primary2004 = 0`) equals β_2. Thus, the coefficient for the interaction term β_3 represents the additional average treatment effect the first group of voters receive relative to the second group.

More generally, an example of the linear regression model with an interaction term is

$$Y = \alpha + \beta_1 X_1 + \beta_2 X_2 + \beta_3 X_1 X_2 + \epsilon,$$

where the coefficient for the interaction term β_3 represents how the effect of X_1 depends on X_2 (or vice versa). To see this, set $X_2 = x_2$ and then compute the predicted value when $X_1 = x_1$. This is given by $\hat{\alpha} + \hat{\beta}_1 x_1 + \hat{\beta}_2 x_2 + \hat{\beta}_3 x_1 x_2$. Now, compare this with the predicted value when X_1 is increased by one unit, i.e., $X_1 = x_1 + 1$. Under this scenario, the predicted value is $\hat{\alpha} + \hat{\beta}_1(x_1 + 1) + \hat{\beta}_2 x_2 + \hat{\beta}_3(x_1 + 1)x_2$. Then, subtracting the previous predicted value from this one, we obtain the following expression for how the change in the average outcome associated with a one-unit increase in X_1 depends on the value of X_2:

$$\hat{\beta}_1 + \hat{\beta}_3 x_2.$$

This is another linear equation. The intercept β_1 represents the increase in the average outcome associated with a one-unit increase in X_1 when $X_2 = 0$. Then, each one-unit increase in X_2 has the effect of further increasing X_1 by the slope $\hat{\beta}_3$.

An example of a linear regression model with an **interaction term** is

$$Y = \alpha + \beta_1 X_1 + \beta_2 X_2 + \beta_3 X_1 X_2 + \epsilon.$$

The model assumes that the effect of X_1 linearly depends on X_2. That is, as we increase X_2 by one unit, the change in the average outcome associated with a one-unit increase of X_1 goes up by β_3.

In R, an interaction term can be represented by a colon : with the syntax `x1:x2` producing an interaction term between the two variables `x1` and `x2`. We illustrate the use of interaction terms by focusing on the `Neighbors` and `Control` groups.

```
## subset Neighbors and Control groups
social.neighbor <- subset(social, (messages == "Control") |
                          (messages == "Neighbors"))
## standard way to generate main and interaction effects
fit.int <- lm(primary2008 ~ primary2004 + messages + primary2004:messages,
              data = social.neighbor)
fit.int

##
## Call:
## lm(formula = primary2008 ~ primary2004 + messages + primary2004:messages,
##     data = social.neighbor)
##
## Coefficients:
##                   (Intercept)
##                       0.23711
##                   primary2004
##                       0.14870
##             messagesNeighbors
##                       0.06930
## primary2004:messagesNeighbors
##                       0.02723
```

Since the `Control` group is the baseline condition, the slope coefficients are estimated only for the `Neighbors` condition and its interaction with the `primary2004` variable.

Alternatively, an asterisk * generates two *main effect* terms as well as one interaction effect term. That is, the syntax `x1*x2` produces `x1`, `x2`, and `x1:x2`. In most applications, one should include the corresponding main effects when the model has an interaction term. The same regression model as above can be fitted using the following syntax.

```
lm(primary2008 ~ primary2004 * messages, data = social.neighbor)
```

To interpret each estimated coefficient, it is again helpful to consider the predicted average outcome. Among those who voted in the 2004 primary election, the estimated average effect of the `Neighbors` treatment can be written as the difference in the estimated average outcome between the treatment and control groups. In terms of model parameters, this difference is equal to $(\hat{\alpha} + \hat{\beta}_1 + \hat{\beta}_2 + \hat{\beta}_3) - (\hat{\alpha} + \hat{\beta}_1) = \hat{\beta}_2 + \hat{\beta}_3$, where $\hat{\beta}_2$ and $\hat{\beta}_3$ are excluded from the second part of the equation because for the control group, `Neighbors` equals 0. In contrast, the estimated average treatment effect among those who did not vote is given by $(\hat{\alpha} + \hat{\beta}_2) - \hat{\alpha} = \hat{\beta}_2$. Thus, the difference in the estimated average treatment effect between those who voted in the 2004 primary election and those who did not equals the estimated coefficient for the interaction effect term, i.e., $(\hat{\beta}_2 + \hat{\beta}_3) - \hat{\beta}_2 = \hat{\beta}_3$. This implies that the coefficient for the interaction effect term β_3 characterizes how the average treatment effect varies as a function of the covariate.

While we have so far focused on a factor or categorical variable, it is also possible to use a continuous variable as a predictor. The use of continuous variables requires a stronger linearity assumption that a one-unit increase in the predictor leads to an increase of the same size in the outcome, regardless of the baseline value. In the current application, we consider the age of the voter in 2008 as a predictor. We first compute this variable by subtracting the year of birth variable from the year of election.

```
social.neighbor$age <- 2008 - social.neighbor$yearofbirth
summary(social.neighbor$age)
##    Min. 1st Qu.  Median     Mean 3rd Qu.     Max.
##   22.00   43.00   52.00    51.82   61.00   108.00
```

Thus, in this subset of the data, the ages of voters vary from 22 to 108. We now explore how the average causal effect of the `Neighbors` treatment changes as a function of age. To do this, we use the `age` variable instead of the `primary2004` variable in the linear regression model given in equation (4.9):

$$Y = \alpha + \beta_1 \, \text{age} + \beta_2 \, \text{Neighbors} + \beta_3 \, (\text{age} \times \text{Neighbors}) + \epsilon.$$

We can use the same computation strategy as above to understand how the average treatment effect changes as a function of age. Consider a group of voters who are x years old. The estimated average treatment effect of the `Neighbors` message for these voters is given by $(\hat{\alpha} + \hat{\beta}_1 x + \hat{\beta}_2 + \hat{\beta}_3 x) - (\hat{\alpha} + \hat{\beta}_1 x) = \hat{\beta}_2 + \hat{\beta}_3 x$. In contrast, among the voters who are $(x + 1)$ years old, the estimated average effect is $\{\hat{\alpha} + \hat{\beta}_1(x + 1) + \hat{\beta}_2 + \hat{\beta}_3(x + 1)\} - \{\hat{\alpha} + \hat{\beta}_1(x + 1)\} = \hat{\beta}_2 + \hat{\beta}_3(x + 1)$. Thus, the estimated coefficient for the interaction effect term $\hat{\beta}_3 = \{\hat{\beta}_2 + \hat{\beta}_3(x + 1)\} - (\hat{\beta}_2 + \hat{\beta}_3 x)$ represents the estimated difference in the average treatment effect between two groups of voters whose ages differ by one year.

To compute this estimated difference in R, we first fit the linear regression model with the interaction term between the `age` and `Neighbors` variables. We use the syntax `age * messages`, which produces the main terms and the interaction term.

```
fit.age <- lm(primary2008 ~ age * messages, data = social.neighbor)
fit.age

##
## Call:
## lm(formula = primary2008 ~ age * messages, data = social.neighbor)
##
## Coefficients:
##           (Intercept)                       age
##             0.0894768                 0.0039982
##     messagesNeighbors    age:messagesNeighbors
##             0.0485728                 0.0006283
```

The result suggests that the estimated difference in the average treatment effect between two groups of voters whose ages differ by one year is equal to 0.06 percentage points. Based on this regression model, we can also compute the estimated average treatment effect for different ages. We choose 25, 45, 65, and 85 years old for illustration. We use the `predict()` function by providing the `newdata` argument with a data frame that contains these ages as separate observations.

```
## age = 25, 45, 65, 85 in Neighbors group
age.neighbor <- data.frame(age = seq(from = 25, to = 85, by = 20),
                           messages = "Neighbors")
## age = 25, 45, 65, 85 in Control group
age.control <- data.frame(age = seq(from = 25, to = 85, by = 20),
                          messages = "Control")
## average treatment effect for age = 25, 45, 65, 85
ate.age <- predict(fit.age, newdata = age.neighbor) -
    predict(fit.age, newdata = age.control)
ate.age

##          1          2          3          4
## 0.06428051 0.07684667 0.08941283 0.10197899
```

Researchers have found that the linearity assumption is inappropriate when modeling turnout. While people become more likely to vote as they get older, their likelihood of voting starts decreasing in their 60s or 70s. One common strategy to address this phenomenon is to model turnout as a *quadratic function* of age by including the square of age as an additional predictor. Consider the following model, which also includes interaction terms:

$$Y = \alpha + \beta_1\,\mathsf{age} + \beta_2\,\mathsf{age}^2 + \beta_3\,\mathsf{Neighbors} + \beta_4\,(\mathsf{age} \times \mathsf{Neighbors})$$
$$+ \beta_5\,(\mathsf{age}^2 \times \mathsf{Neighbors}) + \epsilon. \tag{4.10}$$

In R, a formula can contain mathematical functions such as a square or natural logarithm using the `I()` function. For example, to include a square of the x variable in a formula, we can use the syntax `I(x^2)`. The `I()` function enables other arithmetic operations such as `I(sqrt(x))` and `I(log(x))`. We now fit the model specified in equation (4.10).

```
fit.age2 <- lm(primary2008 ~ age + I(age^2) + messages + age:messages +
               I(age^2):messages, data = social.neighbor)
fit.age2

##
## Call:
## lm(formula = primary2008 ~ age + I(age^2) + messages + age:messages +
##     I(age^2):messages, data = social.neighbor)
##
## Coefficients:
##             (Intercept)                        age
##              -9.700e-02                  1.172e-02
##                I(age^2)           messagesNeighbors
##              -7.389e-05                 -5.275e-02
##     age:messagesNeighbors  I(age^2):messagesNeighbors
##               4.804e-03                 -3.961e-05
```

In a complicated model like this one, the coefficients no longer have an easy interpretation. In such situations, it is best to predict the average outcome under various scenarios using the `predict()` function and then compute quantities of interest. Here, we predict the average turnout rate for voters of different ages, ranging from 25 to 85, under the `Neighbors` and `Control` conditions. We then compute the average treatment effect as the difference between the two conditions and characterize it as a function of age. The following syntax accomplishes this task.

```
## predicted turnout rate under the Neighbors treatment condition
yT.hat <- predict(fit.age2,
                  newdata = data.frame(age = 25:85, messages = "Neighbors"))
## predicted turnout rate under the Control condition
yC.hat <- predict(fit.age2,
                  newdata = data.frame(age = 25:85, messages = "Control"))
```

For ease of interpretation, we plot the results. The first plot displays the predicted turnout as a function of age separately for the `Neighbors` and `Control` groups. The second plot shows the estimated average treatment effect as a function of age.

```
## plotting the predicted turnout rate under each condition
plot(x = 25:85, y = yT.hat, type = "l", xlim = c(20, 90), ylim = c(0, 0.5),
     xlab = "Age", ylab = "Predicted turnout rate")
lines(x = 25:85, y = yC.hat, lty = "dashed")
text(40, 0.45, "Neighbors condition")
text(45, 0.15, "Control condition")
## plotting the average treatment effect as a function of age
plot(x = 25:85, y = yT.hat - yC.hat, type = "l", xlim = c(20, 90),
     ylim = c(0, 0.1), xlab = "Age",
     ylab = "Estimated average\n treatment effect")
```

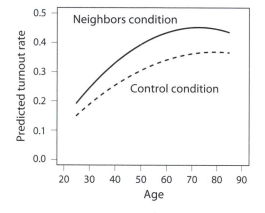 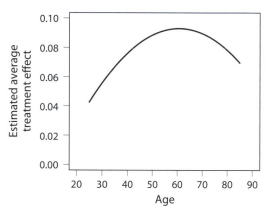

We find that according to this model, the estimated average treatment effect peaks around 60 years old, and the effect size is much smaller among young and old voters.

4.3.4   REGRESSION DISCONTINUITY DESIGN

The discussion in chapter 2 implies that we can interpret the association between treatment and outcome variables as causal if there is no confounding variable. This was the case in the experimental studies we analyzed in sections 4.3.1–4.3.3. In observational studies, however, the treatment assignment is not randomized. As a result, confounding factors, rather than the treatment variable, may explain the outcome difference between the treatment and control groups. In section 2.5, we discussed several research design strategies to address this potential selection bias problem. Here, we introduce another research design for observational studies called *regression discontinuity design* (RD design).

Table 4.8. Members of the British Parliament Personal Wealth Data

Variable	Description
surname	surname of the candidate
firstname	first name of the candidate
party	party of the candidate (labour or tory)
ln.gross	log gross wealth at the time of death
ln.net	log net wealth at the time of death
yob	year of birth of the candidate
yod	year of death of the candidate
margin.pre	margin of the candidate's party in the previous election
region	electoral region
margin	margin of victory (vote share)

As an application of RD design, we consider how much politicians can increase their personal wealth due to holding office. Scholars investigated this question by analyzing members of Parliament (MPs) in the United Kingdom.[6] The authors of the original study collected information about personal wealth at the time of death for several hundred competitive candidates who ran for office in general elections between 1950 and 1970. The data are contained in the CSV file MPs.csv. The names and descriptions of the variables in this data set appear in table 4.8.

A naive comparison of MPs and non-MPs in terms of their wealth is unlikely to yield valid causal inference because those who became MPs differ from those who did not in terms of many observable and unobservable characteristics. Instead, the key intuition behind RD design is to compare those candidates who narrowly won office with those who barely lost it. The idea is that when one's margin of victory switches from a negative number to a positive number, we would expect a large, discontinuous, positive jump in the personal wealth of electoral candidates if serving in office actually financially benefits them. Assuming that nothing else is going on at this point of discontinuity, we can identify the average causal effect of being an MP at this threshold by comparing the candidates who barely won the election with those who barely lost it. Regression is used to predict the average personal wealth at the point of discontinuity.

A simple scatter plot with regression lines is the best way to understand RD design. To do this, we plot the outcome variable, log net wealth at the time of death, against the margin of victory. We take the natural logarithmic transformation of wealth because this variable is quite skewed by a small number of politicians accumulating a large amount of wealth (see the discussion in section 3.4.1). We then separately fit a linear regression model to the observations with a positive margin (i.e., the candidates who won elections and became MPs) and another regression model to those with a negative margin (the candidates who lost). The difference in predicted values at the point of

---

[6] This application is based on Andrew C. Eggers and Jens Hainmueller (2009) "MPs for sale? Returns to office in postwar British politics." *American Political Science Review*, vol. 103, no. 4, pp. 513–533.

discontinuity, i.e., a zero margin of victory, between the two regressions represents the average causal effect on personal wealth of serving as an MP.

We begin by subsetting the data based on party (Labour and Tory) and then fit two regressions for each data set.

```r
## load the data and subset them into two parties
MPs <- read.csv("MPs.csv")
MPs.labour <- subset(MPs, subset = (party == "labour"))
MPs.tory <- subset(MPs, subset = (party == "tory"))
## two regressions for Labour: negative and positive margin
labour.fit1 <- lm(ln.net ~ margin,
                  data = MPs.labour[MPs.labour$margin < 0, ])
labour.fit2 <- lm(ln.net ~ margin,
                  data = MPs.labour[MPs.labour$margin > 0, ])
## two regressions for Tory: negative and positive margin
tory.fit1 <- lm(ln.net ~ margin, data = MPs.tory[MPs.tory$margin < 0, ])
tory.fit2 <- lm(ln.net ~ margin, data = MPs.tory[MPs.tory$margin > 0, ])
```

To predict the outcome using a specific value of predictor, we can use the `predict()` function by specifying a new data frame, `newdata`, as the argument. We conduct a separate analysis for Labour and Tory candidates to estimate each party's causal effect of interest.

```r
## Labour: range of predictions
y11.range <- c(min(MPs.labour$margin), 0) # min to 0
y21.range <- c(0, max(MPs.labour$margin)) # 0 to max
## prediction
y1.labour <- predict(labour.fit1, newdata = data.frame(margin = y11.range))
y2.labour <- predict(labour.fit2, newdata = data.frame(margin = y21.range))
## Tory: range of predictions
y1t.range <- c(min(MPs.tory$margin), 0) # min to 0
y2t.range <- c(0, max(MPs.tory$margin)) # 0 to max
## predict outcome
y1.tory <- predict(tory.fit1, newdata = data.frame(margin = y1t.range))
y2.tory <- predict(tory.fit2, newdata = data.frame(margin = y2t.range))
```

We can now plot the predicted values for each party in the scatter plot of log net wealth and electoral margin.

```r
## scatter plot with regression lines for Labour
plot(MPs.labour$margin, MPs.labour$ln.net, main = "Labour",
     xlim = c(-0.5, 0.5), ylim = c(6, 18), xlab = "Margin of victory",
     ylab = "log net wealth at death")
```

```
abline(v = 0, lty = "dashed")
## add regression lines
lines(y1l.range, y1.labour, col = "blue")
lines(y2l.range, y2.labour, col = "blue")
## scatter plot with regression lines for Tory
plot(MPs.tory$margin, MPs.tory$ln.net, main = "Tory", xlim = c(-0.5, 0.5),
    ylim = c(6, 18), xlab = "Margin of victory",
    ylab = "log net wealth at death")
abline(v = 0, lty = "dashed")
## add regression lines
lines(y1t.range, y1.tory, col = "blue")
lines(y2t.range, y2.tory, col = "blue")
```

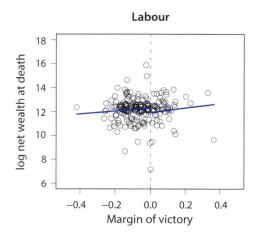

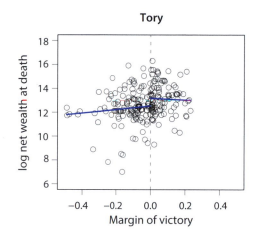

The result suggests that Tory MPs financially benefit from serving in office whereas Labour MPs do not. How large is the effect for Tory candidates? We can numerically compute the differences in prediction at the zero margin and put them back on the original scale (pounds) since net wealth is measured on a log scale. Recall from section 3.4.1 that the *inverse function* of the natural logarithm is the exponential function, given by exp() in R.

```
## average net wealth for Tory MP
tory.MP <- exp(y2.tory[1])
tory.MP

##            1
## 533813.5

## average net wealth for Tory non-MP
tory.nonMP <- exp(y1.tory[2])
```

```
tory.nonMP

##       2
## 278762.5

## causal effect in pounds
tory.MP - tory.nonMP

##       1
## 255050.9
```

The estimated effect of being an MP on the personal wealth of Tory candidates is a little above 250,000 pounds. Since the average net wealth for Tory non-MPs is predicted to be a little above 270,000 pounds, the estimated effect is quite substantial. Being an MP almost doubles one's net wealth at death.

How should one examine the *internal validity* of regression discontinuity design? One way is a *placebo test*. A placebo test finds a case where the effect is theoretically known to be zero and then shows that the estimated effect is indeed close to zero. The name comes from the fact that in a medical study a placebo is supposed to have zero effect on health outcomes (though much evidence suggests that a placebo often has effects, perhaps via psychological mechanisms). In the current application, we estimate the average treatment effect on the margin of victory for the same party in the *previous* election. Since being an MP in the future should not affect the past election result, this effect should be zero if the RD design is valid. If the estimated effect is far from zero, on the other hand, it would suggest a possible violation of the assumption of regression discontinuity. For example, the incumbent party may be engaged in election fraud in order to win close elections.

```
## two regressions for Tory: negative and positive margin
tory.fit3 <- lm(margin.pre ~ margin, data = MPs.tory[MPs.tory$margin < 0, ])
tory.fit4 <- lm(margin.pre ~ margin, data = MPs.tory[MPs.tory$margin > 0, ])
## the difference between two intercepts is the estimated effect
coef(tory.fit4)[1] - coef(tory.fit3)[1]

## (Intercept)
## -0.01725578
```

The estimated effect on the previous margin of victory is less than 2 percentage points. This small effect size gives empirical support for the claim that RD design is applicable to this study. In chapter 7, we will more formally answer the question of how small is small enough to reach this conclusion.

While RD design can overcome the main difficulty of observational studies, i.e., potential confounding bias, this strength of *internal validity* comes at the cost of *external validity*. Specifically, the estimated causal effects obtained under this design apply only to the observations near the point of discontinuity. In our application, these observations represent candidates who narrowly won or lost elections. The degree to which MPs benefit financially from serving in office may be quite different for those who won elections by a larger margin. Thus, although RD requires weaker assumptions than other approaches, the resulting estimates may not be generalizable to a larger population of interest.

> **Regression discontinuity design** (RD design) is a research design strategy for causal inference in observational studies with possible confounding factors. RD design assumes that the change in outcome at the point of discontinuity can be attributed to the change in the treatment variable alone. While RD design often has strong internal validity, it may lack external validity because the result may not be generalizable to observations away from the point of discontinuity.

4.4 Summary

We began this chapter with a discussion of election forecasting. We showed that preelection polls can be used to obtain relatively accurate, though not perfect, **predictions** of election outcomes in the context of US presidential elections. We introduced **prediction error** and explained how the accuracy of prediction can be measured using statistics such as **bias** and the **root-mean-squared error**. We also discussed the problem of **classification**, which is the prediction of categorical outcomes. Two types of **misclassification** are possible—false positives and false negatives. For example, a voter who did turn out being classified as a nonvoter would be a false negative, whereas a voter who did not turn out being classified as a voter would be a false positive. There is a clear trade-off between the two: minimizing false positives tends to increase false negatives and vice versa.

We then introduced a **linear regression model** as a commonly used method to predict an outcome variable of interest using another variable. The model enables researchers to predict an outcome variable based on the values of explanatory variables or predictors. Predictions based on the linear regression model are typically obtained through the **method of least squares** by minimizing the sum of squared prediction errors. We discussed the exact relationship between linear regression and **correlation**, and the phenomenon called **regression towards the mean**. Finally, we presented several ways to assess model fit through the examination of the **coefficient of determination** and residuals. It is important to avoid overfitting one's model to the data at hand so that the model does not capture any idiosyncratic characteristics of the sample and instead identifies the systematic features of the data-generating process.

Despite our intuition, association discovered through regression does not necessarily imply **causation**. A regression's ability to predict observable outcomes does not necessarily entail ability to predict counterfactual outcomes. Yet, valid causal inference requires the latter. At the end of the chapter, we discussed the use of regression in the analysis of experimental and observational data. We discussed how to estimate heterogenous treatment effects using the linear regression model with **interaction terms**. We also discussed the **regression discontinuity design**. By exploiting the discontinuity in the treatment assignment mechanism, this design enables researchers

Table 4.9. Intrade Prediction Market Data from 2008 and 2012.

Variable	Description
day	date of the session
statename	full name of each state (including District of Columbia in 2008)
state	abbreviation of each state (including District of Columbia in 2008)
PriceD	closing price (predicted vote share) of the Democratic nominee's market
PriceR	closing price (predicted vote share) of the Republican nominee's market
VolumeD	total session trades of the Democratic Party nominee's market
VolumeR	total session trades of the Republican Party nominee's market

to credibly identify causal effects in observational studies. The main disadvantage of the regression discontinuity design, however, is the potential lack of **external validity**. Specifically, the empirical conclusions based on this design may not be applicable beyond the observations close to the discontinuity threshold.

4.5 Exercises

4.5.1 PREDICTION BASED ON BETTING MARKETS

Earlier in the chapter, we studied the prediction of election outcomes using polls. Here, we study the prediction of election outcomes based on betting markets. In particular, we analyze data for the 2008 and 2012 US presidential elections from the online betting company called Intrade. At Intrade, people trade contracts such as "Obama to win the electoral votes of Florida." Each contract's market price fluctuates based on its sales. Why might we expect betting markets like Intrade to accurately predict the outcomes of elections or of other events? Some argue that the market can aggregate available information efficiently. In this exercise, we will test this *efficient market hypothesis* by analyzing the market prices of contracts for Democratic and Republican nominees' victories in each state.

The data files for 2008 and 2012 are available in CSV format as `intrade08.csv` and `intrade12.csv`, respectively. Table 4.9 presents the names and descriptions of these data sets. Each row of the data sets represents daily trading information about the contracts for either the Democratic or Republican Party nominee's victory in a particular state. We will also use the election outcome data. These data files are `pres08.csv` (table 4.1) and `pres12.csv` (table 4.5).

1. We will begin by using the market prices on the day before the election to predict the 2008 election outcome. To do this, subset the data such that it contains the market information for each state and candidate on the day before the election only. Note that in 2008, Election Day was November 4. We compare the closing prices for the two candidates in a given state and classify a candidate whose contract has a higher price as the predicted winner of that state. Which states

were misclassified? How does this compare to the classification by polls presented earlier in this chapter? Repeat the same analysis for the 2012 election, which was held on November 6. How well did the prediction market do in 2012 compared to 2008? Note that in 2012 some less competitive states have missing data on the day before the election because there were no trades on the Republican and Democratic betting markets. Assume Intrade predictions would have been accurate for these states.

2. How do the predictions based on the betting markets change over time? Implement the same classification procedure as above on each of the last 90 days of the 2008 campaign rather than just the day before the election. Plot the predicted number of electoral votes for the Democratic Party nominee over this 90-day period. The resulting plot should also indicate the actual election result. Note that in 2008, Obama won 365 electoral votes. Briefly comment on the plot.

3. Repeat the previous exercise but this time use the seven-day *moving-average* price, instead of the daily price, for each candidate within a state. Just as in section 4.1.3, this can be done with a loop. For a given day, we take the average of the Session Close prices within the past seven days (including that day). To answer this question, we must first compute the seven-day average within each state. Next, we sum the electoral votes for the states Obama is predicted to win. Using the `tapply()` function will allow us to efficiently compute the predicted winner for each state on a given day.

4. Create a similar plot for 2008 statewide poll predictions using the data file `polls08.csv` (see table 4.2). Notice that polls are not conducted daily within each state. Therefore, within a given state, for each of the last 90 days of the campaign, we compute the average margin of victory from the most recent poll(s) conducted. If multiple polls occurred on the same day, average these polls. Based on the most recent predictions in each state, sum Obama's total number of predicted electoral votes. One strategy to answer this question is to program two loops—an inner loop with 51 iterations (for each state) and an outer loop with 90 iterations (for each day).

5. What is the relationship between the price margins of the Intrade market and the actual margin of victory? Using the market data from the day before the election in 2008 only, regress Obama's actual margin of victory in each state on Obama's price margin from the Intrade markets. Similarly, in a separate analysis, regress Obama's actual margin of victory on Obama's predicted margin from the latest polls within each state. Interpret the results of these regressions.

6. Do the 2008 predictions of polls and Intrade accurately predict each state's 2012 elections results? Using the fitted regressions from the previous question, forecast Obama's actual margin of victory for the 2012 election in two ways. First, use the 2012 Intrade price margins from the day before the election as the predictor in each state. Recall that the 2012 Intrade data do not contain market prices for all

Table 4.10. 2012 US Presidential Election Polling Data.

Variable	Description
state	abbreviated name of the state in which the poll was conducted
Obama	predicted support for Obama (percentage)
Romney	predicted support for Romney (percentage)
Pollster	name of the organization conducting the poll
middate	middate of the period when the poll was conducted

states. Ignore states without data. Second, use the 2012 poll-predicted margins from the latest polls in each state as the predictor, found in `polls12.csv`. Table 4.10 presents the names and descriptions of the 2012 US presidential election polling data.

4.5.2   ELECTION AND CONDITIONAL CASH TRANSFER PROGRAM IN MEXICO

In this exercise, we analyze the data from a study that seeks to estimate the electoral impact of *Progresa*, Mexico's *conditional cash transfer program* (CCT program).[7] The original study relied on a randomized evaluation of the CCT program in which eligible villages were randomly assigned to receive the program either 21 months (early Progresa) or 6 months (late Progresa) before the 2000 Mexican presidential election. The author of the original study hypothesized that the CCT program would mobilize voters, leading to an increase in turnout and support for the incumbent party (PRI, or Partido Revolucionario Institucional, in this case). The analysis was based on a sample of precincts that contain at most one participating village in the evaluation.

The data we analyze are available as the CSV file `progresa.csv`. Table 4.11 presents the names and descriptions of variables in the data set. Each observation in the data represents a precinct, and for each precinct the file contains information about its treatment status, the outcomes of interest, socioeconomic indicators, and other precinct characteristics.

1. Estimate the impact of the CCT program on turnout and support for the incumbent party (PRI) by comparing the average electoral outcomes in the "treated" (early Progresa) precincts versus the ones observed in the "control" (late Progresa) precincts. Next, estimate these effects by regressing the outcome variable on the treatment variable. Interpret and compare the estimates under these approaches. Here, following the original analysis, use the turnout and support rates as shares of the eligible voting population (`t2000` and `pri2000s`, respectively). Do the results support the hypothesis? Provide a brief interpretation.

---

[7] This exercise is based on the following articles: Ana de la O (2013) "Do conditional cash transfers affect voting behavior? Evidence from a randomized experiment in Mexico." *American Journal of Political Science*, vol. 57, no. 1, pp. 1–14 and Kosuke Imai, Gary King, and Carlos Velasco (2015) "Do nonpartisan programmatic policies have partisan electoral effects? Evidence from two large scale randomized experiments." Working paper.

Table 4.11. Conditional Cash Transfer Program (Progresa) Data.

Variable	Description
treatment	whether an electoral precinct contains a village where households received early Progresa
pri2000s	PRI votes in the 2000 election as a share of precinct population above 18
pri2000v	official PRI vote share in the 2000 election
t2000	turnout in the 2000 election as a share of precinct population above 18
t2000r	official turnout in the 2000 election
pri1994	total PRI votes in the 1994 presidential election
pan1994	total PAN votes in the 1994 presidential election
prd1994	total PRD votes in the 1994 presidential election
pri1994s	total PRI votes in the 1994 election as a share of precinct population above 18
pan1994s	total PAN votes in the 1994 election as a share of precinct population above 18
prd1994s	total PRD votes in the 1994 election as a share of precinct population above 18
pri1994v	official PRI vote share in the 1994 election
pan1994v	official PAN vote share in the 1994 election
prd1994v	official PRD vote share in the 1994 election
t1994	turnout in the 1994 election as a share of precinct population above 18
t1994r	official turnout in the 1994 election
votos1994	total votes cast in the 1994 presidential election
avgpoverty	precinct average of village poverty index
pobtot1994	total population in the precinct
villages	number of villages in the precinct

2. In the original analysis, the author fits a linear regression model that includes, as predictors, a set of pretreatment covariates as well as the treatment variable. Here, we fit a similar model for each outcome that includes the average poverty level in a precinct (avgpoverty), the total precinct population in 1994 (pobtot1994), the total number of voters who turned out in the previous election (votos1994), and the total number of votes cast for each of the three main competing parties in the previous election (pri1994 for PRI, pan1994 for Partido Acción Nacional or PAN, and prd1994 for Partido de la Revolución Democrática or PRD). Use the same outcome variables as in the original analysis, which are based on the shares of the voting age population. According to this model, what are the estimated average effects of the program's availability on turnout and support for the incumbent party? Are these results different from those you obtained in the previous question?

3. Next, we consider an alternative, and more natural, model specification. We will use the original outcome variables as in the previous question. However, our model should include the previous election outcome variables measured as shares of the voting age population (as done for the outcome variables t1994, pri1994s, pan1994s, and prd1994s) instead of those measured in counts. In addition, we apply the natural logarithmic transformation to the precinct population variable when including it as a predictor. As in the original model, our model includes the average poverty index as an additional predictor. Are the results based on these new model specifications different from those we obtained in the previous question? If the results are different, which model fits the data better?

4. We examine the balance of some pretreatment variables used in the previous analyses. Using box plots, compare the distributions of the precinct population (on the original scale), average poverty index, previous turnout rate (as a share of the voting age population), and previous PRI support rate (as a share of the voting age population) between the treatment and control groups. Comment on the patterns you observe.

5. We next use the official turnout rate t2000r (as a share of the registered voters) as the outcome variable rather than the turnout rate used in the original analysis (as a share of the voting age population). Similarly, we use the official PRI's vote share pri2000v (as a share of all votes cast) rather than the PRI's support rate (as a share of the voting age population). Compute the average treatment effect of the CCT program using a linear regression with the average poverty index, the log-transformed precinct population, and the previous official election outcome variables (t1994r for the previous turnout; pri1994v, pan1994v, and prd1994v for the previous PRI, PAN, and PRD vote shares). Briefly interpret the results.

6. So far we have focused on estimating the average treatment effects of the CCT program. However, these effects may vary from one precinct to another. One important dimension to consider is poverty. We may hypothesize that since individuals in precincts with higher levels of poverty are more receptive to cash transfers, they are more likely to turn out in the election and support the incumbent party when receiving the CCT program. Assess this possibility by examining how the average treatment effect of the policy varies by different levels of poverty for precincts. To do so, fit a linear regression with the following predictors: the treatment variable, the log-transformed precinct population, the average poverty index and its square, the interaction between the treatment and the poverty index, and the interaction between the treatment and the squared poverty index. Estimate the average effects for unique observed values and plot them as a function of the average poverty level. Comment on the resulting plot.

Table 4.12. Brazilian Government Transfer Data.

Variable	Description
pop82	population in 1982
poverty80	poverty rate of the state in 1980
poverty91	poverty rate of the state in 1991
educ80	average years in education of the state in 1980
educ91	average years in education of the state in 1991
literate91	literacy rate of the state in 1991
state	state
region	region
id	municipal ID
year	year of measurement

4.5.3 GOVERNMENT TRANSFER AND POVERTY REDUCTION IN BRAZIL

In this exercise, we estimate the effects of increased government spending on educational attainment, literacy, and poverty rates.[8] Some scholars argue that government spending accomplishes very little in environments of high corruption and inequality. Others suggest that in such environments, accountability pressures and the large demand for public goods will drive elites to respond. To address this debate, we exploit the fact that until 1991, the formula for government transfers to individual Brazilian municipalities was determined in part by the municipality's population. This meant that municipalities with populations below the official cutoff did not receive additional revenue, while states above the cutoff did. The data set transfer.csv contains the variables shown in table 4.12.

1. We will apply the regression discontinuity design to this application. State the required assumption for this design and interpret it in the context of this specific application. What would be a scenario in which this assumption is violated? What are the advantages and disadvantages of this design for this specific application?

2. Begin by creating a variable that determines how close each municipality was to the cutoff that determined whether states received a transfer or not. Transfers occurred at three separate population cutoffs: 10,188, 13,584, and 16,980. Using these cutoffs, create a single variable that characterizes the difference from the *closest* population cutoff. Following the original analysis, standardize this measure by dividing the difference by the corresponding cutoff, and multiplying it by 100. This will yield a normalized percentage score for the difference between the population of each state and the cutoff, relative to the cutoff value.

---

[8] This exercise is based on Stephan Litschig and Kevin M. Morrison (2013) "The impact of intergovernmental transfers on education outcomes and poverty reduction." *American Economic Journal: Applied Economics*, vol. 5, no. 4, pp. 206–240.

3. Begin by subsetting the data to include only those municipalities within 3 points of the funding cutoff on either side. Using regressions, estimate the average causal effect of government transfer on each of the three outcome variables of interest: educational attainment, literacy, and poverty. Give a brief substantive interpretation of the results.

4. Visualize the analysis performed in the previous question by plotting data points, fitted regression lines, and the population threshold. Briefly comment on the plot.

5. Instead of fitting linear regression models, we compute the difference-in-means of the outcome variables between the groups of observations above the threshold and below it. How do the estimates differ from what you obtained in question 3? Is the assumption invoked here identical to the one required for the analysis conducted in question 3? Which estimates are more appropriate? Discuss.

6. Repeat the analysis conducted in question 3 but vary the width of the analysis window from 1 to 5 percentage points below and above the threshold. Obtain the estimate for every percentage point. Briefly comment on the results.

7. Conduct the same analysis as in question 3 but this time using the measures of poverty rate and educational attainment taken in 1980, before the population-based government transfers began. What do the results suggest about the validity of the analysis presented in question 3?

Chapter 5

Discovery

The greatest value of a picture is when it forces us to notice what we never expected to see.
— John W. Tukey, *Exploratory Data Analysis*

Over the last couple of decades, the variety as well as volume of data analyzed in quantitative social science research has dramatically increased. In this chapter, we introduce three types of data that were not analyzed in previous chapters: textual, network, and spatial data. We conduct *exploratory data analysis* to inductively learn about the underlying patterns and structure of these data. We saw an example of such analysis applied to the degree of political polarization in chapter 3. In this chapter, we first analyze textual data to discover topics and predict authorship of documents based on the frequency of word usage. Our application is the disputed authorship of *The Federalist Papers*. Second, we analyze network data, which record the relationships among units. As examples, we will explore the marriage network in Renaissance Florence and social media data from Twitter. Finally, we visualize spatial data and examine changes in patterns across time and space. Our examples are the cholera outbreak in the 19th century and the expansion of Walmart retail stores in the 21st century.

5.1 Textual Data

The widespread use of the Internet has led to an astronomical amount of digitized textual data accumulating every second through email, websites, and social media outlets. The analysis of blog sites and social media posts can give new insights into human behavior and opinions. At the same time, large-scale efforts to digitize published articles, books, and government documents have been underway, providing exciting opportunities to revisit previously studied questions, by analyzing new data.

5.1.1 THE DISPUTED AUTHORSHIP OF *THE FEDERALIST PAPERS*

While new opportunities for text analysis have grown in recent years, we begin by revisiting one of the earliest examples of text analysis in the statistics literature. We analyze the text of *The Federalist*, more commonly known as *The Federalist*

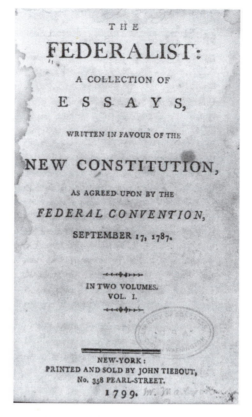

THE

FEDERALIST:

A COLLECTION OF

E S S A Y S,

WRITTEN IN FAVOUR OF THE

NEW CONSTITUTION,

AS AGREED-UPON BY THE

FEDERAL CONVENTION,

SEPTEMBER 17, 1787.

IN TWO VOLUMES.
VOL. I.

NEW-YORK:
PRINTED AND SOLD BY JOHN TIEBOUT,
No. 358 PEARL-STREET.
1799.

Figure 5.1. The Title Page of *The Federalist*, Vol. 1. Source: Library of Congress.

Papers.[1] *The Federalist*, whose title page is displayed in figure 5.1, consists of 85 essays attributed to Alexander Hamilton, John Jay, and James Madison from 1787 to 1788 in order to encourage people in New York to ratify the newly drafted US Constitution. Because both Hamilton and Madison helped draft the Constitution, scholars regard *The Federalist Papers* as a primary document reflecting the intentions of the authors of the Constitution.

The Federalist Papers were originally published in various New York state newspapers under the pseudonym of "Publius." For this reason, the authorship of each paper has been the subject of scholarly research. According to the Library of Congress,[2] experts believe that Hamilton wrote 51 essays while Madison authored 15.[3] In addition, Hamilton and Madison jointly authored 3 papers whereas John Jay wrote 5.[4] The remaining 11 essays were written by either Hamilton or Madison, though

---

[1] This section is in part based on F. Mosteller and D.L. Wallace (1963) "Inference in an authorship problem." *Journal of the American Statistical Association*, vol. 58, no. 302, pp. 275–309.

[2] See the website https://www.congress.gov/resources/display/content/The+Federalist+Papers#TheFederalistPapers-1.

[3] *The Federalist Papers* known to be written by Hamilton: nos. 1, 6–9, 11–13, 15–17, 21–36, 59–61, and 65–85. Papers known to be written by Madison: nos. 10, 14, 37–48, and 58.

[4] *The Federalist Papers* known to be jointly written by Hamilton and Madison: nos. 18–20. *The Federalist Papers* known to be written by John Jay: nos. 2–5 and 64.

Table 5.1. *The Federalist Papers* Data.

AFTER an unequivocal experience of the inefficiency
of the subsisting federal government, you are called
upon to deliberate on a new Constitution for the
United States of America.

$$\vdots$$

This shall accordingly constitute the subject of my next
address.

Note: The data consists of the raw text of each of 85 essays in *The Federalist Papers*. The first and last sentences of *The Federalist Paper* no. 1 appear here as an example.

scholars dispute which one.[5] Below, we analyze the text of *The Federalist Papers* to predict their authorship.

The text of the 85 essays is scraped from the Library of Congress website and stored as `fpXX.txt`, where `XX` represents the essay number ranging from `01` to `85`. *Scraping* refers to an automated method of data collection from websites using a computer program. Each data file contains the textual data of its corresponding essay. See table 5.1, which displays the first and last sentences of *The Federalist Paper* no. 1 as an example.

Before analyzing the data, we need to preprocess it. The **tm** package provides a number of useful *natural language processing* functionalities in R. One functionality eliminates unnecessary white space between words. Another, called stemming, strips away prefixes and suffixes to produce stem words so that different forms of the same word can be recognized. For example, the stem form of "government" is "govern." Note that the stemming functionality in the **tm** package requires another package called **SnowballC**. Be sure to install these packages by utilizing the `install.packages()` function or clicking the `Install` icon under the `Packages` tab in the bottom-right window of **RStudio** (see section 1.3.7 for more detailed instructions). The installation of a package needs only to occur once. However, in order to use a package, you must load it once in each new R session using the `library()` function. Load multiple packages simultaneously by separating them with commas.

```
## load two required libraries
library(tm, SnowballC)
```

We begin by loading the text *corpus*, or collection of texts, into R using the `Corpus()` function. The `DirSource()` function specifies the directory and pattern of corpus file names. The `directory` argument indicates the files' location, in this case the working directory's subdirectory called `federalist`, a folder you must create

---

[5] *The Federalist Papers* with disputed authorship are nos. 49, 50–57, 62, and 63.

Table 5.2. Commonly Used Functions to Preprocess Raw Texts.

Function	Description
tolower()	transform to lower case
stripWhitespace()	remove white space
removePunctuation()	remove punctuation
removeNumbers()	remove numbers
removeWords()	remove specified words
stemDocument()	stem the words in a document for specified language

before running the code. The `pattern` argument identifies a pattern contained in the names of all data files, in this case `fp` (`fp01.txt`, `fp10.txt`, etc.).

```
## load the raw corpus
corpus.raw <- Corpus(DirSource(directory = "federalist", pattern = "fp"))
corpus.raw

## <<VCorpus>>
## Metadata:  corpus specific: 0, document level (indexed): 0
## Content:   documents: 85
```

We now preprocess our corpus. We use the `tm_map()` function, which enables various natural language processing operations on corpora. The first argument of this function is the name of a corpus, while the second argument is a function that transforms text. Table 5.2 summarizes these functions. We first turn all letters to lower case by using the `tolower()` function. Since `tolower()` is a function in the R **base** package rather than in the **tm** package, it must pass through the wrapper function called `content_transformer()` (as of version 0.6–1).[6] Next, we eliminate unnecessary white space with the `stripWhitespace()` function, remove punctuation with the `removePunctuation()` function, and remove numbers with the `removeNumbers()` function.

```
## make lower case
corpus.prep <- tm_map(corpus.raw, content_transformer(tolower))
## remove white space
corpus.prep <- tm_map(corpus.prep, stripWhitespace)
## remove punctuation
corpus.prep <- tm_map(corpus.prep, removePunctuation)
## remove numbers
corpus.prep <- tm_map(corpus.prep, removeNumbers)
```

[6] Note that older versions of the **tm** package do not require the use of the `content_transformer()` function.

Next, to remove the most commonly used words such as a and the, we first use the stopwords() function to obtain a list of stop words for the input language. The beginning of the English list appears below.

```
head(stopwords("english"))
## [1] "i"       "me"       "my"       "myself" "we"       "our"
```

We will then pass this list through the removeWords() function. Finally, we stem each word.

```
## remove stop words
corpus <- tm_map(corpus.prep, removeWords, stopwords("english"))
## finally stem remaining words
corpus <- tm_map(corpus, stemDocument)
```

We can extract a specific essay by using double square brackets [[and]] with an integer indicating the element to be extracted (see section 3.7.2 for more details about the use of double square brackets). In addition, the content() function prints out the actual text of the selected document.

```
## the output is truncated here to save space
content(corpus[[10]]) # essay no. 10

##    [1] "among   numer advantag promis   wellconstruct union none"
##    [2] " deserv     accur develop   tendenc   break "
##    [3] " control   violenc  faction   friend  popular  govern never"
...
```

Compare this preprocessed document with the corresponding section of the original text, which is displayed here.

```
AMONG the numerous advantages promised by a well-constructed
   Union, none
     deserves to be more accurately developed than its tendency
   to break and
     control the violence of faction. The friend of popular
   governments never
```

We observe from the above text that all preprocessing was done as specified in our prior code. That is, all letters were transformed to lower case, punctuation marks such as hyphens and commas were taken out, stop words and white space were removed, and words were stemmed to be reduced to their stem word (e.g., transform numerous to numer and promised to promis).

5.1.2 DOCUMENT-TERM MATRIX

One quick way to explore textual data is to simply count occurrences of each word or term. The number of times a particular word appears in a given document is called *term frequency* (*tf*). The tf statistic can be summarized in a *document-term matrix*, which is a rectangular array with rows representing documents and columns representing unique terms. The (i, j) element of this matrix gives the counts of the jth term (column) in the ith document (row). We can also flip rows and columns and convert a document-term matrix to a *term-document matrix* where rows and columns represent terms and documents, respectively. A document-term matrix can be created by the `DocumentTermMatrix()` function in R (similarly, the `TermDocumentMatrix()` function creates a term-document matrix).

```
dtm <- DocumentTermMatrix(corpus)
dtm

## <<DocumentTermMatrix (documents: 85, terms: 4849)>>
## Non-/sparse entries: 44917/367248
## Sparsity           : 89%
## Maximal term length: 18
## Weighting          : term frequency (tf)
```

Because the output of the `DocumentTermMatrix()` function is a special matrix, R prints the document-term matrix's summary rather than the document-term matrix itself. The summary contains the number of documents as well as the number of terms. In addition, the number of nonsparse or nonzero entries and the number of sparse entries in the document-term matrix are provided. `Sparsity` refers to the proportion of zero entries in the document-term matrix. As is the case in this example, a document-term matrix is typically *sparse*. That is, the vast majority of its entries are zero because most terms appear in only a small number of documents. In the case of *The Federalist Papers*, 89% of the elements of the document-term matrix are 0. Finally, the summary output provides the maximal term length and quantity by which the entries of this matrix are weighted. In the current example, each entry represents the tf statistic.

To take a closer look at the actual entries of this matrix, we use the `inspect()` function, which displays detailed information on a corpus or term-document matrix. We can subset these matrix objects just like we subset a data frame object using square brackets `[,]`. As an example, the following syntax inspects the first 5 rows and first 8 columns of the document-term matrix.

```
inspect(dtm[1:5, 1:8])

## <<DocumentTermMatrix (documents: 5, terms: 8)>>
## Non-/sparse entries: 4/36
## Sparsity           : 90%
## Maximal term length: 7
## Weighting          : term frequency (tf)
##
```

```
##            Terms
## Docs      abandon abat abb abet abhorr abil abject abl
##   fp01.txt      0    0   0    0      0    0      0   1
##   fp02.txt      0    0   0    0      0    1      0   0
##   fp03.txt      0    0   0    0      0    0      0   2
##   fp04.txt      0    0   0    0      0    0      0   1
##   fp05.txt      0    0   0    0      0    0      0   0
```

Alternatively, we can coerce this object into a standard `matrix` object using the `as.matrix()` function, and print it directly.

```
dtm.mat <- as.matrix(dtm)
```

5.1.3 TOPIC DISCOVERY

We begin by visualizing and analyzing the document-term matrix created above. Our analysis of word frequency critically relies on the commonly used *bag-of-words* assumption, which ignores the grammar and ordering of words. This means that our analysis is unlikely to detect subtle meanings of texts. The distribution of *term frequency* (tf) should, however, allow us to infer *topics* discussed in the documents. A common way to visualize this distribution is a *word cloud* where more frequently used words appear in a larger font. The `wordcloud()` function in the **wordcloud** package creates a word cloud, which may serve as a useful visualization tool because the document-term matrix often contains too many columns to visually inspect.

Like clustering, covered in section 3.7, topic discovery is an example of *unsupervised learning* because we lack access to true information about topic assignment. That is, we do not know, a priori, what topics exist in the corpus and characterize each document. We wish to discover topics by analyzing the distribution of term frequency within a given document and across documents. In contrast, in *supervised learning*, researchers use a sample with an observed outcome variable to learn about the relationship between the outcome and predictors. For example, we may have human coders read some documents and assign topics. We can then use this information to predict the topics of other documents that have not been read. Clearly, the lack of information about outcome variables makes unsupervised learning problems more challenging than supervised problems.

We begin by visualizing *The Federalist Papers* nos. 12 and 24 with word clouds in order to infer their topics. Both papers are known to be authored by Alexander Hamilton. In the **wordcloud** package, which we must install, the `wordcloud()` function takes two main arguments. The first argument takes a vector of words while the second argument takes the frequencies of those words. To avoid clutter, we limit the maximum number of words to be plotted by setting `max.words` to `20`.

```
library(wordcloud)

wordcloud(colnames(dtm.mat), dtm.mat[12, ], max.words = 20)  # essay no. 12
wordcloud(colnames(dtm.mat), dtm.mat[24, ], max.words = 20)  # essay no. 24
```

nation must upon
countri commerc trade import
duti will
excis part
object far govern
great tax
revenu direct
state land

must nation
will constitut
twogarrison
withoutpower
state
time peac even
one appear
upon object
establish armi
necess
legislatur

The comparison of the two word clouds shows that the left-hand plot for paper no. 12 contains words related to economy such as `revenu` (the root form of `revenue`), `commerc` (`commerce`), `trade`, `tax`, `land`, and so on. In contrast, the right-hand plot for paper no. 24 contains more words about security including `power`, `peac` (the root form of `peace`), `garrison`, and `armi` (`army`). Recall that the `stemDocument()` function stems documents. We now can use the `stemCompletion()` function to recover the full version of a stemmed word. The function's first argument takes the stem word or words, while the second argument takes candidate full words. Our candidate full words here come from the unstemmed corpus, `corpus.prep`.

```
stemCompletion(c("revenu", "commerc", "peac", "army"), corpus.prep)

##      revenu    commerc        peac        army
##   "revenue" "commerce"     "peace"      "army"
```

These discovered topics are indeed consistent with the actual content of the papers. Paper no. 12 is entitled, "The utility of the Union in respect to revenue" and discusses the economic benefits of the 13 colonies forming one nation. In contrast, the title of no. 24 is "The powers necessary to the common defense further considered" and discusses the creation of a national army as well as the relationship between legislative power and federal forces.

In the above analysis, we visualized the distribution of term frequency within each document. However, a certain term's high frequency within a document means little if that term often appears across the documents of the corpus. To address this issue, we should downweight the terms that occur frequently across documents. This can be done by computing the statistic called *term frequency–inverse document frequency*, or *tf–idf* in short. The tf–idf statistic is another measure of the importance of each term in a given document. For a given document d and term w, we define tf–idf(w, d) as

$$\text{tf–idf}(w, d) = \text{tf}(w, d) \times \text{idf}(w). \tag{5.1}$$

In the above equation, tf(w, d) represents *term frequency* or the number of occurrences of term w in document d. In some cases, we convert tf(w, d) to a log scale when it takes a positive value. Note that tf(w, d) equals 0 when term w never occurs in document d.

The other factor in equation (5.1), idf(w), is the *inverse document frequency*, which is typically defined as

$$\text{idf}(w) = \log\left(\frac{N}{\text{df}(w)}\right).$$

In this equation, N is the total number of documents and df(w) is the *document frequency* or the number of documents that contain term w. Dividing by df(w) implies that idf(w) takes a smaller value when term w is used more frequently across documents. As a consequence, common terms across documents receive less weight in tf–idf.

We can compute the tf–idf measure using the `weightTfIdf()` function, which takes as its input the document-term matrix output from the `DocumentTermMatrix()` function. Note that the `weightTfIdf()` function has an argument `normalize`, for which the default value is `FALSE`. If this argument is set to `TRUE`, then term frequency tf(w, d) will be divided by the total number of terms in document d.

```r
dtm.tfidf <- weightTfIdf(dtm) # tf-idf calculation
```

Below, we list the 10 most important terms for *The Federalist Papers* nos. 12 and 24 using the tf–idf measure. The `sort()` function helpfully identifies the terms with the largest tf–idf values. We sort a vector in decreasing (increasing) order by specifying the `decreasing` argument as `TRUE` (`FALSE`). Since the class of `dtm.tfidf` is still `DocumentTermMatrix`, we need to convert it to a matrix before applying the `sort()` function.

```r
dtm.tfidf.mat <- as.matrix(dtm.tfidf)   # convert to matrix
## 10 most important words for paper no. 12
head(sort(dtm.tfidf.mat[12, ], decreasing = TRUE), n = 10)

##      revenu contraband      patrol      excis       coast
## 0.01905877 0.01886965 0.01886965 0.01876560 0.01592559
##       trade         per         tax        cent       gallon
## 0.01473504 0.01420342 0.01295466 0.01257977 0.01257977
```

```
## 10 most important words for paper no. 24
head(sort(dtm.tfidf.mat[24, ], decreasing = TRUE), n = 10)

##    garrison   dockyard settlement       spain       armi
## 0.02965511 0.01962294 0.01962294 0.01649040 0.01544256
##    frontier     arsenal     western        post      nearer
## 0.01482756 0.01308196 0.01306664 0.01236780 0.01166730
```

The results clearly show that the most important terms for *The Federalist Paper* no. 12 concern the economy whereas those for paper no. 24 relate to security policies, though such word association is done by the researcher.

> The analysis of documents based on term frequency relies on the **bag-of-words** assumption that ignores the order of words. To measure the relative importance of a term in a document, we can compute the **term frequency–inverse document frequency** (tf–idf), which represents the relative frequency of the term inversely weighted by the number of documents in which the term appears (document frequency).

Finally, we consider an alternative approach to topic discovery, by identifying clusters of similar essays, based on the tf–idf measure. We focus on the essays written by Hamilton. Following section 3.7, we apply the *k*-means algorithm to this weighted document-term matrix. After some experimentation, we choose the number of clusters to be 4. While arbitrary, this choice produces clusters that seem reasonable. We check the number of iterations to convergence to make sure that it does not exceed the default maximum value 10.

```
k <- 4  # number of clusters
## subset the Federalist papers written by Hamilton
hamilton <- c(1, 6:9, 11:13, 15:17, 21:36, 59:61, 65:85)
dtm.tfidf.hamilton <- dtm.tfidf.mat[hamilton, ]
## run k-means
km.out <- kmeans(dtm.tfidf.hamilton, centers = k)
km.out$iter # check the convergence; number of iterations may vary

## [1] 2
```

We next summarize the results by printing out the 10 most important terms at the centroid of each of the resulting clusters. We also show which essays of *The Federalist Papers* belong to each cluster. Since we must perform the same operation for each cluster, we use a loop (see section 4.1.1).

```
## label each centroid with the corresponding term
colnames(km.out$centers) <- colnames(dtm.tfidf.hamilton)
for (i in 1:k) { # loop for each cluster
    cat("CLUSTER", i, "\n")
    cat("Top 10 words:\n") # 10 most important terms at the centroid
    print(head(sort(km.out$centers[i, ], decreasing = TRUE), n = 10))
    cat("\n")
    cat("Federalist Papers classified:\n") # extract essays classified
    print(rownames(dtm.tfidf.hamilton)[km.out$cluster == i])
    cat("\n")
}

## CLUSTER 1
## Top 10 words:
##     vacanc     recess      claus      senat    session
## 0.06953047 0.04437713 0.04082617 0.03408008 0.03313305
##       fill    appoint     presid      expir    unfound
## 0.03101140 0.02211662 0.01852025 0.01738262 0.01684465
##
## Federalist Papers classified:
## [1] "fp67.txt"
##
## CLUSTER 2
## Top 10 words:
##         armi       upon    militia     revenu       land
## 0.004557667 0.003878185 0.003680496 0.003523467 0.003410589
##    militari        war confederaci      taxat     esourc
## 0.003378875 0.003035943 0.003021217 0.002835844 0.002699460
##
## Federalist Papers classified:
##  [1] "fp01.txt" "fp06.txt" "fp07.txt" "fp08.txt" "fp09.txt"
##  [6] "fp11.txt" "fp12.txt" "fp13.txt" "fp15.txt" "fp16.txt"
## [11] "fp17.txt" "fp21.txt" "fp22.txt" "fp23.txt" "fp24.txt"
## [16] "fp25.txt" "fp26.txt" "fp27.txt" "fp28.txt" "fp29.txt"
## [21] "fp30.txt" "fp31.txt" "fp34.txt" "fp35.txt" "fp36.txt"
## [26] "fp60.txt" "fp80.txt" "fp85.txt"
##
## CLUSTER 3
## Top 10 words:
##       senat     presid      claus      offic    impeach
## 0.008267389 0.007114606 0.005340963 0.005134467 0.005124293
##       nomin   governor     appoint       upon     magistr
## 0.004568173 0.004490385 0.003965382 0.003748606 0.003667998
##
## Federalist Papers classified:
##  [1] "fp32.txt" "fp33.txt" "fp59.txt" "fp61.txt" "fp65.txt"
##  [6] "fp66.txt" "fp68.txt" "fp69.txt" "fp70.txt" "fp71.txt"
```

```
## [11] "fp72.txt" "fp73.txt" "fp74.txt" "fp75.txt" "fp76.txt"
## [16] "fp77.txt" "fp78.txt" "fp79.txt" "fp84.txt"
##
## CLUSTER 4
## Top 10 words:
##     court       juri      appel  jurisdict     suprem
## 0.05119100 0.03715999 0.01948060 0.01865612 0.01474737
##     tribun      trial     cogniz   inferior     appeal
## 0.01448872 0.01383180 0.01343695 0.01155172 0.01139125
##
## Federalist Papers classified:
## [1] "fp81.txt" "fp82.txt" "fp83.txt"
```

Examining the 10 most important terms at the centroid of each cluster suggests that cluster 2 relates to war and taxation, as indicated by terms like `armi`, `taxat`, and `war`, while cluster 1 covers only one document. Cluster 3 addresses institutional design and cluster 4 appears to be concerned with judicial systems. Comparing these topics with the actual contents of *The Federalist Papers* shows a decent degree of validity for the results of the *k*-means clustering algorithm.

We have been using *The Federalist Papers* to illustrate how text analyses can reveal topics. Of course, since we can easily read all of *The Federalist Papers*, the automated text analysis may not be necessary in this case. However, similar and more advanced techniques can be applied to a much larger corpus that humans would struggle to read in full over a short amount of time. In such situations, automated text analysis can play an essential role in helping researchers extract meaningful information from textual data.

5.1.4 AUTHORSHIP PREDICTION

As mentioned earlier, the authorship of some of *The Federalist Papers* is unknown. We will use the 66 essays attributed to either Hamilton or Madison to predict the authorship of the 11 disputed papers. Since each *Federalist* paper deals with a different topic, we focus on the usage of articles, prepositions, and conjunctions. In particular, we analyze the frequency of the following 10 words: `although`, `always`, `commonly`, `consequently`, `considerable`, `enough`, `there`, `upon`, `while`, `whilst`. We select these words based on the analysis presented in the academic paper that inspired this section (see footnote 1). As a result, we must use the unstemmed corpus, `corpus.prep`. We first compute the term frequency (per 1000 words) separately for each term and document and then subset the resulting term-frequency matrix to contain only these words.

```
## document-term matrix converted to matrix for manipulation
dtm1 <- as.matrix(DocumentTermMatrix(corpus.prep))
tfm <- dtm1 / rowSums(dtm1) * 1000 # term frequency per 1000 words
```

```
## words of interest
words <- c("although", "always", "commonly", "consequently",
           "considerable", "enough", "there", "upon", "while", "whilst")
## select only these words
tfm <- tfm[, words]
```

We then calculate the average term frequency separately for Hamilton and Madison across each author's entire body of documents.

```
## essays written by Madison: "hamilton" defined earlier
madison <- c(10, 14, 37:48, 58)
## average among Hamilton/Madison essays
tfm.ave <- rbind(colSums(tfm[hamilton, ]) / length(hamilton),
                 colSums(tfm[madison, ]) / length(madison))
tfm.ave
##         although    always  commonly consequently
## [1,] 0.01756975 0.7527744 0.2630876   0.02600857
## [2,] 0.27058809 0.2006710 0.0000000   0.44878468
##      considerable    enough     there       upon      while
## [1,]    0.5435127 0.3955031 4.417750 4.3986828 0.3700484
## [2,]    0.1601669 0.0000000 1.113252 0.2000269 0.0000000
##           whilst
## [1,] 0.007055719
## [2,] 0.380113114
```

The results suggest that Hamilton prefers to use terms such as `there` and `upon`, which Madison seldom uses, preferring instead to use `consequently` and `whilst`. We will use the frequency of these 4 words as the predictors of a linear regression model, where the outcome variable is the authorship of an essay. We first fit this linear regression model to the 66 essays whose authorship is known to estimate the coefficients. The resulting fitted model can then be used to predict the unknown authorship of the 11 essays based on the 4 words' frequencies. For the linear regression model, we first create the outcome variable by coding essays authored by Hamilton as `1` and those written by Madison as `-1`. We then construct a data frame object, which contains this authorship variable as well as the term-frequency matrix `tfm` for all essays whose authorship is known.

```
author <- rep(NA, nrow(dtm1)) # a vector with missing values
author[hamilton] <- 1   # 1 if Hamilton
author[madison] <- -1   # -1 if Madison
## data frame for regression
author.data <- data.frame(author = author[c(hamilton,madison)],
                          tfm[c(hamilton, madison), ])
```

To predict the authorship, we use the term frequency of the 4 words selected based on our preliminary analysis, i.e., upon, there, consequently, and whilst. The data frame object we created above contains the term frequency of the 10 words including these 4. We estimate the coefficients using the 66 essays with known authorship.

```
hm.fit <- lm(author ~ upon + there + consequently + whilst,
        data = author.data)
hm.fit

##
## Call:
## lm(formula = author ~ upon + there + consequently + whilst, data = author.data)
##
## Coefficients:
## (Intercept)           upon             there   consequently
##    -0.26288        0.16678          0.09494       -0.44012
##        whilst
##    -0.65875
```

The results are consistent with the preliminary analysis we conducted above. The estimated coefficients for upon and there are positive while those for consequently and whilst are negative, implying that the first two words are associated with Hamilton whereas the latter pair are associated with Madison. Interestingly, the estimated coefficient for whilst has the largest magnitude. Holding the term frequency of the other 3 words constant, one additional use of whilst (per 1000 words) in an essay decreases the predicted authorship score by 0.66. To put this number into perspective, we compute the standard deviation of fitted values using the fitted() and sd() functions.

```
hm.fitted <- fitted(hm.fit) # fitted values
sd(hm.fitted)

## [1] 0.7180769
```

We find that the magnitude of this coefficient is large and close to 1 standard deviation of fitted values. That is, one additional use of whilst (per 1000 words) accounts for approximately 1 standard deviation of variation in our predicted value for the authorship score.

5.1.5 CROSS VALIDATION

How well is this model fitting the data? We classify each essay using its fitted value and compute the *classification error*. To do this, we compute the proportion of positive fitted values among the essays authored by Hamilton. Similarly, we compute the proportion of negative fitted values among those written by Madison. The results represent the classification success rate (see section 4.1.3).

```
## proportion of correctly classified essays by Hamilton
mean(hm.fitted[author.data$author == 1] > 0)

## [1] 1

## proportion of correctly classified essays by Madison
mean(hm.fitted[author.data$author == -1] < 0)

## [1] 1
```

The results show that the model perfectly classifies the authorship of these essays. Like the coefficient of determination introduced in chapter 4, however, this measure of prediction accuracy is based on *in-sample prediction*. That is, the same data we used to fit the model are again used for assessing the prediction accuracy. This is not necessarily a good idea because we can *overfit* a model to the data at hand. Overfitting occurs when a model captures idiosyncratic features of a specific sample while muddling up systematic patterns that exist across different samples.

Let us instead consider *out-of-sample prediction*. The idea is that we use new observations to assess the predictive performance of a model. In chapter 4, we performed out-of-sample prediction by forecasting election results using preelection polls. Similarly, here, we employ a procedure called *leave-one-out cross validation*. Specifically, we set aside one observation and predict its outcome variable value after fitting the model to the remaining observations. We repeat this procedure for each observation in the sample and compute the classification error. Cross validation enables us to assess the accuracy of model prediction without relying on in-sample prediction.

Cross validation is a methodology to assess the accuracy of model prediction without relying on in-sample prediction, which often leads to overfitting. Suppose that we have a sample of n observations. Then, the leave-one-out cross-validation procedure repeats the following steps for each observation $i = 1, \ldots, n$:

1. Take out the ith observation and set it aside.
2. Fit the model using the remaining $n - 1$ observations.
3. Using the fitted model, predict the outcome for the ith observation and compute the prediction error.

Finally, compute the average prediction error across n observations as a measure of prediction accuracy.

In R, we can cross validate using a *loop*, where each iteration fits the model to the data after excluding one observation, then predicts that observation's outcome variable value. A convenient way of setting aside the ith observation is to use the minus sign, i.e., `-i`, to remove a certain row of the data frame. As we saw in section 4.3.4, the `predict()` function can compute the predicted value $\widehat{Y}$. In this function, the `newdata` argument should specify a data frame whose only row is the observation of interest.

```
n <- nrow(author.data)
hm.classify <- rep(NA, n) # a container vector with missing values
for (i in 1:n) {
    ## fit the model to the data after removing the ith observation
    sub.fit <- lm(author ~ upon + there + consequently + whilst,
                  data = author.data[-i, ]) # exclude ith row
    ## predict the authorship for the ith observation
    hm.classify[i] <- predict(sub.fit, newdata = author.data[i, ])
}
```

The results below show that even when the cross validation procedure is used, the model continues to perfectly classify the authorship of each essay.

```
## proportion of correctly classified essays by Hamilton
mean(hm.classify[author.data$author == 1] > 0)

## [1] 1

## proportion of correctly classified essays by Madison
mean(hm.classify[author.data$author == -1] < 0)

## [1] 1
```

Finally, we use this fitted model to predict the unknown authorship of the 11 essays. When using `predict()` for prediction, don't forget to coerce the term-frequency matrix into a data frame through the `as.data.frame()` function. Note that this function differs from the `data.frame()` function, which creates a data frame.

```
disputed <- c(49, 50:57, 62, 63) # 11 essays with disputed authorship
tf.disputed <- as.data.frame(tfm[disputed, ])
## prediction of disputed authorship
pred <- predict(hm.fit, newdata = tf.disputed)
pred # predicted values

##     fp49.txt     fp50.txt     fp51.txt     fp52.txt     fp53.txt
## -0.99831799 -0.06759254 -1.53243206 -0.26288400 -0.54584900
##     fp54.txt     fp55.txt     fp56.txt     fp57.txt     fp62.txt
##  -0.56566555  0.04376632 -0.57115610 -1.22289415 -1.00675456
##     fp63.txt
##  -0.21939646
```

For ease of presentation, we plot the predicted values using different colors. Red squares signify essays known to be written by Hamilton, while blue circles indicate those by Madison. Black triangles represent papers with disputed authorship. Points above (below) the dashed horizontal line, indicating zero, correspond to essays classified as written by Hamilton (Madison).

```
## fitted values for essays authored by Hamilton; red squares
plot(hamilton, hm.fitted[author.data$author == 1], pch = 15,
     xlim = c(1, 85), ylim  = c(-2, 2), col = "red",
     xlab = "Federalist Papers", ylab = "Predicted values")
abline(h = 0, lty = "dashed")
## essays authored by Madison; blue circles
points(madison, hm.fitted[author.data$author == -1],
       pch = 16, col = "blue")
## disputed authorship; black triangles
points(disputed, pred, pch = 17)
```

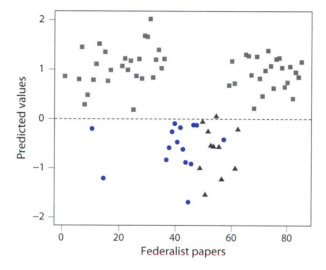

The plot above uses gray squares instead of red squares for the essays authored by Hamilton. See page C4 for the full-color version. As our plot shows, the model predicts that Madison wrote all of the 11 essays except one. That one was barely classified as written by Hamilton, having a predicted value near zero.

5.2 Network Data

Next, we consider *network data*, which describes relationships among units rather than units in isolation. Examples include friendship networks among people, citation networks among academic articles, and trade and alliance networks among countries. Analysis of network data differs from the data analyses we have covered so far in that the unit of analysis is a relationship.

5.2.1 MARRIAGE NETWORK IN RENAISSANCE FLORENCE

We introduce the basic concepts and methods for network data by analyzing a well-known data set about the marriage network in Renaissance Florence.[7] The CSV data

---

[7] This section is in part based on John F. Padgett and Christopher K. Ansell (1993) "Robust action and the rise of the Medici, 1400–1434." *American Journal of Sociology*, vol. 98, no. 6, pp. 1259–1319.

Table 5.3. Florence Marriage Network Data.

FAMILY	ACCIAIUOL	ALBIZZI	⋯	LAMBERTES	MEDICI	⋯	STROZZI	TORNABUON
ACCIAIUOL	0	0	⋯	0	1	⋯	0	0
ALBIZZI	0	0	⋯	0	1	⋯	0	0
⋮			⋮			⋮		
LAMBERTES	0	0	⋯	0	0	⋯	0	0
MEDICI	1	1	⋯	0	0	⋯	0	1
⋮			⋮			⋮		
STROZZI	0	0	⋯	0	0	⋯	0	0
TORNABUON	0	0	⋯	0	1	⋯	0	0

Note: The data are in the form of an adjacency matrix where each entry represents whether a family in its row has a marriage relationship with another family in its column.

file, `florentine.csv`, contains an *adjacency matrix* whose entries represent the existence of relationships between two units (one unit represented by the row and the other represented by the column). Specifically, there are 16 elite Florentine families in the data, leading to a 16×16 adjacency matrix. If the (i, j) entry of this adjacency matrix is 1, then it implies that the ith and jth Florentine families had a marriage relationship. In contrast, a value of 0 indicates the absence of a marriage. Table 5.3 displays part of this data set. Below, we print out the part of the adjacency matrix corresponding to the first 5 families.

```
## the first column "FAMILY" of the CSV file represents row names
florence <- read.csv("florentine.csv", row.names = "FAMILY")
florence <- as.matrix(florence) # coerce into a matrix
## print out the adjacency (sub)matrix for the first 5 families
florence[1:5, 1:5]
##             ACCIAIUOL ALBIZZI BARBADORI BISCHERI CASTELLAN
## ACCIAIUOL           0       0         0        0         0
## ALBIZZI             0       0         0        0         0
## BARBADORI           0       0         0        0         1
## BISCHERI            0       0         0        0         0
## CASTELLAN           0       0         1        0         0
```

The submatrix shows that there was only one marriage relationship among these 5 families. The marriage was between the Barbadori and Castellan families. This adjacency matrix represents an *undirected network* because the matrix contains no directionality. We could add directionality by incorporating which family proposed a marriage if such information were available. In contrast, the Twitter data we analyze later are an example of a *directed network* where any relationship between a pair of units specifies a *sender* and a *receiver*. For an undirected network, the adjacency matrix is symmetric: the (i, j) element has the same value as the (j, i) element. Finally, using the `rowSums()` or `colSums()` function, we can check which family had the largest number of marriage relationships.

```
rowSums(florence)

## ACCIAIUOL    ALBIZZI BARBADORI  BISCHERI CASTELLAN    GINORI
##         1          3         2         3         3         1
## GUADAGNI LAMBERTES    MEDICI     PAZZI   PERUZZI     PUCCI
##         4          1         6         1         3         0
##   RIDOLFI   SALVIATI   STROZZI TORNABUON
##         3          2         4         3
```

The result shows that the Medici family had 6 marriage relationships. It turns out that through this marriage network, the Medici family made themselves the most powerful faction in Renaissance Florence and eventually took over the state.

> Network data carry information about the relationships between units. A **directed network** contains directionality, with senders and receivers, whereas an **undirected network** does not. An **adjacency matrix**, whose entries indicate the existence or absence of a relationship between two units, is one way to represent network data. An undirected network yields a symmetric adjacency matrix, whereas a directed network does not.

5.2.2 UNDIRECTED GRAPH AND CENTRALITY MEASURES

The most common tool for visualizing network data is a *graph*, which is also a mathematical object, as well as a visualization tool. A graph $\mathcal{G}$ consists of a set of *nodes* (or *vertices*) V and a set of *edges* (or *ties*) E, i.e., $\mathcal{G} = (V, E)$. A node represents an individual unit, or a family in our current example, and is typically depicted as a solid circle. An edge, on the other hand, represents the existence of a relationship between any pair of nodes (e.g., a marriage relationship between two families) via a line connecting those nodes.

The **igraph** package makes it easy to visualize network data as a graph. Be sure to install the package if you have not done so already. We first use the graph.adjacency() function to turn an adjacency matrix into an igraph object, meaning an object that the **igraph** package can use. We set the mode argument to "undirected" since we are analyzing an undirected network. We also specify diag = FALSE to indicate the assumption that there is no marriage within a family, resulting in a value of zero for every diagonal element of the adjacency matrix. Finally, we can visualize the marriage network data as a graph by applying the plot() function to the igraph object.

```
library("igraph")  # load the package

florence <- graph.adjacency(florence, mode = "undirected", diag = FALSE)
plot(florence) # plot the graph
```

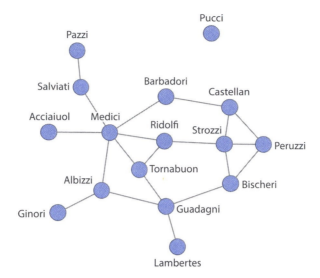

The Medici family appears to occupy the center of the Florentine marriage network, being connected to various parts of the graph. We now introduce a variety of graph-based measures that can quantify *centrality*, or the extent to which each node is connected to other nodes and appears in the center of a graph. The number of edges, or *degree*, is perhaps the most crude measure of how well a node is connected to the other nodes in a graph. Figure 5.2a illustrates this measure using a simple undirected network example, where degree is indicated as an integer value within each node. Above, we found that the Medici family had the largest number of marriage relationships, so it has the highest degree. The degree of every node can be calculated by applying the degree() function to the igraph object.

```
degree(florence)

## ACCIAIUOL    ALBIZZI BARBADORI   BISCHERI CASTELLAN     GINORI
##         1          3         2          3         3          1
## GUADAGNI LAMBERTES     MEDICI       PAZZI   PERUZZI      PUCCI
##        4          1         6          1         3          0
## RIDOLFI   SALVIATI    STROZZI  TORNABUON
##        3          2         4          3
```

Degree is problematically a local measure because it simply counts the number of edges that come out of a given node. As a result, it does not account for the structure of the graph beyond its immediate neighbors. As an alternative, we can count the sum of edges from a given node to all other nodes in a graph, including the ones that are not directly connected. This measure, called *farness*, describes how far apart a given node is from each one of all other nodes in the graph. This contrasts with degree, which counts the number of connected nodes. The inverse of farness, *closeness*, represents another

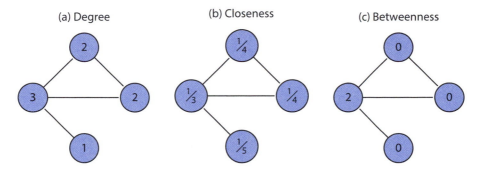

Figure 5.2. Degree, Closeness, and Betweenness in an Undirected Network. This simple example of an undirected network illustrates three alternative measures of centrality: degree, closeness, and betweenness.

measure of centrality. The closeness for node v is defined as

$$\text{closeness}(v) = \frac{1}{\text{farness}(v)}$$

$$= \frac{1}{\sum_{u \in V,\, u \neq v} \text{distance between } v \text{ and } u},$$

where the summation is taken over all nodes other than v itself. The distance between two nodes is the number of edges in the shortest path, which is the shortest sequence of connected nodes, between the two nodes of interest. Figure 5.2b shows the values of this measure for each node in a simple example of an undirected network. In R, we can use the `closeness()` function to compute this measure.

```
closeness(florence)

##      ACCIAIUOL       ALBIZZI      BARBADORI       BISCHERI      CASTELLAN
##    0.018518519   0.022222222    0.020833333    0.019607843    0.019230769
##         GINORI      GUADAGNI      LAMBERTES          MEDICI          PAZZI
##    0.017241379   0.021739130    0.016949153    0.024390244    0.015384615
##        PERUZZI          PUCCI        RIDOLFI       SALVIATI        STROZZI
##    0.018518519   0.004166667    0.022727273    0.019230769    0.020833333
##      TORNABUON
##    0.022222222
```

As with degree, we find that the Medici family has the largest value of closeness. To facilitate the interpretation of this measure, we can calculate the average number of edges from a given node to another node. This is done by dividing the farness by the number of other nodes on a graph. In the current example, we have a total of 16 nodes and so we divide the farness by 15. The results below imply that on average, there are 2.7 edges between the Medici family and another family in this network, which is the lowest among all families considered in this network data.

```
1 / (closeness(florence) * 15)

## ACCIAIUOL     ALBIZZI  BARBADORI    BISCHERI  CASTELLAN      GINORI
##   3.600000    3.000000   3.200000    3.400000   3.466667    3.866667
##   GUADAGNI  LAMBERTES      MEDICI       PAZZI    PERUZZI       PUCCI
##   3.066667    3.933333   2.733333    4.333333   3.600000   16.000000
##    RIDOLFI    SALVIATI     STROZZI   TORNABUON
##   2.933333    3.466667   3.200000    3.000000
```

A different type of centrality measure is *betweenness*. According to this measure, a node is considered to be central if it is responsible for connecting other nodes. In particular, if we assume that communication between a pair of nodes occurs through the shortest path between them, a node that lies on many such shortest paths may possess special leverage within a network. For a given node v, we calculate betweenness in three steps. First, compute the proportion of the shortest paths between two other nodes, t and u, that contain v. For example, two shortest paths occur between the Albizzi family and Tornabuon family, but we want only the proportion that contain v. Second, calculate this proportion for every unique pair of nodes t and u in the graph, excluding v. Third, sum all proportions. The formal definition is given by

$$\text{betweenness}(v) = \sum_{(t,u) \in V, \; t \neq v, \; u \neq v} \frac{\text{number of shortest paths that contain node } v}{\text{number of shortest paths between nodes } t \text{ and } u}.$$

Figure 5.2c illustrates this centrality measure in the same undirected network example used for the other two measures.

The betweenness() function can be used to compute this measure. We find that by far, the Medici family has the highest value of betweenness. In fact, since any given node can be uniquely paired with 105 other nodes, the Medici family lies in the shortest path of more than 45% of all possible pairs of other nodes.

```
betweenness(florence)

## ACCIAIUOL     ALBIZZI  BARBADORI    BISCHERI  CASTELLAN      GINORI
##   0.000000   19.333333   8.500000    9.500000   5.000000    0.000000
##   GUADAGNI  LAMBERTES      MEDICI       PAZZI    PERUZZI       PUCCI
## 23.166667    0.000000  47.500000    0.000000   2.000000    0.000000
##    RIDOLFI    SALVIATI     STROZZI   TORNABUON
## 10.333333   13.000000   9.333333    8.333333
```

A **graph** is another way to represent network data where nodes (vertices) represent units and an edge (or tie) between two nodes indicates that a relationship exists between them. There are various **centrality** measures, including degrees, closeness, and betweenness. These measures evaluate the extent to which each node plays a central role in a graph.

We visualize the Florentine marriage network data by making the size of each node proportional to two centrality measures, closeness and betweenness. The values of closeness are relatively small, and so we multiply them by 1000 in order to enlarge the nodes of the graph.

```
plot(florence, vertex.size = closeness(florence) * 1000,
    main = "Closeness")
plot(florence, vertex.size = betweenness(florence),
    main = "Betweenness")
```

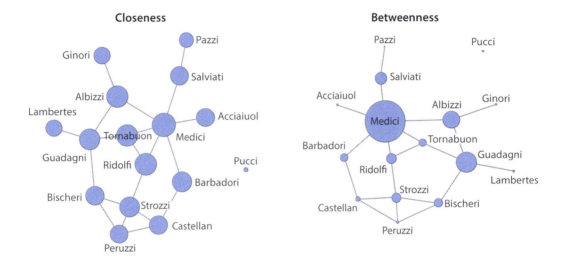

The graphs illustrate that the Medici family stands out especially in terms of betweenness, while the closeness measure suggests they are one of several well-connected families. In sum, using three measures of centrality—degree, closeness, and betweenness—we find that the Medici family is the most connected and central in the network of Florentine marriage relationships. In Renaissance Florence, the Medici family had the largest number of marriage relationships, was closely connected to other families, and occupied a critical position in marriages among other families.

5.2.3 TWITTER-FOLLOWING NETWORK

The Florentine marriage network data exemplify an *undirected* network where each edge has no directionality. Next, we analyze Twitter-following data among US senators as *directed* network data. In this data set, an edge represents an instance of a senator following another senator's Twitter account.[8] The data consist of two files, one listing pairs of the Twitter screen names of the following and followed politicians, twitter-following.csv, and the other containing information about

---

[8] This data set is generously provided by Pablo Barberá.

Table 5.4. Twitter Following Data.

Variable	Description
Twitter-following data	
`following`	Twitter screen name of the following senator
`followed`	Twitter screen name of the followed senator
Twitter senator data	
`screen_name`	Twitter screen name
`name`	name of senator
`party`	party (`D` = Democrat, `R` = Republican, `I` = Independent)
`state`	state abbreviation

Note: The data are in two files, one listing the pairs of following and followed senators and the other containing information about each senator.

each politician, `twitter-senator.csv`. Table 5.4 lists the names and descriptions of variables in these two data files.

```
twitter <- read.csv("twitter-following.csv")
senator <- read.csv("twitter-senator.csv")
```

We begin by creating an adjacency matrix with these two data sets. For directed network data, the (i, j)th element of the adjacency matrix is 1 if an edge connects node i to node j. A value of 0 indicates the absence of any relationship. Consequently, unlike the case of undirected network data, the adjacency matrix is asymmetric: the (i, j)th element of this matrix may not equal its (j, i)th element. We create this adjacency matrix by initializing it with a matrix of zeros and then changing the value of its (i, j)th element from 0 to 1 if the ith politician follows the jth politician.

```
n <- nrow(senator) # number of senators
## initialize adjacency matrix
twitter.adj <- matrix(0, nrow = n, ncol = n)
## assign screen names to rows and columns
colnames(twitter.adj) <- rownames(twitter.adj) <- senator$screen_name
## change "0" to "1" when edge goes from node "i" to node "j"
for (i in 1:nrow(twitter)) {
    twitter.adj[twitter$following[i], twitter$followed[i]] <- 1
}
```

Finally, as before, we use the `graph.adjacency()` function to turn the adjacency matrix into an `igraph` object. This time, however, we need to specify its `mode` argument as `"directed"` to indicate that the input is a directed network data set.

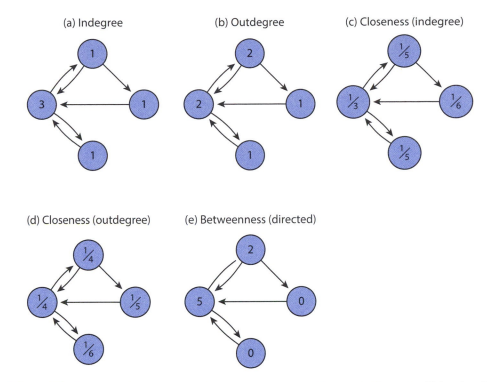

Figure 5.3. Degree, Closeness, and Betweenness in a Directed Network. This simple example of directed network data illustrates three alternative measures of centrality: degree, closeness, and betweenness.

```
twitter.adj <- graph.adjacency(twitter.adj, mode = "directed", diag = FALSE)
```

5.2.4 DIRECTED GRAPH AND CENTRALITY

We can define the three centrality measures discussed earlier for a directed network. We now have two types of *degree* measures. The sum of edges coming to a node (i.e., the number of times a politician's Twitter account is followed by another politician) is called *indegree*, whereas the sum of edges coming out of a node (i.e., the number of times a politician follows the Twitter account of another politician) is called *outdegree*. Figures 5.3a and 5.3b illustrate the two degree measures using a simple directed network. The `degree()` function accepts an argument `mode` with three options, `"in"` for indegree, `"out"` for outdegree, and `"total"` (the default when `mode` is unspecified) for total degree, which is the sum of indegree and outdegree. We compute and store indegree and outdegree as additional variables in the `senator` data frame. By construction, the `twitter.adj` matrix has the same ordering of senators as the `senator` data frame. As a result, one can insert the output of the `degree()` function without sorting them.

```
senator$indegree <- degree(twitter.adj, mode = "in")
senator$outdegree <- degree(twitter.adj, mode = "out")
```

Next, we extract the cases with the 3 greatest values of indegree and outdegree. To do this, we use the `order()` function, which returns the ordering index vector. Like the `sort()` function, the `order()` function allows one to sort in decreasing or increasing order by specifying the `decreasing` argument as `TRUE` or `FALSE`, respectively. The key difference is that the `order()` function returns the ordering index vector while the `sort()` function returns the ordered vector itself. This ordering index can then be used to extract details about the cases of interest. Recall from section 3.7.2 that the `$` operator extracts an element from a list. Below, we identify the 3 politicians who have the greatest values of indegree and another set of 3 politicians who have the greatest values of outdegree.

```
in.order <- order(senator$indegree, decreasing = TRUE)
out.order <- order(senator$outdegree, decreasing = TRUE)
## 3 greatest indegree
senator[in.order[1:3], ]

##           screen_name                name party state indegree
## 68      SenPatRoberts        Pat Roberts     R    KS         63
## 8   SenJohnBarrasso     John Barrasso       R    WY         60
## 75        SenStabenow Debbie Stabenow       D    MI         58
##      outdegree
## 68          68
## 8           87
## 75          43

## 3 greatest outdegree
senator[out.order[1:3], ]

##           screen_name                name party state indegree
## 57      lisamurkowski Lisa Murkowski        R    AK         55
## 8   SenJohnBarrasso   John Barrasso         R    WY         60
## 43      SenatorIsakson Johnny Isakson       R    GA         22
##      outdegree
## 57          88
## 8           87
## 43          87
```

The other two measures of centrality introduced above, *closeness* and *betweenness*, can be defined for directed network data as well. There are three ways to define a path from one node to another. We can ignore directionality as in the case of undirected networks or incorporate it in one of two ways: traveling along an outgoing path in its direction, or traveling along an incoming path against its direction. Closeness for incoming paths corresponds to indegree, while closeness for outgoing paths corresponds to outdegree. Figures 5.3c and 5.3d illustrate the closeness measures based on incoming and outgoing paths, respectively.

To compute closeness in R, therefore, the `closeness()` function has the `mode` argument, which can take either `"in"` (incoming path), `"out"` (outgoing path), or `"total"` (ignore directionality). Betweenness, however, sees only two options (`direct = TRUE` or `FALSE`), because the distinction between incoming and outgoing paths does not make sense from the perspective of a node in the path between two other nodes (see figure 5.3e). In particular, the `betweenness()` function takes a logical value for the `directed` argument, indicating whether to consider directionality. Below, we first graphically compare two closeness measures (incoming versus outgoing path) and then compare directed betweenness against undirected betweenness using another plot. Before making these plots, we set the parameters for colors and symbols based on party. Specifically, we use blue triangles for Democrats, red circles for Republicans, and black crosses for Independents.

```r
n <- nrow(senator)
## color: Democrats = blue, Republicans = red, Independent = black
col <- rep("red", n)
col[senator$party == "D"] <- "blue"
col[senator$party == "I"] <- "black"
## pch: Democrats = triangle, Republicans = circle, Independent = cross
pch <- rep(16, n)
pch[senator$party == "D"] <- 17
pch[senator$party == "I"] <- 4
```

Using these color and symbol parameters, we are now ready to make the plots.

```r
## plot for comparing two closeness measures (incoming vs. outgoing)
plot(closeness(twitter.adj, mode = "in"),
     closeness(twitter.adj, mode = "out"), pch = pch,  col = col,
    main = "Closeness", xlab = "Incoming path", ylab = "Outgoing path")
## plot for comparing directed and undirected betweenness
plot(betweenness(twitter.adj, directed = TRUE),
     betweenness(twitter.adj, directed = FALSE), pch = pch, col = col,
    main = "Betweenness", xlab = "Directed", ylab = "Undirected")
```

The plots below use solid gray circles for Republicans instead of red gray circles. See page C4 for the full-color version.

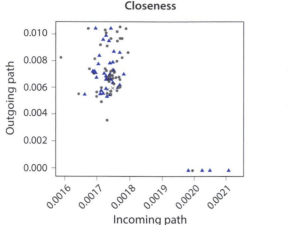

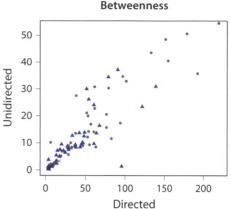

There is little association between the two closeness measures based on incoming and outgoing paths. This suggests that in this Twitter network, a senator's closeness to other senators in terms of being followed by them has little relationship to closeness based on the same senator following them. Interestingly, however, the betweenness measure is quite similar, regardless of whether one incorporates directionality. The two betweenness measures suggest that several Republican senators are well connected and central to the network (see the upper-right corner of the right-hand plot).

As a final alternative measure of centrality, we introduce *PageRank*. PageRank was developed by the cofounders of *Google*, Sergey Brin and Larry Page, to optimize the ranking of websites for their search engine outcomes. PageRank is computed using an iterative algorithm. In section 3.7, we saw *k*-means clustering as an example of an iterative algorithm. PageRank is based on the idea that nodes with a greater number of incoming edges are more important. Intuitively, we can think of incoming edges as votes of support. In the Twitter example, those senators who have a large number of followers are seen as more important. Furthermore, if a node has an incoming edge from another node with a large number of incoming edges, it results in a greater value of PageRank than if it has an incoming edge from a node with fewer incoming edges. In other words, if the Twitter account of a politician is followed by another politician whose account has many followers, they receive a larger PageRank than they would if followed by a politician with fewer followers. Finally, we note that the sum of PageRank values across all nodes equals 1.

The algorithm begins by assigning a set of initial PageRank values to all nodes. At each iteration, the PageRank value for node j will be updated using

$$\text{PageRank}_j = \frac{1-d}{n} + d \times \sum_{i=1}^{n} \underbrace{\frac{A_{ij} \times \text{PageRank}_i}{\text{outdegree}_i}}_{\text{"vote" from node } i \text{ to node } j} . \qquad (5.2)$$

In this equation, A_{ij} is the (i, j)th element of the adjacency matrix indicating whether or not an edge connects node i to node j, d is a constant to be specified (typically set to 0.85), and n is the number of nodes. The equation shows that the PageRank for a given node j equals the sum of "votes" from other nodes that have an incoming edge into node j. If there is no edge from node i to node j, then $A_{ij} = 0$, and therefore no vote is given to node j from node i. However, if $A_{ij} = 1$, then a vote from node i to node j is equal to the PageRank value of node i divided by node i's outdegree. This means that each node must equally allocate its PageRank value across all other nodes to which it has outgoing edges. For example, if a node has a PageRank value of 0.1 and has two outgoing edges, then each receiver obtains 0.05 from this node. This iterative algorithm stops when the PageRank values for all nodes no longer change.

> There are several **centrality measures** for **directed networks**, including indegree and outdegree, closeness (based on incoming edges, outgoing edges, or both), and betweenness (with or without directionality). **PageRank** is an iterative algorithm that produces a centrality measure where each node equally allocates its "votes" to other connected nodes.

In R, we can compute PageRank by the page.rank() function. The function can also be applied to an undirected network by setting the directed argument to FALSE (the default value is TRUE). The output object is a list that includes a numeric vector of PageRank, as an element called vector.

```
senator$pagerank <- page.rank(twitter.adj)$vector
```

Below, we visualize usage of the Twitter network among US senators by setting node size proportional to PageRank. The plot() function for adjacency matrices takes several arguments, including vertex.size (to adjust the size of each node), vertex.color (to adjust the color of each node), vertex.label (to specify the label of each node), edge.arrow.size (to adjust the size of each edge's arrow), and edge.width (to adjust the width of each edge). See ?igraph.plotting for more details.

```
## "col" parameter is defined earlier
plot(twitter.adj, vertex.size = senator$pagerank * 1000,
     vertex.color = col, vertex.label = NA,
     edge.arrow.size = 0.1, edge.width = 0.5)
```

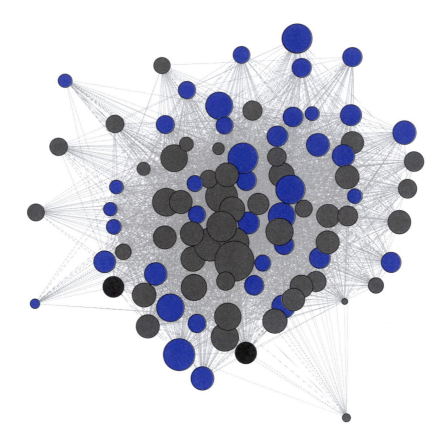

The plot above uses solid gray circles for Republicans instead of red gray circles. See page C5 for the full-color version. The plot shows that this Twitter network is quite dense with many edges connecting senators. While Republican senators appear to have slightly greater PageRank values than Democrats, the partisan difference is minor.

To better understand the algorithm, we consider a function that updates the PageRank at each iteration according to equation (5.2). Let n be the number of nodes in a graph, A be an $n \times n$ adjacency matrix, d be a constant, and pr be a vector of PageRank values from the previous iteration. Then, this function can be defined as follows.

```r
PageRank <- function(n, A, d, pr) { # function takes 4 inputs
    deg <- degree(A, mode = "out") # outdegree calculation
    for (j in 1:n) {
        pr[j] <- (1 - d) / n +  d * sum(A[ ,j] * pr / deg)
    }
    return(pr)
}
```

We will apply this function to the simple network used in figure 5.3. We will use the while() loop so that the algorithm stops when the differences in PageRank

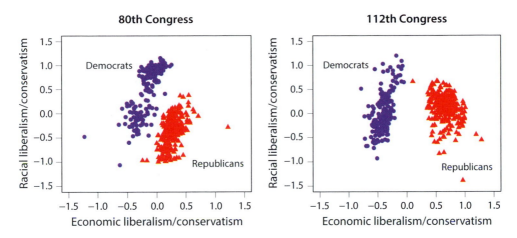

The full-color version of the plots on page 99 in section 3.6.1.

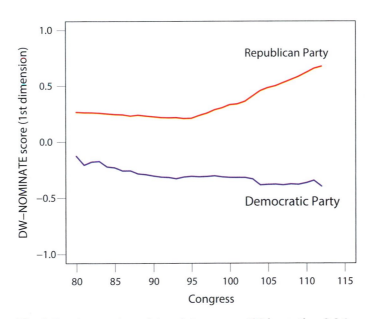

The full-color version of the plot on page 100 in section 3.6.1.

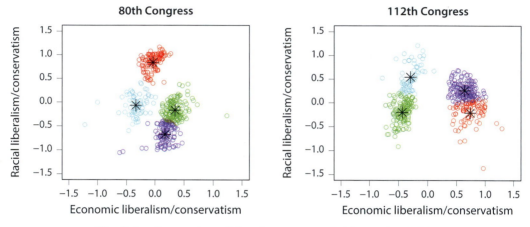

The full-color version of the plots on page 114 in section 3.7.3.

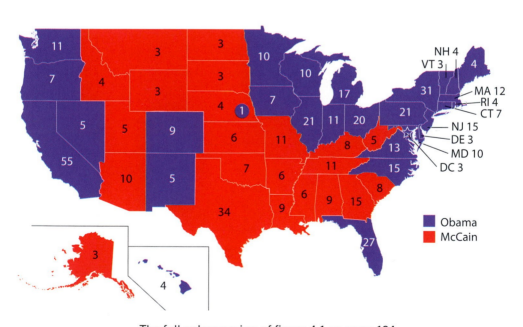

The full-color version of figure 4.1 on page 124.

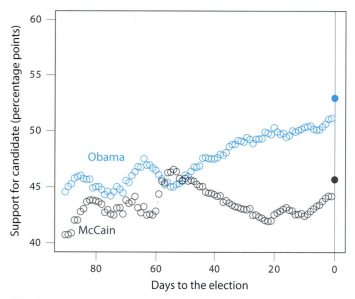

The full-color version of the plot on page 138 in section 4.1.3.

Facial competence and vote share

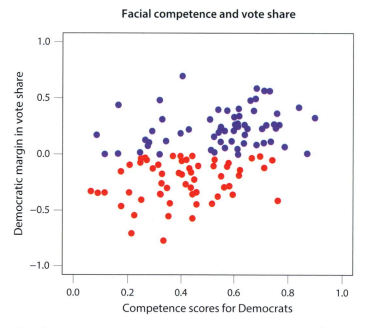

The full-color version of the plot on page 141 in section 4.2.1.

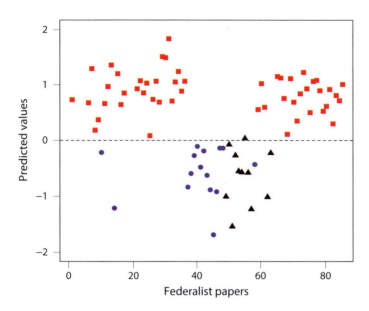

The full-color version of the plot on page 205 in section 5.1.5.

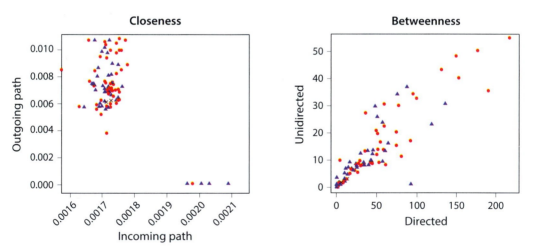

The full-color version of the plots on page 216 in section 5.2.4.

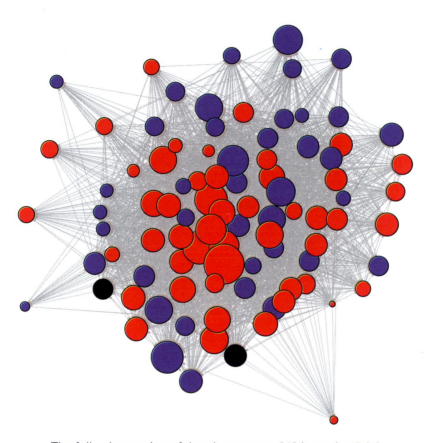

The full-color version of the plot on page 218 in section 5.2.2.

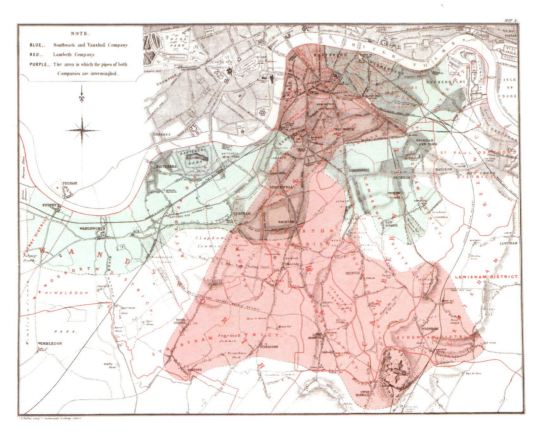

The full-color version of figure 5.5 on page 222.

The full-color version of the maps on page 229 in section 5.3.4.

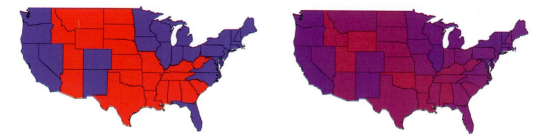

The full-color version of the maps on page 230 in section 5.3.4.

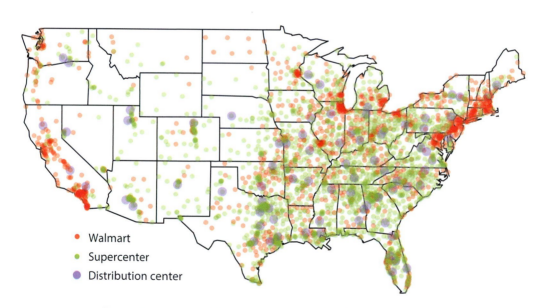

- ● Walmart
- ● Supercenter
- ● Distribution center

The full-color version of the map on page 232 in section 5.3.4

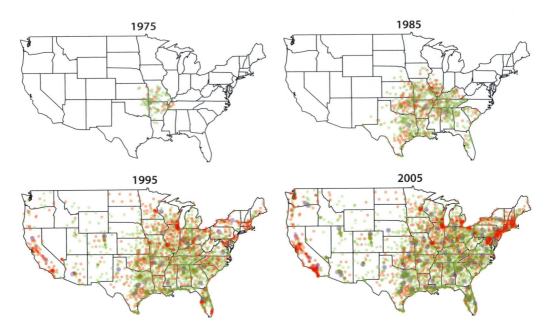

The full-color version of the maps on page 234 in section 5.3.6.

values between two successive iterations become negligible. The `while` loop takes the syntax

```
while (condition) {

    LOOP CONTENTS HERE

}
```

where the loop contents will be executed repeatedly so long as the conditional statement, `condition`, is evaluated to be TRUE. In our application, we will compute the maximum absolute difference in **PageRank** values between two successive iterations and stop the algorithm when this becomes less than a prespecified threshold. To test this script, we first construct an adjacency matrix with arbitrary values.

```
nodes <- 4
## adjacency matrix with arbitrary values
adj <- matrix(c(0, 1, 0, 1, 1, 0, 1, 0, 0, 1, 0, 0, 0, 1, 0, 0),
              ncol = nodes, nrow = nodes, byrow = TRUE)
adj

##      [,1] [,2] [,3] [,4]
## [1,]    0    1    0    1
## [2,]    1    0    1    0
## [3,]    0    1    0    0
## [4,]    0    1    0    0

adj <- graph.adjacency(adj)  # turn it into an igraph object
```

To implement the **PageRank** algorithm, we set the starting values and specify the constant d in the algorithm (we choose 0.85). We then use the `while()` loop to iteratively run the algorithm until a convergence criterion is satisfied. For the convergence criterion, we use 0.001 as the threshold for the maximal absolute difference in the **PageRank** values between two successive iterations. We use equal **PageRank** values across nodes as their starting values.

```
d <- 0.85  # typical choice of constant
pr <- rep(1 / nodes, nodes) # starting values
## maximum absolute difference; use a value greater than threshold
diff <- 100
## while loop with 0.001 being the threshold
while (diff > 0.001) {
    pr.pre <- pr # save the previous iteration
    pr <- PageRank(n = nodes, A = adj, d = d, pr = pr)
    diff <- max(abs(pr - pr.pre))
}
```

```
pr
## [1] 0.2213090 0.4316623 0.2209565 0.1315563
```

The result shows that the second observation has the highest PageRank value. This makes sense because, as shown in the adjacency matrix, this observation has the greatest number of incoming edges, represented by the second column.

5.3 Spatial Data

In addition to texts and networks, we introduce another type of data, *spatial data*. Spatial data are best analyzed by visualization through *maps*. This chapter covers two types of spatial data. One is *spatial point data*, which can be plotted as a set of points on a map. The other is *spatial polygon data*, which represent a sequence of connected points on a map corresponding to the boundaries of certain areas such as counties, districts, and provinces. We also consider *spatial–temporal data*, which are a set of spatial point or polygon data recorded over time, revealing changes in spatial patterns over time.

5.3.1   THE 1854 CHOLERA OUTBREAK IN LONDON

In his book, *Mode of Communication of Cholera*, a British physician John Snow demonstrated the effective use of maps for visualizing the spatial distribution of fatal cholera cases. Snow collected the spatial point data about fatal cases in the Soho neighborhood of London during the 1854 outbreak and plotted this information on a map. Figure 5.4 reproduces the original map. Black rectangle areas indicate fatal cholera cases, which were found to cluster around the Broad Street water pump located at the center of the map. All water pumps are also indicated by solid circles and labeled as such on the map.

From this map, Snow discovered that fatal cholera cases were clustered on and around Broad Street. He speculated that cholera was spread by sewage-contaminated water, a theory the authorities and the water company were reluctant to believe. After extensive research that included close inspection of water and interviews with local residents, Snow concluded that the water pump at the corner of Broad and Cambridge Streets was the source of the cholera outbreak. He concluded by writing,

> The result of the inquiry then was, that there had been no particular outbreak or increase of cholera, in this part of London, except among the persons who were in the habit of drinking the water of the above-mentioned pump-well. (p. 40)

Snow also employed a "grand natural experiment" to show that the water supply of the Southwark and Vauxhall Company was responsible for the spread of cholera in London. Figure 5.5 reproduces the spatial polygon map that Snow used to visualize the area of the *natural experiment*, meaning a situation in the world that resembles an experiment without intervention from researchers. The map shows that the Lambeth

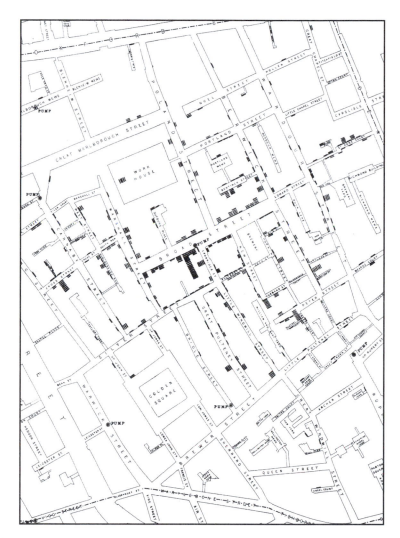

Figure 5.4. John Snow's Map of Fatal Cholera Cases in London. Black rectangle areas indicate fatal cholera cases, which were found to cluster around the Broad Street water pump. All water pumps are also indicated on the map. Original source: John Snow (1855) *Mode of Communication of Cholera*. London: John Churchill, New Burlington Street.

Company supplied cleaner water to the neighborhoods along the River Thames (indicated by the blue region), whereas the Southwark and Vauxhall Company provided contaminated water to the area further south (indicated by the red region). See page C6 for the full-color version. Snow argued that the overlapping area represented a natural experiment where two companies competed for customers: some people received their water supply from one company while their neighbors received water from the other company. Assuming that the two groups of customers were alike in all other respects, any difference in their cholera rates resulted from the choice of company.

After much research, Snow concluded that probably no *confounder* affected this *natural experiment*. Based on the discussion in section 2.5.2, confounding factors

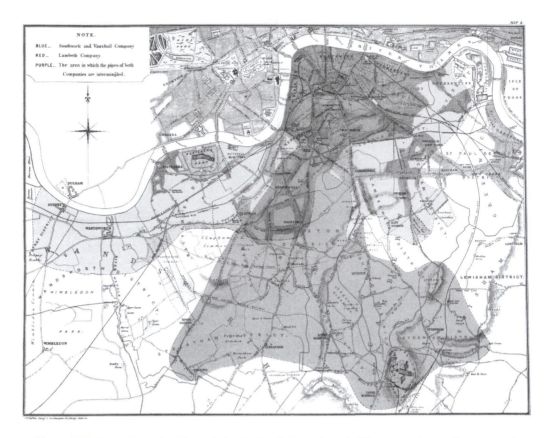

Figure 5.5. John Snow's Map of the Natural Experiment. The map shows the area of the natural experiment where two water companies (the Lambeth Company and the Southwark and Vauxhall Company) compete for customers. This area is represented by the overlap of blue (Lambeth) and red (Southwark and Vauxhall) regions as shown in the full-color version of this figure on page C6.

in this context refer to the variables associated with water companies and cholera outbreak rates of a neighborhood. He describes this experiment succinctly as follows:

> The mixing of the supply is of the most intimate kind. The pipes of each Company go down all the streets, and into nearly all the courts and alleys. A few houses are supplied by one Company and a few by the other, according to the decision of the owner or occupier at that time when the Water Companies were in active competition. In many cases a single house has a supply different from that on either side. Each Company supplies both rich and poor, both large houses and small; there is no difference either in the condition or occupation of the persons receiving the water of the different Companies. . . .
>
> The experiment, too, was on the grandest scale. No fewer than three hundred thousand people of both sexes, of every age and occupation, and of every rank and station, from gentlefolks down to the very poor, were divided into two groups without their choice, and, in most cases, without their knowledge; one

group being supplied with water containing the sewage of London, and amongst it, whatever might have come from the cholera patients, the other group having water quite free from such impurity. (pp. 74–75)

By matching the addresses of persons dying of cholera with the companies that supplied them water, Snow was able to show that the overwhelming majority of deaths had occurred in the households with water supplied by the Southwark and Vauxhall Company.

Snow's book illustrates the power of spatial data analysis. In particular, the visualization of spatial data through maps enables researchers to discover previously unknown patterns and present their findings in a convincing manner.

5.3.2 SPATIAL DATA IN R

In chapter 4, we analyzed the 2008 US presidential election. Figure 4.1 presents a map of the Electoral College, efficiently visualizing the outcome of the election. This is an example of *spatial polygon data*, where each state represents a polygon whose boundaries can be constructed by connecting a series of points. We can then color each polygon or state blue (red) if Barack Obama (John McCain) won the plurality of votes within that state.

In R, the **maps** package provides various mapping tools as well as many spatial databases. The package contains a spatial database of various cities in the world. For example, it includes a data frame of US cities called us.cities. Any built-in data frame can be loaded by using the data() function. Below, we show the first few observations of this data set, which contains the name (as the name variable), state (country.etc), population (pop), latitude (lat), longitude (long), and whether the city is the capital of the country (capital = 1), the capital of a state (capital = 2), or neither (capital = 0).

```
library(maps)

data(us.cities)
head(us.cities)

##          name country.etc    pop   lat    long capital
## 1 Abilene TX           TX 113888 32.45  -99.74       0
## 2   Akron OH           OH 206634 41.08  -81.52       0
## 3 Alameda CA           CA  70069 37.77 -122.26       0
## 4  Albany GA           GA  75510 31.58  -84.18       0
## 5  Albany NY           NY  93576 42.67  -73.80       2
## 6  Albany OR           OR  45535 44.62 -123.09       0
```

Now we can add state capitals to the map of the United States. We can use the map() function to access one spatial database and visualize the data therein. For example, in order to plot the United States, we set the database argument to "usa". Spatial points can be easily added to maps using the points() function with their longitude and latitude information as the inputs for the x and y coordinates, respectively. Each state capital is represented by a solid circle whose size is proportional to its population. We can add a title by using the `title()` function after a map is drawn.

```
map(database = "usa")
capitals <- subset(us.cities, capital == 2) # subset state capitals
## add points proportional to population using latitude and longitude
points(x = capitals$long, y = capitals$lat, col = "blue",
       cex = capitals$pop / 500000, pch = 19)
title("US state capitals") # add a title
```

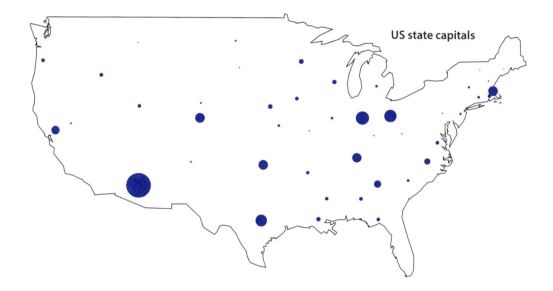

As another example, we plot the state of California. We use the `"state"` database, which contains the spatial polygon data about US states, and specify the `regions` argument to `"California"`.

```
map(database = "state", regions = "California")
```

We will add to a map of California the seven cities that have the largest populations. To extract these cities from the data, we use the `order()` function as before (see section 5.2.4).

```
cal.cities <- subset(us.cities, subset = (country.etc == "CA"))
sind <- order(cal.cities$pop, decreasing = TRUE) # order by population
top7 <- sind[1:7] # seven cities with largest population
```

We now add these cities to the map using the `points()` function, as well as their city names using the `text()` function.

```
map(database = "state", regions = "California")
points(x = cal.cities$long[top7], y = cal.cities$lat[top7], pch = 19)
## add a constant to longitude to avoid overlapping with circles
text(x = cal.cities$long[top7] + 2.25, y = cal.cities$lat[top7],
     label = cal.cities$name[top7])
title("Largest cities of California")
```

Largest cities of California

It is instructive to consider what the spatial polygon data look like in R. To do this, we can set the `plot` argument of the `map()` function to `FALSE` to suppress the plotting. Then, the function will return a list object with a sequence of coordinates saved as x (x-coordinate or *longitude*) and y (y-coordinate or *latitude*). Within the list, NA separates different polygons whose names are stored as names. We use the US map to illustrate this.

```
usa <- map(database = "usa", plot = FALSE) # save map
names(usa)   # list elements

## [1] "x"      "y"       "range" "names"
```

Now, we can check the number of coordinates used to create the US map by computing the length of vector x. We also display the first few after combining the x- and y-coordinates into a matrix using the `cbind()` function.

```
length(usa$x)

## [1] 7252

head(cbind(usa$x, usa$y)) # first five coordinates of a polygon

##            [,1]      [,2]
## [1,] -101.4078 29.74224
## [2,] -101.3906 29.74224
## [3,] -101.3620 29.65056
## [4,] -101.3505 29.63911
## [5,] -101.3219 29.63338
## [6,] -101.3047 29.64484
```

We observe that the map of the United States consists of 7252 pairs of coordinates. The map() function connects these points to construct maps.

> Spatial data contain information about patterns over space and can be visualized through maps. While **spatial point data** represent the locations of events as points on a map, **spatial polygon data** represent geographical areas by connecting points on a map.

5.3.3 COLORS IN R

We next learn how to color maps. Color is important for visualization in general, not simply for maps. So far, we have been specifying colors using names like "red" or "blue". The only exception is section 3.7.3 where we used a set of integers that correspond to different colors through the palette() function. In fact, R knows the names of 657 different colors. To see them all, look at the output of the colors() function.

```
allcolors <- colors()
head(allcolors) # some colors

## [1] "white"         "aliceblue"     "antiquewhite"
## [4] "antiquewhite1" "antiquewhite2" "antiquewhite3"

length(allcolors) # number of color names

## [1] 657
```

However, R can produce many more colors than this. To refer to a color from the full range of possible colors, we can use the *hexadecimal color code*. *Hexadecimal* is a number system whose base is 16, with integers 0–9 and letters A–F representing values from 0 to 15. A hexadecimal color code is a sequence of six characters beginning with a hash sign (#). Each set of two digits represents the strength of the three primary colors—red, green, and blue, or *RGB*—with each taking a value from 0 to 255 (or one of 2^8 levels). For example, half-strength red and blue together yields purple. This can be represented as RGB = (127, 0, 127). Recognizing that 127 is equal to 7F in the base-16 numeral system, we arrive at the hexadecimal color code of #7F007F.

In R, the `rgb()` function helps create hexadecimal color codes from numerical values. The three arguments, `red`, `green`, and `blue`, take the intensity of each color, ranging from 0 to 1, which gets translated into an integer value from 0 to 255 and then represented as a hexadecimal numeral. In addition, we can create more than one color code from `rgb()` at a time. The arguments can take vectors of length longer than 1. Below are some examples of hexadecimal color code. There are also many online sources that help us find the hexadecimal representation of a color. We start with primary colors.

```r
red <- rgb(red = 1, green = 0, blue = 0) # red
green <- rgb(red = 0, green = 1, blue = 0) # green
blue <- rgb(red = 0, green = 0, blue = 1) # blue
c(red, green, blue) # results

## [1] "#FF0000" "#00FF00" "#0000FF"
```

Black and white can be represented by 0% or 100% for each primary color, respectively.

```r
black <- rgb(red = 0, green = 0, blue = 0) # black
white <- rgb(red = 1, green = 1, blue = 1) # white
c(black, white) # results

## [1] "#000000" "#FFFFFF"
```

Finally, we can create purple (50% red and 50% blue) and yellow (100% red and 100% green). The `rgb()` function can take a vector of inputs, as illustrated in this example.

```r
rgb(red = c(0.5, 1), green = c(0, 1), blue = c(0.5, 0))

## [1] "#800080" "#FFFF00"
```

Another advantage of using hexadecimal color codes is that we can make the colors (partly) transparent by adding two additional digits, from 00 to FF, to the end of a hexadecimal color code. This enables us to control the level of transparency. Again, it is easier to think about the intensity scale from 0 to 1 and use the `rgb()` function to transform it to a hexadecimal color code. The function takes a fourth argument `alpha`, which can be used for this purpose. An example is given here.

```
## semitransparent blue
blue.trans <- rgb(red = 0, green = 0, blue = 1, alpha = 0.5)
## semitransparent black
black.trans <- rgb(red = 0, green = 0, blue = 0, alpha = 0.5)
```

Once we know the hexadecimal colors, we can use them (as a character object) in our plots in the same way that we have been using named colors like `"red"` and `"blue"`. In the following plot, semitransparent circles can be easily distinguished even when they overlap, whereas it is harder to distinguish between nontransparent circles. Note that in this plot we suppress the default axis labels in order to avoid distraction by setting the `ann` argument to `FALSE` in the `plot()` function.

```
## completely colored dots; difficult to distinguish
plot(x = c(1, 1), y = c(1, 1.2), xlim = c(0.5, 4.5), ylim = c(0.5, 4.5),
     pch = 16, cex = 5, ann = FALSE, col = black)
points(x = c(3, 3), y = c(3, 3.2), pch = 16, cex = 5, col = blue)
## semitransparent; easy to distinguish
points(x = c(2, 2), y = c(2, 2.2), pch = 16, cex = 5, col = black.trans)
points(x = c(4, 4), y = c(4, 4.2), pch = 16, cex = 5, col = blue.trans)
```

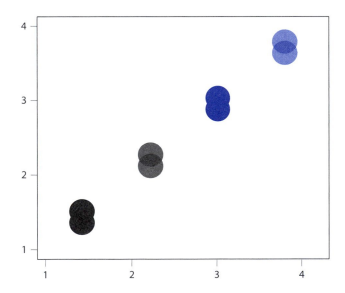

5.3.4 US PRESIDENTIAL ELECTIONS

Now that we understand how color is represented in R, we can color maps. Here, we color the map of the United States using the 2008 presidential election results. The election data were introduced in chapter 4. The names and description of variables in the data file `pres08.csv` are given in table 4.1.

We will color each state in two ways. First, we use blue for the states won by Obama and red for the states won by McCain. This will produce a map just like figure 4.1 with "blue and red states." Second, we exploit the fact that various shades of purple can be produced as a mixture of blue and red in the RGB color scheme. Specifically, we compute the two-party vote share and set the intensity of blue as the Democratic two-party vote share and that of red as the Republican two-party vote share. In this way, the color of a state reflects the degree of support for Democratic and Republican candidates. The following code chunk loads the data set, computes the two-party vote shares, and sets the RGB color scheme for California based on its two-party vote share.

```
pres08 <- read.csv("pres08.csv")
## two-party vote share
pres08$Dem <- pres08$Obama / (pres08$Obama + pres08$McCain)
pres08$Rep <- pres08$McCain / (pres08$Obama + pres08$McCain)
## color for California
cal.color <- rgb(red = pres08$Rep[pres08$state == "CA"],
                 blue = pres08$Dem[pres08$state == "CA"],
                 green = 0)
```

We now color the map of California in two ways. First, we color it as a blue state because Obama won California in 2008. Second, we color it using the RGB color scheme based on the two-party vote share. To add color to a map, we must specify the `col` argument. In addition, we set the `fill` argument to `TRUE` in order to fill each state with the specified color.

```
## California as a blue state
map(database = "state", regions = "California", col = "blue",
    fill = TRUE)
## California as a purple state
map(database = "state", regions = "California", col = cal.color,
    fill = TRUE)
```

The right plot below uses gray instead of purple. See page C6 for the full-color version.

We will repeat this for all states using a loop. The map does not include Hawaii, Alaska, and Washington DC, so we will skip those states. Note that we will set the `add` argument to `TRUE` in order to add a color to each state. A loop is used because we color one state at a time. We first use a dichotomized color scheme where the states Obama won appear blue and those won by McCain are shown as red. In the second map, we use the RGB color scheme based on the two-party vote share for each state. The code chunks used for these two maps are almost identical. The only difference is the way in which color is chosen for each state.

```r
## USA as red and blue states
map(database = "state") # create a map
for (i in 1:nrow(pres08)) {
    if ((pres08$state[i] != "HI") & (pres08$state[i] != "AK") &
        (pres08$state[i] != "DC")) {
        map(database = "state", regions = pres08$state.name[i],
            col = ifelse(pres08$Rep[i] > pres08$Dem[i], "red", "blue"),
            fill = TRUE, add = TRUE)
    }
}
## USA as purple states
map(database = "state") # create a map
for (i in 1:nrow(pres08)) {
    if ((pres08$state[i] != "HI") & (pres08$state[i] != "AK") &
        (pres08$state[i] != "DC")) {
        map(database = "state", regions = pres08$state.name[i],
            col = rgb(red = pres08$Rep[i], blue = pres08$Dem[i],
                green = 0), fill = TRUE, add = TRUE)
    }
}
```

The maps below use gray scale. See page C7 for the full-color version.

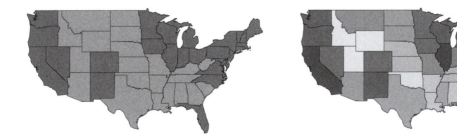

The left-hand map shows that Obama won many states on the West and East Coasts whereas McCain was particularly strong in the Midwest. However, the right-hand map illustrates that no state is completely dominated by either Democrats or Republicans. Each state has both types of voters, and it is the winner-take-all electoral system that is responsible for characterizing each state as either a blue or a red state.

Table 5.5. Walmart Store Opening Data.

Variable	Description
opendate	opening date for the store
st.address	street address of the store
city	city of the store
state	state of the store
type	store type (Wal-MartStore, SuperCenter, DistributionCenter)
long	longitude of the store
lat	latitude of the store

Note: The data set contains spatial and temporal information about Walmart store openings from the first opening on March 1, 1962 until August 1, 2006.

5.3.5 EXPANSION OF WALMART

Shifting from politics to business, we next examine the expansion of Walmart, a successful American multinational chain of retail discount department and warehouse stores.[9] Walmart opened its first store in 1962 in Bentonville, Arkansas. Over the next several decades, it opened many stores within the United States and then around the world. Walmart has become one of the largest retail multinational companies in the world. Table 5.5 shows the names and descriptions of variables in the Walmart store opening data, `walmart.csv`. This data set contains spatial and temporal information about Walmart store openings, from the first opening on March 1, 1962 until August 1, 2006.

We begin by plotting all of the store locations on a map. The data set contains three different types of stores, represented by the variable `type`. `Wal-MartStore` represents a standard Walmart store, whereas `SuperCenter` is a standard Walmart store as well as a full supermarket. Walmart Supercenters often include pharmacies, garden shops, car service centers, and other specialty centers. We also plot `DistributionCenter` data, representing stores that distribute food and goods to standard Walmart stores and Supercenters. To distinguish the three types of stores, we use different colors—red for standard Walmart stores, green for Supercenters, and blue for Distribution Centers. We make the colors transparent so that circles representing different stores can overlap with each other. Distribution Centers, which are fewer than the other two types, will be represented by larger circles so that they stand out. The following code chunk defines these parameters.

```
walmart <- read.csv("walmart.csv")
## red = Wal-MartStore, green = SuperCenter, blue = DistributionCenter
walmart$storecolors <- NA # create an empty vector
walmart$storecolors[walmart$type == "Wal-MartStore"] <-
    rgb(red = 1, green = 0, blue = 0, alpha = 1/3)
```

---

[9] This section is in part based on Thomas J. Holmes (2011) "The diffusion of Wal-Mart and economies of density." *Econometrica*, vol. 79, no. 1, pp. 253–302.

```
walmart$storecolors[walmart$type == "SuperCenter"] <-
    rgb(red = 0, green = 1, blue = 0, alpha = 1/3)
walmart$storecolors[walmart$type == "DistributionCenter"] <-
    rgb(red = 0, green = 0, blue = 1, alpha = 1/3)
## larger circles for DistributionCenter
walmart$storesize <- ifelse(walmart$type == "DistributionCenter", 1, 0.5)
```

Finally, we create a map and add Walmart store locations to it. We also include a legend using the `legend()` function. To use this function, we specify the location of the legend by setting the `x` and `y` coordinates and provide a vector of legend texts as the `legend` argument. A box encloses the legend by default when the `bty` argument is left unspecified, whereas setting the argument to `"n"` eliminates the box. As before, the `pch` argument can be used to specify types of objects to plot. We choose solid circles whose size can be controlled by the `pt.cex` argument.

```
## map with legend
map(database = "state")
points(walmart$long, walmart$lat, col = walmart$storecolors,
       pch = 19, cex = walmart$storesize)
legend(x = -120, y = 32, bty = "n",
       legend = c("Walmart", "Supercenter", "Distribution center"),
       col = c("red", "green", "blue"), pch = 19, # solid circles
       pt.cex = c(0.5, 0.5, 1)) # size of circles
```

The map below uses dark and light gray circles in place of red and green circles. See page C7 for the full-color version.

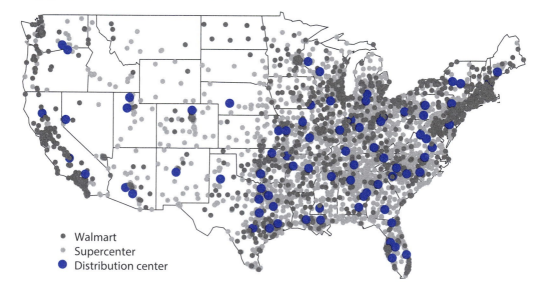

The map clearly shows the business strategy of Walmart. While Supercenters are widespread throughout the Midwest and South, they appear less prevalent in the Northeast and the West Coast, as well as in urban centers more generally. In these areas, Walmart has chosen not to expand past the standard discount store format.

5.3.6 ANIMATION IN R

The previous analysis of Walmart store openings ignored the temporal dimension even though the data set contains the opening date. By examining the spatial–temporal patterns rather than spatial patterns alone, we can better understand how Walmart expanded its stores over time. What visualization strategy should we employ to achieve this goal? We can create a series of maps over time, showing all stores at various points in time.

To do this, it is useful to define a function (see section 1.3.4) that subsets the data given a specified date, and then creates a map of Walmart stores like the one shown above. All we need to do is to include our previous code chunk in a function. Below, we create this function, called `walmart.map()`. The function takes two inputs. The first argument `data` takes a data frame, which should have a variable called `opendate` representing the opening date of the store. This variable should belong to the `Date` class. The second argument `date` takes another `Date` object defining the point in time for which the map should be created. The function subsets all the stores that opened on or before the specified date and then plots their locations on a map.

```
walmart.map <- function(data, date) {
    walmart <- subset(data, subset = (opendate <= date))
    map(database = "state")
    points(walmart$long, walmart$lat, col = walmart$storecolors,
           pch = 19, cex = walmart$storesize)
}
```

Using this function, it is straightforward to create a map at any given point of time. We create a map for every ten years.

```
walmart$opendate <- as.Date(walmart$opendate)
walmart.map(walmart, as.Date("1974-12-31"))
title("1975")
walmart.map(walmart, as.Date("1984-12-31"))
title("1985")
walmart.map(walmart, as.Date("1994-12-31"))
title("1995")
walmart.map(walmart, as.Date("2004-12-31"))
title("2005")
```

The following maps use dark and light gray circles in place of red and green circles. See page C8 for the full-color version.

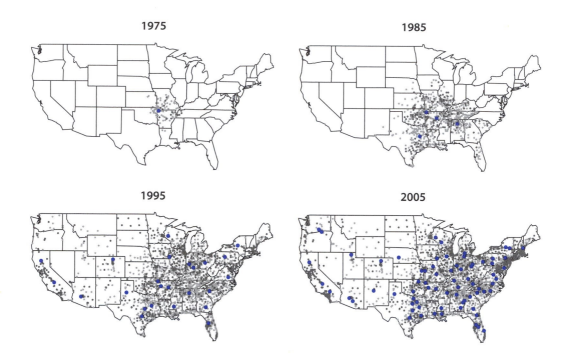

Another method for visualizing spatial–temporal data like the above is *animation*, which dynamically shows how geographical patterns change over time. The **animation** package can show how Walmart has opened its stores at various locations at different times. We first set the number of maps to be animated and then create a vector of equally spaced dates from the beginning to the end of the data set.

```
n <- 25 # number of maps to animate
dates <- seq(from = min(walmart$opendate),
             to = max(walmart$opendate), length.out = n)
```

We are now ready to animate. At its core, using the **animation** package involves little more than writing a loop to create a series of maps over time. In fact, we need just one extra function, saveHTML(), to wrap the loop. The function takes the R code chunk as the main input, enclosed in curly braces { }, and then inserts all plots that are created with the loop into an HTML file. The resulting HTML file can display the animation in a web browser. Useful arguments of the saveHTML() function include htmlfile for the HTML filename, title for the title of the animation, outdir for the name of the directory where the resulting files will be saved, and autobrowse indicating whether or not the output will be automatically displayed on a browser. In addition to HTML, available formats include saveLatex() for LaTeX files and saveVideo() for video files.

The following code chunk creates an animation and saves the HTML file named walmart.html and all other files to the working directory. Note that the saveHTML() function repeatedly calls the walmart.map() function we created earlier through a loop. The getwd() function returns the path to the working directory, and specifying this function as the `outdir` input will save all output files in that directory.

```
library("animation")
saveHTML({
    for (i in 1:length(dates)) {
        walmart.map(walmart, dates[i])
        title(dates[i])
    }
}, title = "Expansion of Walmart", htmlfile = "walmart.html",
        outdir = getwd(), autobrowse = FALSE)
```

We can play the animation by opening a web browser and clicking `File > Open file...` in the menu. While watching, we see quite clearly the Midwestern origins of the Walmart franchise and its gradual spread throughout the region in the 1970s and 1980s. Particularly striking is the speed of the mid-1990s expansion throughout the rest of the country, as well as when and where new Distribution Centers are established in anticipation of regional expansion.

5.4 Summary

This chapter introduced types of data different from those we analyzed in the previous chapters. We focused on how to discover systematic patterns in a variety of data. We began by analyzing **textual data** under the **bag-of-words assumption** that ignores the sequence of words. By focusing on the frequency of different terms within and across documents, we can discover topics that underlie the corpus. We introduced **term frequency–inverse document frequency** as a statistic that measures the importance of each term in a particular document. Using *The Federalist Papers* as an example, we also showed how the frequency of words can predict the authorship of essays via a linear regression model. To assess prediction accuracy while avoiding overfitting, we used **cross validation** (and in particular a leave-one-out cross validation procedure).

The second type of data covered in this chapter was network data. We visualized both **directed** and **undirected network data** with **graphs**, where nodes (or vertices) represent units, and edges (or ties) between nodes represent the relationships between them. We showed how to compute various **centrality measures** in order to identify influential nodes within a given network. These measures include degree, closeness, and betweenness. We also introduced a popular iterative algorithm called **PageRank**, which forms the basis of the Google website ranking algorithm, as another way to measure centrality. These methods were illustrated through the classic example of the Florentine marriage network and a modern example of the Twitter-following network among politicians.

Finally, we considered **spatial** and **spatial–temporal data**. The spatial dimension splits into two types: spatial point and spatial polygon data. We showed how maps can visualize spatial patterns effectively using John Snow's famous study of a cholera outbreak in 19th century London. Snow utilized a natural experiment to uncover

Table 5.6. Constitution Preamble Data.

Variable	Description
country	country name with words separated by underscores
year	year the constitution was created
preamble	raw text of the preamble to the constitution

Note: The data set contains raw textual information about the preambles of constitutions around the world.

the primary cause of the outbreak. We also used maps to visualize the outcome of the US presidential election and the diffusion of Walmart stores over time. Like the analysis of texts and networks, visualization plays a central role in spatial data analysis. To investigate how spatial patterns change over time, we created an **animation** that sequentially displayed a series of maps. This visualization effectively demonstrated the expansion of Walmart stores in the United States over the last several decades.

5.5 Exercises

5.5.1 ANALYZING THE PREAMBLES OF CONSTITUTIONS

Some scholars argue that over the last few centuries, the US Constitution has emerged, either verbatim or paraphrased, in numerous founding documents across the globe.[10] Will this trend continue, and how might one even measure constitutional influence, anyway? One way is to see which constitutional rights (such as free speech) are shared across the founding documents of different countries, and observe how this commonality changes over time. An alternative approach, which we take in this exercise, is to examine textual similarity among constitutions. We focus on the preamble of each constitution, which typically states the guiding purpose and principles of the rest of the constitution. Table 5.6 presents the names and descriptions of the constitution preambles in `constitution.csv`.

1. First, let us visualize the data to better understand how constitutional documents differ. Start by importing the preamble data into a data frame, and then preprocess the text. Before preprocessing, use the `VectorSource()` function inside the `Corpus()` function. Create two data matrices for both the regular document-term frequency, and for the tf–idf weighted term frequency. In both cases, visualize the preamble to the US Constitution with a word cloud. How do the results differ between the two methods? Note that we must normalize the tf–idf weights by document size so that lengthy constitutions do not receive greater weights.

[10] This exercise is in part based on David S. Law and Mila Versteeg (2012) "The declining influence of the United States Constitution." *New York University Law Review*, vol. 87, no. 3, pp. 762–858 and Zachary Elkins, Tom Ginsburg, and James Melton (2012) "Comments on law and Versteeg's the declining influence of the United States Constitution." *New York University Law Review*, vol. 87, no. 6, pp. 2088–2101.

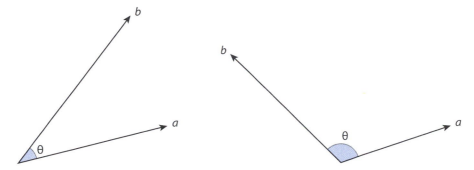

Figure 5.6. Cosine Similarity of Two Vectors. Two two-dimensional vectors a and b have a positive (negative) value of cosine similarity in the left (right) plot.

2. We next apply the k-means algorithm to the rows of the tf–idf matrix and identify clusters of similar constitution preambles. Set the number of clusters to 5 and describe the results. To make each row comparable, divide it by a constant such that each row represents a vector of unit length. Note that the length of a vector $a = (a_1, a_2, \ldots, a_n)$ is given by $||a|| = \sqrt{a_1^2 + a_2^2 + \cdots + a_n^2}$.

3. We will next see whether new foreign constitutions are more similar to the US Constitution preamble than the existing ones. In the document-term matrix, each document is represented as a vector of term frequencies. To compare two documents, we define *cosine similarity* as the cosine of the angle θ between the two corresponding n-dimensional vectors $a = (a_1, a_2, \ldots, a_n)$ and $b = (b_1, b_2, \ldots, b_n)$. Formally, the measure is defined as

$$\text{cosine similarity} = \cos\theta = \frac{a \cdot b}{||a|| \times ||b||} = \frac{\sum_{i=1}^{n} a_i b_i}{\sqrt{\sum_{i=1}^{n} a_i^2}\sqrt{\sum_{i=1}^{n} b_i^2}}.$$

The numerator represents the so-called *dot product* of a and b, while the denominator is the product of the lengths of the two vectors. The measure ranges from -1 (when the two vectors go in opposite directions) to 1 (when they completely overlap). As illustrated in figure 5.6, two vectors have a positive (negative) value of cosine similarity when they point in similar (different) directions. The measure is zero when they are perpendicular to each other.

Below is a function that takes a vector a, alongside a collection of vectors or a matrix b, and computes the cosine similarity between a and each row of b.

```
cosine <- function(a, b) {
    ## t() transposes a matrix ensuring that vector "a" is multiplied
    ## by each row of matrix "b"
    numer <- apply(a * t(b), 2, sum)
    denom <- sqrt(sum(a^2)) * sqrt(apply(b^2, 1, sum))
    return(numer / denom)
}
```

Table 5.7. International Trade Data.

Variable	Description
country1	country name of exporter
country2	country name of importer
year	year
exports	total value of exports (in tens of millions of dollars)

Note: The data are given for 1900, 1920, 1940, 1955, 1980, 2000, and 2009.

Apply this function to identify the 5 constitutions whose preambles most resemble that of the US Constitution.

4. We examine the influence of the US Constitution on other constitutions over time. We focus on the postwar period. Sort the constitutions chronologically and calculate, for every 10 years from 1960 until 2010, the average of cosine similarity between the US Constitution and the constitutions that were created during the previous decade. Plot the result. Each of these averages computed over time is called a *moving average*. Does similarity tend to increase, decrease, or remain the same over time? Comment on the pattern you observe.

5. We next construct directed, weighted network data based on the cosine similarity of constitutions. Specifically, create an adjacency matrix whose (i, j)th entry represents the cosine similarity between the ith and jth constitution preambles, where the ith constitution was created in the same year or after the jth constitution. This entry is zero if the ith constitution was created before the jth constitution. Apply the **PageRank** algorithm to this adjacency matrix. Briefly comment on the result.

5.5.2   INTERNATIONAL TRADE NETWORK

The size and structure of international trade flows vary significantly over time.[11] The volume of goods traded between countries has grown rapidly over the past century, as technological advances have lowered the cost of shipping and countries have adopted more liberal trade policies. At times, however, trade flows have decreased due to disruptive events such as major wars and the adoption of protectionist trade policies. In this exercise, we will explore some of these changes by examining the network of international trade over several time periods. The data file trade.csv contains the value of exports from one country to another in a given year. The names and descriptions of variables in this data set are given in table 5.7.

---

[11] This exercise is based in part on Luca De Benedictis and Lucia Tajoli (2011) "The world trade network." *The World Economy*, vol. 34, no. 8, pp. 1417–1454. The trade data are from Katherine Barbieri and Omar Keshk (2012) *Correlates of War Project Trade Data Set*, version 3.0. Available at http://correlatesofwar.org.

1. We begin by analyzing international trade as an unweighted, directed network. For every year in the data set, create an adjacency matrix whose entry (i, j) equals 1 if country i exports to country j. If this export is zero, then the entry equals 0. We assume that missing data, indicated by NA, represents zero trade. Plot the *network density*, which is defined over time as

$$\text{network density} = \frac{\text{number of edges}}{\text{number of potential edges}}.$$

   The `graph.density()` function can compute this measure given an adjacency matrix. Interpret the result.

2. For the years 1900, 1955, and 2009, compute the measures of centrality based on degree, betweenness, and closeness (based on total degree) for each year. For each year, list the 5 countries that have the largest values of each of these centrality measures. How do the countries on the lists change over time? Briefly comment on the results.

3. We now analyze the international trade network as a weighted, directed network in which each edge has a nonnegative weight proportional to its corresponding trade volume. Create an adjacency matrix for such network data. For the years 1900, 1955, and 2009, compute the centrality measures from above for the weighted trade network. Instead of degree, however, compute the *graph strength*, which in this case equals the sum of imports and exports with all adjacent nodes. The `graph.strength()` function can be used to compute this weighted version of degree. For betweenness and closeness, we use the same function as before, i.e., `closeness()` and `betweenness()`, which can handle weighted graphs appropriately. Do the results differ from those of the unweighted network? Examine the top 5 countries. Can you think of another way to calculate centrality in this network that accounts for the value of exports from each country? Briefly discuss.

4. Apply the PageRank algorithm to the weighted trade network, separately for each year. For each year, identify the 5 most influential countries according to this algorithm. In addition, examine how the ranking of PageRank values has changed over time for each of the following 5 countries—United States, United Kingdom, Russia, Japan, and China. Briefly comment on the patterns you observe.

5.5.3 MAPPING US PRESIDENTIAL ELECTION RESULTS OVER TIME

The partisan identities of many states have been stable over time. For example, Massachusetts is a solidly "blue" state, having pledged its electoral votes to the Democratic candidate in 8 out of the last 10 presidential elections. On the other extreme, Arizona's electoral votes went to the Republican candidate in 9 of the same 10 elections. Still, geography can occasionally be a poor predictor of presidential elections.

Table 5.8. County-Level US Presidential Election Data.

Variable	Description
state	full name of the 48 states (excluding Alaska, Hawaii, and the District of Columbia)
county	county name
year	election year
rep	popular votes for the Republican candidate
dem	popular votes for the Democratic candidate
other	popular votes for other candidates

For instance, in 2008, typically red states—including North Carolina, Indiana, and Virginia—helped elect Barack Obama to the presidency.

In this exercise, we will again map the US presidential election results for 48 states. However, our data will be more detailed in two respects. First, we will analyze data from 14 presidential elections from 1960 to 2012, allowing us to visualize how the geography of party choice has changed over time. Second, we will examine election results at the county level, allowing us to explore the spatial distribution of Democratic and Republican voters within states. The data file is available in CSV format as elections.csv. Each row of the data set represents the distribution of votes in that year's presidential election from each county in the United States. Table 5.8 presents the names and descriptions of variables in this data set.

1. We begin by visualizing the outcome of the 2008 US presidential election at the county level. Begin with Massachusetts and Arizona and visualize the county-level outcome by coloring counties based on the two-party vote share as done in section 5.3.4. The color should range from pure blue (100% Democratic) to pure red (100% Republican) using the RGB color scheme. Use the county database in the **maps** package. The regions argument of the map() function enables us to specify the state and county. The argument accepts a character vector, each entry of which has the syntax state, county. Provide a brief comment.

2. Next, using a loop, visualize the 2008 county-level election results across the United States as a whole. Briefly comment on what you observe.

3. We now examine how the geographical distribution of US presidential election results has changed over time at the county level. Starting with the 1960 presidential election, which saw Democratic candidate John F. Kennedy prevail over Republican candidate Richard Nixon, use animation to visualize the county-level election returns for each presidential election up to 2012. Base your code on what you programmed to answer the previous question.

4. In this exercise, we quantify the degree of partisan segregation for each state. We consider a state to be politically segregated if Democrats and Republicans tend

to live in different counties. A common way to quantify the degree of residential segregation is to use the *dissimilarity index* given by

$$\text{dissimilarity index} = \frac{1}{2}\sum_{i=1}^{N}\left|\frac{d_i}{D} - \frac{r_i}{R}\right|.$$

In the formula, d_i (r_i) is the number of Democratic (Republican) votes in the ith county and D (R) is the total number of Democratic (Republican) votes in the state. N represents the number of counties. This index measures the extent to which Democratic and Republican votes are evenly distributed within states. It can be interpreted as the percentage of one group that would need to move in order for its distribution to match that of the other group. Using data on Democratic and Republican votes from the 2008 presidential election, calculate the dissimilarity index for each state. Which states are among the most (least) segregated according to this measure? Visualize the result as a map. Briefly comment on what you observe.

5. Another way to compare political segregation across states is to assess whether counties within a state are highly unequal in terms of how many Democrats or Republicans they have. For example, a state would be considered segregated if it had many counties filled with Democrats and many with no Democrats at all. In chapter 3, we considered the Gini coefficient as a measure of inequality (see section 3.6.2). Calculate the Gini coefficient for each state based on the percentage of Democratic votes in each county. Give each county the same weight, disregarding its population size. Which states have the greatest (or lowest) value of the index? Visualize the result using a map. What is the correlation between the Gini index and the dissimilarity index you calculated above? How are the two measures conceptually and empirically different? Briefly comment on what you observe and explain the differences between the two indexes. To compute the Gini index, use the `ineq()` function in the **ineq** package by setting its argument `type` to `"Gini"`.

6. Lastly, we examine how the degree of political segregation has changed in each state over time. Use animation to visualize these changes. Briefly comment on the patterns you observe.

Chapter 6

Probability

Probability is the very guide of life.
— Cicero, *De Natura*

Until now, we have studied how to identify patterns in data. While some patterns are indisputably clear, in many cases we must figure out ways to distinguish systematic patterns from noise. Noise, also known as random error, is the irrelevant variation that occurs in every real-world data set. Quantifying the degree of statistical uncertainty of empirical findings is the topic for the *next* chapter, but this requires an understanding of probability. Probability is a set of mathematical tools that measure and model randomness in the world. As such, this chapter introduces the derivation of the fundamental rules of probability, with the use of mathematical notation. In the social sciences, we use probability to model the randomly determined nature of various real-world events, and even human behavior and beliefs. Randomness does not necessarily imply complete unpredictability. Rather, our task is to identify systematic patterns from noisy data.

6.1 Probability

We use *probability* as a measure of uncertainty. Probability is based on a set of three simple axioms, from which a countless number of useful theorems have been derived. In this section, we show how to define, interpret, and compute probability.

6.1.1 FREQUENTIST VERSUS BAYESIAN

In everyday life, we often hear statements such as "the probability of winning a coin toss is 50%" and "the probability of Obama winning the 2008 US presidential election is 80%." What do we mean by "probability"? There are at least two different interpretations. One interpretation, which is called the *frequentist* interpretation, states that probability represents the *limit* of relative frequency, defined as the ratio between the number of times the event occurs and the number of trials, in repeated trials under the same conditions. For example, the above statement about coin tosses can be interpreted as follows: if a coin toss is repeatedly conducted under the same conditions,

Figure 6.1. Reverend Thomas Bayes (1701–1761).

the fraction of times a coin lands on heads approaches 0.5 as the number of coin tosses increases. Here, the mathematical term, "limit," represents the value to which a sequence of relative frequencies converges as the number of (hypothetically) repeated experiments approaches infinity.

The frequentist interpretation of probability faces several difficulties. First, it is unclear what we mean by "the same conditions." In the case of coin flips, such conditions may include initial angle and velocity as well as air pressure and temperature. However, if all conditions are identical, then the laws of physics imply that a coin flip will always yield the same outcome. Second, in practice, we can never conduct experiments like coin flips under the exact same conditions infinitely many times. This means that probability may be unable to describe the randomness of many events in the real world. In fact, coin flips may be among the easiest experiments to repeat under nearly identical conditions. Many other events covered in this book happen in dynamic social environments that are constantly changing.

How should we think about the probability of Obama winning the 2008 US presidential election from the frequentist perspective? Since the 2008 US presidential election occurs only once, it is strange to consider a hypothetical scenario in which this particular election occurs repeatedly under the same conditions. In addition, since Obama either wins the election or not, the probability of his victory should be either 0 or 1. Here, what is random is the election forecast (due to sampling variability etc.) not the actual election outcome.

An alternative framework is the *Bayesian* interpretation of probability, named after an 18th century English mathematician and minister, Thomas Bayes (see figure 6.1). According to this paradigm, probability is a measure of one's subjective belief about the likelihood of an event occurring. A probability of 0 means that an individual thinks an event is impossible, whereas a probability of 1 implies that the individual thinks the event is sure to happen. Any probability value between 0 and 1 indicates the degree to which one feels uncertain about the occurrence of the event. In contrast to the frequentist perspective, the Bayesian framework makes it easy to interpret the statement, "the probability of Obama winning the 2008 US presidential election is x%," because x simply reflects the speaker's subjective belief about the likelihood of Obama's victory.

Critics of Bayesian interpretation argue that if scientists have identical sets of empirical evidence, they should arrive at the same conclusion rather than reporting different probabilities of the same event. Such subjectivity may hinder scientific progress because under the Bayesian framework, probability simply becomes a tool to describe one's belief system. In contrast, Bayesians contend that human beings, including scientists, are inherently subjective, so they should explicitly recognize the role of their subjective beliefs in scientific research.

Regardless of the ongoing controversy about its interpretation, probability was established as a mathematical theory by Soviet mathematician Andrey Kolmogorov in the early 20th century. Since both frequentists and Bayesians use this mathematical theory, the disagreement is about interpretation and is not mathematical.

> There are two dominant ways to interpret probability. According to the **frequentist framework**, probability represents the limit of the relative frequency with which an event of interest occurs when the number of experiments repeatedly conducted under the same conditions approaches infinity. The **Bayesian framework**, in contrast, interprets probability as one's subjective belief about the likelihood of event occurrence.

6.1.2   DEFINITION AND AXIOMS

We define probability using the following three concepts: *experiment*, *sample space*, and *event*.

> The definition of probability requires the following concepts:
>
> 1. **experiment**: an action or a set of actions that produce stochastic events of interest
> 2. **sample space**: a set of all possible outcomes of the experiment, typically denoted by Ω
> 3. **event**: a subset of the sample space

We can briefly illustrate each concept using the aforementioned two examples. Flipping a coin or holding an election would be the experiment, while the sample space would be given by {lands on heads, lands on tails} or {Obama wins, McCain wins, a third-party candidate wins}. The mathematical term *set* refers to a collection of distinct objects. An event represents *any* subset of sample space, and hence it may include multiple outcomes. In fact, the entire sample space that contains all outcomes is also an event. Moreover, an event is said to *occur* if the set that defines the event includes an actual outcome of the experiment. In the election example, events include {Obama wins, McCain wins}, which contains two outcomes and can be understood in English as "either Obama or McCain wins." Since Obama won the election, this event did occur in 2008.

As another example, consider a voter's decision in the 2008 US presidential election as an experiment. The idea is that a voter's decision can be modeled as a stochastic, rather than deterministic, event. By considering all four possible outcomes, we can define the sample space of this experiment as Ω = {abstain, vote for Obama, vote for McCain, vote for a third-party candidate}. Within this sample space, we may consider the occurrence of various events including {vote for Obama, vote for McCain, vote for a third-party candidate} (i.e., "do not abstain") and {abstain, vote for McCain, vote for a third-party candidate} (i.e., "do not vote for Obama").

We now discuss how to compute probability, starting with the simplest case in which all outcomes are equally likely to occur. In this case, the probability of event A occurring, denoted by $P(A)$, can be computed as the ratio of the number of elements in the corresponding set A to that in the entire sample space Ω:

$$P(A) = \frac{\text{number of elements in } A}{\text{number of elements in } \Omega}. \tag{6.1}$$

To illustrate this, consider an experiment of tossing a fair coin 3 times. In this experiment, if we denote {lands on heads} and {lands on tails} as H and T, respectively, then the sample space is equal to the set of 8 outcomes, Ω = $\{HHH, HHT, HTH, HTT, THH, THT, TTH, TTT\}$. We can then compute the probability of, for example, landing on heads at least twice by counting the number of elements in the relevant set, A = $\{HHH, HHT, HTH, THH\}$. In this case, therefore, using the formula above we obtain $P(A) = 4/8 = 0.5$.

Having defined probability, we next consider its basic rules or *axioms*. Modern probability theory rests on the following three simple axioms. Remarkably, from these axioms, the entire theory of probability, including all the existing rules and theorems, can be derived.

The **probability axioms** are given by the following three rules:

1. The probability of any event A is nonnegative:
$$P(A) \geq 0.$$

3. The probability that one of the outcomes in the sample space occurs is 1:
$$P(\Omega) = 1.$$

3. (*Addition rule*) If events A and B are mutually exclusive, then
$$P(A \text{ or } B) = P(A) + P(B). \tag{6.2}$$

The first two axioms together imply that probability ranges from 0 to 1. To understand the last axiom, recall the previous example in which the 2008 US presidential

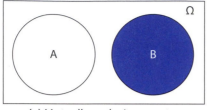
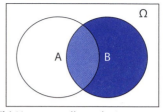

(a) Mutually exclusive events   **(b)** Not mutually exclusive events

Figure 6.2. Venn Diagram. Two events, A and B, can be mutually exclusive, having two disjoint sets of outcomes (left plot) or not mutually exclusive, sharing some outcomes (right plot). The rectangular box represents the sample space Ω. Source: Adapted from example by Uwe Ziegenhagen, http://texample.net.

election is considered as an experiment. "Mutually exclusive" in the last axiom means that two events, A and B, do not share an outcome. As illustrated by the *Venn diagram* (named after John Venn, an English philosopher) in figure 6.2a, mutually exclusive events imply two disjoint sets, meaning that they do not share any element. Consider two events: $A =$ Obama wins and $B =$ McCain wins. Clearly, these two events are mutually exclusive in that both Obama and McCain cannot win at the same time. Hence, we can apply the addition rule to conclude that $P(\{\text{Obama wins}\} \text{ or } \{\text{McCain wins}\}) = P(\text{Obama wins}) + P(\text{McCain wins})$.

Now, consider two events that are not mutually exclusive because they share an outcome: $A =$ Obama loses and $B =$ McCain loses. In this case, the addition rule does not apply because both A and B contain the same outcome: a third-party candidate wins. For events that are not mutually exclusive, we can apply the following general addition rule.

> For any given events A and B, the **addition rule** is given by
>
> $$P(A \text{ or } B) = P(A) + P(B) - P(A \text{ and } B). \qquad (6.3)$$

Applying this to the current example, we have $P(\{\text{Obama loses}\} \text{or} \{\text{McCain loses}\}) = P(\text{Obama loses}) + P(\text{McCain loses}) - P(\{\text{Obama loses}\} \text{ and } \{\text{McCain loses}\})$.

This result can be immediately seen from the *Venn diagram* shown in figure 6.2b. In the diagram, we observe that the event, $\{A \text{ or } B\}$, can be decomposed into three mutually exclusive events, $\{A \text{ and } B^c\}$ (white region), $\{B \text{ and } A^c\}$ (dark blue region), and $\{A \text{ and } B\}$ (overlapped light blue region). The superscript c represents the *complement* of a set, which consists of all elements in the sample space except those in the set. For example, A^c represents the collection of all outcomes in the sample space that do not belong to A. The notation $\{A \text{ and } B^c\}$ translates to "all outcomes of A that do not belong to B." Since any outcome in the sample space belongs either to A or A^c, in general, we have

$$P(A^c) = 1 - P(A). \qquad (6.4)$$

The equation directly follows from the probability axioms since events A and A^c are mutually exclusive and together they constitute the entire sample space.

Using the third probability axiom, given in equation (6.2), we have

$$P(A \text{ or } B) = P(A \text{ and } B^c) + P(B \text{ and } A^c) + P(A \text{ and } B). \qquad (6.5)$$

When A and B are mutually exclusive, $P(A \text{ and } B^c)$ and $P(B \text{ and } A^c)$ reduce to $P(A)$ and $P(B)$, respectively (see figure 6.2a). In addition, we have $P(A \text{ and } B) = 0$ in this mutually exclusive case.

Finally, notice that event A can be decomposed as two mutually exclusive events, $\{A \text{ and } B\}$ (overlapped light blue region) and $\{A \text{ and } B^c\}$ (nonoverlapped white region). This is called the *law of total probability*.

For any given events A and B, the **law of total probability** is given by

$$P(A) = P(A \text{ and } B) + P(A \text{ and } B^c). \qquad (6.6)$$

According to the law of total probability, we can write $P(A \text{ and } B^c) = P(A) - P(A \text{ and } B)$ by subtracting $P(A \text{ and } B)$ from both sides of equation (6.6). Similarly, the law of total probability can be applied to event B, yielding $P(B \text{ and } A^c) = P(B) - P(A \text{ and } B)$. Substituting these results into equation (6.5) and simplifying the expression leads to the general addition rule given in equation (6.3). We emphasize that this result is obtained by using the probability axioms alone. In addition, readers are encouraged to confirm the results shown in equations (6.3)–(6.6) using the Venn diagram of figure 6.2.

6.1.3 PERMUTATIONS

When each outcome is equally likely, in order to compute the probability of event A, we need to count the number of elements in event A as well as the total number of elements in the sample space Ω (see equation (6.1)). We introduce a useful counting technique, called *permutations*. Permutations refer to the number of ways in which objects can be arranged. For example, consider three unique objects A, B, and C. There are 6 unique ways to arrange them: $\{ABC, ACB, BAC, BCA, CAB, CBA\}$.

How can we compute the number of permutations without enumerating every arrangement, especially when the number of objects is large? It turns out that there is an easy way to do this. Let's consider the above example of arranging three objects, A, B, and C. First, there are three ways to choose the first object: A, B, or C. Once the first object is selected, there are two ways to choose the second object. Finally, the third object remains, leaving us only one way to choose this last object. We can conceptualize this process as a tree shown in figure 6.3, where the total number of leaves equals the number of permutations. Thus, to compute the number of leaves, we only need to sequentially multiply the number of branches at each level, i.e., $3 \times 2 \times 1$.

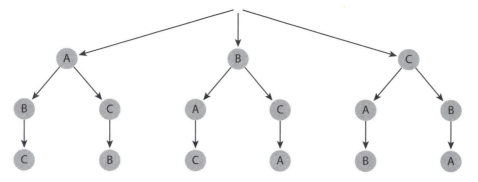

Figure 6.3. A Tree Diagram for Permutations. There are 6 ways to arrange 3 unique objects. Source: Adapted from example by Madit, http://texample.net.

Generalizing this idea, we can compute the number of permutations of k objects out of a set of n unique objects, denoted by $_nP_k$ where $k \leq n$, using the following formula.

The number of **permutations** when arranging k objects out of n unique objects is given by

$$_nP_k = n \times (n - 1) \times \cdots \times (n - k + 2) \times (n - k + 1) = \frac{n!}{(n - k)!}. \quad (6.7)$$

In this equation, ! represents the *factorial* operator. When n is a nonnegative integer, $n! = n \times (n - 1) \times \cdots \times 2 \times 1$. Note that 0! is defined as 1.

In the previous example, $n = 3$ and $k = 3$. Therefore,

$$_3P_3 = \frac{3!}{0!} = \frac{3 \times 2 \times 1}{1} = 6.$$

As another example, compute the number of ways in which you can arrange 4 cards out of 13 unique cards. This can be computed by setting $n = 13$ and $k = 4$ in equation (6.7):

$$_{13}P_4 = \frac{13!}{(13 - 4)!} = 13 \times 12 \times 11 \times 10 = 17160.$$

The *birthday problem* is a well-known counterintuitive example of permutations. The problem asks how many people one needs in order for the probability that at least two people have the same birthday to exceed 0.5, assuming that each birthday is equally likely. What is surprising about this problem is that the answer is only 23 people, which is much lower than what most people guess. To solve this problem using permutations, first notice the following relationship:

$$P(\text{at least two people have the same birthday})$$
$$= 1 - P(\text{nobody has the same birthday}). \quad (6.8)$$

This equality holds because the event {nobody has the same birthday} is the complement of the event {at least two people have the same birthday} (see equation (6.4)). This means that we only need to compute the probability that nobody has the same birthday.

Let k be the number of people. To compute the probability that nobody has the same birthday, we count the number of ways in which k people can have different birthdays. Since each birthday is assumed to be equally likely, we can use permutations to count the number of ways in which k unique birthdays can be arranged out of 365 days. This is given by $_{365}P_k = 365!/(365 - k)!$. Applying equation (6.1), we then divide this number by the total number of elements in the sample space. The latter is equal to the total number of ways to select k possibly nonunique birthdays out of 365 days. The first person could have any of 365 days as his/her birthday, and so could any other person. Hence, the denominator is equal to $365 \times 365 \times \cdots \times 365 = 365^k$. Therefore, we have

$P(\text{nobody has the same birthday})$

$$= \frac{\text{\# of ways in which } k \text{ unique birthdays can be arranged}}{\text{\# of ways in which } k \text{ possibly nonunique birthdays can be arranged}}$$

$$= \frac{_{365}P_k}{365^k} = \frac{365!}{365^k(365 - k)!}. \tag{6.9}$$

Together with equation (6.8), the solution to the birthday problem is $1 - 365!/\{365^k(365 - k)!\}$.

Computing equation (6.9) is not easy even for a moderate value of k because both the denominator and numerator can take extremely large values. In such cases, it is often convenient to use the natural *logarithmic transformation* (see section 3.4.1). For the natural logarithm, $e^A = B$ implies $A = \log B$. In addition, the basic rules of logarithms we use here are

$$\log AB = \log A + \log B, \quad \log \frac{A}{B} = \log A - \log B, \quad \text{and} \quad \log A^B = B \log A.$$

Applying these rules, we have

$$\log P(\text{nobody has the same birthday}) = \log 365! - k \log 365 - \log(365 - k)!.$$

After computing this probability on a logarithmic scale, we then take the exponential transformation of it to obtain the desired probability. In R, we use the `lfactorial()` function to compute the logarithm of a factorial instead of the `factorial()` function, which computes a factorial without the logarithmic transformation. We now create a new function called `birthday`, which computes the probability that at least two people have the same birthday given k. The function is written so that it takes a vector of k values. We plot the results.

```
birthday <- function(k) {
    logdenom <- k * log(365) + lfactorial(365 - k) # log denominator
    lognumer <- lfactorial(365) # log numerator
    ## P(at least two have the same bday) = 1 - P(nobody has the same bday)
```

```
    pr <- 1 - exp(lognumer - logdenom) # transform back
    return(pr)
}
k <- 1:50
bday <- birthday(k)   # call the function
names(bday) <- k   # add labels
plot(k, bday, xlab = "Number of people", xlim = c(0, 50), ylim = c(0, 1),
    ylab = "Probability that at least two\n people have the same birthday")
abline(h = 0.5) # horizontal 0.5 line
bday[20:25]
```

```
##        20        21        22        23        24        25
## 0.4114384 0.4436883 0.4756953 0.5072972 0.5383443 0.5686997
```

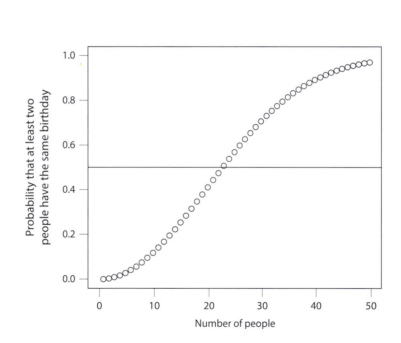

We observe that when the number of people equals 23, the probability of at least two people having the same birthday exceeds 0.5. When the number of people is more than 50, this probability is close to 1.

6.1.4   SAMPLING WITH AND WITHOUT REPLACEMENT

While we derived an exact analytical solution to the birthday problem above, we can also produce an approximate solution using a *Monte Carlo simulation method*. The name originates from the Monte Carlo Casino in Monaco, but we may also simply call it a *simulation* method. The Monte Carlo simulation method refers to a general class of stochastic (as opposed to deterministic) methods that can be used to approximately solve analytical problems by randomly generating quantities of interest.

For the birthday problem, we sample *k* possibly nonunique birthdays out of 365 days and check whether or not the sampled *k* birthdays are all different. We use *sampling with replacement* because for each of *k* draws, every one of 365 days is equally likely to be sampled *regardless of* which dates were sampled before. In other words, the fact that one person is born on a certain day of the year should not exclude someone else from being born on the same day. After repeating this sampling procedure many times, we compute the fraction of simulation trials where at least two birthdays are the same, and this fraction serves as an estimate of the corresponding probability. This simulation procedure is intuitive because it emulates the *data-generating process*, or the actual process in which the data are generated, as described in the birthday problem.

In R, we can use the `sample()` function to implement sampling with or without replacement by setting the `replace` argument to either `TRUE` or `FALSE`. While unused in the birthday problem, *sampling without replacement* means that once an element is sampled, it will not be available for subsequent draws. For example, in the discussion of sample surveys in section 3.4.1, we introduced *simple random sampling* (SRS) as a method to randomly choose a representative sample of respondents from a population. SRS is an example of sampling without replacement because we typically do not interview the same individual multiple times. For sampling with replacement, the basic syntax is `sample(x, size = k, replace = TRUE)`, where `x` is a vector of elements to sample from, and `size` is the number of elements to choose. In addition, we can feed a vector of probability weights into the `prob` argument if unequal probabilities should be used to sample each element.

```r
k <- 23 # number of people
sims <- 1000 # number of simulations
event <- 0 # counter
for (i in 1:sims) {
    days <- sample(1:365, k, replace = TRUE)
    days.unique <- unique(days) # unique birthdays
    ## if there are duplicates, the number of unique birthdays
    ## will be less than the number of birthdays, which is "k"
    if (length(days.unique) < k) {
        event <- event + 1
    }
}
## fraction of trials where at least two bdays are the same
answer <- event / sims
answer

## [1] 0.509
```

While our simulation estimate is close to the analytical solution, which is 0.507, they are not identical. This difference is called the *Monte Carlo error*, but is the inevitable consequence of the simulation approach. The size of the Monte Carlo error depends on the nature of the problem and it differs from one simulation to another. It is difficult to eliminate such an error but it is possible to reduce it. To obtain a more accurate estimate, we increase the number of simulations. In the above code, we set the number of simulations to 1000. Next, we run the same code with the number of simulations set to one million and obtain an estimate of 0.508, which is closer to the true answer.

> The **Monte Carlo simulation method** refers to a general class of repeated random sampling procedures used to approximately solve analytical problems. Commonly used procedures include **sampling with replacement**, in which the same unit can be repeatedly sampled, and **sampling without replacement**, in which each unit can be sampled at most once.

6.1.5 COMBINATIONS

We introduce another useful counting method called *combinations*. Combinations are similar to permutations, but the former ignores ordering while the latter does not. That is, combinations are ways to choose k distinct elements out of n elements without regard to their order. This means that when choosing 2 elements, two *different* permutations, AB and BA, represent one *identical* combination. Since the order in which the elements are arranged does not matter, the number of combinations is never greater than the number of permutations. For example, if we choose 2 distinct elements out of 3 elements, A, B, and C, the number of permutations is $_3P_2 = 6$ (AB, BA, AC, CA, BC, CB), whereas the number of combinations is 3 (AB, AC, BC).

In fact, to compute combinations, we first calculate permutations $_nP_k$ and then divide by $k!$. This is because given k sampled elements, there are $k!$ ways to arrange them in a different order, and yet all these arrangements are counted as a single combination. In the above example, for every set of two sampled elements (e.g., A and B), we have $2!(= 2 \times 1 = 2)$ ways of arranging them (i.e., AB and BA) but these two permutations count as one combination. Here, we obtain the number of combinations through the division of $_3P_2$ by $2!$. In general, the formula for combinations is given as follows.

> The number of **combinations** when choosing k distinct elements from n elements is denoted by either $_nC_k$ or $\binom{n}{k}$ and is computed as
>
> $$_nC_k = \binom{n}{k} = \frac{_nP_k}{k!} = \frac{n!}{k!(n-k)!}. \qquad (6.10)$$

Suppose that we are creating a committee of 5 out of 20 people (10 men and 10 women). Assume that each person is equally likely to be assigned to the committee. What is the probability that at least 2 women are on the committee? To compute this probability, we first note the following equality:

$$P(\text{at least 2 women are on the committee})$$
$$= 1 - P(\text{no woman is on the committee})$$
$$- P(\text{exactly 1 woman is on the committee}).$$

To compute the two probabilities on the right-hand side of this equation, we count the total number of ways we can assign 5 people to the committee out of 20 people regardless of their gender. This is given by $_{20}C_5 = 15,504$. Similarly, the number of

To the Members of the California State Assembly:

I am returning Assembly Bill 1176 without my signature.

For some time now I have lamented the fact that major issues are overlooked while many unnecessary bills come to me for consideration. Water reform, prison reform, and health care are major issues my Administration has brought to the table, but the Legislature just kicks the can down the alley.

Yet another legislative year has come and gone with out the major reforms Californians overwhelmingly deserve. In light of this, and after careful consideration, I believe it is unnecessary to sign this measure at this time.

Sincerely,

Arnold Schwarzenegger

Figure 6.4. California Governor Arnold Schwarzenegger's Veto Message in 2009.

ways in which we can have no woman on the committee is given by $_{10}C_0 \times {}_{10}C_5 = 252$ because there is $_{10}C_0$ way to choose no woman and there are $_{10}C_5$ ways to choose 5 out of 10 men. Thus, the probability of having no woman is 0.016. The number of ways in which we can have exactly 1 woman on the committee is $_{10}C_1 \times {}_{10}C_4 = 2100$, giving a probability of 0.135. Altogether, the probability of having at least 2 women on the committee equals $0.84 = 1 - 0.016 - 0.135$.

As a more complex example of combinations, we discuss an incident that occurred in 2009 when California Governor Arnold Schwarzenegger wrote a message to the state assembly regarding his veto of Assembly Bill 1176.[1] This message is displayed in figure 6.4. When the message was released, many observed that the first letters of each line in the main text, starting with "F" and ending with "u," constitute a sentence of profanity. Asked whether this was intentional, Schwarzenegger's spokesman replied, "My goodness. What a coincidence. I suppose when you do so many vetoes, something like this is bound to happen." Below, we consider the probability of this acrostic happening by chance.

For the sake of simplicity, suppose that the Governor gave his veto message to his secretary who then typed it in her computer but hit the return key at random. That is, the 85 words ("For" to "time") were divided by (random) line breaks into 7 lines, each with at least one word. We further assume that there are no broken words, every way of breaking the lines was equally likely, and the total number of lines is fixed at seven. Under this scenario, what is the probability of the coincidence happening?

To compute this probability using equation (6.1), we first consider the number of ways in which the 85 words can be divided into 7 lines. Note that to end up with 7 lines, 6 line breaks must be inserted. A line break may be inserted before the second word, before the third word, ..., or before the 85th word. There are thus 84 places into which 6 line breaks must be inserted. How many ways can we insert line breaks into 6 out of these 84 places? To compute this number, we use combinations rather than permutations because the order in which 6 line breaks are inserted does not matter. (Of course, the words in the acrostic must be ordered in a particular way to generate the profanity.) Therefore, the application of combinations leads to $_{84}C_6 = 84!/(6!78!)$ equally likely partitions. To compute combinations in R, we use the

---

[1] This section is based on Philip B. Stark (2009) "Null and vetoed: Chance coincidence?" *Chance*, vol. 23, no. 4, pp. 43–46.

choose() function. When the number is large, we may use the lchoose() function so that combinations are calculated on the logarithmic scale.

```
choose(84, 6)

## [1] 406481544
```

Therefore, there are more than 400 million ways to insert 6 line breaks. However, there are only 12 ways to produce this particular acrostic. The break to produce "u" at the beginning of the second line can be in only one place ("unnecessary"). The break to produce "c" at the beginning of the third line can happen in any of 3 places ("come," "consideration," "care"). The break for the "k" can be in only one place ("kicks"). The break for the "y" can be in any of two places ("Yet," "year"). The break for the "o" can be in any of two places ("overwhelmingly," "of"). The break for the "u" can be in only one place ("unnecessary"). These scenarios lead to $12 = 1 \times 3 \times 1 \times 2 \times 2 \times 1$. Hence, the probability that this randomization scheme would produce the acrostic is $12/_{84}C_6$, or about one in 34 million. The analysis suggests that according to this probabilistic model, the "coincidence" is a highly unlikely event.

6.2 Conditional Probability

We next introduce conditional probability, which concerns how the probability of an event changes after we observe other events. Conditional probability follows the rules of probability described in section 6.1. The difference is that conditional probability enables us to take into account observed evidence.

6.2.1 CONDITIONAL, MARGINAL, AND JOINT PROBABILITIES

We begin by defining the conditional probability of event A occurring, given the information that event B has occurred. This conditional probability, denoted as $P(A \mid B)$, has the following definition.

The **conditional probability** of event A occurring given that event B occurred is defined as

$$P(A \mid B) = \frac{P(A \text{ and } B)}{P(B)}. \tag{6.11}$$

In this equation, $P(A \text{ and } B)$ is the **joint probability** of both events occurring, whereas $P(B)$ is the **marginal probability** of event B. By rearranging, we obtain the **multiplication rule**

$$P(A \text{ and } B) = P(A \mid B)P(B) = P(B \mid A)P(A). \tag{6.12}$$

Using this rule, we can derive an alternative form of the *law of total probability* introduced in equation (6.6):

$$P(A) = P(A \mid B)P(B) + P(A \mid B^c)P(B^c). \tag{6.13}$$

To see the importance of conditioning, consider two couples who are both expecting twins. One couple had an ultrasound exam, but the technician was able to determine only that one of the two was a boy. The other couple did not find out the genders of their twins until the delivery when they saw the first baby was a boy. What is the probability that both babies are boys? Is this probability different between the two couples? We begin by noting that there are four outcomes in the sample space. Denoting the baby gender by "G" for girl and "B" for boy, respectively, we can represent the sample space by $\Omega = \{GG, GB, BG, BB\}$. For example, GB means that the elder twin is a girl and the younger one is a boy.

Then, for the first couple, the probability of interest is

$$P(BB \mid \text{at least one is a boy}) = \frac{P(BB \text{ and \{at least one is a boy\}})}{P(\text{at least one is a boy})}$$

$$= \frac{P(BB \text{ and } \{BB \text{ or } BG \text{ or } GB\})}{P(BB \text{ or } BG \text{ or } GB)}$$

$$= \frac{P(BB)}{P(BB \text{ or } BG \text{ or } GB)} = \frac{1/4}{3/4} = \frac{1}{3}.$$

The third equality follows from the fact that event BB is a subset of event {at least one is a boy}, i.e., BB and $\{BB \text{ or } BG \text{ or } GB\} = BB$.

In contrast, for the second couple, we have

$$P(BB \mid \text{elder twin is a boy}) = \frac{P(BB \text{ and \{the elder twin is a boy\}})}{P(\text{elder twin is a boy})}$$

$$= \frac{P(BB \text{ and } \{BB \text{ or } BG\})}{P(BB \text{ or } BG)}$$

$$= \frac{P(BB)}{P(BB \text{ or } BG)} = \frac{1/4}{1/2} = \frac{1}{2}.$$

Therefore, this example illustrates that the information upon which we condition matters. Knowing that the first baby is a boy, as opposed to knowing that at least one is a boy, gives a different conditional probability of the same event.

Probability and conditional probability can also be used to describe the characteristics of a population. For example, if 10% of a population of voters are black, then we may write $P(\text{black}) = 0.1$. We can interpret this probability as stating that if we randomly sample a voter from this population there is a 10% chance this voter is black. Similarly, $P(\text{black} \mid \text{hispanic or black})$ represents the population proportion of blacks among minority (i.e., black and Hispanic) voters.

As an illustration, we will use a random sample of 10,000 registered voters from Florida contained in the CSV file `FLVoters.csv`. Table 6.1 shows the names and descriptions of variables in this sample list of registered voters. To begin, we load the data and remove those voters who contain a missing value using the `na.omit()` function.

Table 6.1. Florida Registered Voter List Sample.

Variable	*Description*
surname	surname
county	county ID of the voter's residence
VTD	voting district ID of the voter's residence
age	age
gender	gender: m = male and f = female
race	self-reported race

```
FLVoters <- read.csv("FLVoters.csv")
dim(FLVoters) # before removal of missing data

## [1] 10000    6

FLVoters <- na.omit(FLVoters)
dim(FLVoters) # after removal

## [1] 9113    6
```

For the sake of illustration, we will treat this sample of 9113 voters as a population of interest. To compute the *marginal probability* for each racial category, we can use the `table()` and `prop.table()` functions (see section 2.5.2) and calculate the proportion of voters who belong to each racial group in this population.

```
margin.race <- prop.table(table(FLVoters$race))
margin.race

##
##       asian       black    hispanic      native       other
## 0.019203336 0.131021617 0.130802151 0.003182267 0.034017338
##       white
## 0.681773291
```

The result shows, for example, that $P(\text{black}) = 0.13$ and $P(\text{white}) = 0.68$. Similarly, we can obtain the marginal probabilities of gender as follows.

```
margin.gender <- prop.table(table(FLVoters$gender))
margin.gender

##
##         f         m
## 0.5358279 0.4641721
```

Therefore, we have $P(\text{female}) = 0.54$ and $P(\text{male}) = 0.46$. Next, to compute the *conditional probability* of race given gender, we can look at the proportion of each racial group among female voters and among male voters, separately.

```
prop.table(table(FLVoters$race[FLVoters$gender == "f"]))

##
##        asian        black     hispanic       native        other
## 0.016997747 0.138849068 0.136391563 0.003481466 0.032357157
##        white
## 0.671922998
```

The result suggests, for example, $P(\text{black} \mid \text{female}) = 0.14$ and $P(\text{white} \mid \text{female}) = 0.67$. Lastly, the *joint probability* of race and gender can be computed by calculating the proportion of voters who belong to specific racial and gender groups.

```
joint.p <- prop.table(table(race = FLVoters$race, gender = FLVoters$gender))
joint.p

##           gender
## race              f           m
##    asian    0.009107868 0.010095468
##    black    0.074399210 0.056622408
##    hispanic 0.073082410 0.057719741
##    native   0.001865467 0.001316800
##    other    0.017337869 0.016679469
##    white    0.360035115 0.321738176
```

This joint probability table gives, for example, $P(\text{black and female}) = 0.07$ and $P(\text{white and male}) = 0.32$. From this joint probability, we can compute the marginal and conditional probability. First, to obtain the marginal probability, we apply the *law of total probability* given in equation (6.6). For example, we can compute the probability of being a black voter by

$$P(\text{black}) = P(\text{black and female}) + P(\text{black and male}).$$

Thus, summing over columns for each row results in the marginal probability of race. This operation yields results identical to those obtained above.

```
rowSums(joint.p)

##        asian        black     hispanic       native        other
## 0.019203336 0.131021617 0.130802151 0.003182267 0.034017338
##        white
## 0.681773291
```

Similarly, we can obtain the marginal probability of gender from the joint probability table by summing over racial categories. Since we have a total of six racial categories, we will extend the law of total probability given in equation (6.6) to

$$P(A) = \sum_{i=1}^{N} P(A \text{ and } B_i), \tag{6.14}$$

where $B_1, \ldots, B_N$ is a set of mutually exclusive events which together cover the entire sample space. In the current setting, for example, since racial categories are mutually exclusive, we have

$$P(\text{female}) = P(\text{female and asian}) + P(\text{female and black})$$

$$+ P(\text{female and hispanic}) + P(\text{female and native})$$

$$+ P(\text{female and other}) + P(\text{female and white}).$$

Therefore, the marginal probability of gender is obtained by summing over rows for each column of the joint probability table.

```
colSums(joint.p)

##         f         m
## 0.5358279 0.4641721
```

Finally, the *conditional probability* can be obtained as the ratio of joint probability to the marginal probability (see equation (6.11)). For example, the conditional probability of being black among female voters is calculated as

$$P(\text{black} \mid \text{female}) = \frac{P(\text{black and female})}{P(\text{female})} \approx \frac{0.074}{0.536} \approx 0.139,$$

which, as expected, is equal to what we computed earlier.

The results of this example are summarized in table 6.2. From the joint probability, both marginal and conditional probabilities can be obtained. To compute marginal probability, we sum over either rows or columns. Once marginal probability is obtained in this way, we can divide joint probability by marginal probability in order to calculate the desired conditional probability.

We can extend the definition of conditional probability to settings with more than two types of events. For events A, B, and C, the joint probability is defined as $P(A \text{ and } B \text{ and } C)$, whereas there are three marginal probabilities $P(A)$, $P(B)$, and $P(C)$. In this case, there are two types of conditional probabilities: the joint probability of two events conditional on the remaining event (e.g., $P(A \text{ and } B \mid C)$) and the

Table 6.2. An Example of a Joint Probability Table.

Racial groups	Gender Female	Male	Marginal prob.
Asian	0.009	0.010	0.019
Black	0.074	0.057	0.131
Hispanic	0.073	0.058	0.131
Native	0.002	0.001	0.003
White	0.360	0.322	0.682
Marginal prob.	0.536	0.464	1

Note: The table is based on Florida voter registration data. The marginal probability of gender (far right column) and that of race (bottom row) can be obtained by summing the joint probabilities over columns and over rows, respectively.

conditional probability of one event given the other two (e.g., $P(A \mid B \text{ and } C)$). These conditional probabilities can be defined analogously to the two-event case as

$$P(A \text{ and } B \mid C) = \frac{P(A \text{ and } B \text{ and } C)}{P(C)}, \tag{6.15}$$

$$P(A \mid B \text{ and } C) = \frac{P(A \text{ and } B \text{ and } C)}{P(B \text{ and } C)} = \frac{P(A \text{ and } B \mid C)}{P(B \mid C)}. \tag{6.16}$$

The second equality in equation (6.16) follows from the equality $P(A \text{ and } B \text{ and } C) = P(A \text{ and } B \mid C)P(C)$, which is obtained by rearranging the terms in equation (6.15).

To illustrate the above conditional probabilities, we create a new `age.group` variable indicating four age groups: 20 and below, 21–40, 41–60, and above 60.

```
FLVoters$age.group <- NA # initialize a variable
FLVoters$age.group[FLVoters$age <= 20] <- 1
FLVoters$age.group[FLVoters$age > 20 & FLVoters$age <= 40] <- 2
FLVoters$age.group[FLVoters$age > 40 & FLVoters$age <= 60] <- 3
FLVoters$age.group[FLVoters$age > 60] <- 4
```

The joint probability of age group, race, and gender can be calculated as a three-way table. Below, this three-way table is displayed as two separate two-way tables: one two-way (race and age group) table for female voters and the other two-way table for male voters.

```
joint3 <-
    prop.table(table(race = FLVoters$race, age.group = FLVoters$age.group,
              gender = FLVoters$gender))
```

```
joint3

## , , gender = f
##
##          age.group
## race              1             2             3
##    asian   0.0001097333  0.0026336004  0.0041698672
##    black   0.0016460002  0.0280917371  0.0257873368
##    hispanic 0.0015362669  0.0260068035  0.0273236036
##    native  0.0001097333  0.0004389334  0.0006584001
##    other   0.0003292000  0.0062548008  0.0058158674
##    white   0.0059256008  0.0796664106  0.1260836168
##          age.group
## race              4
##    asian   0.0021946670
##    black   0.0188741358
##    hispanic 0.0182157358
##    native  0.0006584001
##    other   0.0049380007
##    white   0.1483594864
##
## , , gender = m
##
##          age.group
## race              1             2             3
##    asian   0.0002194667  0.0028530670  0.0051574674
##    black   0.0016460002  0.0228245364  0.0189838692
##    hispanic 0.0016460002  0.0197520026  0.0221661363
##    native  0.0000000000  0.0004389334  0.0003292000
##    other   0.0004389334  0.0069132009  0.0055964007
##    white   0.0040601339  0.0750576100  0.1184022825
##          age.group
## race              4
##    asian   0.0018654669
##    black   0.0131680018
##    hispanic 0.0141556019
##    native  0.0005486667
##    other   0.0037309338
##    white   0.1242181499
```

For example, the proportion of black female voters who are above 60 or P(black and above 60 and female) is equal to 0.019. Suppose that we wish to obtain the conditional probability of being black and female given that a voter is above 60 years old or P(black and female | above 60). Using equation (6.15), we can compute this conditional probability by dividing the joint probability by the marginal probability of being above 60 or P(above 60). To extract a specific joint probability from the above three-way table, we specify the corresponding value for each demographic characteristic.

```
## marginal probabilities for age groups
margin.age <- prop.table(table(FLVoters$age.group))
margin.age

##
##          1          2          3          4
## 0.01766707 0.27093164 0.36047405 0.35092725

## P(black and female | above 60)
joint3["black", 4, "f"] / margin.age[4]

##          4
## 0.05378361
```

According to equation (6.16), the conditional probability of being black given that a voter is female and above 60 years old or P(black | female and above 60) can be computed by dividing the three-way joint probability P(black and above 60 and female) by the two-way joint probability P(above 60 and female). To obtain this two-way joint probability, we can create a two-way joint probability table for age group and gender.

```
## two-way joint probability table for age group and gender
joint2 <- prop.table(table(age.group = FLVoters$age.group,
                           gender = FLVoters$gender))
joint2

##          gender
## age.group          f          m
##         1 0.009656535 0.008010534
##         2 0.143092286 0.127839350
##         3 0.189838692 0.170635356
##         4 0.193240426 0.157686821

joint2[4, "f"] # P(above 60 and female)

## [1] 0.1932404

## P(black | female and above 60)
joint3["black", 4, "f"] / joint2[4, "f"]

## [1] 0.09767178
```

6.2.2 INDEPENDENCE

Having defined conditional probability, we can now formally discuss the concept of *independence*. Intuitively, the independence of two events implies that the knowledge of one event does not give us any additional information about the occurrence of the other event. That is, if events A and B are independent of each other, the conditional probability of A given B does not differ from the marginal probability of A. Similarly, the conditional probability of B given A does not depend on A:

$$P(A \mid B) = P(A) \quad \text{and} \quad P(B \mid A) = P(B). \tag{6.17}$$

Together with equation (6.12), this equality implies the following formal definition of independence between events A and B.

> Events A and B are **independent** if and only if the joint probability is equal to the product of the marginal probabilities:
>
> $$P(A \text{ and } B) = P(A)P(B). \qquad (6.18)$$

We investigate whether race and gender are independent of each other in the sample of Florida registered voters analyzed earlier. Although we do not expect this relationship to be exactly independent, we examine whether the proportion of female voters, for example, is greater than expected in some racial groups. Note that if independence holds, we should have, for example, $P(\text{black and female}) = P(\text{black})P(\text{female})$, $P(\text{white and male}) = P(\text{white})P(\text{male})$, and so on. We compare the products of marginal probabilities for race and female with their joint probabilities using a scatter plot. We use the `c()` function, which combines its inputs into a vector, to coerce a table format into a vector so that its elements can be used in the `plot()` function.

```
plot(c(margin.race * margin.gender["f"]), # product of marginal probs.
     c(joint.p[, "f"]), # joint probabilities
     xlim = c(0, 0.4), ylim = c(0, 0.4),
     xlab = "P(race) * P(female)", ylab = "P(race and female)")
abline(0, 1) # 45-degree line
```

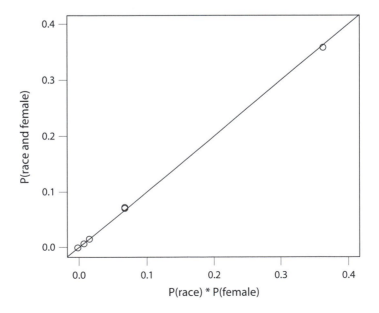

The scatter plot shows that the points fall neatly along the 45-degree line, implying that $P(\text{race})P(\text{female})$ (horizontal axis) and $P(\text{race and female})$ (vertical axis) are approximately equal. This means that race and gender are approximately independent in this sample of registered voters. That is, the knowledge of a voter's gender does not help us predict her race. Similarly, one's race does not predict gender either.

The notion of independence extends to situations with more than two events. For example, if we have three events A, B, and C, the *joint independence* among these events implies that the joint probability can be written as the product of marginal probabilities:

$$P(A \text{ and } B \text{ and } C) = P(A)P(B)P(C). \tag{6.19}$$

Furthermore, we can define the independence between two events conditional on another event. The *conditional independence* of events A and B given event C implies that the joint probability of A and B given C is equal to the product of two conditional probabilities:

$$P(A \text{ and } B \mid C) = P(A \mid C)P(B \mid C). \tag{6.20}$$

Joint independence given in equation (6.19) implies pairwise independence given in equation (6.18). This result can be obtained by applying the *law of total probability*:

$$
\begin{aligned}
P(A \text{ and } B) &= P(A \text{ and } B \text{ and } C) + P(A \text{ and } B \text{ and } C^c) \\
&= P(A)P(B)P(C) + P(A)P(B)P(C^c) \\
&= P(A)P(B)\big(P(C) + P(C^c)\big) = P(A)P(B).
\end{aligned}
$$

In addition, joint independence implies conditional independence, defined in equation (6.20), but the converse is not necessarily true. This result is based on the definition of conditional probability given in equation (6.15):

$$P(A \text{ and } B \mid C) = \frac{P(A \text{ and } B \text{ and } C)}{P(C)} = \frac{P(A)P(B)P(C)}{P(C)} = P(A \mid C)P(B \mid C).$$

The last equality follows from the fact that joint independence implies pairwise independence (and hence equation (6.17) holds for A and C as well as B and C).

To examine joint independence among our sample of registered Florida voters, we compare the elements of the three-way proportion table `joint3` with the corresponding product of marginal probabilities, `margin.race`, `margin.age`, and `margin.gender`. As an illustration, we set the age group to the above 60 category and examine female voters. We also examine conditional independence between race and gender, given age. For this, we again set the age and gender groups to the above 60 and female categories, respectively. The results show that both joint (left-hand plot) and conditional (right-hand plot) independence relationships approximately hold, despite small deviations.

```
## joint independence
plot(c(joint3[, 4, "f"]), # joint probability
     margin.race * margin.age[4] * margin.gender["f"], # product of marginals
     xlim = c(0, 0.3), ylim = c(0, 0.3), main = "Joint independence",
     xlab = "P(race and above 60 and female)",
     ylab = "P(race) * P(above 60) * P(female)")
abline(0, 1)
## conditional independence given female
plot(c(joint3[, 4, "f"]) / margin.gender["f"], # joint prob. given female
     ## product of marginals
     (joint.p[, "f"] / margin.gender["f"]) *
         (joint2[4, "f"] / margin.gender["f"]),
     xlim = c(0, 0.3), ylim = c(0, 0.3), main = "Marginal independence",
     xlab = "P(race and above 60 | female)",
     ylab = "P(race | female) * P(above 60 | female)")
abline(0, 1)
```

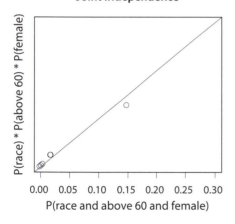

Finally, the well-known *Monty Hall problem* illustrates how tricky conditional probability and independence can be. The problem goes as follows. You are on a game show and must choose one of three doors, where one conceals a new car and two conceal old goats. After you randomly choose one door, the host of the game show, Monty, opens a different door, which does not conceal a car. Then, Monty asks you if you would like to switch to the (unopened) third door. You will win the new car if it is behind the door of your final choice. Should you switch, or stay with your original choice? Does switching make a difference? Most people think switching makes no difference because after Monty reveals one door with a goat, the two remaining doors have a goat or a car behind them. Therefore, the chance of winning a car is 50%. However, it turns out that this seemingly sensible reasoning is incorrect.

Let's think about this problem carefully. Consider the strategy of not switching. In this case, your initial choice determines the outcome regardless of what Monty does. Therefore, the probability of winning the car is 1/3. Now, consider the strategy of switching. There are two scenarios. First, suppose that you initially choose a door with the car. The probability of this event is 1/3. Swapping the door in this scenario is a bad choice because you will not win the car. Next, suppose that the door you selected first has a goat. The probability of your initially choosing a door with a goat is 2/3. Then, since Monty opens another door with a goat, the remaining door to which you will switch contains a car. Hence, under this scenario, you will always win the car. Therefore, switching gives you a probability of winning the car that is twice as high as not switching.

We formalize this logic by applying the rules of probability covered so far. To compute the probability of winning a car given that you switch, we first apply the law of total probability in equation (6.13):

$$P(\text{car}) = P(\text{car} \mid \text{car first})P(\text{car first}) + P(\text{car} \mid \text{goat first})P(\text{goat first})$$

$$= P(\text{goat first}) = \frac{2}{3}.$$

To see why the second equality holds, notice that if you initially select the door with a car then switching makes you lose the car, i.e., $P(\text{car} \mid \text{car first}) = 0$. In contrast, if you first pick a door with a goat, then you have a 100% chance of winning a car by switching, i.e., $P(\text{car} \mid \text{goat first}) = 1$.

This rather counterintuitive problem can also be solved with *Monte Carlo simulations*. For emulating random choice in R, we use the `sample()` function. We set the `size` argument to `1` in order to randomly choose one element from a vector.

```
sims <- 1000
doors <- c("goat", "goat", "car") # order does not matter
result.switch <- result.noswitch <- rep(NA, sims)
for (i in 1:sims) {
    ## randomly choose the initial door
    first <- sample(1:3, size = 1)
    result.noswitch[i] <- doors[first]
    remain <- doors[-first] # remaining two doors
    ## Monty chooses one door with a goat
    monty <- sample((1:2)[remain == "goat"], size = 1)
    result.switch[i] <- remain[-monty]
}
mean(result.noswitch == "car")

## [1] 0.338

mean(result.switch == "car")

## [1] 0.662
```

6.2.3 BAYES' RULE

We discussed different interpretations of probability at the beginning of this chapter. One interpretation, proposed by Reverend Thomas Bayes, was that probability measures one's subjective belief in an event's occurrence. From this Bayesian perspective, it is natural to ask the question of how we should update our beliefs after observing some data. *Bayes' rule* shows how updating beliefs can be done in a mathematically coherent manner.

Bayes' rule is given by

$$P(A \mid B) = \frac{P(B \mid A)P(A)}{P(B)} = \frac{P(B \mid A)P(A)}{P(B \mid A)P(A) + P(B \mid A^c)P(A^c)}. \quad (6.21)$$

In this equation, $P(A)$ is called the **prior probability** and reflects one's initial belief about the likelihood of event A occurring. After observing the data, represented as event B, we update our belief and obtain $P(A \mid B)$, which is called the **posterior probability**.

Regardless of whether we interpret probability as subjective belief, Bayes' rule shows mathematically how the knowledge of $P(A)$ (*prior probability*), $P(B \mid A)$, and $P(B \mid A^c)$ yields that of $P(A \mid B)$ (*posterior probability*). Bayes' rule is simply the result of rewriting the definition of conditional probability given in equation (6.11) using the law of total probability shown in equation (6.13):

$$P(A \mid B) = \frac{P(A \text{ and } B)}{P(B)} = \frac{P(B \mid A)P(A)}{P(B)}.$$

A well-known application of Bayes' rule is the interpretation of medical diagnostic tests, which can have false positives and false negatives (defined in section 4.1.3). Consider the following first-trimester screening test problem. A 35-year-old pregnant woman is told that 1 in 378 women of her age will have a baby with Down syndrome (DS). A first-trimester ultrasound screening procedure indicates that she is in a high-risk category. Of 100 cases of DS, 86 mothers will receive a high-risk result and 14 cases of DS will be missed. Also, there is a 1 in 20 chance for a normal pregnancy to be diagnosed as high risk. Given the result of the screening procedure, what is the probability that her baby has DS? What would the probability be if the result had been negative?

To solve this problem, we first specify the prior probability. Without any testing, the probability that a baby has DS, $P(\text{DS})$, is equal to 1/378 or approximately 0.003. The ultrasound screening procedure gives a high-risk result 86% of times when a baby actually has DS. This is called the *true positive rate* of the test and can be expressed as $P(\text{HR} \mid \text{DS}) = 0.86$, where HR denotes a high-risk result. However, the screening procedure also produces a *false positive rate* of 5%, which can be formally written as $P(\text{HR} \mid \text{not DS}) = 0.05$. Using this information, we can apply Bayes' rule to obtain the posterior probability that the baby has DS, given that the woman received a high-risk result, or the *positive predictive value* of the test:

$$P(\text{DS} \mid \text{HR}) = \frac{P(\text{HR} \mid \text{DS})P(\text{DS})}{P(\text{HR} \mid \text{DS})P(\text{DS}) + P(\text{HR} \mid \text{not DS})P(\text{not DS})}$$

$$= \frac{0.86 \times \frac{1}{378}}{0.86 \times \frac{1}{378} + 0.05 \times \frac{377}{378}} \approx 0.04.$$

Similarly, if the woman received a normal pregnancy result, the posterior probability becomes

$$P(\text{DS} \mid \text{not HR}) = \frac{P(\text{not HR} \mid \text{DS})P(\text{DS})}{P(\text{not HR} \mid \text{DS})P(\text{DS}) + P(\text{not HR} \mid \text{not DS})P(\text{not DS})}$$

$$= \frac{0.14 \times \frac{1}{378}}{0.14 \times \frac{1}{378} + 0.95 \times \frac{377}{378}} \approx 0.0004.$$

We see that even when the woman receives a high-risk result, the posterior probability of having a baby with DS is small. This is because DS is a relatively rare disease, as reflected by a small prior probability. As expected, if the woman receives a normal pregnancy result, then the posterior probability becomes even smaller than the prior probability.

We can use Bayes' rule to solve the Monty Hall problem introduced in section 6.2.2. Let A represent the event that the first door has a car behind it. Define B and C similarly for the second and third doors, respectively. Since each door is equally likely to have a car behind it, the prior probabilities are $P(A) = P(B) = P(C) = 1/3$. Suppose that we choose the first door and let MC represent the event that Monty opens the third door. We want to know whether switching to the second door increases the chance of winning the car, i.e., $P(B \mid \text{MC}) > P(A \mid \text{MC})$. We apply Bayes' rule after noting that $P(\text{MC} \mid A) = 1/2$ (Monty chooses between the second and third door with equal probability), $P(\text{MC} \mid B) = 1$ (Monty has no option but to open the third door, which has a goat), and $P(\text{MC} \mid C) = 0$ (Monty cannot open the third door, which has a car):

$$P(A \mid \text{MC}) = \frac{P(\text{MC} \mid A)P(A)}{P(\text{MC} \mid A)P(A) + P(\text{MC} \mid B)P(B) + P(\text{MC} \mid C)P(C)}$$

$$= \frac{\frac{1}{2} \times \frac{1}{3}}{\frac{1}{2} \times \frac{1}{3} + 1 \times \frac{1}{3} + 0 \times \frac{1}{3}} = \frac{1}{3},$$

$$P(B \mid \text{MC}) = \frac{P(\text{MC} \mid B)P(B)}{P(\text{MC} \mid A)P(A) + P(\text{MC} \mid B)P(B) + P(\text{MC} \mid C)P(C)}$$

$$= \frac{1 \times \frac{1}{3}}{\frac{1}{2} \times \frac{1}{3} + 1 \times \frac{1}{3} + 0 \times \frac{1}{3}} = \frac{2}{3}.$$

Thus, switching doors will give a probability of winning a car that is twice as great as staying with the initial choice.

6.2.4 PREDICTING RACE USING SURNAME AND RESIDENCE LOCATION

This section contains an advanced application of conditional probability and Bayes' rule in the social sciences. Readers may skip this section without affecting their ability to understand the materials in the remainder of the book.

It is often of interest to infer certain unknown attributes of individuals from their known characteristics. We consider the problem of predicting individual race using surname and residence location.[2] Accurate prediction of individual race is useful, for example, when studying turnout rates among racial groups.

The US Census Bureau releases a list of common surnames with their frequency. For example, the most common surname was "Smith" with 2,376,206 occurrences, followed by "Johnson" and "Williams" with 1,857,160 and 1,534,042, respectively. This data set is quite comprehensive, including a total of more than 150,000 surnames that occurred at least 100 times. In addition, the census provides the relative frequencies of individual race within each surname, using a six-category self-reported race measure: non-Hispanic white, non-Hispanic black, non-Hispanic Asian and Pacific Islander, Hispanic origin, non-Hispanic American Indian and Alaskan Native, and non-Hispanic of two or more races. We will combine the last two categories into a single category of non-Hispanic others, so that we have five categories in total. The aggregate information, which can be written as $P(\text{race} \mid \text{surname})$, enables us to predict race given an individual's surname.

Note that $P(\text{race})$, $P(\text{race} \mid \text{surname})$, and $P(\text{race and surname})$ are examples of general ways to represent the marginal, conditional, and joint probabilities, respectively. For example, $P(\text{race})$ represents a collection of marginal probabilities, i.e., $P(\text{white})$, $P(\text{black})$, $P(\text{asian})$, $P(\text{hispanic})$, and $P(\text{others})$. Similarly, $P(\text{race} \mid \text{surname})$ can be evaluated for any given racial group and surname, for example, $P(\text{black} \mid \text{Smith})$. To illustrate the convenience of this general notation, we apply the law of total probability in equation (6.14) to the joint probability of race and surname:

$$P(\text{surname}) = \sum_{\text{race}} P(\text{race and surname}),$$

where the summation is taken over all racial categories (i.e., white, black, asian, hispanic, and others. In terms of the notation used in equation (6.14), A represents any given surname while B_i is a racial category. This equality applies to any surname of interest, and the summation is taken over all five racial categories.

This census name list is contained in the CSV data file `names.csv`. Table 6.3 lists the names and descriptions of variables in this census surname list data set.[3]

---

[2] This section is in part based on Kosuke Imai and Kabir Khanna (2016) "Improving ecological inference by predicting individual ethnicity from voter registration records." *Political Analysis*, vol. 24, no. 2 (Spring), pp. 263–272.

[3] To protect anonymity, the Census Bureau does not reveal small race percentages for given surnames. For the sake of simplicity, we impute these missing values by assuming that residual values will be equally allocated to the racial categories with missing values. That is, for each last name, we subtract the sum of the percentages of all races without missing values from 100% and divide the remaining percentage equally among those races that do have missing values.

Table 6.3. US Census Bureau Surname List Data.

Variable	Description
surname	surname
count	number of individuals with a specific surname
pctwhite	percentage of non-Hispanic whites among those who have a specific surname
pctblack	percentage of non-Hispanic blacks among those who have a specific surname
pctapi	percentage of non-Hispanic Asians and Pacific Islanders among those who have a specific surname
pcthispanic	percentage of Hispanic origin among those who have a specific surname
pctothers	percentage of the other racial groups among those who have a specific surname

```
cnames <- read.csv("names.csv")
dim(cnames)

## [1] 151671       7
```

The total number of surnames contained in this data set is 151,671. For these surnames, the data set gives the probability of belonging to a particular racial group given a voter's surname, i.e., $P(\text{race} \mid \text{surname})$. We begin by using this conditional probability to classify the race of individual voters. To validate the accuracy of our prediction of individual race, we use the sample of 10,000 registered voters from Florida analyzed earlier (see table 6.1). In some Southern states including Florida, voters are asked to self-report their race when registering. This makes the Florida data an ideal validation data set. If the accuracy of a prediction method is empirically validated in Florida, we may use the method to predict individual race in other states where such information is not available.

For matching names between the voter file and census name data, we use the `match()` function. This function takes the syntax of `match(x, y)` and returns a vector of indices of vector y's correspondence to each element of vector x. The function returns `NA` if there is no match found in y for an element of x. Here is a simple example illustrating the use of the `match()` function.

```
x <- c("blue", "red", "yellow")
y <- c("orange", "blue")
## match x with y
match(x, y) # "blue" appears in the 2nd element of y

## [1]  2 NA NA

## match y with x
```

```
match(y, x) # "blue" appears in the first element of x

## [1] NA   1
```

Going back to the problem of predicting individual racial groups, we remove voters whose surnames do not appear in the census surname list. To do so, we utilize the fact that the syntax match(x, y) returns NA if the corresponding element of x is not matched with any element of y.

```
FLVoters <- FLVoters[!is.na(match(FLVoters$surname, cnames$surname)), ]
dim(FLVoters)

## [1] 8022    7
```

The syntax !is.na() represents "not NA," where ! indicates negation, so that only the matched elements are retained. Thus, we focus on the resulting 80% of the original sample. We first compute the proportion of voters whose race is correctly classified in each racial category. Race is considered correctly classified if the racial category with the greatest conditional probability $P(\text{race} \mid \text{surname})$ is identical to the self-reported race. These represent *true positives* of classification (see table 4.3).

We calculate the *true positive rate* for each racial group, which represents, for example, the proportion of white voters who are correctly predicted as white. To compute this, we first subset white voters from the Florida voter file and then match the surname of each voter with the same surname in the census surname data.

```
whites <- subset(FLVoters, subset = (race == "white"))
w.indx <- match(whites$surname, cnames$surname)
head(w.indx)

## [1]   8610    237   4131   2244 27852   3495
```

The outputted row index w.indx contains, for each observation in the whites data frame, the number of the row with the same surname in the cnames data frame. For example, the second observation in the whites data frame has the surname Lynch. This surname appears in the 237th row of the cnames data set. Accordingly, the second value in w.indx is 237. More specifically, for each surname belonging to a white voter in Florida, we use apply(cnames[w.indx, vars], 1, max) to compare the predicted probabilities across the five racial categories in the vector vars, and extract the highest predicted probability. We then check whether the highest predicted probability for that voter is the same as the predicted probability of their being white. If these two numbers are identical, the classification is correct. Finally, we compute the mean of the resulting binary vector to obtain the proportion of correct classifications, the true positive rate.

```
## relevant variables
vars <- c("pctwhite", "pctblack", "pctapi", "pcthispanic", "pctothers")
mean(apply(cnames[w.indx, vars], 1, max) == cnames$pctwhite[w.indx])

## [1] 0.950218
```

The result shows that 95% of white voters are correctly predicted as whites. We repeat the same analysis for black, Hispanic, and Asian voters.

```
## black
blacks <- subset(FLVoters, subset = (race == "black"))
b.indx <- match(blacks$surname, cnames$surname)
mean(apply(cnames[b.indx, vars], 1, max) == cnames$pctblack[b.indx])

## [1] 0.1604824

## Hispanic
hispanics <- subset(FLVoters, subset = (race == "hispanic"))
h.indx <- match(hispanics$surname, cnames$surname)
mean(apply(cnames[h.indx, vars], 1, max) == cnames$pcthispanic[h.indx])

## [1] 0.8465298

## Asian
asians <- subset(FLVoters, subset = (race == "asian"))
a.indx <- match(asians$surname, cnames$surname)
mean(apply(cnames[a.indx, vars], 1, max) == cnames$pctapi[a.indx])

## [1] 0.5642857
```

We find that surname alone can correctly classify 85% of Hispanic voters as Hispanic. In contrast, classification of Asian and black voters is much worse. In particular, only 16% of black voters are correctly classified as African-Americans. The high true positive rate for whites may simply arise from the fact that they far outnumber voters from other racial categories.

We next look at *false positives*. Below, we calculate the *false discovery rate* for each racial group, which, for example, represents the proportion of voters who are not white among those classified as white. We use the same indexing trick as above and compute the proportion of white voters among those classified as whites. Subtracting the resulting value from 1 yields the false discovery rate for whites.

```
indx <- match(FLVoters$surname, cnames$surname)
## white false discovery rate
1 - mean(FLVoters$race[apply(cnames[indx, vars], 1, max) ==
                         cnames$pctwhite[indx]] == "white")

## [1] 0.1973603
```

Table 6.4. Florida Census Data at the Voting District Level.

Variable	Description
county	county census ID of the voting district
VTD	voting district census ID (only unique within the county)
total.pop	total population of the voting district
white	proportion of non-Hispanic whites in the voting district
black	proportion of non-Hispanic blacks in the voting district
api	proportion of non-Hispanic Asians and Pacific Islanders in the voting district
hispanic	proportion of voters of Hispanic origin in the voting district
others	proportion of the other racial groups in the voting district

```
## black false discovery rate
1 - mean(FLVoters$race[apply(cnames[indx, vars], 1, max) ==
                    cnames$pctblack[indx]] == "black")

## [1] 0.3294574

## Hispanic false discovery rate
1 - mean(FLVoters$race[apply(cnames[indx, vars], 1, max) ==
                    cnames$pcthispanic[indx]] == "hispanic")

## [1] 0.2274755

## Asian false discovery rate
1 - mean(FLVoters$race[apply(cnames[indx, vars], 1, max) ==
                    cnames$pctapi[indx]] == "asian")

## [1] 0.3416667
```

The results show that the false discovery rate is the highest for Asian and black voters, while it is much lower for whites and Hispanics.

Next, we attempt to improve the above prediction by taking into account where voters live. This approach should be helpful to the extent that there exists residential segregation based on race. In the United States, voter files contain voters' addresses. Using this information, our data set also provides the voting district where each voter lives. In addition, we will utilize the Florida census data, which contains the racial composition of each voting district. The names and descriptions of variables in this census data set, FLCensusVTD.csv, are given in table 6.4.

How does the knowledge of residence location improve the prediction of individual race? Whereas the census name data set contains information about the conditional probability $P(\text{race} \mid \text{surname})$, the Florida census data set provides additional information about $P(\text{race} \mid \text{residence})$ (proportion of each racial category among residents in a given voting district) and $P(\text{residence})$ (proportion of residents who live in a given voting district). We wish to combine them and compute the desired conditional probability $P(\text{race} \mid \text{surname and residence})$. Recall that these are general ways to represent marginal, conditional, and joint probabilities. Each expression can be evaluated using a specific racial group, surname, and residential location.

Computing $P(\text{race} \mid \text{surname and residence})$ requires Bayes' rule. So far, we have employed Bayes' rule for one event A conditional on an event B, but now we need to use Bayes' rule conditional on both B and another event C:

$$P(A \mid B, C) = \frac{P(B \mid A \text{ and } C) P(A \mid C)}{P(B \mid C)},$$

where every probability on the right-hand side is defined conditional on another event C (see equation (6.21)). Applying this rule yields

$$\begin{aligned} & P(\text{race} \mid \text{surname and residence}) \\ &= \frac{P(\text{surname} \mid \text{race and residence}) P(\text{race} \mid \text{residence})}{P(\text{surname} \mid \text{residence})}. \end{aligned} \quad (6.22)$$

In this equation, while $P(\text{race} \mid \text{residence})$ is available from the Florida census data, the other two conditional probabilities, $P(\text{surname} \mid \text{race and residence})$ and $P(\text{surname} \mid \text{residence})$, are not directly given either in the census name data set or the Florida census data set.

To overcome this difficulty, we make an additional assumption that a voter's surname and residence location are independent of each other, given race. This *conditional independence* assumption implies that once we know a voter's race, their residence location does not give us any additional information about their surname. So long as there is no strong geographical concentration of certain surnames in Florida within a racial category, this assumption is reasonable. The assumption is violated, for example, if Hispanic Cubans tend to have distinct names and are concentrated in certain neighborhoods. Unfortunately, our data cannot tell us whether this assumption is appropriate, but we will proceed assuming it is. Applying equation (6.20), the assumption can be written as

$$\begin{aligned} P(\text{surname} \mid \text{race and residence}) &= \frac{P(\text{surname and race} \mid \text{residence})}{P(\text{race} \mid \text{residence})} \\ &= \frac{P(\text{surname} \mid \text{residence}) P(\text{race} \mid \text{residence})}{P(\text{race} \mid \text{residence})} \\ &= P(\text{surname} \mid \text{race}). \end{aligned} \quad (6.23)$$

The first equality follows from the definition of conditional probability, whereas the second equality is due to the application of equation (6.20).

The assumption transforms equation (6.22) into

$$P(\text{race} \mid \text{surname and residence}) = \frac{P(\text{surname} \mid \text{race}) P(\text{race} \mid \text{residence})}{P(\text{surname} \mid \text{residence})}.$$

We should keep this key version of the equation in mind as the one we will ultimately use.

Note that applying the law of total probability defined in equation (6.14) and then invoking the assumption given in equation (6.23), the denominator of equation (6.22) can be written as the following equation, which sums over all racial categories:

$$P(\text{surname} \mid \text{residence}) = \sum_{\text{race}} P(\text{surname} \mid \text{race and residence}) P(\text{race} \mid \text{residence})$$

$$= \sum_{\text{race}} P(\text{surname} \mid \text{race}) P(\text{race} \mid \text{residence}). \qquad (6.24)$$

In the above equations, we use $\sum_{\text{race}}$ to indicate summation over all categories of the race variable (i.e., black, white, Asian, Hispanic, and others).

While the census surname list gives $P(\text{race} \mid \text{surname})$, the prediction of individual race based on equation (6.22) requires the computation of $P(\text{surname} \mid \text{race})$, which is included in both the numerator and the denominator (see equation (6.24)). Fortunately, we can use Bayes' rule to obtain

$$P(\text{surname} \mid \text{race}) = \frac{P(\text{race} \mid \text{surname}) P(\text{surname})}{P(\text{race})}. \qquad (6.25)$$

The two terms in the numerator of equation (6.25) can be computed using the census name list. We compute $P(\text{race})$, which is not included in that data, from the Florida census data by using the law of total probability:

$$P(\text{race}) = \sum_{\text{residence}} P(\text{race} \mid \text{residence}) P(\text{residence}). \qquad (6.26)$$

In this equation, $\sum_{\text{residence}}$ indicates summation over all values of the residence variable (i.e., all voting districts in the data).

To implement this prediction methodology in R, we first compute $P(\text{race})$ using equation (6.26). We do so by calculating a *weighted average* of percentages for each racial category across voting districts with the population of the voting district, which is proportional to $P(\text{residence})$, as the weight. The `weighted.mean()` function can be used to compute weighted averages, in which the `weights` argument takes a vector of weights.

```
FLCensus <- read.csv("FLCensusVTD.csv")
## compute proportions by applying weighted.mean() to each column
race.prop <-
    apply(FLCensus[, c("white", "black", "api", "hispanic", "others")],
        2, weighted.mean, weights = FLCensus$total.pop)
race.prop # race proportions in Florida

##      white        black          api      hispanic        others
## 0.60451586 0.13941679 0.02186662 0.21279972 0.02140101
```

We can now compute P(surname | race) using equation (6.25) and the census name list.

```
total.count <- sum(cnames$count)
## P(surname | race) = P(race | surname) * P(surname) / P(race)
cnames$name.white <- (cnames$pctwhite / 100) *
    (cnames$count / total.count) / race.prop["white"]
cnames$name.black <- (cnames$pctblack / 100) *
    (cnames$count / total.count) / race.prop["black"]
cnames$name.hispanic <- (cnames$pcthispanic / 100) *
    (cnames$count / total.count) / race.prop["hispanic"]
cnames$name.asian <- (cnames$pctapi / 100) *
    (cnames$count / total.count) / race.prop["api"]
cnames$name.others <- (cnames$pctothers / 100) *
    (cnames$count / total.count) / race.prop["others"]
```

Next, we compute the denominator of equation (6.22), P(surname | residence), using equation (6.24). To do this, we merge the census data into the voter file data using the `county` and `VTD` variables. In the `merge()` function, we set the `all` argument to `FALSE` so that nonmatching rows in both data sets will be dropped (see section 4.2.5). Since the census data includes P(race | residence) as a variable for each racial category, the merged data set will as well.

```
FLVoters <- merge(x = FLVoters, y = FLCensus, by = c("county", "VTD"),
                  all = FALSE)
## P(surname | residence) = sum_race P(surname | race) P(race | residence)
indx <- match(FLVoters$surname, cnames$surname)
FLVoters$name.residence <- cnames$name.white[indx] * FLVoters$white +
    cnames$name.black[indx] * FLVoters$black +
    cnames$name.hispanic[indx] * FLVoters$hispanic +
    cnames$name.asian[indx] * FLVoters$api +
    cnames$name.others[indx] * FLVoters$others
```

We have now calculated every quantity contained in our key version of equation (6.22): P(surname | race), P(race | residence), and P(surname | residence). Finally, we plug the quantities into the equation to compute the predicted probability that an individual belongs to a particular race, given his or her surname and residence.

```
## P(race | surname, residence) = P(surname | race) * P(race | residence)
##                              / P(surname | residence)
FLVoters$pre.white <- cnames$name.white[indx] * FLVoters$white /
    FLVoters$name.residence
```

```
FLVoters$pre.black <- cnames$name.black[indx] * FLVoters$black /
    FLVoters$name.residence
FLVoters$pre.hispanic <- cnames$name.hispanic[indx] * FLVoters$hispanic /
    FLVoters$name.residence
FLVoters$pre.asian <- cnames$name.asian[indx] * FLVoters$api /
    FLVoters$name.residence
FLVoters$pre.others <- 1 - FLVoters$pre.white - FLVoters$pre.black -
    FLVoters$pre.hispanic - FLVoters$pre.asian
```

We evaluate the accuracy of this prediction methodology and assess how much improvement knowledge of the voters' location of residence yields. We begin by examining true positives for each race using the same programming trick as before.

```
## relevant variables
vars1 <- c("pre.white", "pre.black", "pre.hispanic", "pre.asian",
           "pre.others")
## white
whites <- subset(FLVoters, subset = (race == "white"))
mean(apply(whites[, vars1], 1, max) == whites$pre.white)

## [1] 0.9371366

## black
blacks <- subset(FLVoters, subset = (race == "black"))
mean(apply(blacks[, vars1], 1, max) == blacks$pre.black)

## [1] 0.6474954

## Hispanic
hispanics <- subset(FLVoters, subset = (race == "hispanic"))
mean(apply(hispanics[, vars1], 1, max) == hispanics$pre.hispanic)

## [1] 0.85826

## Asian
asians <- subset(FLVoters, subset = (race == "asian"))
mean(apply(asians[, vars1], 1, max) == asians$pre.asian)

## [1] 0.6071429
```

The true positive rate for blacks has jumped from 16% to 65%. Minor improvements are also made for Hispanic and Asian voters. Since African-Americans tend to live close to one another in the United States, the location of voters' residences can be informative. For example, according to the census data, among people whose surname is "White," 27% are black. However, once we incorporate the location of their residence, the predicted probability of such individuals being black ranges from 1% to 98%. This implies that we predict some voters to be highly likely black and others highly likely nonblack.

```
## proportion of blacks among those with surname "White"
cnames$pctblack[cnames$surname == "WHITE"]

## [1] 27.38

## predicted probability of being black given residence location
summary(FLVoters$pre.black[FLVoters$surname == "WHITE"])

##     Min.  1st Qu.   Median     Mean  3rd Qu.     Max.
## 0.005207 0.081150 0.176300 0.264000 0.320000 0.983700
```

Finally, we compute the false positive rate for each race.

```
## white
1 - mean(FLVoters$race[apply(FLVoters[, vars1], 1, max)==
                       FLVoters$pre.white] == "white")

## [1] 0.1187425

## black
1 - mean(FLVoters$race[apply(FLVoters[, vars1], 1, max)==
                       FLVoters$pre.black] == "black")

## [1] 0.2346491

## Hispanic
1 - mean(FLVoters$race[apply(FLVoters[, vars1], 1, max) ==
                       FLVoters$pre.hispanic] == "hispanic")

## [1] 0.2153709

## Asian
1 - mean(FLVoters$race[apply(FLVoters[, vars1], 1, max) ==
                       FLVoters$pre.asian] == "asian")

## [1] 0.3461538
```

We find that the false positive rate for whites is significantly reduced. This is in large part due to the fact that many of the black voters who were incorrectly classified as whites using surname alone are now predicted to be black. In addition, the false positive rate for blacks lowered by a similar amount. This example illustrates the powerful use of conditional probability and Bayes' rule.

6.3 Random Variables and Probability Distributions

We have so far considered various events including a coin landing on heads, twins being both boys, and a voter being African-American. In this section, we introduce the concept of *random variables* and their *probability distributions*, which further widens the scope of mathematical analyses of these events.

6.3.1   RANDOM VARIABLES

A random variable assigns a number to each event. For example, two outcomes of a coin flip can be represented by a binary random variable where 1 indicates landing on heads and 0 denotes landing on tails. Another example is one's income measured in dollars. The values of random variables must represent *mutually exclusive and exhaustive* events. That is, different values cannot represent the same event and all events should be represented by some values. For example, consider a random variable that represents one's racial group using five unique integers: black $= 1$, white $= 2$, hispanic $= 3$, asian $= 4$, and others $= 5$. According to this definition, someone who self-identifies as black and white will be assigned the value of 5 instead of taking the values of 1 and 2 at the same time.

There are two types of random variables, depending on the type of values they take. The first is a *discrete random variable*, which takes a finite (or at most countably infinite) number of distinct values. Examples include categorical or factor variables such as racial groups and number of years of education. The second type is a *continuous random variable*, which takes a value within an interval of the real line. That is, the variable can assume uncountably many values. Examples of continuous random variables include height, weight, and gross domestic product (GDP). The use of random variables, instead of events, facilitates the development of mathematical rules for probability because a random variable takes numeric values. Once we define a random variable, we can formalize a *probability model* using the distribution of the random variable.

> A **random variable** assigns a numeric value to each event of the experiment. These values represent mutually exclusive and exhaustive events, together forming the entire sample space. A **discrete random variable** takes a finite or at most countably infinite number of distinct values, whereas a **continuous random variable** assumes an uncountably infinite number of values.

6.3.2   BERNOULLI AND UNIFORM DISTRIBUTIONS

We first consider the simplest example of a *discrete random variable*: a coin flip. For this experiment, we define a *binary random variable* X, which is equal to 1 if a coin lands on heads, and 0 otherwise. In general, a random variable that takes two distinct values is called a *Bernoulli random variable*. Notice that this setup applies to any experiment with two distinct events. Examples include {vote, abstain}, {win election, lose election}, and {correct classification, misclassification}. Thus, whether a voter turns out ($X = 1$) or not ($X = 0$) can be represented by a Bernoulli random variable. Generically, we consider the event $X = 1$ a success and the event $X = 0$ a failure. We use p to denote the probability of success.

The distribution of a discrete random variable can be characterized by the *probability mass function (PMF)*. The PMF $f(x)$ of a random variable X is defined as the probability that the random variable takes a particular value x, i.e., $f(x) = P(X = x)$. That is, given the input x, which is a specific value of choice, the PMF $f(x)$ returns as

Probability mass function

Cumulative distribution function

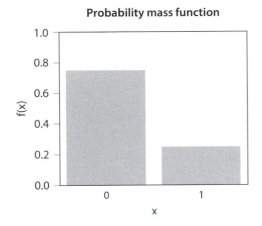
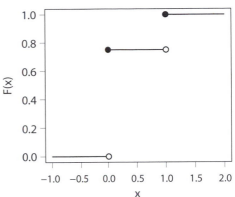

Figure 6.5. The Probability Mass and Cumulative Distribution Functions for a Bernoulli Random Variable. The probability of success is 0.25. The open and solid circles represent the exclusion and inclusion of the corresponding points, respectively.

the output the probability that a random variable X takes that value x. In the case of a Bernoulli random variable, the PMF takes the value of p when $x = 1$ and that of $1 - p$ when $x = 0$. The function is zero at all other values of x.

Another important function related to probability distribution is the *cumulative distribution function (CDF)*. The CDF $F(x)$ represents the cumulative probability that a random variable X takes a value equal to or less than a specific value x, i.e., $F(x) = P(X \leq x)$. The CDF, therefore, represents the sum of the PMF $f(x)$ evaluated at all values up to x. Formally, the relationship between the PMF $f(x)$ and the CDF $F(x)$ for a discrete random variable can be written as

$$F(x) = P(X \leq x) = \sum_{k \leq x} f(k),$$

where k represents all values the random variable X can take that are less than or equal to x. That is, the CDF equals the sum of the PMFs. The CDF ranges from 0 to 1 for any random variable, whether continuous or discrete. It is a nondecreasing function because as x increases, more probability will be added.

The CDF $F(x)$ for a Bernoulli random variable is simple. It is zero for all negative values of x because the random variable never assumes any of those values. The CDF then takes the value of $1 - p$ when $x = 0$, which is the probability that X equals 0. The function stays flat at $1 - p$ when $0 \leq x < 1$ because none of these values will be realized. At $x = 1$, the CDF equals 1 because the random variable takes either the value of 0 or 1, and stays at this value when $x \geq 1$ because X does not take any value greater than 1. Figure 6.5 graphically displays the PMF and CDF of a Bernoulli random variable when $p = 0.25$. The open and solid circles represent the exclusion and inclusion of the corresponding points, respectively.

Probability density function

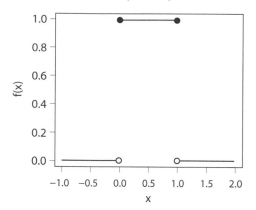

Cumulative distribution function

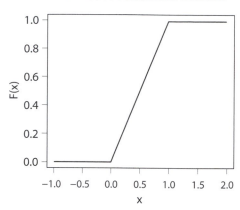

Figure 6.6. The Probability Density and Cumulative Distribution Functions for a Uniform Random Variable. The interval is set to $[0, 1]$. The open and solid circles represent the exclusion and inclusion of the corresponding points, respectively.

The **probability mass function** (PMF) of a **Bernoulli random variable** with success probability p is given by

$$f(x) = \begin{cases} p & \text{if } x = 1, \\ 1 - p & \text{if } x = 0, \\ 0 & \text{otherwise,} \end{cases}$$

where $f(1)$ and $f(0)$ represent the probability of success and failure, respectively. The **cumulative distribution function** (CDF) is given by

$$F(x) = \begin{cases} 0 & \text{if } x < 0, \\ 1 - p & \text{if } 0 \leq x < 1, \\ 1 & \text{if } x \geq 1. \end{cases}$$

We now discuss a *uniform random variable* as a simple example of a *continuous random variable*. A uniform random variable takes every value within a given interval $[a, b]$ with equal likelihood. The PMF is not defined for a continuous random variable because this variable assumes an uncountably infinite number of values. Instead, we use the *probability density function (PDF)* $f(x)$ (or simply, density function), which quantifies the likelihood that a continuous random variable X will take a specific value x. We have already seen the concept of *density*, which is used to measure the height of bins in a histogram (see section 3.3.2). The value of the PDF is nonnegative and can be greater than 1. Moreover, like density in histograms, the area under the PDF must sum to 1.

Since each value within the interval is equally likely to be realized, the PDF for the uniform distribution is a flat horizontal line defined by $1/(b - a)$. In other words, the PDF does not depend on x and always equals $1/(b - a)$ within the interval. The height is determined so that the area below the line equals 1 as required. The left-hand plot of figure 6.6 graphically displays the PDF for a uniform distribution when the interval is set to [0, 1].

We can also define the *cumulative distribution function* (CDF) for a continuous random variable. The definition of the CDF is the same as the case of discrete random variables. That is, the CDF $F(x)$ represents the probability that a random variable X takes a value less than or equal to a specific value x, i.e., $P(X \leq x)$. Graphically, the CDF corresponds to the area under the probability density function curve up to the value x (from negative infinity). Mathematically, this notion can be expressed using integration instead of summation:

$$F(x) = P(X \leq x) = \int_{-\infty}^{x} f(t)\,dt.$$

Since the entire area under the probability density curve has to sum to 1, we have $F(x) = 1$ when $x = \infty$. The CDF for the uniform distribution is shown in the right-hand plot of figure 6.6. In this case, the CDF is a straight line, as shown in the right-hand plot of the figure, because the area under the PDF increases at a constant rate.

The **probability density function** (PDF) of a **uniform random variable** with interval $[a, b]$ is given by

$$f(x) = \begin{cases} \frac{1}{b-a} & \text{if } a \leq x \leq b, \\ 0 & \text{otherwise.} \end{cases}$$

The **cumulative probability function** (CDF) is given by

$$F(x) = \begin{cases} 0 & \text{if } x < a, \\ \frac{x-a}{b-a} & \text{if } a \leq x < b, \\ 1 & \text{if } x \geq b. \end{cases}$$

We can easily compute the PDF and CDF of a uniform distribution in R. For the PDF $f(x)$, we use the `dunif()` function where the main argument is the value x at which the function is evaluated and the interval is specified using the `min` and `max` arguments. We can compute the CDF in a similar manner using the `punif()` function. The `d` in `dunif()` indicates density, whereas the `p` in `punif()` stands for probability.

```
## uniform PDF: x = 0.5, interval = [0, 1]
dunif(0.5, min = 0, max = 1)

## [1] 1

## uniform CDF: x = 1, interval = [-2, 2]
punif(1, min = -2, max = 2)

## [1] 0.75
```

The two distributions we have introduced here share a useful connection. We can use a uniform random variable to generate a Bernoulli random variable. To do this, notice that under the uniform distribution with unit interval [0, 1], the CDF is given by the 45-degree line, i.e., $F(x) = x$. Therefore, the probability that this uniform random variable X takes a value less than or equal to x is equal to x when $0 \leq x \leq 1$. Thus, in order to generate a Bernoulli random variable Y with success probability p, we can first sample a uniform random variable X and then set $Y = 1$ when X is less than p (similarly, set $Y = 0$ if $X \geq p$) so that Y takes a value of 1 with probability p. To do this *Monte Carlo simulation* in R, we use the `runif()` function to generate a uniform random variable by setting the `min` and `max` arguments to 0 and 1, respectively.

```
sims <- 1000
p <- 0.5 # success probabilities
x <- runif(sims, min = 0, max = 1) # uniform [0, 1]
head(x)

## [1] 0.292614295 0.619951024 0.004618747 0.162426728
## [5] 0.001157040 0.655518809

y <- as.integer(x <= p) # Bernoulli; turn TRUE/FALSE to 1/0
head(y)

## [1] 1 0 1 1 1 0

mean(y) # close to success probability p, proportion of 1s vs. 0s

## [1] 0.521
```

6.3.3 BINOMIAL DISTRIBUTION

The *binomial distribution* is a generalization of the Bernoulli distribution. Instead of a single coin flip, we consider an experiment in which the same coin is flipped independently and multiple times. That is, a binomial random variable can represent the number of times a coin lands on heads in multiple trials of independent coin flips.

More generally, a binomial random variable X records the number of successes in a total of n independent and identical trials with success probability p. In other words, a binomial random variable is the sum of n *independently and identically distributed* (or *i.i.d.* in short) Bernoulli random variables. Recall that a Bernoulli random variable equals either 1 or 0 with success probability p. Thus, X can take an integer value from 0 to n. Since the binomial distribution is discrete, its PMF can be interpreted as the probability of X taking a specific value x. The CDF represents the cumulative probability that a binomial random variable has x or fewer successes out of n trials. The PMF and CDF of a binomial random variable are given by the following formulas, which involve combinations (see equation (6.10)). No simple expression exists for the CDF, which is written as the sum of the PMFs.

Probability mass function

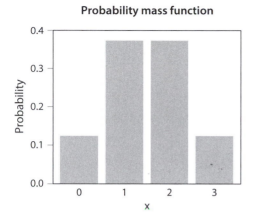

Cumulative distribution function

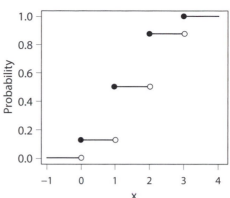

Figure 6.7. The Probability Mass and Cumulative Distribution Functions for a Binomial Random Variable. The success probability is 0.5 and the total number of trials is 3. The open and solid circles represent the exclusion and inclusion of the corresponding points, respectively. Source: Adapted from example by Paul Gaborit, http://texample.net.

The probability mass function (PMF) of a **binomial random variable** with success probability p and n trials is given by

$$f(x) = P(X = x) = \binom{n}{x} p^x (1 - p)^{n-x}. \tag{6.27}$$

The cumulative distribution function (CDF) can be written as

$$F(x) = P(X \leq x) = \sum_{k=0}^{x} \binom{n}{k} p^k (1 - p)^{n-k},$$

for $x = 0, 1, \ldots, n$.

Figure 6.7 shows the PMF and CDF when $p = 0.5$ and $n = 3$. For example, we can compute the probability that we obtain two successes out of three trials, which is the height of the third bar in the left-hand plot of the figure:

$$f(2) = P(X = 2) = \binom{3}{2} \times 0.5^2 \times (1 - 0.5)^{3-2} = \frac{3!}{(3 - 2)!2!} \times 0.5^3 = 0.375.$$

Calculating the PMF of a binomial distribution is straightforward. The `dbinom()` function takes the number of successes as the main argument, and the `size` and `prob` arguments specify the number of trials and success probability, respectively.

```
## PMF when x = 2, n = 3, p = 0.5
dbinom(2, size = 3, prob = 0.5)

## [1] 0.375
```

The CDF, shown in the right-hand plot of the figure, is a *step function* where the function is flat and then jumps at each nonnegative integer value. The size of each jump equals the height of the PMF at the corresponding integer value. Using the CDF, we can compute the cumulative probability that we have at most one success out of three trials:

$$F(1) = P(X \leq 1) = P(X = 0) + P(X = 1) = f(0) + f(1) = 0.125 + 0.375 = 0.5.$$

We can compute the CDF of a binomial distribution in R using the `pbinom()` function.

```
## CDF when x = 1, n = 3, p = 0.5
pbinom(1, size = 3, prob = 0.5)

## [1] 0.5
```

An intuitive explanation covers why the PMF of a binomial distribution looks like equation (6.27). When we flip a coin n times, each unique sequence of n outcomes is equally likely. For example, if $n = 5$, then the event that only the last two coin flips land on tails $\{HHHTT\}$ is equally as likely as the event that the flips alternate landing on heads and tails $\{HTHTHT\}$, where we use H and T to denote the events that a coin lands on heads and tails, respectively. However, for the binomial distribution only the number of heads matters. As a result, these two events represent the same outcome. We use combinations to count the number of ways we can have x successes out of n trials, which is equal to $_nC_x = \binom{n}{x}$. We multiply this by the probability of x successes, which is equal to p^x (because each trial is independent), and the probability of $n - x$ failures, which is given by $(1 - p)^{n-x}$ (again because of independence).

As an application of the binomial distribution, consider the probability that one's vote is pivotal in an election. Your vote is pivotal if the election is tied before you cast your ballot. Suppose that in a large population exactly 50% of voters support an incumbent while the other half support a challenger. Further, assume that whether voters turn out or not has nothing to do with their vote choice. Under this scenario, what is the probability that the election ends up with an exact tie? We compute this probability when the number of voters who turn out equals 1000, then 10,000, and then 100,000. To compute this probability, we can evaluate the PMF of the binomial distribution by setting the success probability to 50% and the size to the total number of voters who turn out. We then evaluate the PMF at exactly half of all voters who turn out. We find that the probability of a tie is quite small, even when the population of voters is evenly divided.

```
## number of voters who turn out
voters <- c(1000, 10000, 100000)
dbinom(voters / 2, size = voters, prob = 0.5)

## [1] 0.025225018 0.007978646 0.002523126
```

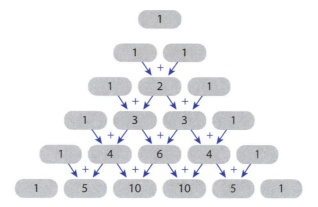

Figure 6.8. Pascal's Triangle. Binomial coefficients can be represented as Pascal's triangle, where the xth element of the nth row returns the binomial coefficient $\binom{n-1}{x-1}$. Source: Adapted from example by Paul Gaborit, http://texample.net.

Where does the name "binomial distribution" come from? The name of this distribution is based on the following *binomial theorem*.

> The **binomial theorem** shows how to compute the coefficient of each term when expanding the power of a binomial, i.e., $(a + b)^n$. That is, the coefficient for the term $a^x b^{n-x}$ when expanding $(a + b)^n$ is equal to $\binom{n}{x}$.

For example, according to the binomial theorem, when $n = 4$, the coefficient for the term $a^2 b^2$ when expanding $(a + b)^4$ is equal to $\binom{4}{2} = 6$. This result is confirmed by writing out the entire expansion:

$$(a + b)^4 = a^4 + 4a^3 b + 6a^2 b^2 + 4ab^3 + b^4. \tag{6.28}$$

These binomial coefficients can be organized as *Pascal's triangle*, as shown in figure 6.8. For example, the coefficients for the terms resulting from the expansion of $(a + b)^4$ in equation (6.28) are shown in the fifth row of Pascal's triangle. More generally, in Pascal's triangle, the xth element of the nth row represents the binomial coefficient $\binom{n-1}{x-1}$. In addition, as shown in the figure, each element equals the sum of the two elements just above it, leading to a straightforward sequential computation of binomial coefficients. This makes sense because, for example, $(a + b)^4$ can be written as the product of $(a + b)^3$ and $(a + b)$,

$$(a + b)^4 = (a^3 + 3a^2 b + 3ab^2 + b^3)(a + b).$$

In this example, the coefficient for $a^2 b^2$ is based on the sum of two products, i.e., $3a^2 b \times b$ and $3ab^2 \times a$, and hence is equal to $6 = 3 + 3$. In general, to obtain x

Probability density function

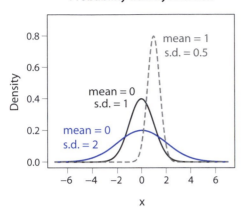

Cumulative distribution function

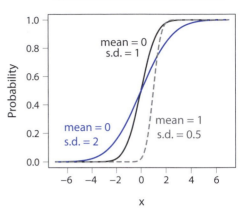

Figure 6.9. The Probability Density and Cumulative Distribution Functions of the Normal Distribution.

success combinations out of n trials, we consider two scenarios—the last trial ending in a success or ending in a failure—and add the total number of combinations under each scenario:

$$\binom{n-1}{x} + \binom{n-1}{x-1} = \frac{(n-1)!}{x!(n-x-1)!} + \frac{(n-1)!}{(x-1)!(n-x)!}$$

$$= (n-1)! \times \frac{(n-x)+x}{x!(n-x)!} = \binom{n}{x}.$$

The first (second) term corresponds to the scenario where there are x $(x-1)$ successes out of $(n-1)$ trials and the last trial ends in a failure (success).

6.3.4   NORMAL DISTRIBUTION

As another important example of a continuous random variable, we introduce the *normal distribution*. This distribution is also called the *Gaussian distribution*, named after German mathematician Carl Friedrich Gauss. As implied by its name, the normal distribution is special because, as section 6.4.2 will explore, the sum of many random variables from the same distribution tends to follow the normal distribution even when the original distribution is not normal.

A normal random variable can take any number on the real line $(-\infty, \infty)$. The normal distribution has two parameters, mean μ and standard deviation σ. If X is a normal random variable, we may write $X \sim \mathcal{N}(\mu, \sigma^2)$, where σ^2 represents the variance (the square of standard deviation). The PDF and the CDF of the normal distribution are given by the following formulas.

The probability density function (PDF) of a **normal random variable** is given by

$$f(x) = \frac{1}{\sqrt{2\pi}\sigma} \exp\left\{-\frac{1}{2\sigma^2}(x - \mu)^2\right\},$$

for any x on the real line. The cumulative probability distribution (CDF) has no analytically tractable form and is given by

$$F(x) = P(X \le x) = \int_{-\infty}^{x} f(t)\,dt = \int_{-\infty}^{x} \frac{1}{\sqrt{2\pi}\sigma} \exp\left\{-\frac{1}{2\sigma^2}(t - \mu)^2\right\} dt,$$

(6.29)

where $X \sim \mathcal{N}(\mu, \sigma^2)$ and $\exp(\cdot)$ is the exponential function (see section 3.4.1). The CDF represents the area under the PDF from negative infinity up to x.

Figure 6.9 plots the PDF (left-hand plot) and CDF (right-hand plot) for the normal distribution, with three different sets of the mean and standard deviation. The PDF of the normal distribution is bell shaped and centered around its mean, with the standard deviation controlling the spread of the distribution. When the mean is 0 and standard deviation is 1, we have the *standard normal distribution*. The PDF is symmetric around the mean. Different means shift the PDF and CDF without changing their shape. In contrast, a larger standard deviation means more variability, yielding a flatter PDF and a more gradually increasing CDF.

The normal distribution has two important properties. First, adding a constant to (or subtracting it from) a normal random variable yields a normal random variable with appropriately shifted mean. Second, multiplying (or dividing) a normal random variable by a constant also yields another normal random variable with an appropriately scaled mean and standard deviation. Accordingly, the z-score of a normal random variable follows the standard normal distribution. We formally state these properties below.

Suppose X is a normal random variable with mean μ and standard deviation σ, i.e., $X \sim \mathcal{N}(\mu, \sigma^2)$. Let c be an arbitrary constant. Then, the following properties hold:

1. A random variable defined by $Z = X + c$ also follows a normal distribution, with $Z \sim \mathcal{N}(\mu + c, \sigma^2)$.
2. A random variable defined by $Z = cX$ also follows a normal distribution, with $Z \sim \mathcal{N}(c\mu, (c\sigma)^2)$.

These properties imply that the z-**score** of a normal random variable follows the standard normal distribution, which has zero mean and unit variance:

$$z\text{-score} = \frac{X - \mu}{\sigma} \sim \mathcal{N}(0, 1).$$

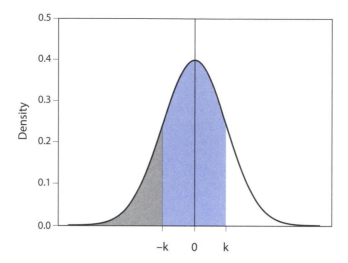

Figure 6.10. The Area under the Probability Density Function Curve of the Normal Distribution. The blue area can be computed as the difference between the cumulative distribution function (CDF) evaluated at k and $-k$ (i.e., the gray and blue areas minus the gray area).

In addition, it is important to note that if the data are distributed according to the normal distribution, about two-thirds are within 1 standard deviation from the mean and approximately 95% are within 2 standard deviations from the mean. Let us compute the probability that a normal random variable with mean μ and standard deviation σ lies within k standard deviations from the mean for a positive constant $k > 0$. To simplify the computation, consider the *z-score*, which has the standard normal distribution:

$$P(\mu - k\sigma \leq X \leq \mu + k\sigma) = P(-k\sigma \leq X - \mu \leq k\sigma)$$

$$= P\left(-k \leq \frac{X - \mu}{\sigma} \leq k\right)$$

$$= P(-k \leq Z \leq k),$$

where Z is a standard normal random variable. The first equality holds because we subtract μ from each term whereas the second inequality holds since we divide each term by a positive constant σ.

Thus, the desired probability equals the probability that a standard normal random variable lies between $-k$ and k. As illustrated in figure 6.10, this probability can be written as the difference in the CDF evaluated at k and $-k$:

$$P(-k \leq Z \leq k) = P(Z \leq k) - P(Z \leq -k) = F(k) - F(-k),$$

where $F(k)$ represents the sum of the blue and gray areas in the figure, whereas $F(-k)$ equals the gray area. These results can be confirmed in R with the `pnorm()` function, which evaluates the CDF at its input value. This function takes the mean (mean) and standard deviation (sd) as two important arguments. The default is the standard normal distribution with mean = 0 and sd = 1.

```
## plus minus 1 standard deviation from the mean
pnorm(1) - pnorm(-1)

## [1] 0.6826895

## plus minus 2 standard deviations from the mean
pnorm(2) - pnorm(-2)

## [1] 0.9544997
```

The result suggests that, under the standard normal distribution, approximately 2/3 are within 1 standard deviation from the mean and about 95% are within 2 standard deviations from the mean. We can also directly specify mean and standard deviation without transforming a variable into a standard normal random variable. Suppose that the original distribution has a mean of 5 and standard deviation of 2, i.e., $\mu = 5$ and $\sigma = 2$. We can compute the same probabilities as above in the following way.

```
mu <- 5
sigma <- 2
## plus minus 1 standard deviation from the mean
pnorm(mu + sigma, mean = mu, sd = sigma) - pnorm(mu - sigma, mean = mu, sd = sigma)

## [1] 0.6826895

## plus minus 2 standard deviations from the mean
pnorm(mu + 2*sigma, mean = mu, sd = sigma) - pnorm(mu - 2*sigma, mean = mu, sd = sigma)

## [1] 0.9544997
```

As an application of the normal distribution, consider the *regression towards the mean* phenomenon discussed in section 4.2.4. In that section, we presented evidence from US presidential elections demonstrating that in states where Obama received a large share of votes in 2008, he was likely to receive a *smaller* share of votes in 2012 (see section 4.2.5). Recall that our regression model used Obama's 2008 statewide vote share to predict his vote share for the same state in the 2012 election. We use the regression object fit1, as created in section 4.2.5.

```
## see the page reference above
## "Obama2012.z" is Obama's 2012 standardized vote share
## "Obama2008.z" is Obama's 2008 standardized vote share
fit1

##
## Call:
## lm(formula = Obama2012.z ~ -1 + Obama2008.z, data = pres)
```

```
##
## Coefficients:
## Obama2008.z
##      0.9834
```

We examine the distribution of *residuals* and compare it with the normal distribution (see section 4.2.3 for the definition of residuals). We first present a histogram and overlay the PDF of the normal distribution using the `dnorm()` function. We then use a *quantile–quantile plot* (*Q–Q plot*) to directly compare the distribution of residuals with the normal distribution. The `qqnorm()` function creates a quantile–quantile plot using the *standard normal distribution*, whose mean is 0 and standard deviation is 1. To make the standard normal distribution and the distribution of residuals comparable, we use the `scale()` function to compute the *z-score* of residuals, or *standardized residuals*, whose mean is 0 and standard deviation is 1 (see section 3.7.3). Since residuals always have a mean of 0 (see section 4.2.3), we need only divide them by their standard deviation to obtain standardized residuals.

```
e <- resid(fit1)
## z-score of residuals
e.zscore <- scale(e)
## alternatively we can divide residuals by their standard deviation
e.zscore <- e / sd(e)
hist(e.zscore, freq = FALSE, ylim = c(0, 0.4),
     xlab = "Standardized residuals",
     main = "Distribution of standardized residuals")
x <- seq(from = -3, to = 3, by = 0.01)
lines(x, dnorm(x)) # overlay the normal density
qqnorm(e.zscore, xlim = c(-3, 3), ylim = c(-3, 3)) # quantile-quantile plot
abline(0, 1) # 45-degree line
```

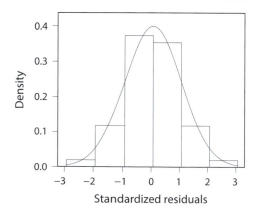

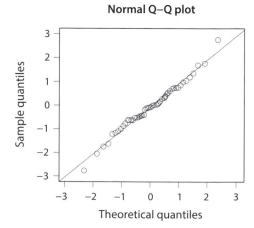

Both the histogram and Q–Q plot show that the distribution of standardized residuals is remarkably close to the standard normal distribution. Now, consider the following probability model:

Obama's 2012 standardized vote share

$$= 0.983 \times \text{Obama's 2008 standardized vote share} + \epsilon, \qquad (6.30)$$

where 0.983 is the estimated slope coefficient, and the error term ϵ follows a normal distribution with mean and standard deviation equal to 0 and 0.18, respectively. The value of standard deviation is obtained as follows.

```
e.sd <- sd(e)
e.sd

## [1] 0.1812239
```

Thus, this probability model describes a potential data-generating process for Obama's 2012 vote share given his vote share in the previous election. Because both the outcome variable and the predictor are standardized, the intercept is estimated to be exactly zero and hence is not included in the coef(fit1) object (recall that the regression line always goes through the means of the outcome variable and the predictor).

We first analyze California where, in 2008, Obama won 61% of the votes, or a standardized vote share of 0.87. According to the above model, what is the probability that Obama wins a greater share of California votes in 2012? Using the pnorm() function, we can compute the area corresponding to the 2008 vote share under the normal distribution derived for Obama's 2012 votes from the probability model given in equation (6.30). We set the lower.tail argument in the pnorm() function to FALSE in order to compute the probability that Obama wins a *greater* vote share in 2012 than in 2008.

```
CA.2008 <- pres$Obama2008.z[pres$state == "CA"]
CA.2008

## [1] 0.8720631

CA.mean2012 <- coef(fit1) * CA.2008
CA.mean2012

## Obama2008.z
##   0.8576233

## area to the right; greater than CA.2008
pnorm(CA.2008, mean = CA.mean2012, sd = e.sd, lower.tail = FALSE)

## [1] 0.4682463
```

Thus, Obama is somewhat unlikely to win a larger share of California votes in 2012 than he won in 2008. In fact, the probability of this event is only 46.8%. Now consider Texas, where in 2008 Obama received only 44% of the votes, or a standardized vote share of -0.67. Again, under the probability model specified in equation (6.30), we compute the probability that Obama wins a greater share of Texas votes in 2012 than he did in the previous election.

```
TX.2008 <- pres$Obama2008.z[pres$state == "TX"]
TX.mean2012 <- coef(fit1) * TX.2008
TX.mean2012

## Obama2008.z
##  -0.6567543

pnorm(TX.2008, mean = TX.mean2012, sd = e.sd, lower.tail = FALSE)

## [1] 0.5243271
```

In the case of Texas, this probability is 52.4%, which is higher than the probability for California. This illustrates the regression towards the mean phenomenon under the probability model based on linear regression with a normally distributed error.

6.3.5   EXPECTATION AND VARIANCE

We have introduced several commonly used random variables by defining their PDF/PMF and CDF. These functions completely characterize the distribution of a random variable, but often it is helpful to obtain a more concise summary of a distribution. Previously, we used means and standard deviations in order to measure the center and spread of a distribution. We begin by examining the *expectation*, or mean, of a random variable. We should not confuse this with the *sample mean* discussed earlier in this book. The sample mean refers to the average of a variable in a particular data set, whereas the expectation or *population mean* represents the mean value under a probability distribution. The sample mean fluctuates from one sample to another, but the expectation of a random variable is of a theoretical nature and is fixed given a probability model.

Before we examine the formal definition of expectation, a few examples will prove instructive. Consider a Bernoulli random variable with success probability p (e.g., a single coin flip with the probability of landing on heads being p). What is the expectation? This random variable can take only two values, 0 (tail) and 1 (heads), and so the expectation can be computed as the weighted average of these two values with $(1-p)$ and p (i.e., the PMF) as weights, respectively. Let $\mathbb{E}(X)$ represent the expectation of a random variable X. Then, the expectation of a Bernoulli random variable can be computed as

$$\mathbb{E}(X) = 0 \times P(X = 0) + 1 \times P(X = 1) = 0 \times f(0) + 1 \times f(1) = 0 \times (1-p) + 1 \times p = p.$$
(6.31)

Similarly, consider a binomial random variable with success probability p and size n (e.g., the number of heads out of n independent and identical coin flips). This random variable can take any nonnegative integer up to n (i.e., $0, 1, \ldots, n$). The expectation of this binomial random variable is also defined as the weighted average of these values with the weights given by the corresponding values of the PMF:

$$\mathbb{E}(X) = 0 \times f(0) + 1 \times f(1) + \cdots + n \times f(n) = \sum_{x=0}^{n} x \times f(x). \qquad (6.32)$$

While we use the weighted average to define expectation for a discrete random variable, we need a different way of defining the expectation for a continuous variable. We still compute the weighted average of each value in which the weights are given by the PDF. However, the difference is that a continuous random variable can take an uncountably infinite number of distinct values. This is done through the mathematical operation called *integration*. Readers who are not familiar with calculus can skip the details, but, for example, the expectation of a uniform random variable with interval $[a, b]$ is calculated as

$$\mathbb{E}(X) = \int_{a}^{b} x \times f(x)\,dx = \int_{a}^{b} \frac{x}{b-a}\,dx = \frac{x^2}{2(b-a)}\bigg|_{a}^{b} = \frac{a+b}{2}. \qquad (6.33)$$

Since each point within the interval is equally likely, the expectation of a uniform random variable equals the midpoint of the interval.

We now summarize the general definition of expectation for discrete and continuous random variables.

> The **expectation** of a random variable is denoted by $\mathbb{E}(X)$ and is defined as
>
> $$\mathbb{E}(X) = \begin{cases} \sum_{x} x \times f(x) & \text{if } X \text{ is discrete,} \\ \int x \times f(x)\,dx & \text{if } X \text{ is continuous,} \end{cases} \qquad (6.34)$$
>
> where $f(x)$ is the probability mass function or PMF (probability density function or PDF) of the discrete (continuous) random variable X.

In the definition of expectation, the summation and integration are taken with respect to all possible values of X. The set of all possible values that X takes is called the *support* of the distribution. We now introduce the basic rules of the expectation operator $\mathbb{E}$.

Let X and Y be random variables, and a and b be arbitrary constants. The **expectation** is a linear operator that satisfies the following equalities:

1. $\mathbb{E}(a) = a$.
2. $\mathbb{E}(aX) = a\mathbb{E}(X)$.
3. $\mathbb{E}(aX + b) = a\mathbb{E}(X) + b$.
4. $\mathbb{E}(aX + bY) = a\mathbb{E}(X) + b\mathbb{E}(Y)$.
5. If X and Y are independent, then $\mathbb{E}(XY) = \mathbb{E}(X)\mathbb{E}(Y)$. But generally, $\mathbb{E}(XY) \neq \mathbb{E}(X)\mathbb{E}(Y)$.

Now, using these rules, we can easily compute the expectation of a binomial random variable. Recall that a binomial random variable X with success probability p and size n is the sum of n independently and identically distributed (i.i.d.) Bernoulli random variables, $Y_1, \ldots, Y_n$, with the same success probability p. This suggests that we can obtain the expectation of the binomial random variable as

$$\mathbb{E}(X) = \mathbb{E}\left(\sum_{i=1}^{n} Y_i\right) = \sum_{i=1}^{n} \mathbb{E}(Y_i) = np.$$

This derivation is much more straightforward than the calculation that would be required (i.e., the sum of binomial PMFs evaluated at many values) if we used the definition of expectation given in equation (6.32).

Another useful statistic is the *standard deviation* and its square, *variance*, of a random variable. Both concepts have already been introduced in section 2.6.2. Like the expectation, it is important to distinguish between the standard deviation of a particular sample and the theoretical standard deviation of a random variable. Their interpretations match in that standard deviation is defined as the root mean square (RMS) of deviation from the mean (see section 2.6.2). In the current context, however, we use the expectation, rather than the sample average, to represent the mean.

The **variance** of a random variable X is defined as

$$\mathbb{V}(X) = \mathbb{E}[\{X - \mathbb{E}(X)\}^2].$$

The square root of $\mathbb{V}(X)$ is called the **standard deviation**.

Using the basic rules of expectation, we can write the variance as the difference between the expectation of X^2 and the expectation of X. The expectation of X^2 is called the *second moment*, while the expectation of X, or the mean, is called the *first moment*:

$$\begin{aligned}
\mathbb{V}(X) &= \mathbb{E}[\{X - \mathbb{E}(X)\}^2] \\
&= \mathbb{E}[X^2 - 2X\mathbb{E}(X) + \{\mathbb{E}(X)\}^2] \\
&= \mathbb{E}(X^2) - 2\mathbb{E}(X)\mathbb{E}(X) + \{\mathbb{E}(X)\}^2 \\
&= \mathbb{E}(X^2) - \{\mathbb{E}(X)\}^2.
\end{aligned} \tag{6.35}$$

This alternative expression of variance is useful. For example, the variance of a Bernoulli random variable can be derived by noting that $X = X^2$ regardless of whether X equals 1 or 0 (because $1^2 = 1$ and $0^2 = 0$):

$$\mathbb{V}(X) = \mathbb{E}(X) - \{\mathbb{E}(X)\}^2 = p(1 - p). \tag{6.36}$$

This variance is greatest when $p = 0.5$. This makes intuitive sense because when p is smaller, for example, a Bernoulli random variable is more likely to equal 0 and hence has a smaller variance and hence less variation.

Similarly, using equation (6.35), we can also calculate the variance of a uniform random variable with the interval $[a, b]$, though readers unfamiliar with integration may ignore the details of the following derivation:

$$\mathbb{V}(X) = \mathbb{E}(X^2) - \{\mathbb{E}(X)\}^2 = \int_a^b \frac{x^2}{b-a} \, dx - \left(\frac{a+b}{2}\right)^2$$

$$= \frac{x^3}{3(b-a)} \Big|_a^b - \left(\frac{a+b}{2}\right)^2 = \frac{1}{12}(b-a)^2. \tag{6.37}$$

Like expectation, variance can be approximated through Monte Carlo simulation. Using the set of Bernoulli draws we generated earlier, we compute the sample variance, which should approximate the population variance.

```
## theoretical variance: p was set to 0.5 earlier
p * (1 - p)

## [1] 0.25

## sample variance using "y" generated earlier
var(y)

## [1] 0.2498088
```

Variance has several important properties. For example, since variance involves the expectation of squared distance from the mean, adding a constant to a random variable only shifts the variable and its mean by the same amount without altering its variance. However, the multiplication of a constant and a random variable changes its variance:

$$\mathbb{V}(aX) = \mathbb{E}[\{aX - a\mathbb{E}(X)\}^2] = a^2\mathbb{V}(X). \tag{6.38}$$

We summarize these properties below.

> Let X and Y be random variables, and a and b be arbitrary constants. The **variance** operator $\mathbb{V}$ has the following properties:
>
> 1. $\mathbb{V}(a) = 0$.
> 2. $\mathbb{V}(aX) = a^2 \mathbb{V}(X)$.
> 3. $\mathbb{V}(X + b) = \mathbb{V}(X)$.
> 4. $\mathbb{V}(aX + b) = a^2 \mathbb{V}(X)$.
> 5. If X and Y are independent, $\mathbb{V}(X + Y) = \mathbb{V}(X) + \mathbb{V}(Y)$.

To compute the variance of a binomial random variable X, we use its status as the sum of n independently and identically distributed (i.i.d.) Bernoulli random variables, $Y_1, Y_2, \ldots, Y_n$, with success probability p:

$$\mathbb{V}(X) = \mathbb{V}\left(\sum_{i=1}^{n} Y_i\right) = \sum_{i=1}^{n} \mathbb{V}(Y_i) = np(1 - p).$$

As another example, consider two independent normal random variables X and Y. Suppose that X has mean μ_X and variance σ_X^2, whereas Y has mean μ_Y and variance σ_Y^2. We write this setting compactly as $X \sim \mathcal{N}(\mu_X, \sigma_X^2)$ and $Y \sim \mathcal{N}(\mu_Y, \sigma_Y^2)$. What is the distribution of $Z = aX + bY + c$? The discussion in section 6.3.4 implies that Z is also a normal random variable. Using the rules of expectation and variance, we can derive the mean and variance as

$$\mathbb{E}(Z) = a\mathbb{E}(X) + b\mathbb{E}(Y) + c = a\mu_X + b\mu_Y + c,$$

$$\mathbb{V}(Z) = \mathbb{V}(aX + bY + c) = a^2\mathbb{V}(X) + b^2\mathbb{V}(Y) = a^2\sigma_X^2 + b^2\sigma_Y^2,$$

respectively. Therefore, we have $Z \sim \mathcal{N}(a\mu_X + b\mu_Y + c, a^2\sigma_X^2 + b^2\sigma_Y^2)$.

6.3.6   PREDICTING ELECTION OUTCOMES WITH UNCERTAINTY

We next revisit the prediction of election outcomes using preelection polls. In section 4.1's introduction of the topic, our prediction did not include a measure of uncertainty. However, polling has *sampling variability* because we interview only a fraction of a large population. Suppose that we conduct a preelection poll under the exact same conditions multiple times. Each time, we obtain a representative sample of the target population and yet the sample consists of different voters. This means that the estimated support for a candidate will differ for each sample.

To capture this sampling variability, consider the following probability model. Suppose that the Election Day outcome represents the true proportion of Obama and McCain supporters in the population of voters within each state. We further assume that the fraction of voters who support a third-party candidate is negligible. We therefore focus on the two-party support rate for Obama, p_j, and McCain, $1 - p_j$, within each state j. The CSV data file, `pres08.csv`, contains the 2008 US presidential election results (see table 4.1). We first compute the two-party support rate for Obama.

```r
pres08 <- read.csv("pres08.csv")
## two-party vote share
pres08$p <- pres08$Obama / (pres08$Obama + pres08$McCain)
```

We assume that for each hypothetical sampling, we interview 1000 voters who are randomly selected from the population. The binomial distribution with success probability p and size 1000 within each state is our model for Obama's support estimate based on a preelection poll. Using *Monte Carlo simulation*, we estimate Obama's support within each state, then allocate that state's Electoral College votes to the winning candidate. We will repeat this procedure many times to describe the uncertainty in preelection polling estimates that is due to sampling variability.

To sample from the binomial distribution in R, we use the `rbinom()` function. The `prob` argument of this function can take a vector of success probabilities. For each success probability, the function will return a vector of binomial random variable realizations. That is, given a p_j probability of success and $n = 1000$ voters, R will generate the number of votes for Obama. If a majority of these 1000 voters support Obama, we assign the state's Electoral College votes to Obama. We construct a histogram of these predicted Electoral College votes for Obama.

```r
n.states <- nrow(pres08) # number of states
n <- 1000 # number of respondents
sims <- 10000 # number of simulations
## Obama's electoral votes
Obama.ev <- rep(NA, sims)
for (i in 1:sims) {
    ## samples number of votes for Obama in each state
    draws <- rbinom(n.states, size = n, prob = pres08$p)
    ## sums state's Electoral College votes if Obama wins the majority
    Obama.ev[i] <- sum(pres08$EV[draws > n / 2])
}
hist(Obama.ev, freq = FALSE, main = "Prediction of election outcome",
     xlab = "Obama's Electoral College votes")
abline(v = 364, col = "blue") # actual result
```

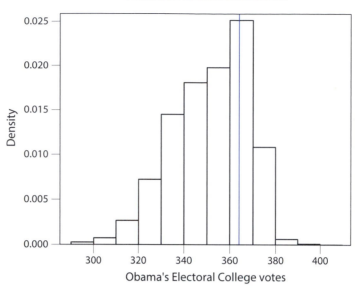

We find that all prediction draws are above the winning threshold of 270 votes. While the highest density of the histogram roughly corresponds to the actual number of Electoral College votes Obama won, the distribution of predictions is skewed. As a result, the mean and median values are lower than the actual number of Obama's votes.

```
summary(Obama.ev)

##    Min. 1st Qu.  Median    Mean 3rd Qu.    Max.
##   291.0   340.0   353.0   352.2   364.0   401.0
```

We can also analytically compute the expected value of Obama's Electoral College votes under this probability model. Let S_j represent the number of respondents (among a total of 1000 respondents) to a preelection poll who express support for Obama in state j. We use v_j to denote the number of Electoral College votes for state j. Then, the expected number of Obama's Electoral College votes is

$$\mathbb{E}(\text{Obama's votes}) = \sum_{j=1}^{51} v_j \times P(\text{Obama wins state } j) = \sum_{j=1}^{51} v_j \times P(S_j > 500).$$

(6.39)

To compute this expectation in R, we use the `pbinom()` function, which evaluates the CDF of the binomial distribution at its input value. As in `dbinom()`, the function takes as its arguments `size` and `prob`. In addition, we set the `lower.tail` argument to `FALSE` so that the function can be used to evaluate $P(S_j > 500)$ rather than $P(S_j \leq 500)$. The threshold 500 is based on the fact that we predict Obama as a winner for a state if more than half of 1000 respondents support him.

```
mean(Obama.ev)

## [1] 352.1646

## probability of binomial random variable taking greater than n/2 votes
sum(pres08$EV * pbinom(n / 2, size = n, prob = pres08$p, lower.tail = FALSE))

## [1] 352.1388
```

As expected, the analytically derived expected value is close to the approximate value based on Monte Carlo simulations. Similarly, we can compute the variance of Obama's electoral votes:

$$\mathbb{V}(\text{Obama's predicted votes}) = \sum_{j=1}^{51} \mathbb{V}(v_j \mathbf{1}\{S_j > 500\})$$

$$= \sum_{j=1}^{51} v_j^2 P(S_j > 500)\bigl(1 - P(S_j > 500)\bigr).$$

In this derivation, $\mathbf{1}\{\cdot\}$ represents the *indicator function*, which returns 1 (0) if the statement inside the curly braces is true (false). In addition, the first equality follows from the fact that the variance of the sum of independent random variables equals the sum of their respective variances. We also used the expression for the variance of a Bernoulli random variable given in equation (6.36) because we are evaluating the variance of a Bernoulli random variable $\mathbf{1}\{S_j > 500\}$. We compute the variance first with the theoretical expression above and then with Monte Carlo simulation draws.

```
## approximate variance using Monte Carlo draws
var(Obama.ev)

## [1] 268.7592

## theoretical variance
pres08$pb <- pbinom(n / 2, size = n, prob = pres08$p, lower.tail = FALSE)
V <- sum(pres08$pb * (1 - pres08$pb) * pres08$EV^2)
V

## [1] 268.8008

## approximate standard deviation using Monte Carlo draws
sd(Obama.ev)

## [1] 16.39388

## theoretical standard deviation
sqrt(V)

## [1] 16.39515
```

The result implies that with 1000 respondents in each state, our poll-based pre-diction of Obama's Electoral College votes varies from one sample to another. The standard deviation of our prediction is about 16 Electoral College votes. Given that Obama won the election with a much greater margin, this sampling variation did not significantly impact the preelection polls' ability to predict the winner.

6.4   Large Sample Theorems

As the final topic of this chapter, we introduce two important probabilistic regu-larities in large samples. In a wide range of probabilistic models, certain patterns will emerge as the sample size increases. These regularities will quantify the uncertainty of our data analysis in the next chapter. In this section, we discuss two *large sample theorems* (*asymptotic theorems*): the law of large numbers and the central limit theorem.

6.4.1   THE LAW OF LARGE NUMBERS

The *law of large numbers* states that as the sample size increases, the sample average converges to the expectation or population average.

Suppose that we obtain a random sample of n independently and identically distributed (i.i.d.) observations, $X_1, X_2, \ldots, X_n$, from a probability distribution with expectation $\mathbb{E}(X)$. The **law of large numbers** states

$$\overline{X}_n = \frac{1}{n} \sum_{i=1}^{n} X_i \to \mathbb{E}(X), \tag{6.40}$$

where we use $\to$ as shorthand for convergence.

In the theorem, X without subscript i represents a generic random variable, whereas X_i is the random variable for the ith observation. Although the precise mathematical meaning of convergence, as well as the precise conditions under which this theorem holds, are beyond the scope of this book, we emphasize that this theorem is applicable to a wide range of probability distributions. Intuitively speaking, the law states that the sample average, $\overline{X}_n$, will better approximate the expectation, $\mathbb{E}(X)$, as the sample size increases. The law of large numbers is powerful because it can be applied in most settings without knowledge of the underlying probability distribution.

We have already implicitly used the law of large numbers in a variety of contexts. The law of large numbers justifies the use of random sampling in surveys (see section 3.4.1). As we increase the number of randomly sampled respondents, the average response among them becomes closer to the true average of the population. In preelection polls, so long as the sample size is sufficiently large, the sample fraction of those who support Obama approximates the population fraction of voters who are Obama supporters. The law of large numbers enables researchers to talk to a small fraction of randomly sampled individuals in order to infer the opinion of the entire population.

In terms of a probability model, we can think of preelection polling as the sum of independently and identically distributed (i.i.d.) Bernoulli random variables, where a respondent is randomly drawn from a population of Obama supporters and non-supporters. That is, we define X_i as an indicator variable of voter i being an Obama supporter, i.e., $X_i = 1$ if voter i is an Obama supporter and $X_i = 0$ otherwise. The proportion of Obama supporters in the population is given by p. Then, the law of large numbers given in equation (6.40) can be directly applied. The sample fraction of Obama's supporters approaches the expectation, or the population proportion of Obama supporters, i.e., $\mathbb{E}(X) = p$.

Similarly, we can rely on the law of large numbers in randomized experiments when computing the difference-in-means between the (randomly divided) treatment and control groups to estimate the average treatment effect (see section 2.4.1). If we consider a population of potential outcomes, as the sizes of the treatment and control groups increase, the sample average of the observed outcome better approximates the expected potential outcome. In other words, we can apply the law of large numbers shown in equation (6.40) by setting X to each potential outcome, $Y(1)$ in the treatment group and $Y(0)$ in the control group.

The law of large numbers can also justify the use of *Monte Carlo simulations*. For example, in the birthday problem described in section 6.1.4, we computed the fraction of simulation trials where at least two birthdays were the same, in order to approximate the true probability of the event occurrence. When applying the law of large numbers shown in equation (6.40), this probability can be written as the expectation by defining a Bernoulli random variable that equals 1 if at least two birthdays match and 0 otherwise. We can then think of the fraction of simulation trials as the sample mean. Similarly, we solved the Monty Hall problem by computing the fraction of simulation trials in which a contender won a car rather than a goat (see section 6.2.2).

To illustrate the law of large numbers, we conduct a Monte Carlo simulation. We randomly sample from a binomial distribution with success probability $p = 0.2$ and size $n = 10$. We then examine, as the number of binomial draws increases, how the sample mean approaches the expectation, which equals $\mathbb{E}(X) = np = 2$ in this case. To calculate the sample mean after a single draw, two draws, and so on, all the way up to 1000 draws, we apply the `cumsum()` function. This function computes the *cumulative sum*, which combines all values up to and including the current value, for each position in a vector. For example, for a vector of length 3, $(5, 3, 4)$, the `cumsum()` function will return another vector of length 3 that contains the cumulative sum $(5, 8, 12)$. We obtain the desired average for each sample size $(5, 4, 4)$ by dividing the cumulative sum vector by a vector that contains the number of elements used for the summation, i.e., $(1, 2, 3)$. According to the law of large numbers, a large number of draws should produce a sample mean close to the expectation.

```
sims <- 1000
## 3 separate simulations for each
x.binom <- rbinom(sims, p = 0.2, size = 10)
## computing sample mean with varying sample size
mean.binom <- cumsum(x.binom) / 1:sims
```

In addition, we use the uniform distribution as an example of continuous random variables. The `runif()` function generates a random sample from this distribution.

```
## default runif() is uniform(0, 1)
x.unif <- runif(sims)
mean.unif <- cumsum(x.unif) / 1:sims
```

Finally, we plot the results. As the sample size increases, the sample mean approaches the expectation.

```
## plot for binomial
plot(1:sims, mean.binom, type = "l", ylim = c(1, 3),
     xlab = "Sample size", ylab = "Sample mean", main = "Binomial(10, 0.2)")
abline(h = 2, lty = "dashed") # expectation
## plot for uniform
plot(1:sims, mean.unif, type = "l", ylim = c(0, 1),
     xlab = "Sample size", ylab = "Sample mean", main = "Uniform(0, 1)")
abline(h = 0.5, lty = "dashed") # expectation
```

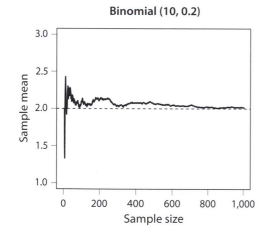
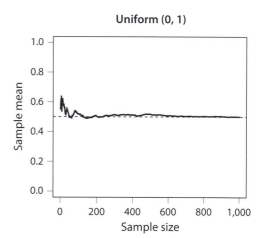

6.4.2   THE CENTRAL LIMIT THEOREM

The law of large numbers is useful but cannot quantify how good the approximation becomes as the sample size increases. For example, in the above figure, convergence appears to occur more quickly in the case of the uniform distribution than the binomial distribution. In practice, however, we observe only the sample mean and do not know the expectation. The former is something we compute from the data but the latter is a theoretical concept. Therefore, we need a different tool to know how well our sample mean approximates the expectation.

Figure 6.11. The Quincunx as a Machine to Illustrate the Central Limit Theorem.

The *central limit theorem* shows that the distribution of the sample mean approaches the *normal distribution* as the sample size increases. This is a remarkable result because, like the law of large numbers, it applies to a wide range of distributions. The result is useful, as shown in the next chapter, when quantifying the uncertainty of our estimates.

Before we explain the central limit theorem more formally, we discuss the *quincunx*, invented by Sir Francis Galton who first demonstrated the regression towards the mean phenomenon (section 4.2.4), as a machine that illustrates the theorem. Figure 6.11 presents a picture of a quincunx owned by the author. Red balls are dropped, one at a time, from the tiny hole at the top. The balls, as they fall, bounce off each peg either to its right or left before settling into one of the slots at the bottom of the machine. As seen in the figure, the balls will cluster in the middle, forming a bell-shaped curve that looks like a normal distribution.

Why does the quincunx create a bell-shaped curve? When a ball hits a peg, the ball has a 50–50 chance of bouncing off to its right or left. Although each path from the top to the bottom of the quincunx is equally likely, the ball has more ways to fall into a middle slot than a side slot. More formally, the total number of ways in which a ball reaches a particular slot can be computed using Pascal's triangle, as shown in figure 6.8. As illustrated in the figure, for example, if there are 5 lines of pegs in the quincunx, there are 20 ways for a ball to fall into the middle two slots.

We can understand the quincunx as a machine that generates a sequence of independently and identically distributed (i.i.d.) binomial random variables X with success probability 0.5 and size n, where n is the number of lines of pegs. Recall that a binomial random variable is the sum of n i.i.d. Bernoulli random variables. This means that if the central limit theorem holds, then we expect a binomial random variable to approximate the normal distribution as the sample size, or the number of balls in this case, increases. In fact, this is exactly what we observe.

The central limit theorem applies not only to the binomial distribution but also to other distributions. This is important because in most practical settings we do not know the probability distribution that generates the data. We now more formally state the central limit theorem.

Suppose that we obtain a random sample of n independently and identically distributed (i.i.d.) observations, $X_1, X_2, \ldots, X_n$, from a probability distribution with mean $\mathbb{E}(X)$ and variance $\mathbb{V}(X)$. Let us denote the sample average by $\overline{X}_n = \sum_{i=1}^{n} X_i / n$. Then, the **central limit theorem** states

$$\frac{\overline{X}_n - \mathbb{E}(X)}{\sqrt{\mathbb{V}(X)/n}} \rightsquigarrow \mathcal{N}(0, 1). \tag{6.41}$$

In the theorem, $\rightsquigarrow$ indicates "convergence in distribution" as the sample size n increases.

While formula (6.41) appears complex at first glance, it has a straightforward interpretation. The theorem says that the *z-score* of the sample mean converges in distribution to the standard normal distribution or $\mathcal{N}(0, 1)$ as the sample size increases. Recall the definition of z-score given in equation (3.1). In order to standardize a random variable, we subtract its mean from it and then divide it by its standard deviation. As a result, any z-score has zero mean and unit variance.

To show that the left-hand side of formula (6.41) represents the z-score of the sample mean, we first note that the expectation of the sample mean $\overline{X}_n$ is the expectation of the original random variable X. Using the rules of the expectation operator, we obtain

$$\mathbb{E}(\overline{X}_n) = \mathbb{E}\left(\frac{1}{n}\sum_{i=1}^{n}\right) = \frac{1}{n}\sum_{i=1}^{n}\mathbb{E}(X_i) = \mathbb{E}(X). \tag{6.42}$$

We next exploit the fact that the variance of two independent random variables equals the sum of their variances. The variance of the sample mean then is given by

$$\mathbb{V}(\overline{X}_n) = \mathbb{V}\left(\frac{1}{n}\sum_{i=1}^{n} X_i\right) = \frac{1}{n^2}\sum_{i=1}^{n}\mathbb{V}(X_i) = \frac{1}{n}\mathbb{V}(X). \tag{6.43}$$

To derive this expression, we also used formula (6.38). This shows that the denominator of the left-hand side of formula (6.41) represents the standard deviation of the sample mean. Hence, the entire quantity in the left-hand side of formula (6.41) corresponds to the z-score of the sample mean.

Monte Carlo simulations can illustrate the central limit theorem. We consider two distributions as examples: the binomial distribution with success probability $p = 0.2$ and size $n = 10$, and the uniform distribution with the range $[0, 1]$. Recall that the mean and variance of this binomial distribution are $np = 10 \times 0.2 = 2$ and $np(1 - p) = 10 \times 0.2 \times (1 - 0.2) = 1.6$, respectively. For this uniform distribution, the mean and variance are $(a + b)/2 = 1/2$ and $(b - a)^2/12 = 1/12$, respectively. We use these results to compute the z-scores and see whether their distributions can be approximated by the standard normal distribution.

```
## sims = number of simulations
n.samp <- 1000
z.binom <- z.unif <- rep(NA, sims)
for (i in 1:sims) {
    x <- rbinom(n.samp, p = 0.2, size = 10)
    z.binom[i] <- (mean(x) - 2) / sqrt(1.6 / n.samp)
    x <- runif(n.samp, min = 0, max = 1)
    z.unif[i] <- (mean(x) - 0.5) / sqrt(1 / (12 * n.samp))
}
## histograms; nclass specifies the number of bins
hist(z.binom, freq = FALSE, nclass = 40, xlim = c(-4, 4), ylim = c(0, 0.6),
     xlab = "z-score", main = "Binomial(0.2, 10)")
x <- seq(from = -3, to = 3, by = 0.01)
lines(x, dnorm(x)) # overlay the standard normal PDF
hist(z.unif, freq = FALSE, nclass = 40, xlim = c(-4, 4), ylim = c(0, 0.6),
     xlab = "z-score", main = "Uniform(0, 1)")
lines(x, dnorm(x))
```

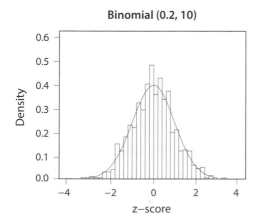

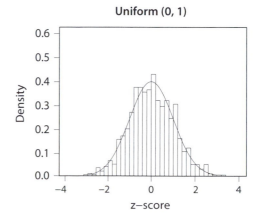

The above simulations are based on a sample size of 1000. We see that the standard normal distribution approximates the distribution of the z-score well. What about for a smaller sample size? Below, we conduct the same simulation using a sample size of 100 (the code is identical to the one above, aside from the change in sample size, and therefore omitted).

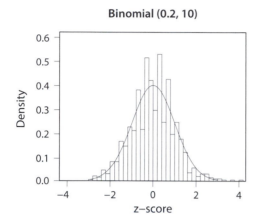

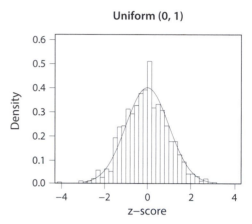

We observe that the approximation is poorer than before for the binomial distribution, whereas the central limit theorem holds well for the uniform distribution. The theorem does not tell us how large the sample size must be for a good approximation. As shown here, the answer to this question depends on the distribution of the original random variables. Nevertheless, what is incredible about the central limit theorem is that the z-score of the sample mean converges in distribution to the standard normal distribution *regardless of* the distribution of the original random variable.

6.5 Summary

In this chapter, we studied probability. We first introduced two different interpretations of probability, **frequentist** and **Bayesian**. Despite its competing interpretations, probability has a unified mathematical foundation with its basic definition and axioms. We then covered the basic rules of probability, including the **law of total probability**, the definition of **conditional probability**, the concept of **independence**, and **Bayes' rule**. We applied these rules to various problems including the prediction of an individual's race from their surname and residence location.

Next, we examined the concepts of **random variables** and their **probability distributions**. We introduced basic distributions such as **uniform**, **binomial**, and **normal** distributions. These distributions can be characterized by the **probability density function** and **probability mass function** for continuous and discrete random variables, respectively. The **cumulative distribution function** represents the cumulative probability that a random variable takes a value less than or equal to a specified value. Using the probability mass and density functions, we showed how to compute the

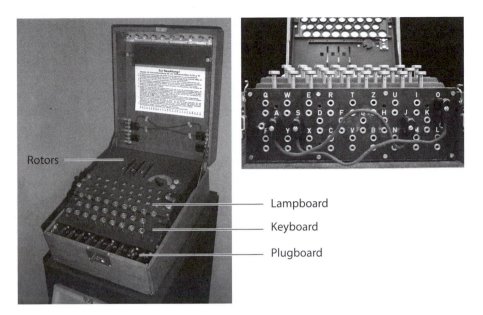

Figure 6.12. The Enigma Machine and its Plugboard. Photographer: Karsten Sperling, http://spiff.de/photo.

expectation and **variance** of a random variable. We used these tools to quantify the sampling uncertainty regarding the polling prediction of election results.

Lastly, we discussed the two fundamental large sample approximation theorems. The power of these theorems is that they can be applied to the sample mean of virtually any random variable given a sufficient sample size. The **law of large numbers** states that the sample mean approaches the expectation or the population mean as the sample size increases. This justifies the use of the sample mean as an estimator of the population mean in survey sampling and randomized experiments. The **central limit theorem** states that the z-score of the sample mean is approximately distributed according to the standard normal distribution. In the next chapter, we will use these large sample theorems to quantify the degree of uncertainty regarding the empirical conclusions drawn from our data analyses.

6.6   Exercises

6.6.1   THE MATHEMATICS OF ENIGMA

The Enigma machine is the most famous cipher machine to date. Nazi Germany used it during World War II to encrypt messages so that enemies could not understand them. The story of the British cryptanalysts who successfully deciphered Enigma has become the subject of multiple movies (*Enigma* (2001), *The Imitation Game* (2014)). In this exercise, we will focus our attention on a simplified version of the Enigma machine, which we name "Little Enigma." Like the real Enigma machine shown in the left panel of figure 6.12, this machine consists of two key components. First, the Little Enigma machine has 5 different *rotors*, each of which comes with 10 pins with numbers ranging from 0 to 9. Second, as shown in the right panel of figure 6.12, the *plugboard* contains 26 holes, corresponding to the 26 letters of the alphabet. In addition, 13 cables connect all possible pairs of letters. Since a cable has two ends, one can connect, for example, the letter A with any of the other 25 letters present in the plugboard.

To either encode a message or decode an encrypted message, one must provide the Little Enigma machine with the correct 5-digit passcode to align the rotors, and the correct configuration of the plugboard. The rotors are set up just like many combination locks. For example, the passcode 9–4–2–4–9 means that the 5 rotors display the numbers 9, 4, 2, 4, and 9 in that order. In addition, the 13 cables connecting the letters in the plugboard must be appropriately configured. The purpose of the plugboard is thus to scramble the letters. For example, if B is connected to W, the Little Enigma machine will switch B with W and W with B to encode a message or decode an encoded message. Thus, a sender types a message on the keyboard, the plugboard scrambles the letters, and the message is sent in its encrypted form. A receiver decodes the encrypted message by retyping it on a paired Little Enigma machine that has the same passcode and plugboard configuration.

1. How many different 5-digit passcodes can be set on the 5 rotors?

2. How many possible configurations does the plugboard provide? In other words, how many ways can 26 letters be divided into 13 pairs?

3. Based on the previous two questions, what is the total number of possible settings for the Little Enigma machine?

4. Five cryptanalytic machines have been developed to decode 1500 messages encrypted by the Little Enigma machine. The table below presents information on the number of messages assigned to each machine and the machine's failure rate (i.e., the percentage of messages the machine was unable to decode). Aside from this information, we do not know anything about the assignment of each message to a machine or whether the machine was able to correctly decode the message.

Machine	Number of messages	Failure rate
Banburismus	300	10%
Bombe	400	5%
Herivel tip	250	15%
Crib	340	17%
Hut 6	210	20%

Suppose that we select one message at random from the pool of all 1500 messages but find out this message was not properly decoded. Which machine is most likely responsible for this mistake?

5. Write an R function that randomly configures the plugboard. This function will take no input but will randomly select a set of 13 pairs of letters. The output object should be a 2 × 13 matrix for which each column represents a pair of letters. You may use the built-in R object `letters`, which contains the 26 letters of the alphabet as a character vector. Name the function `plugboard`.

6. Write an R function that encodes and decodes a message given a plugboard configuration set by the `plugboard()` function from the previous question. This function should take as inputs the output of the `plugboard()` function, as well as a message to be encoded (decoded), and return an encoded (decoded) message. You may wish to use the `gsub()` function, which replaces a pattern in a character string with another specified pattern. The `tolower()` function, which makes characters in a character vector lowercase, and `toupper()` function, which capitalizes characters in a character vector, can also help.

6.6.2 A PROBABILITY MODEL FOR BETTING MARKET ELECTION PREDICTION

Earlier in this chapter, we used preelection polls with a probability model to predict Obama's electoral vote share in the 2008 US election. In this exercise, we will apply a similar procedure to the Intrade betting market data analyzed in an exercise in chapter 4 (see section 4.5.1).[4] The 2008 Intrade data are available as `intrade08.csv`. The variable names and descriptions of this data set are available in table 4.9. Recall that each row of the data set represents daily trading information about the contracts for either the Democratic or Republican Party nominee's victory in a particular state. The 2008 election results data are available as `pres08.csv`, with variable names and descriptions appearing in table 4.1.

1. We analyze the contract of the Democratic Party nominee winning a given state j. Recall from section 4.5.1 that the data set contains the contract price of the market for each state on each day i leading up to the election. We will interpret `PriceD` as the probability p_{ij} that the Democrat would win state j if the election were held on day i. To treat `PriceD` as a probability, divide it by 100 so it ranges from 0 to 1. How accurate is this probability? Using only the data from the day before Election Day (November 4, 2008) within each state, compute the expected number of electoral votes Obama is predicted to win and compare it with the actual number of electoral votes Obama won. Briefly interpret the result. Recall that the actual total number of electoral votes for Obama is 365, not 364, which is the sum of electoral votes for Obama based on the results data. The total of 365 includes a single electoral vote that Obama garnered from Nebraska's 2nd Congressional District. McCain won Nebraska's 4 other electoral votes because he won the state overall.

[4] This exercise is based on David Rothschild (2009) "Forecasting elections: Comparing prediction markets, polls, and their biases." *Public Opinion Quarterly*, vol. 73, no. 5, pp. 895–916.

2. Next, using the same set of probabilities used in the previous question, simulate the total number of electoral votes Obama is predicted to win. Assume that the election in each state is a Bernoulli trial where the probability of success (Obama winning) is p_{ij}. Display the results using a histogram. Add the actual number of electoral votes Obama won as a solid line. Briefly interpret the result.

3. In prediction markets, people tend to exaggerate the likelihood that the trailing or "long shot" candidate will win. This means that candidates with a low (high) p_{ij} have a true probability that is lower (higher) than their predicted p_{ij}. Such a discrepancy could introduce bias into our predictions, so we want to adjust our probabilities to account for it. We do so by reducing the probability for candidates who have a less than 0.5 chance of winning, and increasing the probability for those with a greater than 0.5 chance. We will calculate a new probability p_{ij}^* using the following formula proposed by a researcher: $p_{ij}^* = \Phi(1.64 \times \Phi^{-1}(p_{ij}))$ where $\Phi(\cdot)$ is the CDF of a standard normal random variable and $\Phi^{-1}(\cdot)$ is its inverse, the quantile function. The R functions `pnorm()` and `qnorm()` can be used to compute $\Phi(\cdot)$ and $\Phi^{-1}(\cdot)$, respectively. Plot p_{ij}, used in the previous questions, against p_{ij}^*. In addition, plot this function itself as a line. Explain the nature of the transformation.

4. Using the new probabilities p_{ij}^*, repeat questions 1 and 2. Do the new probabilities improve predictive performance?

5. Compute the expected number of Obama's electoral votes using the new probabilities p_{ij}^* for each of the last 120 days of the campaign. Display the results as a time-series plot. Briefly interpret the plot.

6. For each of the last 120 days of the campaign, conduct a simulation as in question 2, using the new probabilities p_{ij}^*. Compute the quantiles of Obama's electoral votes at 2.5% and 97.5% for each day. Represent the range from 2.5% to 97.5% for each day as a vertical line, using a loop. Also, add the estimated total number of Obama's electoral votes across simulations. Briefly interpret the result.

6.6.3   ELECTION FRAUD IN RUSSIA

In this exercise, we use the rules of probability to detect election fraud by examining voting patterns in the 2011 Russian State Duma election.[5] The State Duma is the federal legislature of Russia. The ruling political party, United Russia, won this election, but to many accusations of election fraud, which the Kremlin, or Russian government, denied. As shown in figure 6.13, some protesters highlighted irregular patterns of voting as evidence of election fraud. In particular, the protesters pointed out the

---

[5] This exercise is based on Arturas Rozenas (2016) "Inferring election fraud from distributions of vote-proportions." Working paper.

Figure 6.13. Protesters in the Aftermath of the 2011 State Duma Election. The poster says, "We don't believe Churov! We believe Gauss!" Churov is the head of the Central Electoral Commission, and Gauss refers to an 18th century German mathematician, Carl Friedrich Gauss, whom the Gaussian (normal) distribution was named after. Source: Maxim Borisov, trv-science.ru.

Table 6.5. Russian and Canadian Election Data.

Variable	Description
N	total number of voters in a precinct
turnout	total turnout in a precinct
votes	total number of votes for the winner in a precinct

Note: The results of each election are stored in a data frame. The RData file `fraud.RData` contains data on four elections: the 2007 and 2011 Russian Duma elections, the 2012 Russian presidential election, and the 2011 Canadian election.

relatively high frequency of common fractions such as 1/4, 1/3, and 1/2 in the official vote shares.

We analyze the official election results, contained in the `russia2011` data frame in the RData file `fraud.RData`, to investigate whether there is any evidence for election fraud. The RData file can be loaded using the `load()` function. Besides `russia2011`, the RData file contains the election results from the 2003 Russian Duma election, the 2012 Russian presidential election, and the 2011 Canadian election, as separate data frames. Table 6.5 presents the names and descriptions of variables used in each data frame. **Note:** Part of this exercise may require computationally intensive code.

1. To analyze the 2011 Russian election results, first compute United Russia's vote share as a proportion of the voters who turned out. Identify the 10 most frequently occurring fractions for the vote share. Create a histogram that sets the number of bins to the number of unique fractions, with one bar created for each uniquely observed fraction, to differentiate between similar fractions like 1/2 and 51/100. This can be done by using the `breaks` argument in the `hist()` function. What does this histogram look like at fractions with low numerators and denominators such as 1/2 and 2/3?

2. The mere existence of high frequencies at low fractions may not imply election fraud. Indeed, more numbers are divisible by smaller integers like 2, 3, and 4 than by larger integers like 22, 23, and 24. To investigate the possibility that the low fractions arose by chance, assume the following probability model. The turnout for a precinct has a binomial distribution, whose size equals the number of voters and success probability equals the turnout rate for the precinct. The vote share for United Russia in this precinct is assumed to follow a binomial distribution, conditional on the turnout, where the size equals the number of voters who turned out and the success probability equals the observed vote share in the precinct. Conduct a Monte Carlo simulation under this alternative assumption (1000 simulations should be sufficient). What are the 10 most frequent vote share values? Create a histogram similar to the one in the previous question. Briefly comment on the results you obtain. **Note:** This question requires a computationally intensive code. Write a code with a small number of simulations first and then run the final code with 1000 simulations.

3. To judge the Monte Carlo simulation results against the actual results of the 2011 Russian election, we compare the observed fraction of observations within a bin of certain size with its simulated counterpart. To do this, create histograms showing the distribution of question 2's four most frequently occurring fractions, i.e., 1/2, 1/3, 3/5, and 2/3, and compare them with the corresponding fractions' proportion in the actual election. Briefly interpret the results.

4. We now compare the relative frequency of observed fractions with the simulated ones beyond the four fractions examined in the previous question. To do this, we choose a bin size of 0.01 and compute the proportion of observations that fall into each bin. We then examine whether or not the observed proportion falls within the 2.5 and 97.5 percentiles of the corresponding simulated proportions. Plot the result with the horizontal axis as the vote share and vertical axis as the estimated proportion. This plot will attempt to reproduce the one held by protesters in figure 6.13. Also, count the number of times that the observed proportions fall outside the corresponding range of simulated proportions. Interpret the results.

5. To put the results of the previous question into perspective, apply the procedure developed in the previous question to the 2011 Canadian elections and the 2003 Russian election, where no major voting irregularities were reported. In addition, apply this procedure to the 2012 Russian presidential election, where election fraud allegations were reported. No plot needs to be produced. Briefly comment on the results you obtain. **Note:** This question requires a computationally intensive code. Write a code with a small number of simulations first and then run the final code with 1000 simulations.

Chapter 7

Uncertainty

As far as the laws of mathematics refer to reality, they are not certain; and as far as they are certain, they do not refer to reality.
— Albert Einstein, *Geometry and Experience*

Thus far, we have studied various data analysis techniques that can extract useful information from data. We have used these methods to draw causal inferences, measure quantities of interest, make predictions, and discover patterns in data. One important remaining question, however, is how certain we can be of our empirical findings. For example, if in a randomized controlled trial the average outcome differs between the treatment and control groups, when is this difference large enough for us to conclude that the treatment of interest affects the outcome, on average? Did the observed difference result from chance? In this chapter, we consider how to separate signals from noise in data by quantifying the degree of uncertainty. We do so by applying the laws of probability introduced in the previous chapter. We cover several concepts and methodologies to formally quantify the level of uncertainty. These include bias, standard errors, confidence intervals, and hypothesis testing. Finally, we describe ways to make inferences from linear regression models with measures of uncertainty.

7.1 Estimation

In earlier chapters, we showed how to infer public opinion in a population through survey sampling (chapter 3) and estimate causal effects through randomized controlled trials (chapter 2). In these examples, researchers want to estimate the unknown value of a quantity of interest using observed data. We refer to the quantity of interest as a *parameter* and the method to compute its estimate as an *estimator*. For example, in the analysis of survey data presented in chapter 3, we are interested in estimating the proportion of Obama supporters in the population of American voters (parameter) based on a relatively small number of survey respondents (data). We use the sample proportion of Obama supporters as our estimator. Similarly, in randomized controlled trials, the average outcome difference between the treatment and control groups represents an estimator for the average causal effect, which is our parameter.

How good is our estimate of the parameter? This is a difficult question to answer because we do not know the true value of the parameter. However, it turns out that we can characterize how well the estimator will perform over hypothetically repeated sampling. This section shows how statistical theory can help us investigate the performance of the estimators we used in the earlier parts of the book.

7.1.1 UNBIASEDNESS AND CONSISTENCY

Consider a survey for which a certain number of respondents are selected from a population using the *simple random sampling* procedure. Simple random sampling implies that each individual in the population is equally likely to be selected into a sample. As discussed in chapter 3, such random sampling benefits us by producing a representative sample of a target population (see section 3.4.1).

To give further context to these ideas, recall the preelection polling example in the 2008 US presidential election (see section 4.1.3). In that example, our parameter was the proportion of voters in the population of American voters that supported Obama. We used simple random sampling to obtain a representative sample of n voters from the population. The survey asked whether each of the respondents supported Obama or not. We used the sample proportion of those who supported Obama as our estimate of the population proportion of Obama supporters.

To formalize the content of the previous paragraph, let p denote the population proportion of Obama supporters. We use a random variable X to represent a response to the question. If voter i supports (does not support) Obama, then we denote this observation with $X_i = 1$ ($X_i = 0$). Since each respondent is sampled independently from the same population, we can assume that $\{X_1, X_2, \ldots, X_n\}$ are independently and identically distributed (i.i.d.) Bernoulli random variables with success probability p (see section 6.3.2). Our estimator is the sample proportion, $\overline{X}_n = \sum_{i=1}^{n} X_i / n$, which we use to estimate the unknown parameter p. The specific value of this estimator we obtain from our sample represents the estimate of p.

How good is this estimate? Ideally, we would like to compute the *estimation error*, which is defined as the difference between our estimate and the truth:

$$\text{estimation error} = \text{estimate} - \text{truth} = \overline{X}_n - p.$$

However, the estimation error can never be computed because we do not know p. In fact, if we know the truth, there is no need to estimate the parameter in the first place!

While we never know the size of the estimation error specific to our sample, it is sometimes possible to compute the *average* magnitude of the estimation error. To do this, we consider the hypothetical scenario of conducting the same preelection poll infinitely many times in exactly the same manner. This scenario is purely hypothetical because in reality we obtain only one sample and can never conduct sampling in an identical manner multiple times. Under this scenario, each hypothetical poll would draw a different set of n voters from the sample population and yield a different proportion of sampled voters who express support for Obama. This means that the sample proportion, represented by a random variable $\overline{X}_n$, would take a different value for each poll. As a result, the estimation error would also differ from one poll to another and hence is a random variable.

More formally, the sample proportion can be considered as a random variable that has its own distribution over the repeated use of simple random sampling. This distribution is called the *sampling distribution* of the estimator. In this particular example, each hypothetical sample is drawn independently from the same population. Therefore, the sample proportion, $\overline{X}_n$, is a binomial random variable, divided by n, with success probability p and size n where n represents the number of respondents in a poll (recall from section 6.3.3 that the sum of i.i.d. Bernoulli random variables is a binomial random variable).

We now compute the average estimation error or *bias* over this repeated simple random sampling procedure using the concept of *expectation* (see section 6.3.5). Under the binomial model, the success probability equals p. Therefore, we can show that the bias, or the average estimation error, of the sample mean is zero:

$$\text{bias} = \mathbb{E}(\text{estimation error}) = \mathbb{E}(\text{estimate} - \text{truth}) = \mathbb{E}(\overline{X}_n) - p = p - p = 0.$$

This result implies that the sample proportion under simple random sampling is an *unbiased* estimator for the population proportion. That is, while the sample proportion based on a specific sample may deviate from the population proportion, it gives, on average, the right answer. More precisely, if we were to conduct the same preelection poll infinitely many times under identical conditions, the average of the sample proportions of Obama supporters would exactly equal their population proportion. Thus, unbiasedness refers to the accuracy of the average estimate over repeated sampling rather than the accuracy of an estimate based on the observed data.

Similar logic applies to nonbinary variables. We can show that the expectation of the sample mean equals the population average so long as each survey respondent is randomly sampled from a large population. An example of a nonindependent sampling procedure is respondent-driven sampling, in which one respondent introduces another respondent to the interviewer. Using the fact that expectation is a linear operator (see section 6.3.5), we obtain the following general result for the sample mean:

$$\mathbb{E}(\overline{X}_n) = \frac{1}{n} \sum_{i=1}^{n} \mathbb{E}(X_i) = \mathbb{E}(X). \tag{7.1}$$

The final equality follows because each of the n observations is randomly sampled from the same population whose mean is denoted by $\mathbb{E}(X)$. Therefore, regardless of the distribution of a variable, random sampling provides a way to use the sample average as an unbiased estimator of the population mean. In other words, equation (7.1) shows that random sampling eliminates bias.

In general, random sampling plays an essential role in obtaining an unbiased estimate. In the absence of random sampling or other ways to obtain a representative sample, it is difficult to estimate a population characteristic without bias. For example, item and unit *nonresponse*, discussed in section 3.4.2, can yield biased estimates.

In section 6.4.1, we introduced the *law of large numbers*, which states that as sample size increases, the sample mean converges to the population mean. In the current context, this implies that the estimation error, which is the difference between the sample mean and the population mean, becomes smaller as the sample size increases. The estimator is said to be *consistent* if it converges to the parameter as the sample size goes to infinity. Thus, the discussion so far implies that the sample mean is a good estimator for the population mean because it is an unbiased and consistent estimator of the population mean. That is, the sample mean on average correctly estimates the population mean, and the estimation error decreases as the sample size increases.

An estimator is said to be **unbiased** if its expectation equals the parameter. An estimator is said to be **consistent** if it converges to the parameter as the sample size increases. For example, the sample average $\overline{X}_n = \sum_{i=1}^{n} X_i/n$ is unbiased and consistent for the population mean $\mathbb{E}(X)$ under simple random sampling:

$$\mathbb{E}(\overline{X}_n) = \mathbb{E}(X) \quad \text{and} \quad \overline{X}_n \to \mathbb{E}(X).$$

We next show that the difference-in-means estimator used to analyze *randomized controlled trials* (see section 2.4) is unbiased for the average treatment effect. Suppose that we have a sample of n units for which we conduct a randomized experiment. This experiment features a single binary treatment T_i which equals 1 if unit i receives the treatment and 0 if the unit is assigned to the control group. We randomly choose n_1 units out of this sample and assign them to the treatment group, and the remaining $n - n_1$ units belong to the control group. This treatment assignment procedure is called *complete randomization*, which fixes a priori the total number of units that receive the treatment. In contrast, *simple randomization* randomly assigns treatment to each unit independently, and so the total number of treated units will vary from one randomization to another. Thus, under complete randomization, there exists a total of $\binom{n}{n_1}$ ways of assigning n_1 units to the treatment group and the remaining units to the control group (see section 6.1.5 for the definition of combinations). Each of these treatment assignment combinations is equally likely but only one of them is realized.

The first parameter we consider, the *sample average treatment effect* (SATE), is defined in equation (2.1) and reproduced here:

$$\text{SATE} = \frac{1}{n} \sum_{i=1}^{n} \{Y_i(1) - Y_i(0)\}.$$

In this equation, $Y_i(1)$ and $Y_i(0)$ are the potential outcomes under the treatment and control conditions for unit i, respectively. As discussed in section 2.3, $Y_i(1)$ ($Y_i(0)$) represents the outcome that would be observed for unit i if it were assigned to the treatment (control) condition. Since $Y_i(1) - Y_i(0)$ represents the treatment effect for unit i, the SATE is the average of this treatment effect across all units in the sample. But because only one potential outcome can be observed for each unit, we cannot observe the treatment effect for any unit, so the SATE is unknown.

In section 2.4, we learned that randomization of treatment assignment makes the treatment and control groups identical on average. As a result, we can use the *difference-in-means estimator* to estimate average treatment effect. Let's formalize this argument here. The difference-in-means estimator $\widehat{\text{SATE}}$ can be written as

$$\widehat{\text{SATE}} = \text{average of the treated} - \text{average of the untreated}$$

$$= \frac{1}{n_1} \sum_{i=1}^{n} T_i Y_i - \frac{1}{n - n_1} \sum_{i=1}^{n} (1 - T_i) Y_i. \tag{7.2}$$

Recall that n_1 represents the number of units in the treatment group and hence $n - n_1$ is the size of the control group. The expression $\sum_{i=1}^{n} T_i Y_i$, for example, gives the sum of the observed outcome variable across all treated units because the treatment variable T_i is 1 when unit i is treated and 0 if it belongs to the control group. This means that $T_i Y_i = Y_i$ and $(1 - T_i) Y_i = 0$ when observation i is in the treatment group, and $T_i Y_i = 0$ and $(1 - T_i) Y_i = Y_i$ when it is in the control group.

We now show that the difference-in-means estimator is unbiased for the SATE. As discussed earlier, in survey sampling, the unbiasedness of an estimator means that over repeated sampling the average value of the estimator is identical to the unknown true value of the parameter. In randomized controlled trials, we consider how an estimator behaves over the repeated randomization of treatment assignment. That is, suppose that using a sample of the same n units, a researcher conducts a randomized control trial (infinitely) many times by randomizing the treatment assignment. A given unit will receive the treatment in some of these trials while in others it will be assigned to the control group. Each time, a researcher will compute the difference-in-means estimator after randomizing the treatment assignment and observing the outcome. Throughout the hypothetical repeated experiments, the potential outcomes remain fixed and only the treatment assignment changes. Thus, unbiasedness implies that the average value of the difference-in-means estimator over repeated trials is equal to the true value of the SATE.

To show the unbiasedness more formally, we can take the expectation of the difference-in-means estimator with respect to T_i since in this framework the randomized treatment assignment T_i is the only random variable. Since T_i is a Bernoulli random variable, its expectation equals $P(T_i = 1)$, which is the proportion of subjects who are treated, or n_1/n in this case:

$$\mathbb{E}(\widehat{\text{SATE}}) = \mathbb{E}\left(\frac{1}{n_1} \sum_{i=1}^{n} T_i Y_i(1) - \frac{1}{n - n_1} \sum_{i=1}^{n} (1 - T_i) Y_i(0) \right)$$

$$= \frac{1}{n_1} \sum_{i=1}^{n} \mathbb{E}(T_i) Y_i(1) - \frac{1}{n - n_1} \sum_{i=1}^{n} \mathbb{E}(1 - T_i) Y_i(0)$$

$$= \frac{1}{n_1} \sum_{i=1}^{n} \frac{n_1}{n} Y_i(1) - \frac{1}{n - n_1} \sum_{i=1}^{n} \left(1 - \frac{n_1}{n} \right) Y_i(0)$$

$$= \frac{1}{n} \sum_{i=1}^{n} \{ Y_i(1) - Y_i(0) \} = \text{SATE}. \tag{7.3}$$

The first equality follows because for a treated unit, the potential outcome under the treatment condition is observed, i.e., $Y_i = Y_i(1)$, while a control unit reveals the other potential outcome, i.e., $Y_i = Y_i(0)$. The second equality holds because the expectation is a linear operator and is taken with respect to the treatment assignment. That is, the potential outcomes are treated as fixed constants. The derivation above shows that the difference-in-means estimator is unbiased for the SATE.

We can combine the advantage of the above random treatment assignment with that of random sampling. Suppose that we first randomly sample n individuals from a large population of interest. Within this sample, we randomly assign the treatment to n_1 individuals and measure the outcome for each one. This two-step procedure ensures the experimental results are generalizable to the population because the experiment's sample is representative of the population. To see this formally, consider the *population average treatment effect* or PATE, which represents the average of the treatment effect among all individuals in the population. Here, we use the expectation to represent the population average:

$$\text{PATE} = \mathbb{E}(Y(1) - Y(0)). \tag{7.4}$$

Recall that the sample is representative of the population because of random sampling. This means that while the SATE is unobservable, its expectation equals the PATE. Since the difference-in-means estimator is unbiased for the SATE, the estimator is also unbiased for the PATE. It is also clear from equation (7.3) that the difference-in-means estimator is consistent for the PATE. This result emerges from applying the *law of large numbers* to the sample average of the treatment group and that of the control group, separately. In sum, the combination of random sampling and random assignment enables us to make causal inferences about a target population.

> In randomized controlled trials, the average outcome difference between the treatment and control groups is an unbiased estimator of the **sample average treatment effect** (SATE). The estimator is also unbiased and consistent for the **population average treatment effect** (PATE).

A *Monte Carlo simulation* can illustrate the idea of unbiasedness. Suppose that the potential outcome under the control condition $Y_i(0)$ is distributed according to the *standard normal distribution* in a population (i.e., a normal distribution with zero mean and unit variance). We further assume that in the population the individual-level treatment effect follows another normal distribution with both mean and variance equal to 1. Formally, we can write this hypothetical *data-generating process* as

$$Y_i(0) \sim \mathcal{N}(0, 1) \quad \text{and} \quad Y_i(1) \sim \mathcal{N}(1, 1). \tag{7.5}$$

The treatment assignment is randomized, where a randomly selected half of the sample receives the treatment and the other half does not. Finally, we can define the treatment effect for unit i as $\tau_i = Y_i(1) - Y_i(0)$. For each unit, we observe the potential outcome under the realized treatment condition. Under this model, we can analytically compute the PATE as

$$\mathbb{E}(\tau_i) = \mathbb{E}(Y_i(1)) - \mathbb{E}(Y_i(0)) = 1 - 0 = 1. \qquad (7.6)$$

In contrast, the value of the SATE depends on which units are sampled.

We now implement this simulation in R. We follow the above equations to generate one sample of units with potential outcomes from the population. This process requires the `rnorm()` function, which randomly draws a sample, of the size specified in the first argument, from a normal distribution with specified mean and standard deviation. We next compute the true value of the SATE for that sample. This is, of course, possible only in this hypothetical simulation exercise. In the real world, we would never observe both potential outcomes at the same time for any given observation and hence the true value of the SATE is unknown.

```r
## simulation parameters
n <- 100 # sample size
mu0 <- 0 # mean of Y_i(0)
sd0 <- 1 # standard deviation of Y_i(0)
mu1 <- 1 # mean of Y_i(1)
sd1 <- 1 # standard deviation of Y_i(1)
## generate a sample
Y0 <- rnorm(n, mean = mu0, sd = sd0)
Y1 <- rnorm(n, mean = mu1, sd = sd1)
tau <- Y1 - Y0 # individual treatment effect
## true value of the sample average treatment effect
SATE <- mean(tau)
SATE

## [1] 1.046216
```

We then use a *loop* to simulate a large number of hypothetical randomized controlled trials by randomly assigning the treatment to the units in the sample and selecting one of the potential outcomes according to the realized treatment condition. For each replication of the randomized controlled trials, we compute the difference-in-means estimator and examine its average performance. In order to randomize the treatment, we use the `sample()` function to randomly sample one half of elements from a vector that contains 0s and 1s in equal proportion. We will conduct a Monte Carlo simulation with a sample size arbitrarily set at 100. The entire procedure, therefore, is equivalent to randomly assigning 50 observations to the treatment group and the other 50 to the control group where we observe $Y_i(1)$ for the treatment group and $Y_i(0)$ for the control group.

```r
## repeatedly conduct randomized controlled trials
sims <- 5000 # repeat 5000 times, we could do more
diff.means <- rep(NA, sims)  # container
```

```
for (i in 1:sims) {
    ## randomize the treatment by sampling of a vector of 0s and 1s
    treat <- sample(c(rep(1, n / 2), rep(0, n / 2)), size = n, replace = FALSE)
    ## difference-in-means
    diff.means[i] <- mean(Y1[treat == 1]) - mean(Y0[treat == 0])
}
## estimation error for SATE
est.error <- diff.means - SATE
summary(est.error)

##       Min.    1st Qu.     Median       Mean    3rd Qu.
## -0.4414000 -0.0891500 -0.0004482  0.0010830  0.0908500
##       Max.
##  0.5029000
```

We observe that the bias, which is the mean of the estimation error, is 0.001, close to zero. It is not exactly zero as the theory implies because Monte Carlo simulation adds some noise due to its inherent variability. This deviation from the theoretical value is called *Monte Carlo error*. If we were to conduct this simulation infinitely many times, we could eliminate the Monte Carlo error. In this simulation, the estimation error of the difference-in-means estimator ranges from -0.441 to 0.503. Thus, while the estimator is on average very close to the true value of the SATE, it may be far off in any given randomized controlled trial.

To consider the bias of estimating the PATE, we must modify the above simulation procedure. Specifically, we add the step of sampling potential outcomes to the loop. This simulates the process where researchers sample individuals from a population and then conduct a randomized experiment. We then repeat this two-step procedure many times. Such a procedure contrasts with the above simulation setting in which we conducted a randomized experiment on the same sample. To compute the new bias, we compare the average value of the difference-in-means estimator over repeated simulations with the true value of PATE, which equals 1 in the current example. The R code for this PATE simulation is shown below.

```
## PATE simulation
PATE <- mu1 - mu0
diff.means <- rep(NA, sims)
for (i in 1:sims) {
    ## generate a sample for each simulation: this used to be outside loop
    Y0 <- rnorm(n, mean = mu0, sd = sd0)
    Y1 <- rnorm(n, mean = mu1, sd = sd1)
    treat <- sample(c(rep(1, n / 2), rep(0, n / 2)), size = n, replace = FALSE)
    diff.means[i] <- mean(Y1[treat == 1]) - mean(Y0[treat == 0])
}
## estimation error for PATE
est.error <- diff.means - PATE
```

```
## unbiased
summary(est.error)

##      Min.   1st Qu.    Median      Mean   3rd Qu.      Max.
## -0.757900 -0.140900 -0.003669 -0.002793  0.134400  0.650100
```

The average estimation error is close to zero, reflecting the unbiasedness. The variability is greater than in the case of the SATE because random sampling adds more noise.

7.1.2   STANDARD ERROR

We have focused on the mean of the estimation error, but an unbiased estimator with a large degree of variability is of little use in practice. In the above simulation example, the difference-in-means estimator was unbiased but its estimation error was sometimes large. We can plot the sampling distribution of the difference-in-means estimator. The histogram shows that while the estimator is accurate on average, it varies significantly from one randomized treatment assignment to another.

```
hist(diff.means, freq = FALSE,xlab = "Difference-in-means estimator",
     main = "Sampling distribution")
abline(v = SATE, col = "blue") # true value of SATE
```

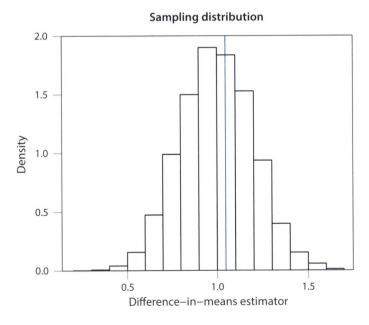

How much would an estimator vary over the hypothetically repeated data-generating process? We have used the standard deviation to characterize the spread of distribution in earlier parts of the book, and we can do the same here. In the above simulation example, this amounts to calculating the standard deviation of the sampling distribution of the difference-in-means estimator.

```
sd(diff.means)

## [1] 0.2003772
```

The result implies that in this example, the difference-in-means estimator is on average 0.2 points away from its mean. This mean equals the true value of the SATE, since the difference-in-means estimator is unbiased for the SATE. Accordingly, the mean of the sampling distribution equals the true value of the SATE, implying that the standard deviation of the sampling distribution (i.e., the deviation from the mean) in this case is equal to the *root-mean-squared error* (RMSE; i.e., the deviation from the truth) (see section 4.1.3 for the definition of RMSE). In our simulation example, we can compute the RMSE as follows.

```
sqrt(mean((diff.means - SATE)^2))

## [1] 0.2062641
```

The result implies that the estimator is on average 0.206 points away from the true value of the SATE. The small difference between the standard deviation and the RMSE reflects the Monte Carlo error in which the sample average differs from its expectation by a small amount.

However, if an estimator is biased, then the standard deviation of its sampling distribution will differ from the RMSE. Formally, we can show that the *mean-squared error* (MSE), which is the square of the RMSE, equals the sum of the variance and squared bias. Let θ be a parameter and $\hat{\theta}$ be its estimator. We can derive this decomposition as follows:

$$\mathsf{MSE} = \mathbb{E}\{(\hat{\theta} - \theta)^2\}$$
$$= \mathbb{E}[\{(\hat{\theta} - \mathbb{E}(\hat{\theta})) + (\mathbb{E}(\hat{\theta}) - \theta)\}^2]$$
$$= \mathbb{E}[\{\hat{\theta} - \mathbb{E}(\hat{\theta})\}^2] + \{\mathbb{E}(\hat{\theta}) - \theta\}^2$$
$$= \mathsf{variance} + \mathsf{bias}^2.$$

The second equality follows because we simply added and subtracted $\mathbb{E}(\hat{\theta})$. The third equality is based on the fact that the cross-product term obtained by expanding the square, i.e., $2\mathbb{E}\{(\hat{\theta} - \mathbb{E}(\hat{\theta}))(\mathbb{E}(\hat{\theta}) - \theta)\}$, can be shown to equal zero.[1]

The decomposition implies that when assessing the accuracy of an estimator, we care about variance as well as bias. An unbiased estimator can have a greater MSE than a biased estimator if the variance of the former is sufficiently larger than that of the latter.

The above discussion suggests that we can characterize the variability of an estimator by computing the standard deviation of the *sampling distribution*. Unfortunately, this

---

[1] Specifically, using the rules of expectation, we have $\mathbb{E}\{(\hat{\theta} - \mathbb{E}(\hat{\theta}))(\mathbb{E}(\hat{\theta}) - \theta)\} = \mathbb{E}[\hat{\theta}\mathbb{E}(\hat{\theta}) - \hat{\theta}\theta - \{\mathbb{E}(\hat{\theta})\}^2 + \mathbb{E}(\hat{\theta})\theta] = \{\mathbb{E}(\hat{\theta})\}^2 - \mathbb{E}(\hat{\theta})\theta - \{\mathbb{E}(\hat{\theta})\}^2 + \mathbb{E}(\hat{\theta})\theta = 0.$

standard deviation cannot be directly obtained from the data because it is defined over hypothetical repeated random sampling and/or random treatment assignment. In the above simulations, we were able to compute it because we generated multiple data sets from the assumed data-generating process. In reality, we obtain only one sample and that is from an unknown data-generating process. However, it turns out that we can estimate the standard deviation of the sampling distribution of an estimator from the observed data. The resulting estimated standard deviation of the sampling distribution is called *standard error* and describes the (estimated) average degree to which an estimator deviates from its expected value.

> To characterize the variability of an estimator, we can use the **standard error**, which is an estimated standard deviation of the sampling distribution. One measure of accuracy is the **root-mean-squared error** (RMSE), which measures the average deviation of an estimator $\hat{\theta}$ from the true parameter value θ. The mean-squared error (MSE) of any estimator is equal to the sum of its variance and squared bias:
>
> $$\mathbb{E}\{(\hat{\theta} - \theta)^2\} = \mathbb{V}(\hat{\theta}) + \{\mathbb{E}(\hat{\theta} - \theta)\}^2.$$

As an example, consider the preelection polling described earlier in this chapter. The parameter is the population proportion of voters who support Obama, denoted by p. We have a simple random sample of n voters from this population. We can represent each response as an independently and identically distributed (i.i.d.) Bernoulli random variable X_i with success probability p, indicating whether respondent i supports Obama ($X_i = 1$) or not ($X_i = 0$). We use the sample proportion $\overline{X}_n = \sum_{i=1}^{n} X_i / n$ as our estimator. Thus, using the rules of variance (see section 6.3.5), we can calculate the variance of this estimator as

$$\mathbb{V}(\overline{X}_n) = \frac{1}{n^2} \mathbb{V}\left(\sum_{i=1}^{n} X_i\right) = \frac{1}{n^2} \sum_{i=1}^{n} \mathbb{V}(X_i) = \frac{\mathbb{V}(X)}{n} = \frac{p(1-p)}{n}. \qquad (7.7)$$

In this derivation, the second and third equalities are due to the fact that each observation is an i.i.d. random variable. The last equality follows from the fact that the variance of a Bernoulli random variable is $p(1 - p)$. When p equals 0.5 (i.e., the population is split into two exact halves), the standard deviation of the sampling distribution is greatest. Thus, the variance of the estimator is a function of the unknown parameter p. While we do not know p, we can estimate it from the observed data. Since, as shown earlier, the sample proportion $\overline{X}_n$ is an unbiased and consistent estimator of p, we can use it to construct the following standard error:

$$\text{standard error of sample proportion} = \sqrt{\frac{\overline{X}_n(1 - \overline{X}_n)}{n}}. \qquad (7.8)$$

For example, if the sample size is 1000 and 600 individuals said they supported Obama, then our estimate of Obama's support rate in the population is 0.6 and the standard error is $0.015 \approx \sqrt{0.6(1 - 0.6)/1000}$. This implies that our estimate deviates from the true population proportion of Obama supporters by 1.5 percentage points on average.

In general, the standard error must be derived for each statistic because each statistic typically has a unique sampling distribution. For example, the standard error formula given in equation (7.8) applies only to the sample proportion of n i.i.d. Bernoulli random variables. The derivation in equation (7.7) shows that a more general formula for the standard error of the sample mean, when X is possibly nonbinary, is given by the following formula.

Suppose that we have a sample of n independently and identically distributed random variables, $\{X_1, X_2, \ldots, X_n\}$. The **standard error** of the sample mean $\overline{X}_n = \sum_{i=1}^{n} X_i/n$ is given by

$$\text{standard error of sample mean} = \sqrt{\widehat{\mathbb{V}(\overline{X}_n)}} = \sqrt{\frac{\widehat{\mathbb{V}(X)}}{n}}. \qquad (7.9)$$

When X is a Bernoulli random variable, the formula can be simplified as shown in equation (7.8) by setting $\widehat{\mathbb{V}(X)} = \overline{X}_n(1 - \overline{X}_n)$.

Thus, we can compute the standard error by estimating the population variance $\mathbb{V}(X)$ with the sample variance $\sum_{i=1}^{n}(X_i - \overline{X}_n)^2/(n - 1)$, where the denominator is $n - 1$ rather than n because the estimation of variance requires the estimation of mean, resulting in the loss of one *degree of freedom* (see section 4.3.2).

Finally, we can also obtain the standard error of the difference-in-means estimator used in a randomized controlled trial. To do this, we note that the variance of the difference-in-means estimator is the sum of the variances of the sample means for the treatment and control groups. We estimate these latter two variances. Here, we can assume statistical independence between the two sample means because they are based on different groups of observations. Our calculations yield the standard error for the difference-in-means estimator when one sample mean is compared with another sample mean.

Suppose that we have a sample of n independently and identically distributed random variables, $\{X_1, X_2, \ldots, X_n\}$. We also have another sample of m independently and identically distributed random variables, $\{Y_1, Y_2, \ldots, Y_m\}$. Then, the **standard error** of the difference-in-means estimator, $\sum_{i=1}^{n} X_i/n - \sum_{i=1}^{m} Y_i/m$, is given by

$$\text{standard error of the difference-in-means} = \sqrt{\frac{\widehat{\mathbb{V}(X)}}{n} + \frac{\widehat{\mathbb{V}(Y)}}{m}}. \qquad (7.10)$$

We now revisit the simulation conducted at the end of section 7.1.1. In this simulation, the quantity of interest is the PATE rather than the SATE, which is based on a particular sample. We add the standard error calculation to each simulation and obtain 5000 standard errors. These standard errors should on average estimate the standard deviation of the sampling distribution of the difference-in-means estimator.

```
## PATE simulation with standard error
sims <- 5000
diff.means <- se <- rep(NA, sims)   # container for standard error added
for (i in 1:sims) {
    ## generate a sample
    Y0 <- rnorm(n, mean = mu0, sd = sd0)
    Y1 <- rnorm(n, mean = mu1, sd = sd1)
    ## randomize the treatment by sampling of a vector of 0s and 1s
    treat <- sample(c(rep(1, n / 2), rep(0, n / 2)), size = n, replace = FALSE)
    diff.means[i] <- mean(Y1[treat == 1]) - mean(Y0[treat == 0])
    ## standard error
    se[i] <- sqrt(var(Y1[treat == 1]) / (n / 2) + var(Y0[treat == 0]) / (n / 2))
}
## standard deviation of difference-in-means
sd(diff.means)

## [1] 0.1966406

## mean of standard errors
mean(se)

## [1] 0.1992668
```

As expected from the definition of standard error, the average of the standard errors is close to the standard deviation of the sampling distribution of the difference-in-means estimator. In the current case, we can analytically derive the exact standard deviation of the sampling distribution of this estimator because we know the true data-generating process. Using the distributions of $Y(1)$ and $Y(0)$ in equation (7.5), we compute it as

$$\sqrt{\frac{\mathbb{V}(Y(1))}{n_1} + \frac{\mathbb{V}(Y(0))}{n - n_1}} = \sqrt{\frac{1}{50} + \frac{1}{50}} = \frac{1}{5}. \tag{7.11}$$

We see that our simulation procedure approximates this true value very well.

7.1.3 CONFIDENCE INTERVALS

In order to study the properties of an estimator, we have used the mean and standard deviation of its sampling distribution. Next, we consider characterizing the entire sampling distribution rather than its mean and standard deviation. In some special cases, this can be done easily. For example, suppose that $\{X_1, X_2, \ldots, X_n\}$ are independently and identically distributed according to a normal distribution with mean μ and variance σ^2. Since the sum of normal random variables follows another normal distribution, the sampling distribution of the sample mean $\overline{X}_n = \sum_{i=1}^{n} X_i/n$ is also a normal distribution, with mean $\mathbb{E}(\overline{X}_n) = \mathbb{E}(X) = \mu$ and variance $\mathbb{V}(\overline{X}_n) = \sigma^2/n$.

While the derivation works out nicely in the case of the normal distribution, it is unclear how to characterize the sampling distribution of an estimator in other cases. This is problematic because in practice we do not know the true data-generating process. Fortunately, in many cases of practical interest, there is a way to *approximate* the sampling distribution of an estimator. Specifically, we use the *central limit theorem* introduced in section 6.4.2. The theorem implies that the sampling distribution of the sample mean is approximately normally distributed:

$$\overline{X}_n \stackrel{\text{approx.}}{\sim} \mathcal{N}\left(\mathbb{E}(X), \frac{\mathbb{V}(X)}{n}\right). \tag{7.12}$$

We can derive this result from equation (6.41) of section 6.4.2 by multiplying both sides by the standard deviation, $\sqrt{\mathbb{V}(X)/n}$ (this changes the variance from 1 to $\mathbb{V}(X)/n$), and adding the mean, $\mathbb{E}(X)$ (this changes the mean from 0 to $\mathbb{E}(X)$). If the random variable is binary, then $\overline{X}_n$ represents the sample proportion, and therefore we have $\mathbb{E}(X) = p$ and $\mathbb{V}(X) = p(1 - p)$. For a large enough sample, this result enables us to characterize the sampling distribution of the sample mean using a normal distribution. Equation (7.12) is useful because it holds regardless of the distribution of the original random variable X.

Using this result, we can construct another measure of uncertainty called a *confidence interval*. Confidence intervals give a range of values that are likely to include the true value of the parameter. They are also referred to as *confidence bands* or *error bands*. To compute the confidence interval, researchers decide the *confidence level*, or the degree to which they would like to be certain that the interval actually contains the true value. More precisely, over a hypothetically repeated data-generating process, confidence intervals contain the true value of the parameter with the probability specified by the confidence level. Many applied researchers choose the 95% confidence level as a matter of convention but other choices such as 90% and 99% can also be used. The confidence level is often written as $(1 - \alpha) \times 100\%$, where α can take any value between 0 and 1. For example, $\alpha = 0.05$ corresponds to the 95% confidence level.

Formally, the $(1 - \alpha) \times 100\%$ asymptotic (i.e., large sample) confidence interval, $\text{CI}(\alpha)$, for the sample mean is defined as

$$\text{CI}(\alpha) = \left[\overline{X}_n - z_{\alpha/2} \times \text{standard error}, \quad \overline{X}_n + z_{\alpha/2} \times \text{standard error}\right]. \tag{7.13}$$

In this definition, $z_{\alpha/2}$ is the *critical value*, which equals the $(1 - \alpha/2)$ quantile of the standard normal distribution such that $P(Z > \alpha/2) = 1 - P(Z \leq \alpha/2) = 1 - \alpha/2$, where Z is a standard normal random variable. Thus, the probability that a standard normal random variable is greater than this critical value is equal to $\alpha/2$. Figure 7.1

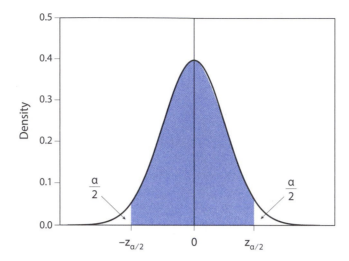

Figure 7.1. Critical Values Based on the Standard Normal Distribution. The lower and upper critical values, $-z_{\alpha/2}$ and $z_{\alpha/2}$, are shown on the horizontal axis. The area under the density curve between these critical values (highlighted in blue) equals $1 - \alpha$. These critical values are symmetric.

Table 7.1. Commonly Used Critical Values Based on the Normal Distribution for Confidence Intervals.

α	Confidence level	Critical value $z_{\alpha/2}$	R expression
0.01	99%	2.58	`qnorm(0.995)`
0.05	95%	1.96	`qnorm(0.975)`
0.1	90%	1.64	`qnorm(0.95)`

graphically illustrates these critical values, where the area under the density curve between the lower and upper critical values, highlighted in blue, equals $1 - \alpha$.

The critical values that correspond to commonly chosen confidence levels are shown along with R expressions in table 7.1. Thus, as the confidence level decreases, the critical value decreases and consequently the width of confidence interval narrows. This is because the width of the confidence interval is $2 \times$ standard error $\times z_{\alpha/2}$ (see equation (7.13)). The trend makes sense because for the same observed data, a shorter confidence interval gives us less confidence that the interval contains the true value. As the table shows, the confidence level corresponds to the argument of the `qnorm()` function. Mathematically, this function computes the inverse of the CDF of a standard normal random variable X. To use the `qnorm()` function, we input a probability p, and the function returns the quantile q such that $p = P(X \le q)$.

Going back to the survey sampling example, if 600 out of 1000 respondents support Obama, then the estimate of the population proportion of voters who support Obama, or point estimate, is $\overline{X}_n = 0.6$ with a standard error of $0.02 = \sqrt{0.6 \times (1 - 0.6)/1000}$. Thus, the 99%, 95%, and 90% confidence intervals can be computed as follows.

```
n <- 1000 # sample size
x.bar <- 0.6 # point estimate
s.e. <- sqrt(x.bar * (1 - x.bar) / n) # standard error
## 99% confidence intervals
c(x.bar - qnorm(0.995) * s.e., x.bar + qnorm(0.995) * s.e.)

## [1] 0.5600954 0.6399046

## 95% confidence intervals
c(x.bar - qnorm(0.975) * s.e., x.bar + qnorm(0.975) * s.e.)

## [1] 0.5696364 0.6303636

## 90% confidence intervals
c(x.bar - qnorm(0.95) * s.e., x.bar + qnorm(0.95) * s.e.)

## [1] 0.574518 0.625482
```

We observe that a greater confidence level yields a wider confidence interval.

How should we interpret confidence intervals? It is tempting to think, for example, that the probability that the particular 95% confidence interval computed based on the observed data contains the true value of the parameter is 0.95. However, this interpretation is incorrect. The reason is that the true value of the parameter is unknown and fixed, and hence the probability that a particular confidence interval contains this value is either 1 (when it actually contains it) or 0 (when it does not). We should note that since confidence intervals are a function of observed data, they are random and vary from one (hypothetical) random sample to another. The correct interpretation of confidence intervals is, therefore, that 95% confidence intervals contain the true value of the parameter 95% of the time during a hypothetically repeated data-generating process. In other words, if we had an infinite number of random samples, then 95% of them yield a 95% confidence interval that contains the truth. The probability that a (random) confidence interval includes the true value is called the *coverage probability* (or *coverage rate*). Confidence intervals are valid when they have a coverage probability equal to the nominal value (e.g., 95% in the current example).

We now explain why the confidence interval given in equation (7.13) has a proper coverage rate. Consider the probability that a $(1 - \alpha/2) \times 100\%$ confidence interval contains the true parameter value $\mathbb{E}(X)$ (or p when X is a Bernoulli random variable), i.e., the probability that the true parameter is between the lower and upper confidence limits. This probability does not change even if we subtract the sample mean $\overline{X}_n$ from each term and divide it by its standard error:

$$P\left(\overline{X}_n - z_{\alpha/2} \times \text{standard error} \leq \mathbb{E}(X) \leq \overline{X}_n + z_{\alpha/2} \times \text{standard error}\right)$$

$$= P\left(-z_{\alpha/2} \leq \frac{\mathbb{E}(X) - \overline{X}_n}{\text{standard error}} \leq z_{\alpha/2}\right)$$

$$= P\left(-z_{\alpha/2} \leq \frac{\overline{X}_n - \mathbb{E}(X)}{\text{standard error}} \leq z_{\alpha/2}\right)$$

$$= 1 - \alpha. \tag{7.14}$$

The middle probability term, $\{\mathbb{E}(X) - \overline{X}_n\}/$standard error, equals the negative z-score of the sample mean, which has the same sampling distribution as the z-score because of symmetry. The central limit theorem implies that the z-score of the sample mean follows the standard normal distribution when the sample size is sufficiently large:

$$\frac{\overline{X}_n - \mathbb{E}(X)}{\sqrt{\mathbb{V}(X)/n}} \approx \frac{\overline{X}_n - \mathbb{E}(X)}{\text{standard error}} \sim \mathcal{N}(0, 1). \tag{7.15}$$

Therefore, the probability in equation (7.14) equals the blue area of figure 7.1.

We now summarize the standard procedure for constructing asymptotic confidence intervals based on the central limit theorem. The procedure applies to any estimator so long as its asymptotic sampling distribution can be approximated by the normal distribution. Such a normal approximation holds for many cases of interest including almost all the examples in this book.

The **confidence interval** of an estimate $\hat{\theta}$ can be obtained by using the following procedure:

1. Choose the desired level of confidence $(1 - \alpha) \times 100\%$ by specifying a value of α between 0 and 1: the most common choice is $\alpha = 0.05$, which gives a 95% confidence level.
2. Derive the sampling distribution of the estimator by computing its mean and variance: in the case of the sample mean, this is given by equation (7.12).
3. Compute the standard error based on this sampling distribution.
4. Compute the critical value $z_{\alpha/2}$ as the $(1 - \alpha) \times 100$ percentile value of the standard normal distribution: see table 7.1.
5. Compute the lower and upper confidence limits as $\hat{\theta} - z_{\alpha/2} \times$ standard error and $\hat{\theta} + z_{\alpha/2} \times$ standard error, respectively.

The resulting confidence interval covers the true parameter value θ over a hypothetically repeated data-generating process $(1 - \alpha) \times 100\%$ of the time.

Several applications of this procedure will be given throughout this section. Here, we conduct Monte Carlo simulations to further illustrate the idea of confidence intervals. First we revisit the PATE simulation shown in section 7.1.2. Given the estimates and standard errors we computed, we can obtain the 90% and 95% confidence intervals for each of the 5000 simulations.

```r
## empty container matrices for 2 sets of confidence intervals
ci95 <- ci90 <- matrix(NA, ncol = 2, nrow = sims)
## 95% confidence intervals
ci95[, 1] <- diff.means - qnorm(0.975) * se # lower limit
ci95[, 2] <- diff.means + qnorm(0.975) * se # upper limit
```

```
## 90% confidence intervals
ci90[, 1] <- diff.means - qnorm(0.95) * se # lower limit
ci90[, 2] <- diff.means + qnorm(0.95) * se # upper limit
```

If these confidence intervals are valid, then they should contain the true value of the PATE, which is equal to 1 in this simulation, approximately 95% and 90% of time, respectively. That is exactly what we find below.

```
## coverage rate for 95% confidence interval
mean(ci95[, 1] <= 1 & ci95[, 2] >= 1)

## [1] 0.9482

## coverage rate for 90% confidence interval
mean(ci90[, 1] <= 1 & ci90[, 2] >= 1)

## [1] 0.9038
```

As another illustration, we use the polling example described earlier. Again, over repeated random sampling, 95% of the 95% confidence intervals should contain the true parameter value. As the sample size increases, we should observe that the approximation improves with the coverage probability approaching its nominal rate. In the code chunk below, we use a double loop. The outer loop is defined for different sample sizes and the inner loop conducts a simulation and examines, for each simulation, whether the confidence interval contains the truth.

```
p <- 0.6 # true parameter value
n <- c(10, 100, 1000) # 3 sample sizes to be examined
alpha <- 0.05
sims <- 5000 # number of simulations
results <- rep(NA, length(n)) # a container for results
## loop for different sample sizes
for (i in 1:length(n)) {
    ci.results <- rep(NA, sims) # a container for whether CI includes truth
    ## loop for repeated hypothetical survey sampling
    for (j in 1:sims) {
        data <- rbinom(n[i], size = 1, prob = p) # simple  random sampling
        x.bar <- mean(data) # sample proportion as  an estimate
        s.e. <- sqrt(x.bar * (1 - x.bar) / n[i]) # standard errors
        ci.lower <- x.bar - qnorm(1 - alpha / 2) * s.e.
        ci.upper <- x.bar + qnorm(1 - alpha / 2) * s.e.
        ci.results[j] <- (p >= ci.lower) & (p <= ci.upper)
    }
    ## proportion of CIs that contain the true value
    results[i] <- mean(ci.results)
}
```

```
results
```

```
## [1] 0.8980 0.9552 0.9486
```

As the sample size increases, the proportion of 95% confidence intervals that contain the true population proportion approaches their nominal value, 95%.

7.1.4 MARGIN OF ERROR AND SAMPLE SIZE CALCULATION IN POLLS

In the world of polling, the phrase *margin of error* typically refers to the half width of 95% confidence intervals. That is, when we say that Obama's approval rate is 60% with margin of error plus or minus 3 percentage points, we mean that the 95% confidence interval is [57, 63]. In general, we can define the margin of error in polling as

$$\text{margin of error} = \pm z_{0.025} \times \text{standard error} \approx \pm 1.96 \times \sqrt{\frac{\overline{X}_n(1 - \overline{X}_n)}{n}}. \quad (7.16)$$

Now consider the case where the standard deviation of the sampling distribution, i.e., $\sqrt{p(1 - p)}$, is the largest. This happens when exactly half of voters support Obama and the other do not, i.e., $p = 0.5$. Then, assuming that we have a large enough sample to ensure $\overline{X} \approx p$, the margin of error becomes approximately $\pm 1/\sqrt{n} \approx \pm 1.96 \times \sqrt{0.5 \times (1 - 0.5)/n}$. From this result, we can derive the *rule of thumb* commonly applied when researchers are deciding the number of respondents to interview. This rule of thumb states that if you compute the reciprocal of the squared margin of error, it gives the sample size necessary to achieve the specified level of precision, i.e., $n \approx 1/\text{margin of error}^2$. For example, if we want to obtain an estimate with margin of error plus or minus 3 percentage points, then we need approximately $1/0.03^2 \approx 1111$ observations. More generally, by rearranging the terms in equation (7.16), the approximate relationship between the margin of error and sample size can be written as follows.

The **margin of error** of the estimated proportion in polling $\overline{X}_n$ refers to the half width of the 95% confidence interval or $z_{0.025} \times \text{standard error} = 1.96 \times \sqrt{\overline{X}_n(1 - \overline{X}_n)/n}$. The approximate relationship between sample size n and margin of error is

$$n \approx \frac{1.96^2 p(1 - p)}{\text{margin of error}^2}, \quad (7.17)$$

where p is the population proportion. The formula can be used to determine the sample size necessary for conducting a survey.

We can use this formula to determine the sample size for a survey given the desired level of precision, or margin of error, and our prior information about the population proportion p. This calculation, conducted before fielding a survey, is called the *sample size calculation* and represents an important planning component of survey sampling. Below, we plot the sample size as a function of the population proportion (the horizontal axis) and the margin of error (different line types). In the plot below, we observe that a large sample size is required to obtain a margin of error of plus or minus 1 percentage point, particularly when the population proportion is close to 0.5. In contrast, a moderate sample size is sufficient if the desired margin of error is plus or minus 3 percentage points or more.

```
MoE <- c(0.01, 0.03, 0.05)  # the desired margin of error
p <- seq(from = 0.01, to = 0.99, by = 0.01)
n <- 1.96^2 * p * (1 - p) / MoE[1]^2
plot(p, n, ylim = c(-1000, 11000),  xlab = "Population proportion",
     ylab = "Sample size", type = "l")
lines(p, 1.96^2 * p * (1 - p) / MoE[2]^2, lty = "dashed")
lines(p, 1.96^2 * p * (1 - p) / MoE[3]^2, lty = "dotted")
text(0.5, 10000, "margin of error = 0.01")
text(0.5, 1800, "margin of error = 0.03")
text(0.5, -200, "margin of error = 0.05")
```

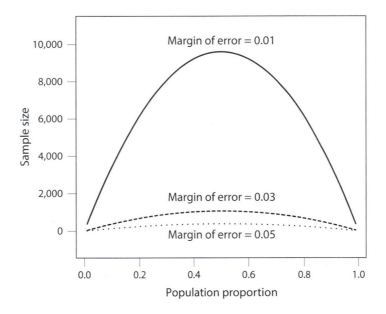

Finally, we revisit the statewide preelection polls analyzed in chapter 4. We analyze the 2008 presidential election polling data set `polls08.csv`, whose variable names and descriptions are given in table 4.2. In section 4.1.3, we computed our estimated margin of victory for Obama within each state and plotted it against his margin of victory on Election Day. Here, we conduct a similar analysis but include the 95% confidence interval for each estimate and plot it as a vertical line. Note that the official election results are contained in the data file `pres08.csv`, the variable names and descriptions of which are shown in table 4.1. Our code modifies the code chunk that appeared in section 4.1.3 by focusing on Obama's support share and adding the 95% confidence intervals. We assume that the sample size for each poll is 1000.

```r
## election and polling results, by state
pres08 <- read.csv("pres08.csv")
polls08 <- read.csv("polls08.csv")
## convert to a Date object
polls08$middate <- as.Date(polls08$middate)
## number of days to Election Day
polls08$DaysToElection <- as.Date("2008-11-04") - polls08$middate
## create a matrix place holder
poll.pred <- matrix(NA, nrow = 51, ncol = 3)
## state names which the loop will iterate through
st.names <- unique(pres08$state)
## add labels for easy interpretation later on
row.names(poll.pred) <- as.character(st.names)
## loop across 50 states plus DC
for (i in 1:51){
    ## subset the ith state
    state.data <- subset(polls08, subset = (state == st.names[i]))
    ## subset the latest polls within the state
    latest <- state.data$DaysToElection == min(state.data$DaysToElection)
    ## compute the mean of latest polls and store it
    poll.pred[i, 1] <- mean(state.data$Obama[latest]) / 100
}
## upper and lower confidence limits
n <- 1000 # sample size
alpha <- 0.05
s.e. <- sqrt(poll.pred[, 1] * (1 - poll.pred[, 1]) / n) # standard error
poll.pred[, 2] <- poll.pred[, 1] - qnorm(1 - alpha / 2) * s.e.
poll.pred[, 3] <- poll.pred[, 1] + qnorm(1 - alpha / 2) * s.e.
```

We now compare the polling prediction of Obama's support share (the vertical axis) against Obama's vote share on Election Day (the horizontal axis). The idea is that the latter represents the true parameter value within each state. If our 95% confidence intervals are appropriate, 95% of them, which is about 48 states, should contain the actual Election Day result. We use the `lines()` function repeatedly to draw the confidence interval for each state, with the confidence limits marking each end.

```r
alpha <- 0.05
plot(pres08$Obama / 100, poll.pred[, 1], xlim = c(0, 1),  ylim = c(0, 1),
     xlab = "Obama's vote share", ylab = "Poll prediction")
abline(0, 1)
```

```
## adding 95% confidence intervals for each state
for (i in 1:51) {
    lines(rep(pres08$Obama[i] / 100, 2), c(poll.pred[i, 2], poll.pred[i, 3]))
}
## proportion of confidence intervals that contain the Election Day outcome
mean((poll.pred[, 2] <= pres08$Obama / 100) &
        (poll.pred[, 3] >= pres08$Obama / 100))

## [1] 0.5882353
```

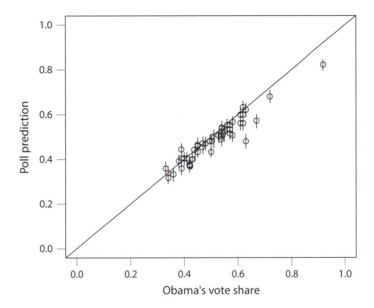

The result suggests that the coverage rate is 58.8%, far below the nominal level. One possible reason for under-coverage is that the poll estimates of Obama's support are biased. If the confidence intervals are not centered around the true parameter value, the coverage rate will be low even if their widths are appropriate. Such bias, if it exists, can affect the confidence intervals by systematically shifting them in one direction and altering the standard error. To investigate this possibility, we first compute the bias and then correct our point estimates by subtracting this bias from the original estimates.

```
## bias
bias <- mean(poll.pred[, 1] - pres08$Obama / 100)
bias

## [1] -0.02679739

## bias corrected estimate
poll.bias <- poll.pred[, 1] - bias
```

Using this bias-corrected estimate, we can retrospectively compute the standard error and the 95% "bias-corrected" confidence intervals. This retrospective procedure differs from prospective bias correction, which estimates the magnitude of bias without observing the true parameter values (i.e., the Election Day result in this application). Finally, we examine the coverage rate of the bias-corrected confidence intervals.

```
## bias-corrected standard error
s.e.bias <- sqrt(poll.bias * (1 - poll.bias) / n)
## bias-corrected 95% confidence interval
ci.bias.lower <- poll.bias - qnorm(1 - alpha / 2) * s.e.bias
ci.bias.upper <- poll.bias + qnorm(1 - alpha / 2) * s.e.bias
## proportion of bias-corrected CIs that contain the Election Day outcome
mean((ci.bias.lower <= pres08$Obama / 100) &
        (ci.bias.upper >= pres08$Obama / 100))

## [1] 0.7647059
```

The bias correction dramatically improves the coverage rate by almost 20 percentage points. Nevertheless, it is still far from the nominal coverage rate of 95%.

Although the standard errors and confidence intervals represent useful measures of uncertainty, they account only for uncertainty due to random sampling. In practice, other sources of uncertainty remain unaccounted for in the standard error calculation. For example, there may exist systematic bias due to *unit nonresponse*. While beyond the scope of this book, statistical methods have been developed to adjust such bias and underestimation of uncertainty.

7.1.5 ANALYSIS OF RANDOMIZED CONTROLLED TRIALS

We next consider the quantification of uncertainty with respect to estimates of causal effects. We revisit the analysis of data from the STAR (Student–Teacher Achievement Ratio) project introduced in section 2.8.1. The STAR project conducted a randomized controlled trial in the 1980s. In the experiment, students were randomly assigned to a small class, regular class, or regular class with an aid. We are interested in knowing whether small class size improves students' test performance. The data in the file STAR.csv have the variable names and descriptions given in table 2.6. We begin by creating a histogram for our outcome variable, the fourth-grade standardized reading test score, separately for students assigned to a regular class and those in a small class. We estimate the average score for each group (after deleting observations with missing values) and add it to each graph as a blue line.

```
## read in data
STAR <- read.csv("STAR.csv", head = TRUE)
hist(STAR$g4reading[STAR$classtype == 1], freq = FALSE, xlim = c(500, 900),
     ylim = c(0, 0.01), main = "Small class",
     xlab = "Fourth-grade reading test score")
abline(v = mean(STAR$g4reading[STAR$classtype == 1], na.rm = TRUE),
       col = "blue")
```

```
hist(STAR$g4reading[STAR$classtype == 2], freq = FALSE, xlim = c(500, 900),
     ylim = c(0, 0.01), main = "Regular class",
     xlab = "Fourth-grade reading test score")
abline(v = mean(STAR$g4reading[STAR$classtype == 2], na.rm = TRUE),
       col = "blue")
```

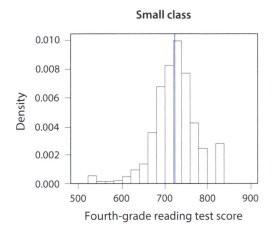

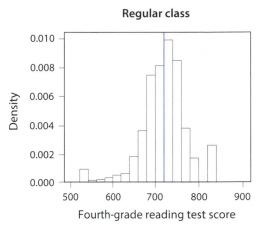

We first compute the estimated average test score for each treatment group by taking its sample average. These estimates of the average test scores are shown in the above plots using blue lines. We also compute the standard error for each estimator. Since the standard error is the estimated standard deviation of the sampling distribution, it is given by $\sqrt{\widehat{\mathbb{V}(\overline{X}_n)}} = \sqrt{\hat{\sigma}^2/n}$ in this case. We can use the sample variance as our estimate of the variance parameter σ^2. When computing the sample size, we need to be careful not to count observations with missing reading scores.

```
## estimate and standard error for small class
n.small <-
sum(STAR$classtype == 1 & !is.na(STAR$g4reading))
est.small <- mean(STAR$g4reading[STAR$classtype == 1], na.rm = TRUE)
se.small <- sd(STAR$g4reading[STAR$classtype == 1], na.rm = TRUE) /
    sqrt(n.small)
est.small

## [1] 723.3912

se.small

## [1] 1.913012

## estimate and standard error for regular class
n.regular <- sum(STAR$classtype == 2 & !is.na(STAR$classtype) &
                 !is.na(STAR$g4reading))
```

```
est.regular <- mean(STAR$g4reading[STAR$classtype == 2], na.rm = TRUE)
se.regular <- sd(STAR$g4reading[STAR$classtype == 2], na.rm = TRUE) /
    sqrt(n.regular)
est.regular

## [1] 719.89

se.regular

## [1] 1.83885
```

How should one construct a confidence interval for each estimate? As before, we can rely on the central limit theorem and obtain an approximate confidence interval for each estimate.

```
alpha <- 0.05
## 95% confidence intervals for small class
ci.small <- c(est.small - qnorm(1 - alpha / 2) * se.small,
              est.small + qnorm(1 - alpha / 2) * se.small)
ci.small

## [1] 719.6417 727.1406

## 95% confidence intervals for regular class
ci.regular <- c(est.regular - qnorm(1 - alpha / 2) * se.regular,
                est.regular + qnorm(1 - alpha / 2) * se.regular)
ci.regular

## [1] 716.2859 723.4940
```

These confidence intervals overlap with each other. Does this mean that the estimated average difference between the two groups, or the estimated PATE of small class size, is not statistically significant? An estimated effect is statistically significant if it reflects true patterns in the population, rather than arising from mere chance. To find out the answer to this question, it would be best to compute the confidence interval directly for the estimated average difference. Recall the standard error of the difference-in-means estimator given in equation (7.10). Using this standard error formula, we can compute the 95% confidence interval for the estimated PATE.

```
## difference-in-means estimator
ate.est <- est.small - est.regular
ate.est

## [1] 3.501232

## standard error and 95% confidence interval
ate.se <- sqrt(se.small^2 + se.regular^2)
```

```
ate.se

## [1] 2.653485

ate.ci <- c(ate.est - qnorm(1 - alpha / 2) * ate.se,
            ate.est + qnorm(1 - alpha / 2) * ate.se)
ate.ci

## [1] -1.699503  8.701968
```

We find that the average treatment effect of small class size on the fourth-grade reading score is estimated to be 3.50 with a standard error of 2.65. The 95% confidence interval is $[-1.70, 8.70]$, containing zero. This finding suggests that although the estimated average treatment effect is positive, it features a considerable degree of uncertainty.

7.1.6   ANALYSIS BASED ON STUDENT'S t-DISTRIBUTION

The calculation of confidence intervals has so far relied upon the central limit theorem. This is why we used the quantiles of the standard normal distribution when computing confidence intervals, assuming that we have a large enough sample to invoke the central limit theorem. This assumption is useful because the central limit theorem applies to a wide variety of distributions. Given that we often do not know the distribution of an outcome variable, the procedure of constructing confidence intervals described earlier is quite general.

Here, we consider an alternative assumption, that the outcome variable (rather than its sample mean) is generated from a normal distribution. As an illustration, we apply this assumption to the STAR experiment just analyzed in section 7.1.5. We assume that the test scores for each group follow a normal distribution, with possibly different means and variances. While the histograms shown earlier suggest that the distribution of test scores for each group may not satisfy this assumption, the inference resulting from this assumption proves more conservative than the asymptotic inference we have been using based on the central limit theorem. Because many researchers prefer conservative inferences, they often use confidence intervals under this normally distributed outcome assumption even when the assumption is not justifiable.

When a random variable is normally distributed, we can obtain an exact confidence interval for the sample mean using *Student's t-distribution*, also simply called the *t-distribution*. The name of the distribution originates from the fact that its British creator William Gossett, a researcher at beer producer Guinness, published the paper introducing it under the pseudonym "Student." We use t_ν to represent the t-distribution with ν degrees of freedom. Specifically, the z-score of the sample mean is called the *t-statistic* and is distributed according to the t-distribution with $n - 1$ *degrees of freedom*. Roughly, the degrees of freedom represent the number of independent observations used for estimation minus the number of parameters to be estimated (see section 4.3.2). The current case involves one parameter to estimate: we use the standard error to estimate the standard deviation of the sampling distribution. This result holds exactly so we do not resort to asymptotic approximation.

Suppose that $\{X_1, X_2, \ldots, X_n\}$ are n independently and identically distributed random variables from a normal distribution with mean μ and variance σ^2. Then, the z-score of the sample mean $\overline{X}_n$, which is called the t-**statistic**, follows **Student's** t-**distribution** with $n - 1$ degrees of freedom:

$$t\text{-statistic of sample mean} = \frac{\overline{X}_n - \text{mean}}{\text{standard error}} = \frac{\overline{X}_n - \mu}{\hat{\sigma}} \sim t_{n-1}.$$

The t-distribution is quite similar to the standard normal distribution but has heavier tails. In the left-hand plot below, we graphically compare the density function of the t-distribution with 3 different degrees of freedom (dashed lines) to the standard normal distribution. The t-distribution with v degrees of freedom has mean zero. The variance is given by $v/(v - 2)$ when the number of degrees of freedom is greater than 2. It turns out that the variance does not exist when v is less than or equal to 2.

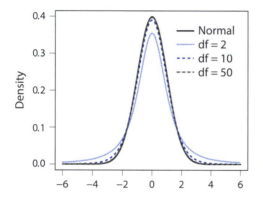
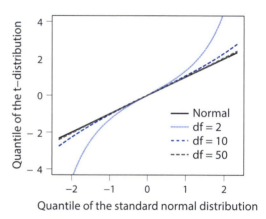

Like the standard normal distribution (black solid line), the t-distribution density function is symmetric and centered around zero. However, the t-distribution has more mass in the tail areas than the standard normal distribution, especially when the degrees of freedom are small. As the degrees of freedom increase, however, the t-distribution approaches the standard normal distribution. This makes sense because according to the *central limit theorem*, the z-score of the sample mean follows the standard normal distribution regardless of the distribution of the original random variable. Therefore, the standard normal distribution should approximate the sampling distribution of the t-statistic well for a sufficiently large sample size.

The construction of the confidence intervals under this setting is the same as for the sample mean, except that we use the t-distribution with $n - 1$ degrees of freedom when computing the *critical values*. That is, the $(1 - \alpha) \times 100\%$ confidence interval for the sample mean is given by equation (7.13) except that $z_{\alpha/2}$ now equals the $1 - \alpha/2$ quantile of the t-distribution. This results in a wider, and hence more conservative, confidence interval because the critical values based on the t-distribution are greater than those based on the standard normal distribution (see the *quantile–quantile plot* or Q–Q plot in the right-hand panel above). For example, when $\alpha = 0.05$ and $n = 50$, the critical value based on the t-distribution is equal to 2.01, which is slightly greater than the one based on the standard normal distribution, 1.96.

We now go back to the analysis of the STAR data and compute the 95% confidence intervals for the estimated average reading score under each treatment condition. To compute critical values for t-statistics in R, we can use the qt() function with the df argument specifying the degrees of freedom, rather than the qnorm() function we used for the normal approximation.

```
## 95% CI for small class
c(est.small - qt(0.975, df = n.small - 1) * se.small,
  est.small + qt(0.975, df = n.small - 1) * se.small)

## [1] 719.6355 727.1469

## 95% CI based on the central limit theorem
ci.small

## [1] 719.6417 727.1406

## 95% CI for regular class
c(est.regular - qt(0.975, df = n.regular - 1) * se.regular,
  est.regular + qt(0.975, df = n.regular - 1) * se.regular)

## [1] 716.2806 723.4993

## 95% CI based on the central limit theorem
ci.regular

## [1] 716.2859 723.4940
```

These confidence intervals are slightly wider than those obtained using the central limit theorem. The differences are tiny because the sample size is relatively large. To compute the confidence interval for the difference-in-means estimator, suppose that $\{X_1, X_2, \ldots, X_n\}$ are n independently and identically distributed normal random variables with mean μ_X and variance σ_X^2, and $\{Y_1, Y_2, \ldots, Y_m\}$ are m i.i.d. normal random variables with mean μ_Y and variance σ_Y^2. Then, the t-statistic is given by

$$t\text{-statistic of difference-in-means} = \frac{(\overline{X}_n - \overline{Y}_m) - (\mu_X - \mu_Y)}{\sqrt{\hat{\sigma}_X^2/n + \hat{\sigma}_Y^2/m}}. \tag{7.18}$$

Although this t-statistic also follows Student's t-distribution, the degrees of freedom calculation is complicated. The details of this calculation are beyond the scope of this book, but we can construct the confidence interval based on Student's t-distribution. We employ the t.test() function, which we will also use later to conduct a hypothesis test. For now, we focus on the part of the output that shows the confidence interval.

```
t.ci <- t.test(STAR$g4reading[STAR$classtype == 1],
               STAR$g4reading[STAR$classtype == 2])
t.ci

##
##  Welch Two Sample t-test
##
## data:STAR$g4reading[STAR$classtype==1] and STAR$g4reading[STAR$classtype == 2]
## t = 1.3195, df = 1541.2, p-value = 0.1872
## alternative hypothesis: true difference in means is not equal to 0
## 95 percent confidence interval:
##  -1.703591  8.706055
## sample estimates:
## mean of x mean of y
##  723.3912  719.8900
```

The degrees of freedom are calculated as 1541.2. Because the size of our sample is not too small, the resulting confidence interval is only slightly wider than the one based on the normal approximation reported above.

7.2   Hypothesis Testing

In section 6.1.5, we presented an analysis of Arnold Schwarzenegger's 2009 veto message to the California legislature, and showed that the particular order of words in his message was highly unlikely to be a consequence of coincidence alone. This was done by examining the likelihood of observing the event that actually happened under a particular probability model. In section 6.6.3, a similar method was used to detect election fraud in Russia, where we generated hypothetical election results and compared them with the actual election outcome to investigate whether the latter was anomalous. In this section, we formalize this logic and introduce a general principle of statistical *hypothesis testing* that underlies such analysis. This principle enables us to determine whether or not the occurrence of an observed event is likely to be due to chance alone.

7.2.1   TEA-TASTING EXPERIMENT

In his classic book *The Design of Experiments*, Ronald Fisher introduced the idea of a statistical hypothesis test. During an afternoon tea party at the University of Cambridge, a lady declared that tea tastes different depending on whether the tea is poured into the milk or the milk is poured into the tea. Fisher examined this claim by using a randomized experiment in which 8 identical cups were prepared and 4 were randomly selected for milk to be poured into the tea. For the remaining 4 cups, the milk was poured first. The lady was then asked to identify, for each cup, whether the tea or the milk had been poured first. To everyone's surprise, the lady correctly classified all the cups. Did this happen by luck or did the lady actually possess the ability to detect the order, as she claimed?

Table 7.2. Tea-Tasting Experiment.

Cups	Lady's guess	Actual order	Scenarios			$\cdots$
1	M	M	T	T	T	
2	T	T	T	T	M	
3	T	T	T	T	M	
4	M	M	T	M	M	
5	M	M	M	M	T	
6	T	T	M	M	T	
7	T	T	M	T	M	
8	M	M	M	M	T	
Number of correct guesses		8	4	6	2	$\cdots$

Note: "M" and "T" represent two scenarios, "milk is poured first" and "tea is poured first," respectively. Under the hypothesis that the lady has no ability to distinguish the order in which milk and tea were poured into each cup, her guess will be identical regardless of which cups had milk/tea poured first.

To analyze this randomized experiment, we draw on potential outcomes as explained in chapter 2. For each of the 8 cups, we consider two potential guesses given by the lady, which may or may not depend on whether milk or tea was actually poured into the cup first. If we hypothesize that the lady had no ability to distinguish whether milk or tea was poured into the cup first, then her guess should not depend on the actual order in which milk and tea were poured. In other words, under this hypothesis, the two potential outcomes should be identical. Recall the *fundamental problem of causal inference*, which states that only one of the two potential outcomes can be observed. Here, the hypothesis that the lady possesses no ability to distinguish the two types of tea with milk reveals her responses under counterfactual scenarios.

Fisher's analysis proceeds under this hypothesis and involves computing the number of correctly guessed cups under every possible assignment combination. As discussed in section 7.1.1, this experiment is an example of *complete randomization*, where the number of observations assigned to each condition is fixed a priori. In contrast, *simple randomization* would randomize each cup independently without such a constraint. Table 7.2 illustrates Fisher's method. The second column of the table shows the lady's actual guess for each cup, which is identical to the true order (third column) in which milk and tea were poured into the cup. In the remaining columns, we show three arbitrarily selected combinations of assigning 4 cups to "milk first" and the other 4 to "tea first." Although these counterfactual assignment combinations did not occur in the actual experiment, we can compute the number of correctly guessed cups under each scenario with the aforementioned hypothesis that the lady lacks the ability to distinguish between the two types of tea with milk and thus different assignments do not affect the lady's guess. This is done by simply comparing the lady's guess (second column), which is assumed to remain unchanged, with each counterfactual assignment. For example, if the cups had received the assignments in the fifth column of the table, then the number of correctly classified cups would have been 6.

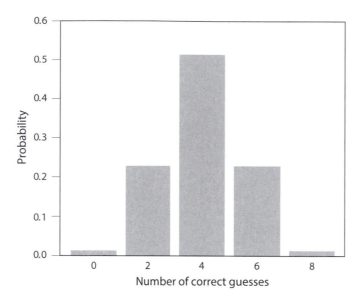

Figure 7.2. Sampling Distribution for the Tea-Tasting Experiment. The bar plot shows the distribution of the number of correctly classified cups.

Under this setup, the key question concerns the likelihood that the lady would have classified all 8 cups correctly if she had not had the ability to distinguish the taste difference. Since each assignment combination is equally likely in this randomized experiment, we can compute the probability of perfect classification by counting the number of ways in which we assign 4 cups to the "milk first" condition and the remaining 4 cups to the "tea first" condition (see equation (6.1)). The number of combinations is given by $_8C_4 = 8!/(4! \times (8-4)!) = 70$ because 4 cups out of 8 were selected to have tea poured in first. Thus, under the assumption that the lady has no ability to distinguish the taste difference, the probability that she guesses all cups correctly is 1/70, or approximately 0.01, which is quite small. We conclude from this analysis that the lady's perfect classification is unlikely to have occurred due to chance alone.

Moreover, as shown in figure 7.2, we can characterize the exact distribution of the number of correctly specified cups over all possible assignment combinations. How is this distribution derived? First, there is only one assignment combination, presented as the actual order in the third column of the table, that makes the lady's guesses a set of perfect classifications. Similarly, there is one assignment combination that makes all of her guesses incorrect. In this experiment, the number of ways in which the lady guesses 2 cups correctly is equivalent to the product of two things: the number of ways in which the lady correctly classifies one of the 4 "milk first" conditions and the number of ways in which the lady incorrectly classifies 3 of them. We can compute this as $_4C_1 \times _4C_3 = 16$. The same calculation applies to the number of assignment combinations that leads to 6 correctly classified cups. Similarly, we can compute the number of combinations that lead to 4 correctly classified cups, which is given by $_4C_2 \times _4C_2 = 36$. Finally, because by design the number of cups assigned to each condition is equal, there is no instance where the number of correctly classified cups is odd. Below, we compute the probability of each event by using the `choose()` function, which enables us to compute combinations.

```
## truth: enumerate the number of assignment combinations
true <- c(choose(4, 0) * choose(4, 4),
          choose(4, 1) * choose(4, 3),
          choose(4, 2) * choose(4, 2),
          choose(4, 3) * choose(4, 1),
          choose(4, 4) * choose(4, 0))
true

## [1]  1 16 36 16  1

## compute probability: divide it by the total number of events
true <- true / sum(true)
## number of correctly classified cups as labels
names(true) <- c(0, 2, 4, 6, 8)
true

##          0          2          4          6          8
## 0.01428571 0.22857143 0.51428571 0.22857143 0.01428571
```

As done in chapter 6, we can also approximate this distribution using Monte Carlo simulations. We generate 1000 hypothetical experiments to approximate the sampling distribution of the number of correctly classified cups. To do this, we use the `sample()` function and *sample without replacement* 8 elements from a vector of 4 M's and 4 T's. This is equivalent to randomly assigning 4 cups to the "milk first" condition and the remaining 4 to the "tea first" condition. We then compute the fraction of trials that yield a certain number of correctly specified cups. The following code chunk shows this simulation approach. We find that the differences between the simulation results and the analytical answers are quite small.

```
## simulations
sims <- 1000
## lady's guess: M stands for "milk first," T stands for "tea first"
guess <- c("M", "T", "T", "M", "M", "T", "T", "M")
correct <- rep(NA, sims) # place holder for number of correct guesses
for (i in 1:sims) {
    ## randomize which cups get milk/tea first
    cups <- sample(c(rep("T", 4), rep("M", 4)), replace = FALSE)
    correct[i] <- sum(guess == cups) # number of correct guesses
}
## estimated probability for each number of correct guesses
prop.table(table(correct))

## correct
##     0     2     4     6     8
## 0.015 0.227 0.500 0.248 0.010
```

```
## comparison with analytical answers; the differences are small
prop.table(table(correct)) - true

## correct
##              0             2             4             6
##    0.0007142857 -0.0015714286 -0.0142857143  0.0194285714
##              8
## -0.0042857143
```

The major advantage of Fisher's analysis is that the inference is solely based on the randomization of treatment assignment. Such inference is called *randomization inference*. Methods based on randomization inference typically do not require a strong assumption about the data-generating process because researchers control the randomization of treatment assignment, which alone serves as the basis of inference.

7.2.2 THE GENERAL FRAMEWORK

The tea-tasting experiment described above illustrates a general framework called statistical hypothesis testing. Statistical hypothesis testing is based on probabilistic *proof by contradiction*. Proof by contradiction is a general strategy of mathematical proof in which one demonstrates that assuming the contrary of what we would like to prove leads to a logical contradiction. For example, consider the proposition that there is no smallest positive *rational number*. To prove this proposition, we assume that the conclusion is false. That is, suppose that there exists a smallest positive rational number a. Recall that any rational number can be expressed as the fraction of two integers: $a = p/q > 0$ where both the numerator p and the nonzero denominator q are positive integers. But, for example, $b = a/2$ is smaller than a, and yet b is also a rational number. This contradicts the hypothesis that a is the smallest positive rational number.

In the case of statistical hypothesis testing, we can never reject a hypothesis with 100% certainty. Consequently, we use a probabilistic version of proof by contradiction. We begin by assuming a hypothesis we would like to eventually refute. This hypothesis is called a *null hypothesis*, often denoted by H_0. In the current application, the null hypothesis is that the lady has no ability to tell whether milk or tea is poured first into a cup. This is an example of *sharp null hypothesis* because all potential outcomes for each observation are determined, and therefore known, under this hypothesis. In contrast, we will later consider a nonsharp null hypothesis, which fixes the *average* potential outcome rather than every potential outcome.

Second, we choose a *test statistic*, which is some function of observed data. For the tea-tasting experiment, the test statistic is the number of correctly specified cups. Next, under the null hypothesis, we derive the *sampling distribution* of the test statistic, which is given in figure 7.2 for our application. This distribution is also called the *reference distribution*. Finally, we ask whether the observed value of the test statistic

Table 7.3. Type I and Type II Errors in Hypothesis Testing.

	Reject H_0	Retain H_0
H_0 is true	**type I error**	correct
H_0 is false	correct	**type II error**

Note: H_0 represents the null hypothesis.

is likely to occur under the reference distribution. In the current experiment, the number of correctly classified cups is observed to be 8. If 8 is likely under the reference distribution, we retain the null hypothesis. If it is unlikely, then we reject the null hypothesis.

In this textbook, we prefer to use phrases such as "fail to reject the null hypothesis" and "retain the null hypothesis" instead of "accept the null hypothesis." Philosophical views on this issue differ, but we adopt a perspective that failure to reject the null hypothesis is evidence for some degree of consistency between the data and the hypothesis, but does not necessarily indicate the correctness of the null hypothesis. Others, however, argue that the failure to reject the null hypothesis implies acceptance of the hypothesis. Regardless of one's stance on this issue, statistical hypothesis testing provides empirical support for scientific theories.

How should we quantify the degree to which the observed value of the test statistic is unlikely to occur under the null hypothesis? We use the *p-value* for this purpose. The *p*-value can be understood as the probability that under the null hypothesis, we observe a value of the test statistic at least as extreme as the one we actually observed. A smaller *p*-value provides stronger evidence against the null hypothesis. Importantly, the *p*-value does not represent the probability that the null hypothesis is true. This probability is actually either 1 or 0 because the null hypothesis is either true or false, though researchers do not know which.

In order to decide whether or not to reject the null hypothesis, we must specify the *level of test* α (as explained later, this α is the same as the confidence level α for confidence intervals discussed earlier). If the *p*-value is less than or equal to α, then we reject the null hypothesis. The level of test represents the probability of false rejection if the null hypothesis is true. This error is called *type I error*. Typically, we would like the level of test to be low. Commonly used values of α are 0.05 and 0.01.

Table 7.3 shows two types of errors in hypothesis testing. While researchers can specify the degree of type I error by choosing the level of test α, it is not possible to directly control *type II error*, which results when researchers retain a false null hypothesis. Notably, there is a clear trade-off between type I and type II errors in that minimizing type I error usually increases the risk of type II error. As an extreme example, suppose that we never reject the null hypothesis. Under this scenario, the probability of type I error is 0 if the null hypothesis is true, but the probability of type II error is 1 if the null hypothesis is false.

In the case of the tea-tasting experiment, the test statistic is the number of correctly classified cups. Since the observed value of this test statistic was 8, which is the most extreme value, the *p*-value equals the probability that the number of correct guesses is 8 or $1/70 \approx 0.014$. If the lady correctly classified 6 cups instead of 8, two values are at least as extreme as the observed value: 6 and 8. Therefore, in this case, the *p*-value is $({}_4C_0 \times {}_4C_4 + {}_4C_1 \times {}_4C_3)/70 = (1 + 16)/70 \approx 0.243$.

These *p*-values are *one-sided p-values* (or *one-tailed p-values*) because they consider only the values of the test statistic that are greater than or equal to the observed value. Under this one-sided *alternative hypothesis*, which is the complement of the null hypothesis, we ignore an extreme response on the other side, such as classifying all 8 cups incorrectly. In contrast, if we specify a two-sided alternative hypothesis, then computing the *two-sided p-value* (or *two-tailed p-value*) requires consideration of extreme values on both sides. If the reference distribution is symmetric, then the two-sided *p*-value is twice as great as the one-sided value. In the tea-tasting experiment, the two-sided *p*-value is $2/70 \approx 0.029$. If the lady had correctly guessed 6 cups, then the two-sided *p*-value is $2 \times (1 + 16)/70 \approx 0.486$.

While the framework described here is applicable to any statistical hypothesis testing, the particular hypothesis testing procedure used for the tea-tasting experiment is called *Fisher's exact test*. As explained earlier, this test is an example of randomization inference, where the validity of the test can be justified based on the randomization of treatment assignment.

Fisher's exact test can be implemented in R using the `fisher.test()` function. The main input of this function is a 2×2 contingency table in matrix form, where the rows and columns represent a binary treatment assignment variable and a binary outcome variable, respectively. Here, as examples, we create tables for the tea-tasting experiment: one case with all 8 cups correctly classified and the other case with 6 out of 8 cups correctly classified. In each table, rows represent actual assignments and columns provide reported guesses with the diagonal elements corresponding to the correct guesses.

```r
## all correct
x <- matrix(c(4, 0, 0, 4), byrow = TRUE, ncol = 2, nrow = 2)
## 6 correct
y <- matrix(c(3, 1, 1, 3), byrow = TRUE, ncol = 2, nrow = 2)
## "M" milk first, "T" tea first
rownames(x) <- colnames(x) <- rownames(y)<- colnames(y) <- c("M", "T")
x

##   M T
## M 4 0
## T 0 4

y

##   M T
## M 3 1
## T 1 3
```

We can specify an alternative hypothesis by setting the `alternative` argument to `"two.sided"` (default), `"greater"`, or `"less"`. In the following code chunk, we conduct Fisher's exact test with one-sided and two-sided alternatives. We confirm that the p-values obtained from the `fisher.test()` function are identical to those we calculated on our own.

```
## one-sided test for 8 correct guesses
fisher.test(x, alternative = "greater")

##
##  Fisher's Exact Test for Count Data
##
## data:  x
## p-value = 0.01429
## alternative hypothesis: true odds ratio is greater than 1
## 95 percent confidence interval:
##  2.003768       Inf
## sample estimates:
## odds ratio
##        Inf

## two-sided test for 6 correct guesses
fisher.test(y)

##
##  Fisher's Exact Test for Count Data
##
## data:  y
## p-value = 0.4857
## alternative hypothesis: true odds ratio is not equal to 1
## 95 percent confidence interval:
##    0.2117329 621.9337505
## sample estimates:
## odds ratio
##    6.408309
```

We now summarize the general procedure of statistical hypothesis testing.

In general, **statistical hypothesis testing** consists of the following five steps:

1. Specify a **null hypothesis** and an alternative hypothesis.
2. Choose a test statistic and the **level of test** α.
3. Derive the **reference distribution**, which refers to the sampling distribution of the test statistic under the null hypothesis.
4. Compute the p-**value**, either one-sided or two-sided depending on the alternative hypothesis.
5. Reject the null hypothesis if the p-value is less than or equal to α. Otherwise, retain the null hypothesis (i.e., fail to reject the null hypothesis).

While statistical hypothesis testing is a principled way to quantify uncertainty, the methodology has an important disadvantage. In particular, it forces researchers to make a binary decision about whether to reject the null hypothesis. In many situations, however, we are not interested in the null hypothesis itself. In fact, we may believe that the null hypothesis never strictly holds true. Instead, it could be more fruitful to quantify the degree to which the observed data deviate from the null hypothesis. In the tea-tasting experiment, we may wish to measure the extent to which the lady can taste the difference rather than simply whether or not she possesses any ability in this regard. While the p-value represents the degree to which empirical evidence refutes the null hypothesis, it does not directly correspond to the substantive quantity of interest. In other words, while hypothesis testing can determine *statistical significance*, it often fails to provide a direct measure of *scientific significance*.

7.2.3   ONE-SAMPLE TESTS

Using the general principle of statistical hypothesis testing we have introduced, a variety of hypothesis tests can be developed. We consider one-sample and two-sample tests, which are among the most commonly used tests. *One-sample tests* of means are used to examine the null hypothesis that the population mean equals a specific value. *Two-sample tests*, on the other hand, are based on the null hypothesis that the means of two populations equal each other. Two-sample tests are particularly useful when analyzing randomized controlled trials, enabling researchers to investigate whether or not the observed difference in average outcomes between the treatment and control groups is likely to arise by random chance alone. These tests are used more frequently than Fisher's exact test, described earlier, because they do not rely on the sharp null hypothesis that no unit is affected by the treatment. Instead, two-sample tests concern whether treatment influences an outcome *on average*.

We start, as an example of one-sample tests, with a reanalysis of the sample surveys given in section 7.1.4. Suppose that our null hypothesis is that in the population exactly half of voters support Obama and the other half do not, i.e., $H_0 : p = 0.5$. Let an alternative hypothesis be that Obama's support rate is not 0.5, i.e., $H_1 : p \neq 0.5$. Now, suppose that we conduct a simple random sample and interview 1018 selected individuals, $n = 1018$. In this sample, 550 of them express support for Obama whereas the other individuals do not. This implies that the sample proportion of Obama's supporters is 54%, i.e., $\overline{X}_n = 550/1018$. Clearly, the sample proportion differs from the hypothesized proportion, 0.5, but is this difference statistically significant? Is the difference within the sampling error? Statistical hypothesis testing can answer this question.

We follow the general procedure of hypothesis testing laid out in section 7.2.2. Since the null and alternative hypotheses are defined above, we next choose a test statistic and the level of the test. We use the sample proportion $\overline{X}_n$ as our test statistic and set $\alpha = 0.05$. We then derive the sampling distribution of this test statistic under the null hypothesis. Following the discussion in section 7.1.3 and utilizing equation (7.12), we use the central limit theorem to approximate the reference distribution of $\overline{X}_n$ as $\mathcal{N}(0.5, 0.5(1 - 0.5)/1018)$, where the variance is computed using the formula $\mathbb{V}(X)/n = p(1 - p)/n$. Note that this variance of the reference distribution is constructed using Obama's support rate under the null hypothesis, i.e., $p = 0.5$.

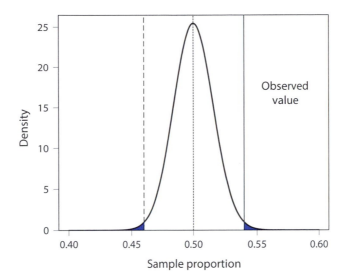

Figure 7.3. One-Sided and Two-Sided *p*-Values. The density curve represents the reference distribution under the null hypothesis that the population proportion is 0.5. The observed value is indicated by the solid vertical line. The two-sided *p*-value equals the sum of the two blue shaded areas under the curve, whereas the one-sided *p*-value is equal to the one of the two blue areas under the curve (depending on the alternative hypothesis).

Under this setup, the *two-sided p-value*, corresponding to our null and alternative hypotheses, can be computed as the probability that under the null hypothesis we observe a value more extreme than the observed value, i.e., $\overline{X}_n = 550/1018$. Figure 7.3 shows this graphically where a more extreme value is indicated by any value either above the observed value (solid line approximately at 0.54) or below its symmetric value (dotted line approximately at 0.46). Thus, the two-sided *p*-value equals the sum of the two blue shaded areas under the density curve. We use the `pnorm()` function to calculate each area where the argument `lower.tail` needs to be set to `FALSE` in order to compute the upper blue area in the figure.

```
n <- 1018
x.bar <- 550 / n
se <- sqrt(0.5 * 0.5 / n) # standard deviation of sampling distribution
## upper blue area in the figure
upper <- pnorm(x.bar, mean = 0.5, sd = se, lower.tail = FALSE)
## lower blue area in the figure; identical to the upper area
lower <- pnorm(0.5 - (x.bar - 0.5), mean = 0.5, sd = se)
## two-sided p-value
upper + lower

## [1] 0.01016866
```

In this particular case, since both the upper and lower shaded areas have the same area (because the normal distribution is symmetric around its mean), we can simply double one of the areas to obtain the two-sided p-value. Note that this may not work in other cases where the reference distribution is not symmetric.

```
2 * upper

## [1] 0.01016866
```

If, on the other hand, our alternative hypothesis is $p > 0.5$ rather than $p \neq 0.5$, then we must compute the one-sided p-value. In this case, there is no need to consider the possibility of an extremely small value because the alternative hypothesis specifies p to be greater than the null value. Hence, the one-sided p-value is given by the blue area under the curve above the observed value in the figure.

```
## one-sided p-value
upper

## [1] 0.005084332
```

Regardless of whether we use the one-sided or two-sided p-value, we reject the null hypothesis that Obama's support in the population is exactly 50%. We conclude that the 4 percentage point difference we observe is unlikely to arise due to chance alone.

When using the normal distribution as the reference distribution, researchers often use the z-score to standardize the test statistic by subtracting its mean and dividing it by its standard deviation. Once this transformation is made, the reference distribution becomes the standard normal distribution. That is, if we use μ_0 to denote the hypothesized mean under the null hypothesis, we have the following result so long as the sample size is sufficiently large (due to the central limit theorem):

$$\frac{\overline{X}_n - \mu_0}{\text{standard error of } \overline{X}_n} \sim \mathcal{N}(0, 1). \tag{7.19}$$

Note that this transformation does not change the outcome of the hypothesis testing conducted above. In fact, the p-value will be identical with or without this transformation. However, one can easily compare the z-score with the critical values shown in table 7.1 in order to determine whether to reject the null hypothesis without computing the p-value. For example, under the two-sided alternative hypothesis, if the z-score is greater than 1.96, then we reject the null hypothesis. We now show, using the current example, that we obtain the same p-value as above.

```
z.score <- (x.bar - 0.5) / se
z.score

## [1] 2.57004

pnorm(z.score, lower.tail = FALSE) # one-sided p-value

## [1] 0.005084332
```

```
2 * pnorm(z.score, lower.tail = FALSE) # two-sided p-value

## [1] 0.01016866
```

This test, which is based on the z-score of the sample mean, is called the *one-sample z-test*. Although we used this test for a Bernoulli random variable in this example, the test can be applied to a wide range of nonbinary random variables so long as the sample size is sufficiently large and the central limit theorem is applicable. For nonbinary random variables, we will use the sample variance to estimate the standard error. If the random variable X is distributed according to the normal distribution, then the same test statistic, i.e., the z-score of the sample mean, follows the t-distribution with $n-1$ degrees of freedom instead of the standard normal distribution. This *one-sample t-test* is more conservative than the one-sample z-test, meaning that the former gives a greater p-value than the latter. Some researchers prefer conservative inference and hence use the one-sample t-test rather than the one-sample z-test.

Suppose that $\{X_1, X_2, \ldots, X_n\}$ are n independently and identically distributed random variables with mean μ and variance σ^2. The **one-sample** z-**test** consists of the following components:

1. Null hypothesis that the population mean μ is equal to a prespecified value μ_0: $H_0 : \mu = \mu_0$
2. Alternative hypothesis: $H_1 : \mu \neq \mu_0$ (two-sided), $H_1 : \mu > \mu_0$ (one-sided), or $H_1 : \mu < \mu_0$ (one-sided)
3. Test statistic (z-statistic): $Z_n = (\overline{X}_n - \mu_0)/\sqrt{\hat{\sigma}^2/n}$, where $\overline{X}_n = \frac{1}{n}\sum_{i=1}^{n} X_i$ (sample mean)
4. Reference distribution: $Z_n \sim \mathcal{N}(0, 1)$ when n is large
5. Variance: $\hat{\sigma}^2 = \frac{1}{n-1}\sum_{i=1}^{n}(X_i - \overline{X}_n)^2$ (sample variance) or $\hat{\sigma}^2 = \mu_0(1 - \mu_0)$ if X is a Bernoulli random variable
6. p-value: $\Phi(-|Z_n|)$ (one-sided) and $2\Phi(-|Z_n|)$ (two-sided), where $\Phi(\cdot)$ is the cumulative distribution function (CDF) of the standard normal distribution

If X is normally distributed, the same test statistic Z_n is called the t-statistic and follows the t-distribution with $n-1$ degrees of freedom. The p-value will be based on the cumulative distribution of this t-distribution. This is called the **one-sample** t-**test**, which is more conservative than the one-sample z-test.

There exists a general one-to-one relationship between confidence intervals and hypothesis tests. Compare equation (7.19) with equation (7.15). The difference is that the unknown population mean $\mathbb{E}(X)$ in the former is replaced with the hypothesized population mean μ_0 in the latter. Note that under a null hypothesis the hypothesized mean μ_0 represents the actual population mean. This suggests that we reject a null hypothesis $H_0 : \mu = \mu_0$ using the α-level two-sided test if and only if the $(1-\alpha) \times 100\%$

confidence interval does not contain μ_0. We can confirm this result using the current example by checking that 0.5 is contained in the 99% confidence interval (since we reject the null hypothesis when $\alpha = 0.1$) but not in the 95% confidence interval (we fail to reject the null when $\alpha = 0.05$).

```
## 99% confidence interval contains 0.5
c(x.bar - qnorm(0.995) * se, x.bar + qnorm(0.995) * se)

## [1] 0.4999093 0.5806408

## 95% confidence interval does not contain 0.5
c(x.bar - qnorm(0.975) * se, x.bar + qnorm(0.975) * se)

## [1] 0.5095605 0.5709896
```

It turns out that this one-to-one relationship between confidence intervals and hypothesis testing holds in general. Many researchers, however, prefer to report confidence intervals rather than p-values because the former also contain information about the magnitude of effects, quantifying *scientific significance* as well as *statistical significance*.

We conducted the one-sample z-test for sample proportion "by hand" above in order to illustrate the underlying idea. However, R has the prop.test() function, which enables us to conduct this test in a single line of R code. For the one-sample test of sample proportion like the one above, the function takes the number of successes as the main argument x and the number of trials as the argument n. In addition, one can specify the success probability under the null hypothesis as p, as well as the alternative hypothesis ("two.sided" for the two-sided alternative hypothesis, and either "less" or "greater" for the one-sided alternative hypothesis). The default confidence level is 95%, which we can change with the conf.level argument.

Finally, the correct argument determines whether a continuity correction should be applied in order to improve the approximation (the default is TRUE). This correction is generally recommended, especially when the sample size is small because the binomial distribution, which is a discrete distribution, is approximated by a continuous distribution, i.e., the normal distribution. We first show that prop.test() without a continuity correction gives a result identical to the one obtained earlier. We then show the result based on the continuity correction.

```
## no continuity correction to get the same p-value as above
prop.test(550, n = n, p = 0.5, correct = FALSE)

##
##  1-sample proportions test without continuity
##  correction
##
## data:  550 out of n, null probability 0.5
## X-squared = 6.6051, df = 1, p-value = 0.01017
## alternative hypothesis: true p is not equal to 0.5
```

```
## 95 percent confidence interval:
##   0.5095661 0.5706812
## sample estimates:
##        p
## 0.540275

## with continuity correction
prop.test(550, n = n, p = 0.5)

##
##  1-sample proportions test with continuity correction
##
## data:  550 out of n, null probability 0.5
## X-squared = 6.445, df = 1, p-value = 0.01113
## alternative hypothesis: true p is not equal to 0.5
## 95 percent confidence interval:
##   0.5090744 0.5711680
## sample estimates:
##        p
## 0.540275
```

The `prop.test()` function also conveniently yields confidence intervals. Note that the standard error used for confidence intervals is different from the standard error used for hypothesis testing. This is because the latter standard error is derived under the null hypothesis $\sqrt{p(1-p)/n}$, whereas the standard error for confidence intervals is computed using the estimated proportion, $\sqrt{\overline{X}_n(1-\overline{X}_n)/n}$. To illustrate a different level of confidence intervals, we can compute 99% confidence intervals using the `conf.level` argument.

```
prop.test(550, n = n, p = 0.5, conf.level = 0.99)

##
##  1-sample proportions test with continuity correction
##
## data:  550 out of n, null probability 0.5
## X-squared = 6.445, df = 1, p-value = 0.01113
## alternative hypothesis: true p is not equal to 0.5
## 99 percent confidence interval:
##   0.4994182 0.5806040
## sample estimates:
##        p
## 0.540275
```

As another example, we revisit the analysis of the STAR project given in section 7.1.5. We first conduct a one-sample t-test just for illustration. Suppose that we test the null hypothesis that the population mean test score is 710, i.e., $H_0 : \mu = 710$.

We use the `t.test()` function where we specify the null value μ_0 using the `mu` argument. The other arguments such as `alternative` and `conf.level` work in the exact same way as for the `prop.test()` function. We use the reading test score for our analysis and conduct a two-sided one-sample t-test. As the result below shows, we retain, at the 0.05 level, the null hypothesis that the population mean of test score is 710. The resulting p-value is small, leading to the rejection of the null hypothesis.

```
## two-sided one-sample t-test
t.test(STAR$g4reading, mu = 710)

##
##   One Sample t-test
##
## data:  STAR$g4reading
## t = 10.407, df = 2352, p-value < 2.2e-16
## alternative hypothesis: true mean is not equal to 710
## 95 percent confidence interval:
##   719.1284 723.3671
## sample estimates:
## mean of x
##   721.2478
```

7.2.4   TWO-SAMPLE TESTS

We now move to a more realistic analysis of the STAR project. When analyzing randomized controlled trials like this, researchers often conduct a statistical hypothesis test with the null hypothesis that the population average treatment effect (PATE) is zero, i.e., $H_0 : \mathbb{E}(Y_i(1) - Y_i(0)) = 0$ with a two-sided alternative hypothesis given by $H_1 : \mathbb{E}(Y_i(1) - Y_i(0)) \neq 0$. If we assume that the PATE cannot be negative, then we employ a one-sided alternative hypothesis, $H_1 : \mathbb{E}(Y_i(1) - Y_i(0)) > 0$. In contrast, if we assume that the PATE cannot be positive, we set $H_1 : \mathbb{E}(Y_i(1) - Y_i(0)) < 0$. In this application, we would like to test whether or not the PATE of small class size on the grade-four reading score (relative to regular class size) is zero.

To test this null hypothesis, we use the difference-in-means estimator as a test statistic. More generally, beyond randomized controlled trials, we can use the two-sample tests based on the difference-in-means estimator to investigate the null hypothesis that the means are equal between these two populations. What is the reference distribution of this test statistic? We can approximate it by appealing to the central limit theorem as in section 7.1.5. The theorem implies that the sample means of the treatment and control groups have a normal distribution. Therefore, under the null hypothesis of equal means between the two populations, the difference between these two sample means is also normally distributed with mean zero. Furthermore, the z-score of the difference in sample means follows the standard normal distribution. We can use this fact to conduct the *two-sample z-test* (see equation (7.18) for the expression of standard error, which serves as the denominator of the test statistic). As in the one-sample tests, if the outcomes are assumed to be normally distributed, the *two-sample t-test* can be used, which yields a more conservative inference.

Suppose that $\{X_1, X_2, \ldots, X_{n_0}\}$ represent n_0 independently and identically distributed random variables with mean μ_0 and variance σ_0^2. Similarly, $\{Y_1, Y_2, \ldots, Y_{n_1}\}$ represent n_1 independently and identically distributed random variables with mean μ_1 and variance σ_1^2. The **two-sample** z-**test** of sample means consists of the following components:

1. Null hypothesis that two populations have the same mean: $H_0 : \mu_0 = \mu_1$
2. Alternative hypothesis: $H_1 : \mu_0 \neq \mu_1$ (two-sided), $H_1 : \mu_0 > \mu_1$ (one-sided), or $H_1 : \mu_0 < \mu_1$ (one-sided)
3. Test statistic (z-statistic): $Z_n = (\overline{Y}_{n_1} - \overline{X}_{n_0})/\sqrt{\frac{1}{n_1}\hat{\sigma}_1^2 + \frac{1}{n_0}\hat{\sigma}_0^2}$
4. Reference distribution: $Z_n \sim \mathcal{N}(0, 1)$ when n_0 and n_1 are large
5. Variance: $\hat{\sigma}_0^2 = \frac{1}{n_0-1}\sum_{i=1}^{n_0}(X_i - \overline{X}_{n_0})^2$ and $\hat{\sigma}_1^2 = \frac{1}{n_1-1}\sum_{i=1}^{n_1}(Y_i - \overline{Y}_{n_1})^2$ (sample variances) or $\hat{\sigma}_0^2 = \hat{\sigma}_1^2 = \hat{p}(1 - \hat{p})$ with $\hat{p} = \frac{n_0}{n_0+n_1}\overline{X}_{n_0} + \frac{n_1}{n_0+n_1}\overline{Y}_{n_1}$ if X and Y are Bernoulli random variables
6. p-value: $\Phi(-|Z_n|)$ (one-sided) and $2\Phi(-|Z_n|)$ (two-sided), where $\Phi(\cdot)$ is the cumulative distribution function (CDF) of the standard normal distribution

If X and Y are normally distributed, the same test statistic Z_n is called the t-statistic and follows the t-distribution. The p-value will be based on the cumulative distribution of this t-distribution. This is called the **two-sample** t-**test**, which is more conservative than the one-sample z-test.

Recall from section 7.1.5 that the estimated PATE is stored as an R object `ate.est` whereas its standard error is given by the R object `ate.se`. Using these objects, we compute the one-sided and two-sided p-values as follows.

```
## one-sided p-value
pnorm(-abs(ate.est), mean = 0, sd = ate.se)

## [1] 0.09350361

## two-sided p-value
2 * pnorm(-abs(ate.est), mean = 0, sd = ate.se)

## [1] 0.1870072
```

Since this p-value is much greater than the typical threshold of 5%, we cannot reject the hypothesis that the average treatment effect of small class size on the fourth-grade reading test score is zero.

The hypothesis test conducted above is based on the large sample approximation because we relied upon the central limit theorem to derive the reference distribution. Similar to the discussion in section 7.1.5, if we assume that the outcome variable is normally distributed, then we could use the t-distribution instead of the normal distribution to conduct a hypothesis test. As a test statistic, we use the z-score for the difference-in-means estimator, which is called the t-statistic in the case of this two-sample t-test. Unlike the one-sample example discussed in section 7.1.5, however, the degrees of freedom must be approximated for the *two-sample t-test*. Because the t-distribution generally has heavier tails than the normal distribution, the *t-test* is more conservative and hence is often preferred even when the outcome variable may not be normally distributed.

In R, we can conduct a two-sample t-test using the `t.test()` function as we did for a one-sample t-test. For the two-sample t-test, the function takes two vectors, each of which contains data for one of the two groups. We can specify the difference between the means of the two groups, or the PATE in this application, under the null hypothesis via the `mu` argument. The default value for this argument is zero, which is what we would like to use in the current example.

```
## testing the null of zero average treatment effect
t.test(STAR$g4reading[STAR$classtype == 1],
       STAR$g4reading[STAR$classtype == 2])

##
##   Welch Two Sample t-test
##
## data:STAR$g4reading[STAR$classtype==1] and STAR$g4reading[STAR$classtype == 2]
## t = 1.3195, df = 1541.2, p-value = 0.1872
## alternative hypothesis: true difference in means is not equal to 0
## 95 percent confidence interval:
##   -1.703591  8.706055
## sample estimates:
## mean of x mean of y
##  723.3912  719.8900
```

The output displays the value of the t-statistic as well as the p-value and the degrees of freedom for Student's t-distribution used for the test. Since the p-value is greater than the standard threshold of $\alpha = 0.05$, we fail to reject the null hypothesis that the average treatment effect of small class size on the fourth-grade reading score is zero. As in the case of `prop.test()`, the output of the `t.test()` function contains the confidence interval for the corresponding level. As expected from the use of the t-distribution, this confidence interval is slightly wider than the confidence interval based on the normal approximation we obtained in section 7.1.5. The confidence interval also contains zero, which is consistent with the fact that we fail to reject the null hypothesis of zero average treatment effect.

As another application of hypothesis tests, we reanalyze the labor market discrimination experiment described in section 2.1. In this experiment, fictitious résumés of job applicants were sent to potential employers. Researchers randomly assigned stereotypically African-American or Caucasian names to each résumé and examined whether or not the callback rate depended on the race of the applicant. The data set we analyze is contained in the CSV file `resume.csv`. The names and descriptions of variables in this data set are given in table 2.1. The outcome variable of interest is call, which indicates whether or not each résumé received a callback. The treatment variable is the race of the applicant, race, and we focus on the comparison between black-sounding and white-sounding names.

We test the null hypothesis that the probability of receiving a callback is the same between résumés with black-sounding names and those with white-sounding names. We use the prop.test() function to implement the two-sample z-test. The input is a table whose columns represent the counts of successes and failures and rows represent the two groups to be compared. We will use a one-sided test because résumés with black-sounding names are hypothesized to receive fewer callbacks.

```
resume <- read.csv("resume.csv")
## organize the data in tables
x <- table(resume$race, resume$call)
x

##
##            0    1
##    black 2278  157
##    white 2200  235

## one-sided test
prop.test(x, alternative = "greater")

##
##   2-sample test for equality of proportions with
##   continuity correction
##
## data:  x
## X-squared = 16.449, df = 1, p-value = 2.499e-05
## alternative hypothesis: greater
## 95 percent confidence interval:
##   0.01881967 1.00000000
## sample estimates:
##     prop 1    prop 2
## 0.9355236 0.9034908
```

Thus, the result supports the alternative hypothesis that résumés with white-sounding names are more likely to receive callbacks than those with black-sounding names. It is instructive to directly compute this p-value without using the prop.test() function. Under the null hypothesis of equal proportions between the two groups, i.e., $H_0 : \mu_0 = \mu_1$, the standard error of the difference-in-means (or more accurately difference-in-proportions) estimator can be computed as

$$\sqrt{\frac{\widehat{\mathbb{V}(X)}}{n_0} + \frac{\widehat{\mathbb{V}(Y)}}{n_1}} = \sqrt{\frac{\hat{p}(1-\hat{p})}{n_0} + \frac{\hat{p}(1-\hat{p})}{n_1}} = \sqrt{\hat{p}(1-\hat{p})\left(\frac{1}{n_0} + \frac{1}{n_1}\right)}, \quad (7.20)$$

where X and Y are the outcome variables for the résumés with black-sounding and white-sounding names, respectively, n_0 and n_1 are sample sizes, and $\hat{p} = \frac{1}{n_0+n_1}(\sum_{i=1}^{n_0} X_i + \sum_{i=1}^{n_1} Y_i)$ is the overall sample proportion. We use the same estimate $\hat{p}(1 - \hat{p})$ for the variances of X and Y because under the null hypothesis of identical proportions, their variances, which are based on the proportions, are also identical.

```
## sample size
n0 <- sum(resume$race == "black")
n1 <- sum(resume$race == "white")
## sample proportions
p <- mean(resume$call) # overall
p0 <- mean(resume$call[resume$race == "black"]) # black
p1 <- mean(resume$call[resume$race == "white"]) # white
## point estimate
est <- p1 - p0
est

## [1] 0.03203285

## standard error
se <- sqrt(p * (1 - p) * (1 / n0 + 1 / n1))
se

## [1] 0.007796894

## z-statistic
zstat <- est / se
zstat

## [1] 4.108412

## one-sided p-value
pnorm(-abs(zstat))

## [1] 1.991943e-05
```

The exact same p-value can be obtained using the prop.test() function without a continuity correction.

```
prop.test(x, alternative = "greater", correct = FALSE)

##
##   2-sample test for equality of proportions without
##   continuity correction
##
## data:  x
## X-squared = 16.879, df = 1, p-value = 1.992e-05
## alternative hypothesis: greater
## 95 percent confidence interval:
```

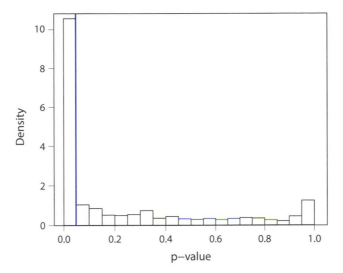

Figure 7.4. The Distribution of *p*-Values for Hypothesis Tests Published in Two Leading Political Science Journals.

```
##   0.01923035 1.00000000
## sample estimates:
##    prop 1    prop 2
## 0.9355236 0.9034908
```

7.2.5 PITFALLS OF HYPOTHESIS TESTING

Since Fisher's tea-tasting experiment, hypothesis testing has been extensively used in the scientific community to determine whether or not empirical findings are statistically significant. Statistical hypothesis testing represents a rigorous methodology to draw a conclusion in the presence of uncertainty. However, the prevalent use of hypothesis testing also leads to *publication bias* because only statistically significant results, and especially the ones that are surprising to the scientific community, tend to be published. In many social science journals, the α-level of 5% is regarded as the cutoff that determines whether empirical findings are statistically significant or not. As a result, researchers tend to submit their papers to journals only when their empirical results have *p*-values smaller than this 5% threshold. In addition, journals may also be more likely to publish statistically significant results than nonsignificant results. This is problematic because even if the null hypothesis is true, researchers have a 5% chance of obtaining a *p*-value less than 5%.

In one study, two researchers examined more than 100 articles published in the two leading political science journals over a decade or so.[2] The researchers collected the *p*-values for the hypotheses tested in those articles. Figure 7.4 shows that a majority of reported findings have *p*-values less than or equal to the 5% threshold, which is

---

[2] Alan Gerber and Neil Malhotra (2008) "Do statistical reporting standards affect what is published? Publication bias in two leading political science journals." *Quarterly Journal of Political Science*, vol. 3, no. 3, pp. 313–326.

(a) Paul the Octopus   (b) Mani the Parakeet

Figure 7.5. Two Animal Oracles that Correctly Predicted the Outcomes of Soccer Matches. Sources: (a) Reuters/Wolfgang Rattay. (b) AP Images/Joan Leong.

indicated by the blue vertical line. In addition, there appears to be a discontinuous jump at the threshold, suggesting that journals are publishing more empirical results that are just below the threshold than results just above it.

Another important pitfall regarding hypothesis testing is *multiple testing*. Recall that statistical hypothesis testing is probabilistic. We never know with 100% certainty whether the null hypothesis is true. Instead, as explained earlier, we typically have type I and type II errors when conducting hypothesis tests (see table 7.3). Multiple testing problems refer to the possibility of *false discoveries* when testing multiple hypotheses.

To see this, suppose that a researcher tests 10 hypotheses when, unbeknown to the researcher, all of these hypotheses are in fact false. What is the probability that the researcher rejects at least one null hypothesis using 5% as the threshold? If we assume independence among these hypotheses tests, we can compute this probability as

$$P(\text{reject at least one hypothesis}) = 1 - P(\text{reject no hypothesis})$$
$$= 1 - 0.95^{10} \approx 0.40.$$

The second equality follows because the probability of not rejecting the null hypothesis when the null hypothesis is true is $1 - \alpha = 0.95$ and we assume independence among these 10 hypothesis tests. Thus, the researcher has a 40% chance of making at least one false discovery. The lesson here is that if we conduct many hypothesis tests, we are likely to falsely find statistically significant results.

To illustrate the multiple testing problem, consider "Paul the Octopus" shown in figure 7.5a. This octopus in a German aquarium attracted media attention during the 2010 World Cup soccer tournament by correctly predicting all seven matches involving Germany, as well as the outcome of the final match between the Netherlands and Spain. Paul predicted by choosing to enter one of two containers with a country flag as shown in the figure. Given this data, we can conduct a hypothesis test with the null hypothesis that Paul does not possess any ability to predict soccer matches. Under this null hypothesis, Paul randomly guesses a winner out of two countries in question. What is the probability that Paul correctly predicts the outcomes of all 8 matches? Since Paul has a 50% chance of correctly predicting each match, this one-sided p-value is equal to $1/2^8 \approx 0.004$. This value is well below the usual 5% threshold and hence can be considered statistically significant.

However, the problem of multiple testing suggests that if we have many animals predict soccer matches, we are likely to find an animal that appears to be prophetic. During the same world cup, another animal, "Mani the Parakeet" shown in figure 7.5b, was reported to have a similar oracle ability. The parakeet correctly predicted only 6 out of 8 matches. Each time, he selected one of two pieces of paper with his beak and flipped it to reveal a winner, without viewing country flags as Paul did. Since no scientific theory suggests animals can possess such predictive ability, we may conclude that Paul and Mani represent false discoveries due to the problem of multiple testing. Although beyond the scope of this book, statisticians have developed various methods that make appropriate adjustments for multiple testing.

> The **multiple testing problem** is that conducting many hypothesis tests is likely to result in false discoveries, i.e., incorrect rejection of null hypotheses.

7.2.6 POWER ANALYSIS

Another problem of hypothesis testing is that null hypotheses are often not interesting. For example, who would believe that the small class in the STAR study has *exactly* zero average causal effect on students' test scores as assumed under the null hypothesis? The effect size might be small, but it is hard to imagine that it is exactly zero. A related problem is that failure to reject the null hypothesis does not necessarily mean that the null hypothesis is true. Failure to reject the null may arise because data are not informative about the null hypothesis. For example, if the sample size is too small, then even if the true average treatment effect is not zero, researchers may fail to reject the null hypothesis of zero average effect because the standard error is too large.

We use *power analysis* in order to formalize the degree of informativeness of data in hypothesis tests. The *power* of a statistical hypothesis test is defined as one minus the probability of *type II error*:

$$\text{power} = 1 - P(\text{type II error}).$$

Recall from the discussion in section 7.2.2 that type II error occurs when researchers retain a false null hypothesis. Therefore, we would like to maximize the power of a statistical hypothesis test so that we can detect departure from the null hypothesis as much as possible.

Power analysis is often used to determine the smallest sample size necessary to estimate the parameter with enough precision that its observed value is distinguishable from the parameter value assumed under the null hypothesis. This is typically done as part of research planning in order to inform data collection. In sample surveys, for example, researchers wish to know the number of people they must interview in order to reject the null hypothesis of an exact tie in support level when one candidate is ahead of the other by a prespecified degree (see also the discussion in section 7.1.4). Moreover, experimentalists use power analysis to compute the number of observations necessary

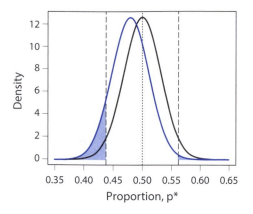 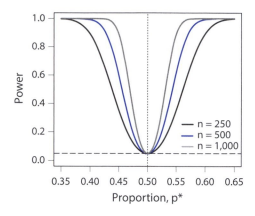

Figure 7.6. Illustration of Power Analysis. In the left-hand plot, the solid black line represents the sampling distribution of sample proportion under the null hypothesis $p = 0.5$ (vertical dotted line). The blue solid line represents the sampling distribution of the test statistic under a hypothetical data-generating process, which has mean 0.48. The sum of the two blue shaded areas equals the power of this statistical test when the significance level is $\alpha = 0.05$. The vertical dashed lines represent thresholds, above or below which the null hypothesis will be rejected. The right-hand plot displays the power function under the same setting with three different sample sizes.

to reject the null hypothesis of zero average treatment effect when the effect is actually not zero. As a result, power analysis is often required for research grant applications in order to justify the budget that researchers are requesting.

Again, we use survey sampling as an example. Suppose that we wish to find out how many respondents we must interview to be able to reject the null hypothesis that the support level for Obama, denoted by p, is exactly 50% when the true support level is at least 2 percentage points away from an exact tie, i.e., 48% or less, or 52% or greater. That is, 2 percentage points is the smallest deviation from the null hypothesis we would like to detect with a high probability. Further assume that we will use the sample proportion as the test statistic, and that the significance level is set to $\alpha = 0.05$ with a two-sided alternative hypothesis.

To compute the power, we need to consider two sampling distributions of the test statistic. The first is the sampling distribution under the null distribution. We have already derived the large sample approximation of this sampling distribution earlier: $\mathcal{N}(p, p(1 - p)/n)$, where p is the null value of the population proportion. In our application, $p = 0.5$. The second is the sampling distribution under a hypothetical data-generating process. In the current case, this distribution is approximated by $\mathcal{N}(p^*, p^*(1 - p^*)/n)$ via the *central limit theorem*, where p^* is either less than or equal to 0.48 or greater than or equal to 0.52.

The left-hand plot of figure 7.6 graphically illustrates the mechanics of power analysis in this case. In the plot, the two sampling distributions of the sample proportion, one centered around 0.5 under the null hypothesis (black solid line) and the other centered around 0.48 under a hypothetical data-generating process (blue solid line), are shown. We choose 0.48 as the mean value under the hypothetical data-generating process because any distribution with a mean less than this value would result in greater statistical power, which is the probability of correctly rejecting the null, and hence would require a smaller sample size. For the meantime, we set the sample size n to 250.

Under this setting, we compute the power of the statistical test, which is the probability of rejecting the null hypothesis. To do this, we first derive the thresholds that determine the rejection region. As shown in section 7.2.3, the threshold is equal to the null value p_0 plus or minus the product of the standard error and critical value $z_{\alpha/2}$, i.e., $p_0 \pm z_{\alpha/2} \times \text{standard error}$, where in the current setting $p_0 = 0.5$ and $z_{\alpha/2} \approx 1.96$. In the left-hand plot of the figure, these thresholds are denoted by black dashed lines and we reject the null hypothesis if an observed value is more extreme than they are.

We use the probability distribution indicated by the blue solid line in the figure when computing the probability of rejection under the hypothetical data-generating process. That is, the power of the test equals the sum of the two blue shaded areas in the figure, one large area below the lower threshold and the other small area above the upper threshold. Formally, it is given by

$$\text{power} = P(\overline{X}_n < p - z_{\alpha/2} \times \text{standard error}) + P(\overline{X}_n > p + z_{\alpha/2} \times \text{standard error}).$$

In this equation, the sample proportion $\overline{X}_n$ is assumed to be approximately distributed according to $\mathcal{N}(p^*, p^*(1 - p^*)/n)$, where in the current application p^* is set to 0.48. We can compute the power of a test in R as follows.

```
## set the parameters
n <- 250
p.star <- 0.48 # data-generating process
p <- 0.5 # null value
alpha <- 0.05
## critical value
cr.value <- qnorm(1 - alpha / 2)
## standard errors under the hypothetical data-generating process
se.star <- sqrt(p.star * (1 - p.star) / n)
## standard error under the null
se <- sqrt(p * (1 - p) / n)
## power
pnorm(p - cr.value * se, mean = p.star, sd = se.star) +
    pnorm(p + cr.value * se, mean = p.star, sd = se.star, lower.tail = FALSE)

## [1] 0.09673114
```

Under these conditions, the power of the test is only 10%. We can examine how the power of this test changes as a function of the sample size and hypothetical data-generating process. The right-hand plot of figure 7.6 presents the *power function*, where the horizontal axis represents the population proportion under the hypothetical data-generating process and each line indicates a different sample size. We observe that the power of a statistical test increases as the sample size becomes greater and the true population proportion p^* shifts away from the null value $p = 0.5$.

The above specific example illustrates the main principle of power analysis. We summarize the general procedure below.

> **Power** is defined as the probability of rejecting the null hypothesis when the null hypothesis is false, which is equal to one minus the probability of type II error. **Power analysis** consists of the following steps:
>
> 1. Select the settings of the statistical hypothesis test you plan to use. This includes the specification of the test statistic, null and alternative hypotheses, and significance level.
> 2. Choose the population parameter value under a hypothetical data-generating process.
> 3. Compute the probability of rejecting the null hypothesis under this data-generating process with a given sample size.
>
> One can then vary the sample size to examine how the power of the test changes to decide the **sample size** necessary for the desired level of power.

The power analysis can be conducted in a similar manner for two-sample tests. Consider the two-sample test of proportions, which can be used to analyze a randomized experiment with a binary outcome variable. The test statistic is the difference in sample proportion between the treatment and control groups, $\overline{Y}_{n_1} - \overline{X}_{n_0}$. Under the null hypothesis that this difference in the population, or the population average treatment effect (PATE), is equal to zero, the sampling distribution of the test statistic is given by $\mathcal{N}(0, p(1-p)(1/n_1 + 1/n_0))$, where p is the overall population proportion (see equation (7.20)), which is equal to the weighted average of the proportions in the two groups, $p = (n_0 p_0 + n_1 p_1)/(n_0 + n_1)$. To compute the power of the statistical test in this case, we must specify the population proportion separately for the treatment and control groups, p_1^* and p_0^*, under a hypothetical data-generating process. Then, the sampling distribution of the test statistic under this data-generating process is given by $\mathcal{N}(p_1^* - p_0^*, p_1^*(1-p_1^*)/n_1 + p_0^*(1-p_0^*)/n_0)$. Using this information, we can compute the probability of rejecting the null.

As an example, consider the résumé experiment analyzed in section 2.1. Suppose that we plan to send out 500 résumés with black-sounding names and another 500 résumés with white-sounding names. Further, assume that we expect the callback rate to be around 5% for black names and 10% for white names.

```
## parameters
n1 <- 500
n0 <- 500
p1.star <- 0.05
p0.star <- 0.1
```

To compute the power of this statistical test, we first compute the overall callback rate as a weighted average of callback rates of the two groups, where the weights are their sample size. We then compute the standard error under the null hypothesis, i.e., standard error $= \sqrt{p(1-p)(1/n_0 + 1/n_1)}$, as well as under the hypothetical data-generating process, i.e., standard error* $= \sqrt{p_1^*(1-p_1^*)/n_1 + p_0^*(1-p_0^*)/n_0}$.

```
## overall callback rate as a weighted average
p <- (n1 * p1.star + n0 * p0.star) / (n1 + n0)
## standard error under the null
se <- sqrt(p * (1 - p) * (1 / n1 + 1 / n0))
## standard error under the hypothetical data-generating process
se.star <- sqrt(p1.star * (1 - p1.star) / n1 + p0.star * (1 - p0.star) / n0)
```

We can now compute the power by calculating the probability that the difference in two proportions, $\overline{Y}_n - \overline{X}_n$, takes a value either less than $-z_{\alpha/2} \times$ standard error or greater than $-z_{\alpha/2} \times$ standard error*, under the hypothetical data-generating process.

```
pnorm(-cr.value * se, mean = p1.star - p0.star, sd = se.star) +
    pnorm(cr.value * se, mean = p1.star - p0.star,
        sd = se.star, lower.tail = FALSE)

## [1] 0.85228
```

While for illustration we computed the power by hand, we can use the `power.prop.test()` function available in R. This function, which is applicable to the two-sample test for proportions, can either compute the power given a set of parameters or determine a parameter value given a target power level. The arguments of this function include the sample size per group (`n`), population proportions for two groups (`p1.star` and `p2.star`), significance level (`sig.level`), and power (`power`). Note that the function assumes the two groups have an identical sample size, i.e., $n_0 = n_1$. To compute the power, we set `power = NULL` (default). The following syntax gives a result identical to what we computed above.

```
power.prop.test(n = 500, p1 = 0.05, p2 = 0.1, sig.level = 0.05)

##
##      Two-sample comparison of proportions power calculation
##
##              n = 500
##             p1 = 0.05
##             p2 = 0.1
##      sig.level = 0.05
##          power = 0.8522797
##    alternative = two.sided
##
## NOTE: n is number in *each* group
```

The `power.prop.test()` function also enables sample size calculation by simply setting the `power` argument to a desired level and setting n to `NULL` (default). For example, if we want to know, under the same conditions as above, the minimum sample size necessary to obtain a 90% level of power, we use the following R syntax. The result below implies that we need at least 582 observations per group in order to achieve this power.

```
power.prop.test(p1 = 0.05, p2 = 0.1, sig.level = 0.05, power = 0.9)

##
##      Two-sample comparison of proportions power calculation
##
##               n = 581.0821
##              p1 = 0.05
##              p2 = 0.1
##       sig.level = 0.05
##           power = 0.9
##     alternative = two.sided
##
## NOTE: n is number in *each* group
```

For continuous variables, we can conduct a power analysis based on *Student's t-test*, introduced in section 7.2.4. The logic is exactly the same as that described above for one-sample and two-sample tests of proportions. The `power.t.test()` function can perform a power analysis where the `type` argument specifies a two-sample (`"two.sample"`) or one-sample (`"one.sample"`) test. For a one-sample *t*-test, we must specify the mean `delta` and standard deviation `sd` of a normal random variable under a hypothetical data-generating process. For a two-sample *t*-test, the function assumes that the standard deviation and sample size are identical for the two groups. We, therefore, specify the true difference-in-means `delta` under a hypothetical data-generating process as well as a standard deviation `sd`. Finally, the function assumes the null hypothesis that the mean is zero for a one-sample test and the mean difference is zero for a two-sample test. If the null value is not zero, then one simply has to adjust the hypothetical data-generating process by subtracting that value from the true mean (or mean difference).

Below, we present two examples of using the `power.t.test()` function. The first is the power calculation for a one-sample test with a true mean of 0.25 and standard deviation of 1. The sample size is 100. Recall that the assumed mean value under the null hypothesis is zero.

```
power.t.test(n = 100, delta = 0.25, sd = 1, type = "one.sample")

##
##      One-sample t test power calculation
##
```

```
##                      n = 100
##                  delta = 0.25
##                     sd = 1
##              sig.level = 0.05
##                  power = 0.6969757
##            alternative = two.sided
```

Under this setting, the power is calculated to be 70%. What is the sample size we need to have a power of 0.9 under the same setting? We can answer this question by specifying the `power` argument in the `power.t.test()` function while leaving the n argument unspecified.

```
power.t.test(power = 0.9, delta = 0.25, sd = 1, type = "one.sample")

##
##        One-sample t test power calculation
##
##                      n = 170.0511
##                  delta = 0.25
##                     sd = 1
##              sig.level = 0.05
##                  power = 0.9
##            alternative = two.sided
```

The minimum sample size for obtaining a power of 0.9 or greater is 171. The second example is the sample size calculation for a one-sided two-sample test with a true mean difference of 0.25 and standard deviation of 1. We set the desired power to be 90%.

```
power.t.test(delta = 0.25, sd = 1, type = "two.sample",
             alternative = "one.sided", power = 0.9)

##
##        Two-sample t test power calculation
##
##                      n = 274.7222
##                  delta = 0.25
##                     sd = 1
##              sig.level = 0.05
##                  power = 0.9
##            alternative = one.sided
##
## NOTE: n is number in *each* group
```

The result shows that we need a minimum of 275 observations per group to achieve a power of 90% under this setting.

7.3   Linear Regression Model with Uncertainty

As the final topic of this book, we consider the uncertainty of estimates based on the linear regression model introduced in chapter 4. In that chapter, we used the linear regression model mainly as a tool to make predictions. We also showed that when applied to a randomized controlled trial with binary treatments, the linear regression model can yield unbiased estimates of average treatment effects. In this section, we introduce another perspective that portrays the linear regression model as an approximation of the *data-generating process* in the real world. Under this framework, we can quantify the uncertainty of our estimates over repeated hypothetical sampling from the specified generative model. Once we view the linear regression model as a generative model, we can compute the standard errors and confidence intervals for our quantities of interest and conduct hypothesis testing.

7.3.1   LINEAR REGRESSION AS A GENERATIVE MODEL

Recall that the linear regression model with p predictors (explanatory or independent variables) is defined as

$$Y_i = \alpha + \beta_1 X_{i1} + \beta_2 X_{i2} + \cdots + \beta_p X_{ip} + \epsilon_i. \tag{7.21}$$

In this model, Y represents the outcome or response variable, X_{ij} is the jth predictor, for $j = 1, 2, \ldots, p$, and ϵ_i denotes the unobserved error term for the ith observation. The model also has a total of $(p + 1)$ coefficients to be estimated, where α represents an intercept and β_j denotes a coefficient for the jth explanatory variable for $j = 1, 2, \ldots, p$.

According to this model, the outcome variable is generated as a linear function of the explanatory variables and the error term. For example, in section 4.2, we modeled the relationship between facial impressions and election outcomes using linear regression. In that application, the election outcome was a linear function of facial impressions and the error term. The error term contains all determinants of election outcomes that we do not observe, such as campaign resources, name recognition, and voter mobilization efforts.

In the model, the only variable we do not directly observe is the error term. As such, the key assumption of the model concerns the distribution of this random variable ϵ_i. Specifically, the linear regression model is based on the following *exogeneity* assumption.

The **exogeneity** assumption for the **linear regression model** is defined as

$$\mathbb{E}(\epsilon_i \mid X_1, X_2, \ldots, X_p) = \mathbb{E}(\epsilon_i) = 0. \tag{7.22}$$

The assumption implies that the unobserved determinants of outcome, contained in the error term ϵ_i, are unrelated to all the observed predictors X_{ij} for $i = 1, 2, \ldots, n$ and $j = 1, 2, \ldots, p$. In this equation, X_j is an $n \times 1$ vector containing the jth covariate of all observations.

The assumption says that the *conditional expectation* of the error term given the explanatory variables, which is the first term in equation (7.22), is equal to its marginal or unconditional expectation, which is the second term in the equation and is equal to zero. The marginal expectation of the error term can always be assumed to be zero in the linear regression model so long as an intercept α is included in the model. The exogeneity assumption implies that the mean of the error term does not depend on the predictors or explanatory variables included in the model. In other words, the unobserved determinants of the outcome variable, which are contained in the error term, should be *uncorrelated* with all the observed predictors. In the election example, this implies that other, unobserved determinants of election outcomes should not be correlated with candidates' facial impressions.

In general, the conditional expectation of a random variable Y given another random variable X, denoted by $\mathbb{E}(Y \mid X)$, is the expectation of Y given a particular value of X. As such, this conditional expectation is a function of X, i.e., $\mathbb{E}(Y \mid X) = g(X)$, where $g(X)$ is called the *conditional expectation function*. All the definitions and rules of expectation introduced in section 6.3.5 hold for conditional expectation, except that we treat the variables in the conditioning set as fixed and compute the expectation with respect to the conditional distribution of Y given X. Thus, under the exogeneity assumption, the linear regression model assumes that the conditional expectation function for the outcome variable given the set of predictors is linear:

$$\mathbb{E}(Y_i \mid \boldsymbol{X}_1, \ldots, \boldsymbol{X}_p) = \alpha + \beta_1 X_{i1} + \cdots + \beta_p X_{ip}.$$

When deriving this result, we used the exogeneity assumption as well as the fact that the conditional expectation of $\beta_j X_{ij}$ given $\boldsymbol{X}_1, \ldots, \boldsymbol{X}_p$ equals itself.

The **conditional expectation** of a random variable Y given another random variable X is denoted by $\mathbb{E}(Y \mid X)$ and is defined as

$$\mathbb{E}(Y \mid X) = \begin{cases} \sum_y y \times f(y \mid X) & \text{if } Y \text{ is discrete,} \\ \int y \times f(y \mid X) dy & \text{if } Y \text{ is continuous,} \end{cases}$$

where $f(Y \mid X)$ is the conditional probability mass function (conditional probability density function) of the discrete (continuous) random variable Y given X.

In *randomized controlled trials*, a violation of exogeneity does not occur because treatment assignment is randomized. In the framework of the linear regression model, this means that the treatment variable, which is represented by X, is statistically independent of all observed and unobserved pretreatment characteristics, which are contained in ϵ. Therefore, the exogeneity assumption is automatically satisfied. Consider the randomized controlled trial about women as policy makers described in section 4.3.1. In this experiment, the explanatory variable of interest, X, is whether seats in the local government, Gram Panchayat (GP), are reserved for female leaders. This variable is randomized and hence statistically independent of all other possible determinants of policy outcomes. For example, the number of new or repaired drinking water facilities in the village is likely to be determined not only by the existence of female leaders but also by numerous other factors such as the population size and the income level. Fortunately, we do not have to worry about these potential *unobserved confounders* because the randomized treatment assignment makes the treatment variable independent of these factors.

In *observational studies*, however, the exogeneity assumption may be violated. Suppose that the reservation of some GPs for female leaders is not randomized. Then, it is possible that villages with high levels of education and liberal ideologies are likely to elect female leaders for their GPs. Under this scenario, we cannot simply attribute the difference in the number of new or repaired drinking water facilities between villages to the gender of their politicians alone. It may be that highly educated villagers want better drinking water facilities and politicians are simply responding to the demands of their constituency. That is, both female and male politicians are responding to their constituencies, but their policy outcomes are different because they have different constituencies rather than because their genders are different. In observational studies, the unobserved confounders may be contained in the error term (e.g., education level of villagers), and if they are correlated with the observed explanatory variables (e.g., gender of politicians), the exogeneity assumption will be violated.

How can we address this problem of unobserved confounding in observational studies? In chapter 2, we learned that one strategy is to compare the treated units with similar control units. Ideally, we would like to find units that did not receive treatment and yet are similar to the treated units in terms of many observed characteristics. In the study on the minimum wage and employment described in section 2.5, researchers chose fast-food restaurants in Pennsylvania (PA), in which the minimum wage was not increased, as the control group for the fast-food restaurants in New Jersey (NJ), for which the minimum wage was raised. The idea was that since these restaurants are quite similar in their patterns of employment, products, and sales, we can use the restaurants in PA to infer the employment level of the restaurants in NJ that would have resulted if the minimum wage had not been increased. If there exist no unobserved factors, other than the treatment in NJ, that influence employment in NJ fast-food restaurants (i.e., no unobserved confounders), then the average difference in employment between the restaurants in NJ and those in PA can be attributed to the increase in NJ's minimum wage. The assumption of no unobserved confounding factors has several different names, including *unconfoundedness*, *selection on observables*, and *no omitted variables*, but they all mean the same thing.

The assumption of no unobserved confounding factors studied in chapter 2, therefore, is directly related to the exogeneity assumption under the linear regression model. Indeed, the exogeneity assumption will be violated whenever unobserved confounding variables exist. In the linear regression model framework, we can address this problem by measuring these confounders and including them as additional predictors in the model in order to adjust for their differences between the treatment and control groups. Although this strategy assumes a linear relationship between the outcome and these confounding variables, conceptually it is the same as comparing treated and control units that have similar characteristics. It can be shown that so long as all confounding variables are included in the model (and the linear relationship between the outcome and all explanatory variables holds), the estimated coefficient for the treatment variable represents an unbiased estimate of the average treatment effect.

In the minimum-wage example, assume that the only confounding factors between the fast-food restaurants in NJ and those in PA are the fast-food chain to which each restaurant belongs, its wage, and the proportion of full-time employment before the minimum wage was increased in NJ. Thus, we adjust for these three variables in the linear model, where the outcome variable is the proportion of full-time employment after the minimum wage was increased in NJ and the treatment variable is whether a restaurant is located in NJ. We use the data set described in table 2.5 and regress the outcome variable and three confounding variables using the `lm()` function. Before we fit the linear regression, we compute the proportion of full-time employment before and after the minimum wage was increased in NJ. We also create an indicator, or "dummy" variable, that equals 1 if a restaurant is located in NJ and 0 if it is in PA.

```r
minwage <- read.csv("minwage.csv")
## compute proportion of full-time employment before minimum wage increase
minwage$fullPropBefore <- minwage$fullBefore /
    (minwage$fullBefore + minwage$partBefore)
## same thing after minimum-wage increase
minwage$fullPropAfter <- minwage$fullAfter /
    (minwage$fullAfter + minwage$partAfter)
## an indicator for NJ: 1 if it's located in NJ and 0 if in PA
minwage$NJ <- ifelse(minwage$location == "PA", 0, 1)
```

We now regress the proportion of full-time employment after the minimum-wage increase on the treatment variable (i.e., whether a restaurant is located in NJ) as well as on 3 other potential confounding variables. We note that `chain` is a factor variable with 4 different chains of fast-food restaurants. When a factor variable is used in the `lm()` function, as we saw in section 4.3.2, the function will automatically create the appropriate number of indicator variables for each category. In this case, since we have an intercept and the factor has 4 categories, the function will create 3 indicator variables. The `lm()` function by default includes an intercept. If we remove the intercept using the `-1` syntax, then it will create 1 indicator variable for each of the four categories. As explained in section 4.3.2, these two models are equivalent and yield an identical predicted value given the same values of the explanatory variables while yielding different estimates of coefficients.

```r
fit.minwage <- lm(fullPropAfter ~ -1 + NJ + fullPropBefore +
                    wageBefore + chain, data = minwage)
## regression result
fit.minwage

##
## Call:
## lm(formula = fullPropAfter ~ -1 + NJ + fullPropBefore + wageBefore +
```

```
##      chain, data = minwage)
##
## Coefficients:
##              NJ    fullPropBefore        wageBefore
##         0.05422           0.16879           0.08133
## chainburgerking           chainkfc         chainroys
##        -0.11563          -0.15080          -0.20639
##     chainwendys
##        -0.22013
```

The result shows that the minimum-wage increase in NJ raised the proportion of full-time employees by 5.4 percentage points (represented by the estimated coefficient for the NJ variable) after adjusting for the proportion of full-time employees and wages before the minimum-wage increase as well as the chains of fast-food restaurants. By excluding the intercept, we can immediately compare the estimated coefficients across fast-food restaurant chains. We find that Burger King is predicted to have the highest proportion of full-time employment after adjusting for the other factors in the model. If we include an intercept, the estimated coefficients need to be interpreted relative to the base category, which will be dropped from the regression model. The base category of a factor variable represents a category to which the other categories of the variable are compared.

```
fit.minwage1 <- lm(fullPropAfter ~ NJ + fullPropBefore +
                   wageBefore + chain, data = minwage)
fit.minwage1

##
## Call:
## lm(formula = fullPropAfter ~ NJ + fullPropBefore + wageBefore +
##       chain, data = minwage)
##
## Coefficients:
##     (Intercept)               NJ    fullPropBefore
##        -0.11563          0.05422           0.16879
##      wageBefore         chainkfc         chainroys
##         0.08133         -0.03517          -0.09076
##     chainwendys
##        -0.10451
```

The lm() function excluded the indicator variable for Burger King from the regression, which means that the estimated coefficients for all other fast-food restaurant chains are relative to Burger King. Consistent with the previous result, we find that all other estimated coefficients are negative, indicating that Burger King is predicted to have the highest proportion of full-time employment after adjusting for the other factors in the model. We emphasize that these two models are equivalent, yielding the same predicted values. For example, we use the outputs of the two regression models to predict the outcome for the first observation in the data yielding an identical predicted value.

```
predict(fit.minwage, newdata = minwage[1, ])

##         1
## 0.2709367

predict(fit.minwage1, newdata = minwage[1, ])

##         1
## 0.2709367
```

> Valid inference under the linear model assumes the **exogeneity assumption** given in equation (7.22). This assumption will be violated if there exist **unobserved confounders**. To make the exogeneity assumption more plausible, researchers can measure confounding variables and include them as additional explanatory variables in the linear regression model.

7.3.2   UNBIASEDNESS OF ESTIMATED COEFFICIENTS

How accurately can we estimate the coefficients of the linear regression model? Under the assumption that the linear regression model actually describes the true data-generating process, we consider the question of how to quantify the uncertainty associated with estimated coefficients. For simplicity, let us consider the model with one predictor only, though the results presented in this section can be generalized to linear regression with more than one predictor:

$$Y_i = \alpha + \beta X_i + \epsilon_i. \tag{7.23}$$

Recall from the discussion given in section 4.2.3 that if the linear regression model contains only an intercept and one predictor, then the least squares estimates are given by

$$\hat{\alpha} = \overline{Y} - \hat{\beta}\overline{X}, \tag{7.24}$$

$$\hat{\beta} = \frac{\sum_{i=1}^{n}(Y_i - \overline{Y})(X_i - \overline{X})}{\sum_{i=1}^{n}(X_i - \overline{X})^2}. \tag{7.25}$$

In this equation, $\overline{X}$ and $\overline{Y}$ represent the sample average of the predictor X_i and the outcome variable Y_i, respectively.

It turns out that under the exogeneity assumption these least squares coefficients, $\hat{\alpha}$ and $\hat{\beta}$, are unbiased for their corresponding true values, α and β, respectively. Formally, we may write $\mathbb{E}(\hat{\alpha}) = \alpha$ and $\mathbb{E}(\hat{\beta}) = \beta$. This means that if we generate the data according to this linear model, the least squares estimates of the coefficients will equal their true values, on average, across the hypothetically repeated data sets. Thus, the method of least squares produces unbiased estimates while minimizing the sum of squared residuals.

For those who are mathematically inclined, we show this important result analytically. Since we assume that the linear regression model is the true data-generating process, we substitute the linear model expression given in equation (7.23) into equation (7.24). Noting that the average outcome is given by $\overline{Y} = \alpha + \beta\overline{X} + \bar{\epsilon}$, we obtain the following expression for the estimated intercept:

$$\hat{\alpha} = \alpha + \beta\overline{X} + \bar{\epsilon} - \hat{\beta}\overline{X} = \alpha + (\beta - \hat{\beta})\overline{X} + \bar{\epsilon}.$$

This equation shows that the estimation error $\hat{\alpha} - \alpha$ is given by $(\beta - \hat{\beta})\overline{X} + \bar{\epsilon}$. Similarly, we use equation (7.23) to rewrite the estimated slope coefficient given in equation (7.25) as the sum of the true value β and the estimation error $\hat{\beta} - \beta$:

$$\hat{\beta} = \frac{\sum_{i=1}^{n}(\beta X_i + \epsilon_i - \beta\overline{X} - \bar{\epsilon})(X_i - \overline{X})}{\sum_{i=1}^{n}(X_i - \overline{X})^2} = \beta + \underbrace{\frac{\sum_{i=1}^{n}(\epsilon_i - \bar{\epsilon})(X_i - \overline{X})}{\sum_{i=1}^{n}(X_i - \overline{X})^2}}_{\text{estimation error}},$$

where we used the fact that $\sum_{i=1}^{n}\beta X_i = \sum_{i=1}^{n}\beta\overline{X}$.

We can further simplify the numerator of this estimation error, i.e., the second term in this equation:

$$\sum_{i=1}^{n}(\epsilon_i - \bar{\epsilon})(X_i - \overline{X}) = \sum_{i=1}^{n}\epsilon_i(X_i - \overline{X}) - \sum_{i=1}^{n}\bar{\epsilon}(X_i - \overline{X})$$

$$= \sum_{i=1}^{n}\epsilon_i(X_i - \overline{X}) - \bar{\epsilon}\underbrace{\left(\sum_{i=1}^{n}X_i - n\overline{X}\right)}_{=0}$$

$$= \sum_{i=1}^{n}\epsilon_i(X_i - \overline{X}).$$

Therefore, we obtain the following final expression for the estimation error of the slope coefficient:

$$\hat{\beta} - \beta = \frac{\sum_{i=1}^{n}\epsilon_i(X_i - \overline{X})}{\sum_{i=1}^{n}(X_i - \overline{X})^2}. \tag{7.26}$$

As discussed in section 7.1.1, to prove the unbiasedness of $\hat{\beta}$, we must show that on average $\hat{\beta}$ equals its true value β over repeated (hypothetical) data-generating processes. Mathematically, we compute the expectation of $\hat{\beta}$ and show it is equal to β, i.e., $\mathbb{E}(\hat{\beta}) = \beta$. In this case, we first compute the conditional expectation of $\hat{\beta}$ given the explanatory variable vector X under the exogeneity assumption given in equation (7.22), then show $\mathbb{E}(\hat{\beta} \mid X) = \beta$. This means that for a given value of X, we consider the hypothetical process of repeatedly generating the outcome variable Y by sampling the error term ϵ independent of X and then compute the least squares estimates $\hat{\alpha}$ and $\hat{\beta}$. While these estimates differ each time, on average they should equal the true values α and β, respectively.

We first calculate the conditional expectation of the estimated slope coefficient. Since the expectation is computed given the predictor vector X, the only random variable is the error term ϵ. This means that the other terms can be considered as constants and taken out of the expectation:

$$\mathbb{E}(\hat{\beta} - \beta \mid X) = \frac{1}{\sum_{i=1}^{n}(X_i - \overline{X})^2} \sum_{i=1}^{n} \mathbb{E}(\epsilon_i \mid X)(X_i - \overline{X}) = 0.$$

The second equality is implied by the exogeneity assumption $\mathbb{E}(\epsilon \mid X) = 0$. Therefore, the estimated slope coefficient for X_i is unbiased conditional on the predictor. Using this result, we can also show that the estimated intercept is unbiased conditional on the predictor vector X:

$$\mathbb{E}(\hat{\alpha} - \alpha \mid X) = \mathbb{E}(\hat{\beta} - \beta \mid X)\overline{X} + \mathbb{E}(\bar{\epsilon} \mid X) = 0.$$

The result follows from the fact that $\mathbb{E}(\hat{\beta} - \beta \mid X) = 0$ (unbiasedness of $\hat{\beta}$) and $\mathbb{E}(\bar{\epsilon} \mid X) = \frac{1}{n}\sum_{i=1}^{n} \mathbb{E}(\epsilon_i \mid X) = 0$ (exogeneity). Since this means that given *any* value of the predictor vector X the estimated coefficients, $\hat{\alpha}$ and $\hat{\beta}$, are unbiased, conditional unbiasedness implies unbiasedness without conditioning, i.e., $\mathbb{E}(\hat{\alpha}) = \alpha$ and $\mathbb{E}(\hat{\beta}) = \beta$.

> Under the exogeneity assumption, the least squares estimates of the coefficients in the linear regression model are unbiased.

The argument we just made, that conditional unbiasedness of estimated coefficients implies (unconditional) unbiasedness, can be made more generally and is called the *law of iterated expectation*.

> The **law of iterated expectation** states that for any two random variables X and Y, the following equality holds:
> $$\mathbb{E}(Y) = \mathbb{E}\{\mathbb{E}(Y \mid X)\}.$$
> The inner expectation averages over Y given X, yielding a function of X, and the outer expectation averages this resulting conditional expectation function over X.

For example, let Y be an individual income and X be the racial group the individual belongs to. Then, in order to obtain the average income in a population, we could simply compute the mean of everyone's income $\mathbb{E}(Y)$ or first compute the average income for each racial category $\mathbb{E}(Y \mid X) = g(X)$ and then obtain the overall mean income by calculating the weighted average of race-specific means, where the weight is proportional to the size of racial group $\mathbb{E}(g(X))$. Applying the law of iterated expectation, we would formally conclude that the estimated coefficients are unbiased:

$$\mathbb{E}(\hat{\alpha}) = \mathbb{E}\{\mathbb{E}(\hat{\alpha} \mid X)\} = \mathbb{E}(\alpha) = \alpha,$$

$$\mathbb{E}(\hat{\beta}) = \mathbb{E}\{\mathbb{E}(\hat{\beta} \mid X)\} = \mathbb{E}(\beta) = \beta.$$

7.3.3 STANDARD ERRORS OF ESTIMATED COEFFICIENTS

Now that we have established the unbiasedness of estimated coefficients, we consider their standard errors. The standard error of each estimated coefficient represents the (estimated) standard deviation of its sampling distribution (see section 7.1.2). The sampling distribution is produced through a hypothetically repeated sampling process, yielding different estimated coefficients across samples. The standard error quantifies the average variability of the estimated coefficient over this repeated sampling procedure.

As in the case of unbiasedness, we consider the linear regression model with one predictor for the sake of simplicity. We derive the variance of the sampling distribution of the estimated slope coefficient $\hat{\beta}$ and then take its square root to obtain the standard error. As in the case of bias, we first compute the conditional variance given the predictor X. Recall the discussion in section 6.3.5 that the variance of a random variable does not change even if we add a constant to it. Thus, the variance of the estimated coefficient $\hat{\beta}$ equals that of the estimation error $\hat{\beta} - \beta$ since β is an (albeit unknown) constant. Using equation (7.26), we obtain

$$
\mathbb{V}(\hat{\beta} \mid X) = \mathbb{V}(\hat{\beta} - \beta \mid X)
$$

$$
= \mathbb{V}\left(\frac{\sum_{i=1}^{n} \epsilon_i (X_i - \overline{X})}{\sum_{i=1}^{n} (X_i - \overline{X})^2} \,\middle|\, X \right)
$$

$$
= \frac{1}{\{\sum_{i=1}^{n} (X_i - \overline{X})^2\}^2} \mathbb{V}\left(\sum_{i=1}^{n} \epsilon_i (X_i - \overline{X}) \,\middle|\, X \right). \tag{7.27}
$$

The third equality follows from equation (6.38) and the fact that the denominator is a function only of the predictor X, which is treated as a constant when computing the conditional variance given X.

To further simplify the expression in equation (7.27), we assume *homoskedasticity* of the error term. That is, we assume that, conditional on the predictor X, the error term of observation i is independent of that of another observation, and that the variance of the error term does not depend on the predictor X.

The assumption of **homoskedastic error** consists of the following two components:

1. ϵ_i is independent of ϵ_j conditional on X for all $i \neq j$.
2. The variance of error does not depend on the predictor:
   $\mathbb{V}(\epsilon_i \mid X) = \mathbb{V}(\epsilon_i)$.

Under this homoskedasticity assumption, we can further simplify the numerator of equation (7.27):

$$\mathbb{V}\left(\sum_{i=1}^{n} \epsilon_i(X_i - \overline{X}) \,\Big|\, \boldsymbol{X}\right) = \sum_{i=1}^{n} \mathbb{V}(\epsilon_i \mid \boldsymbol{X})(X_i - \overline{X})^2 = \mathbb{V}(\epsilon_i)\sum_{i=1}^{n}(X_i - \overline{X})^2. \quad (7.28)$$

Putting this together with equation (7.27), we arrive at the following variance of the estimated slope coefficient $\hat{\beta}$ under the homoskedasticity and exogeneity assumptions:

$$\mathbb{V}(\hat{\beta} \mid \boldsymbol{X}) = \frac{\mathbb{V}(\epsilon_i)}{\sum_{i=1}^{n}(X_i - \overline{X})^2}. \quad (7.29)$$

Although the above expression represents the conditional variance of $\hat{\beta}$ given the predictor X, we can also compute the unconditional variance of $\hat{\beta}$. The former is based on the variability of $\hat{\beta}$ under the hypothetical scenario of repeated sampling of Y_i given X_i (or equivalently ϵ_i given X_i because Y_i is a function of X_i and ϵ_i) for each observation, where X_i is fixed throughout. In contrast, the latter represents the uncertainty of $\hat{\beta}$ under a somewhat more natural data-generating process where Y_i and X_i (or equivalently ϵ_i and X_i) are jointly sampled from the population for each hypothetical realization of the data. To derive the unconditional variance of $\hat{\beta}$, we use the following *law of total variance*.

> The **law of total variance** states that for any two random variables X and Y the following equality holds:
> $$\mathbb{V}(Y) = \mathbb{V}\{\mathbb{E}(Y \mid X)\} + \mathbb{E}\{\mathbb{V}(Y \mid X)\}.$$
> The first term represents the variance of conditional expectation and the second term represents the expectation of conditional variance.

In words, this law implies that the unconditional variance of random variable Y is equal to the sum of the variance of the conditional expectation of Y given X and the expectation of the conditional variance of Y given X. Applying the law of total variance, we can show that the unconditional variance of $\hat{\beta}$ can be derived as

$$\mathbb{V}(\hat{\beta}) = \mathbb{V}(\mathbb{E}(\hat{\beta} \mid \boldsymbol{X})) + \mathbb{E}\{\mathbb{V}(\hat{\beta} \mid \boldsymbol{X})\}$$

$$= \underbrace{\mathbb{V}(\beta)}_{=0} + \mathbb{E}\left(\frac{\mathbb{V}(\epsilon_i)}{\sum_{i=1}^{n}(x_i - \overline{X})^2}\right)$$

$$= \mathbb{V}(\epsilon_i)\mathbb{E}\left[\frac{1}{\sum_{i=1}^{n}(X_i - \overline{X})^2}\right]. \quad (7.30)$$

In the above equation, $\mathbb{V}(\beta) = 0$ because β is a constant. This implies that the unconditional variance of $\hat{\beta}$ is equal to the expected value of the conditional variance of $\hat{\beta}$, i.e., $\mathbb{V}(\hat{\beta}) = \mathbb{E}\{\mathbb{V}(\hat{\beta} \mid \boldsymbol{X})\}$. Thus, a good estimate of the conditional variance is also a good estimate of the unconditional variance.

Given this result, under the assumption of homoskedastic error, we can compute the standard error of $\hat{\beta}$ as an estimate of the unconditional variance given in equation (7.30). We do this by first estimating $\mathbb{V}(\epsilon_i)$ using the sample variance of residuals $\hat{\epsilon}_i = Y_i - \hat{\alpha} - \hat{\beta} X_i$, and then taking the square root of it. That is, if we denote the estimated conditional variance by $\widehat{\mathbb{V}(\hat{\beta})}$, then the standard error of $\hat{\beta}$ is

$$\text{standard error of } \hat{\beta} = \sqrt{\widehat{\mathbb{V}(\hat{\beta})}} = \sqrt{\frac{\frac{1}{n}\sum_{i=1}^{n}\hat{\epsilon}_i^2}{\sum_{i=1}^{n}(X_i - \overline{X})^2}}. \tag{7.31}$$

When estimating $\mathbb{V}(\epsilon_i)$, we used the fact that the sample mean of residuals is always zero,[3] i.e., $\frac{1}{n}\sum_{i=1}^{n}(\hat{\epsilon}_i - \bar{\hat{\epsilon}})^2 = \frac{1}{n}\sum_{i=1}^{n}\hat{\epsilon}_i^2$.

Finally, the standard errors derived above are based on the assumption of homoskedastic errors. If this assumption is violated, then the calculation of standard errors needs to be adjusted. For example, in randomized controlled trials, the variance may differ for the treatment and control groups. In fact, when we computed the standard error for the difference-in-means estimator, we separately calculated the variance for each group (see equation (7.18)). If the error variance depends on the predictor, we say that error is *heteroskedastic*. Although beyond the scope of this book, there are various ways to compute the standard errors that account for heteroskedastic errors. They are called *heteroskedasticity-robust standard errors*.

7.3.4   INFERENCE ABOUT COEFFICIENTS

Given the standard error derived above, we can compute the confidence intervals following the procedure described in section 7.1.3. Specifically, using the *central limit theorem*, we can show that as the sample size increases, the sampling distribution of $\hat{\beta}$ approaches a normal distribution centered around the mean:

$$z\text{-score of } \hat{\beta} = \frac{\hat{\beta} - \beta}{\text{standard error of } \hat{\beta}} \overset{\text{approx.}}{\sim} \mathcal{N}(0, 1). \tag{7.32}$$

Therefore, we can use the critical values based on the standard normal distribution to construct the $(1 - \alpha) \times 100\%$ level confidence interval below:

$$\text{CI}(\alpha) = [\hat{\beta} - z_{\alpha/2} \times \text{standard error}, \ \hat{\beta} + z_{\alpha/2} \times \text{standard error}]. \tag{7.33}$$

We can also conduct a hypothesis test for the slope coefficient. For example, we can test the null hypothesis that the slope coefficient is equal to a particular value β_0. Most often, researchers use zero as the true value under the null hypothesis and ask whether or not the true coefficient for the predictor is equal to zero, i.e., $\beta_0 = 0$. Under the general hypothesis-testing framework developed in section 7.2, our null hypothesis is $H_0 : \beta = \beta_0$. The test statistic is the z-score, i.e., $z^* = (\hat{\beta} - \beta_0)/\text{standard error}$, and the sampling distribution of this test statistic z^* under the null hypothesis is the standard normal distribution. Therefore, we can compute the p-value using the CDF of the standard normal distribution. For example, the two-sided p-value is given by $2 \times P(Z \leq z^*)$, where Z is a standard normal random variable.

---

[3] Since the expectation of the error term is also zero and hence does not need to be estimated, we divide the sum of squared residuals by n instead of $n - 1$ often used for the sample variance calculation (see the discussion in section 2.6.2).

Just as for the analysis of randomized experiments, researchers often use a more conservative confidence interval based on Student's t-distribution (see section 7.1.5). Technically, if we make an additional assumption that the error term is normally distributed with mean zero and homoskedastic variance, then the sampling distribution of z^*, which is called the *t-statistic* in this setting, is given by, without approximation, Student's t-distribution with $n - 2$ degrees of freedom. This contrasts with the asymptotic approximation based on the standard normal distribution without assuming a particular distribution for the error term. The degrees of freedom are $n - 2$ because two parameters, α and β, are estimated from the data. Since Student's t-distribution has thicker tails than the standard normal distribution, we will have a greater critical value and as a result, obtain a wider confidence interval and a greater p-value.

As the first example to illustrate the results described above, we revisit the randomized experiment from chapter 4, examining the effects of women as policy makers in India (see section 4.3.1). The data set we analyze is contained in women.csv and the variable names and descriptions are given in table 4.7. Recall that after loading the data set from this study as a data frame women, we regressed the number of drinking water facilities in a village, water, on a binary variable reserved, indicating whether each GP is reserved for women. Conveniently, in R, all of the necessary information can be obtained by applying the summary() function to the output from the lm() function, which fits a linear regression model.

```
women <- read.csv("women.csv")
fit.women <- lm(water ~ reserved, data = women)
summary(fit.women)

##
## Call:
## lm(formula = water ~ reserved, data = women)
##
## Residuals:
##     Min      1Q  Median      3Q     Max
## -23.991 -14.738  -7.865   2.262 316.009
##
## Coefficients:
##              Estimate Std. Error t value Pr(>|t|)
## (Intercept)    14.738      2.286   6.446 4.22e-10 ***
## reserved        9.252      3.948   2.344   0.0197 *
## ---
## Signif. codes:
## 0 '***' 0.001 '**' 0.01 '*' 0.05 '.' 0.1 ' ' 1
##
## Residual standard error: 33.45 on 320 degrees of freedom
## Multiple R-squared:  0.01688,Adjusted R-squared:  0.0138
## F-statistic: 5.493 on 1 and 320 DF,  p-value: 0.0197
```

We find that the point estimate of the slope coefficient is 9.252 and its standard error is 3.948. This output uses a conservative confidence interval based on Student's t-distribution. The t-statistic for the estimated slope coefficient is, therefore, 2.344. If the null hypothesis is that the slope coefficient is zero, then the two-sided p-value can be computed using Student's t-distribution with 320 degrees of freedom because the sample size is 322. In the summary output, this p-value is shown to be 0.0197. Therefore, using the $\alpha = 0.05$ level of statistical significance, we reject the null hypothesis that the slope coefficient is zero. The asterisks in the summary output indicate the level of statistical significance. We can compute confidence intervals using the `confint()` function, where the default significance level is 0.05. The level of statistical significance can be changed with the `level` argument.

```
confint(fit.women) # 95% confidence intervals

##                  2.5 %    97.5 %
## (Intercept) 10.240240 19.23640
## reserved     1.485608 17.01924
```

The result suggests that having the GP reserved for women is estimated to increase the number of drinking water facilities by 9.25 facilities with a 95% confidence interval of [1.49, 17.02]. As expected, we observe that the 95% confidence interval does not contain zero.

While the mathematical derivation is beyond the scope of this book, we can also compute the standard error and confidence interval of the estimated coefficients in a more general setting with multiple predictors. The `summary()` function can be applied to the output of the `lm()` function even with multiple predictors. For example, we can summarize the results of the linear regression model fitted to the minimum-wage data earlier in section 7.3.1.

```
summary(fit.minwage)

##
## Call:
## lm(formula = fullPropAfter ~ -1 + NJ + fullPropBefore + wageBefore +
##   chain, data = minwage)
## Residuals:
##      Min       1Q    Median       3Q       Max
## -0.48617 -0.18135 -0.02809  0.15127  0.75091
##
## Coefficients:
##                   Estimate Std. Error t value Pr(>|t|)
## NJ                 0.05422    0.03321   1.633  0.10343
## fullPropBefore     0.16879    0.05662   2.981  0.00307 **
## wageBefore         0.08133    0.03892   2.090  0.03737 *
## chainburgerking   -0.11563    0.17888  -0.646  0.51844
```

```
## chainkfc        -0.15080     0.18310   -0.824   0.41074
## chainroys       -0.20639     0.18671   -1.105   0.26974
## chainwendys     -0.22013     0.18840   -1.168   0.24343
## ---
## Signif. codes:
## 0 '***' 0.001 '**' 0.01 '*' 0.05 '.' 0.1 ' ' 1
##
## Residual standard error: 0.2438 on 351 degrees of freedom
## Multiple R-squared:  0.6349,Adjusted R-squared:  0.6277
## F-statistic: 87.21 on 7 and 351 DF,  p-value: < 2.2e-16
```

The summary output contains the relevant information for each of the estimated coefficients. In this observational study, we are interested in the average effect of increasing the minimum wage in NJ, which corresponds to the coefficient of the NJ variable. Thus, the average effect of the minimum-wage increase on the proportion of full-time employees in NJ is estimated to be 5.4 percentage points with a standard error of 3.3 percentage points. According to the result, we fail to reject the null hypothesis that the average effect of the minimum-wage increase is zero. In other words, we cannot preclude the possibility that the nonzero point estimate we obtained may be due to the sampling error under the scenario that the minimum-wage increase did not, on average, change the proportion of full-time employment. The p-values in this case are based on Student's t-distribution with 351 degrees of freedom because we have a total of 358 observations and 7 parameters to be estimated. To obtain the 95% confidence interval for this estimate, we can use the `confint()` function as before.

```
## confidence interval just for the "NJ" variable
confint(fit.minwage)["NJ", ]

##       2.5 %       97.5 %
## -0.01109295   0.11953297
```

As expected, the confidence interval contains zero, consistent with the result of the hypothesis test. However, a large portion of the confidence interval contains positive values, providing evidence that the minimum-wage increase in NJ may not have decreased the proportion of full-time employment.

The above summary output presents various other statistics. They include the *residual standard error*, which is the sample standard deviation of residuals. Since there are $(p + 1)$ parameters to be estimated, the number of degrees of freedom equals $(n - p - 1)$ instead of the usual $(n - 1)$ used when computing average. The residual standard error represents the average magnitude of residuals under the fitted model. The output also includes R^2, or the *coefficient of determination*, which represents the proportion of explained variation in the outcome (see section 4.2.6). As explained in section 4.3.2, the *adjusted R^2* includes the adjustment due to the number of degrees of freedom, penalizing models with large numbers of predictors.

7.3.5 INFERENCE ABOUT PREDICTIONS

As shown in chapter 4, one of the main advantages of regression modeling is its ability to predict outcomes of interest. In the case of linear regression models, once we estimate the coefficients, we can use the model to predict an outcome variable given the values of the predictors in the model. Below, we show how to compute the standard error and construct confidence intervals for a prediction based on the linear regression model.

For the sake of simplicity, consider the linear regression model with a single predictor, i.e., $Y_i = \alpha + \beta X_i + \epsilon_i$. We are interested in obtaining the standard error of the predicted value from this model when the predictor X takes a particular value x:

$$\widehat{Y} = \hat{\alpha} + \hat{\beta} x.$$

To derive the variance of the predicted value $\widehat{Y}$, we must recognize the fact that $\hat{\alpha}$ and $\hat{\beta}$ are possibly correlated with each other. When two random variables, X and Y, are correlated, the variance of their sum is not equal to the sum of their variances. Instead, the variance of their sum includes their *covariance*, defined as follows.

Let X and Y be random variables. Their **covariance** is defined as
$$\mathrm{Cov}(X, Y) = \mathbb{E}\{(X - \mathbb{E}(X))(Y - \mathbb{E}(Y))\}$$
$$= \mathbb{E}(XY) - \mathbb{E}(X)\mathbb{E}(Y).$$

The **correlation**, a standardized version of covariance, is given by
$$\mathrm{Cor}(X, Y) = \frac{\mathrm{Cov}(X, Y)}{\sqrt{\mathbb{V}(X)\mathbb{V}(Y)}}.$$

Sample correlation, or the correlation of a sample, was introduced in chapter 3 (see section 3.6.2). If the two random variables are independent of each other, their covariance and correlation are zero. In addition, the general formula for the variance of the sum of two (possibly dependent) random variables is given as
$$\mathbb{V}(X + Y) = \mathbb{V}(X) + \mathbb{V}(Y) + 2\,\mathrm{Cov}(X, Y).$$

More generally,
$$\mathbb{V}(aX + bY + c) = a^2\mathbb{V}(X) + b^2(Y) + 2ab\,\mathrm{Cov}(X, Y)$$

where a, b, c are constants.

Since $\hat{\alpha}$ and $\hat{\beta}$ may not be independent, using the general formula introduced above, we obtain the following variance of predicted value $\widehat{Y}$ when the predictor X equals a particular value x:

$$\mathbb{V}(\widehat{Y}) = \mathbb{V}(\hat{\alpha} + \hat{\beta}x) = \mathbb{V}(\hat{\alpha}) + \mathbb{V}(\hat{\beta})x^2 + 2x\,\mathrm{Cov}(\hat{\alpha}, \hat{\beta}).$$

We can compute the standard error by estimating each component of this variance and then taking the square root of the estimated variance of $\widehat{Y}$:

$$\text{standard error of } \widehat{Y} = \sqrt{\widehat{\mathbb{V}(\hat{\alpha})} + \widehat{\mathbb{V}(\hat{\beta})}x^2 + 2x\,\widehat{\mathrm{Cov}(\hat{\alpha}, \hat{\beta})}}.$$

Once the standard error is calculated, we can apply the *central limit theorem* to approximate the sampling distribution of the z-score for the predicted value $\widehat{Y}$ using the standard normal distribution:

$$z\text{-score of } \widehat{Y} = \frac{\widehat{Y} - (\alpha + \beta x)}{\text{standard error of } \widehat{Y}} \overset{\text{approx.}}{\sim} \mathcal{N}(0,\ 1). \tag{7.34}$$

From this result, we can obtain a confidence interval and conduct a hypothesis test for a selected level of statistical significance.

As an example of inference with prediction, we revisit the regression discontinuity design introduced in section 4.3.4. In that study, we estimated the average effect of winning an election on a candidate's wealth in the United Kingdom. Instead of comparing members of Parliament (MPs) who won an election with those who lost it, researchers focused on those who narrowly won or narrowly lost an election. The idea was that if winning an election has a large effect on one's wealth, we should expect a substantial gap in the average wealth at the winning threshold, i.e., the winning margin of zero. Two linear regression models were used to predict the average wealth at this threshold, one based on narrow winners and the other fitted to narrow losers. Here, we reproduce the regression analysis conducted in section 4.3.4 separately for the Labour and Tory Parties.

```
## load the data and subset them into two parties
MPs <- read.csv("MPs.csv")
MPs.labour <- subset(MPs, subset = (party == "labour"))
MPs.tory <- subset(MPs, subset = (party == "tory"))
## two regressions for Labour: negative and positive margin
labour.fit1 <- lm(ln.net ~ margin,
                data = MPs.labour[MPs.labour$margin < 0, ])
labour.fit2 <- lm(ln.net ~ margin,
                data = MPs.labour[MPs.labour$margin > 0, ])
## two regressions for Tory: negative and positive margin
tory.fit1 <- lm(ln.net ~ margin, data = MPs.tory[MPs.tory$margin < 0, ])
tory.fit2 <- lm(ln.net ~ margin, data = MPs.tory[MPs.tory$margin > 0, ])
```

The average treatment effect of winning an election results from predicting the average wealth at the winning threshold, i.e., a winning margin of zero. The confidence interval on the predicted value from each regression can be obtained by setting the `interval` argument in the `predict()` function to `"confidence"` rather than to `"none"`, which is the default. Note that as in the `confint()` function, the level of statistical significance can be selected by setting the `level` argument to a desired value (the default is 0.95). We focus on the Tory Party here.

```
## Tory Party: prediction at the threshold
tory.y0 <- predict(tory.fit1, interval = "confidence",
                newdata = data.frame(margin = 0))
```

```
tory.y0

##        fit      lwr      upr
## 1 12.53812 12.11402 12.96221

tory.y1 <- predict(tory.fit2, interval = "confidence",
                 newdata = data.frame(margin = 0))
tory.y1

##        fit      lwr      upr
## 1 13.1878 12.80691 13.56869
```

In this output, the predicted value is given by `fit` and the lower and upper confidence bands are denoted by `lwr` and `upr`, respectively. For example, the average net wealth for non-MPs at the threshold is estimated to be 12.54 log net wealth with a 95% confidence interval of [12.11, 12.96]. Similarly, the average net wealth for MPs at the threshold is estimated to be 13.19 log net wealth with a 95% confidence interval of [12.81, 13.57]. The following code chunk plots these two regression lines (solid lines) with their 95% confidence intervals (dashed lines), using the range of predictor x. To do this, we first define the two ranges of the electoral margin and then compute the predictions for each range with 95% confidence intervals.

```
## range of predictors; min to 0 and 0 to max
y1.range <- seq(from = 0, to = min(MPs.tory$margin), by = -0.01)
y2.range <- seq(from = 0, to = max(MPs.tory$margin),by = 0.01)
## prediction using all the values
tory.y0 <- predict(tory.fit1, interval = "confidence",
                 newdata = data.frame(margin = y1.range))
tory.y1 <- predict(tory.fit2, interval = "confidence",
                 newdata = data.frame(margin = y2.range))
```

Finally, we plot the results where the solid lines represent the predicted values and the dashed lines represent the confidence intervals.

```
## plotting the first regression with losers
plot(y1.range, tory.y0[, "fit"], type = "l", xlim = c(-0.5, 0.5),
     ylim = c(10, 15), xlab = "Margin of victory", ylab = "log net wealth")
abline(v = 0, lty = "dotted")
lines(y1.range, tory.y0[, "lwr"], lty = "dashed") # lower CI
lines(y1.range, tory.y0[, "upr"], lty = "dashed") # upper CI
## plotting the second regression with winners
lines(y2.range, tory.y1[, "fit"], lty = "solid")  # point estimates
lines(y2.range, tory.y1[, "lwr"], lty = "dashed") # lower CI
lines(y2.range, tory.y1[, "upr"], lty = "dashed") # upper CI
```

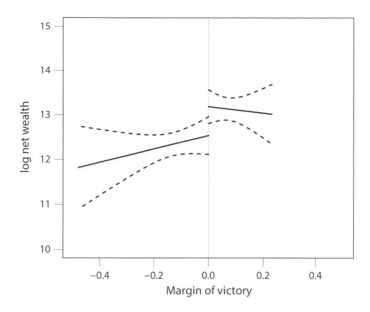

In the plot, we observe that the width of the confidence interval widens as it moves away from the mean value of the predictor. While these two confidence intervals overlap with each other, what we really would like to do is to compute the confidence interval for the difference between these two predicted values. This is because the difference between the two predicted values represents the estimated average treatment effect at the threshold under the regression discontinuity design. Moreover, these two predicted values are assumed to be independent because they are based on two regression models that are fitted to two separate sets of observations. This means that the variance of the difference is the sum of the two variances. To compute the standard error of the difference in the predicted values, we obtain the standard error from each fitted regression. We then use the following formula to compute the standard error of the estimated difference:

$$\text{standard error of } (\widehat{Y}_1 - \widehat{Y}_0) = \sqrt{(\text{standard error of } \widehat{Y}_1)^2 + (\text{standard error of } \widehat{Y}_0)^2}.$$

In R, we obtain the standard error of a predicted value by setting the `se.fit` argument to `TRUE`. There are multiple elements in the output list of the `predict()` function when using this standard error option. Each element can be extracted from this list by using the symbol `$`.

```
## recompute the predicted value and return standard errors
tory.y0 <- predict(tory.fit1, interval = "confidence",  se.fit = TRUE,
                   newdata = data.frame(margin = 0))
tory.y0

## $fit
##          fit       lwr      upr
## 1 12.53812 12.11402 12.96221
```

```
##
## $se.fit
## [1] 0.2141793
##
## $df
## [1] 119
##
## $residual.scale
## [1] 1.434283

tory.y1 <- predict(tory.fit2, interval = "confidence", se.fit = TRUE,
                   newdata = data.frame(margin = 0))
```

Since in this case the predicted value equals the estimated intercept, the standard error one obtains through the `predict()` function is equal to the standard error of the intercept in the summary output.

```
## s.e. of the intercept is the same as s.e. of the predicted value
summary(tory.fit1)

##
## Call:
## lm(formula = ln.net ~ margin, data = MPs.tory[MPs.tory$margin <
##     0, ])
##
## Residuals:
##     Min      1Q  Median      3Q     Max
## -5.3195 -0.4721 -0.0349  0.6629  3.5798
##
## Coefficients:
##             Estimate Std. Error t value Pr(>|t|)
## (Intercept)  12.5381     0.2142  58.540   <2e-16 ***
## margin        1.4911     1.2914   1.155    0.251
## ---
## Signif. codes:
## 0 '***' 0.001 '**' 0.01 '*' 0.05 '.' 0.1 ' ' 1
##
## Residual standard error: 1.434 on 119 degrees of freedom
## Multiple R-squared: 0.01108, Adjusted R-squared: 0.002769
## F-statistic: 1.333 on 1 and 119 DF,  p-value: 0.2506
```

We can now compute the standard error of the estimated difference in the average log net wealth between MPs and non-MPs at the winning threshold. Using this standard error, we compute the confidence interval and conduct a hypothesis test for which the null hypothesis is that winning an election has zero average effect on candidates' net log wealth.

```
## standard error
se.diff <- sqrt(tory.y0$se.fit^2 + tory.y1$se.fit^2)
se.diff

## [1] 0.2876281

## point estimate
diff.est <- tory.y1$fit[1, "fit"] - tory.y0$fit[1, "fit"]
diff.est

## [1] 0.6496861

## confidence interval
CI <- c(diff.est - se.diff * qnorm(0.975), diff.est + se.diff * qnorm(0.975))
CI

## [1] 0.0859455 1.2134268

## hypothesis test
z.score <- diff.est / se.diff
p.value <- 2 * pnorm(abs(z.score), lower.tail = FALSE) # two-sided p-value
p.value

## [1] 0.02389759
```

We find that even though the confidence intervals of the two estimates overlap with each other, the difference between these two estimates is statistically significantly different from zero. Indeed, the average effect of winning an election is estimated to be 0.65 net log wealth with a 95% confidence interval of [0.09, 1.21], which does not contain zero. As a result, the two-sided p-value is less than the conventional statistical significance level, 0.05, allowing us to reject the null hypothesis of zero average effect. Thus, our analysis suggests that winning an election had a positive impact on candidates' net wealth. The overlap of the confidence intervals of the two estimates does not necessarily imply that the confidence interval of the difference between the two estimates contains zero.

7.4 Summary

In this chapter, we introduced a framework for methods of statistical inference that enables us to quantify the degree of uncertainty regarding our estimates. While we can never know how close our estimates are to the unknown truth, we can evaluate the performance of our estimators using a hypothetically repeated randomization of treatment assignment and/or repeated random sampling. We introduced the concept of **unbiasedness**. An unbiased estimator accurately estimates the parameter of interest on average over a hypothetically repeated data-generating process. Using the law of large numbers, we can also show that some estimators have the property of **consistency**, which implies that as the sample size increases, they converge to the true parameter values.

While unbiasedness is an attractive property, we also need to understand the precision of an estimator given that we can obtain only one realization of the estimator. We use **standard error** to quantify how far our estimator is from the true parameter value on average over a repeated data-generating process. Standard error is an estimate of the standard deviation of the sampling distribution of an estimator. Based on standard errors, we can also construct **confidence intervals**, which will contain the true parameter values with a prespecified probability, again over a repeated data-generating process. We also showed how to conduct a statistical **hypothesis test** by specifying a null hypothesis and examining whether or not the observed data are consistent with this hypothesis. We applied these inferential methods to the analysis of randomized experiments and sample surveys from earlier in this book.

Finally, we introduced **model-based inference**. We used a linear regression model as a probabilistic generative model, from which the data are assumed to be drawn. Under this setting, we can quantify the uncertainty of our estimated coefficients and predicted values. We showed that the least squares estimates of coefficients are unbiased and derived their standard errors. Using these results, we also explained how to construct confidence intervals and conduct hypothesis tests. Similarly, we showed how to quantify the uncertainty about our predicted values and applied the methodology to the regression discontinuity design introduced in an earlier chapter. These statistical methods play an essential role in our inference because they enable us to separate signals from noise, extracting systematic patterns from data.

7.5 Exercises

7.5.1 SEX RATIO AND THE PRICE OF AGRICULTURAL CROPS IN CHINA

In this exercise, we consider the effect of a change in the price of agricultural goods whose production and cultivation are dominated by either men or women.[4] Our data come from China, where centrally planned production targets during the Maoist era led to changes in the prices of major staple crops. We focus here on tea, the production and cultivation of which required a large female labor force, as well as orchard fruits, for which the labor force was overwhelmingly male. We use price increases brought on by government policy change in 1979 as a proxy for increases in sex-specific income, and ask the following question: Do changes in sex-specific income alter the incentives for Chinese families to have children of one gender over another? The CSV data file, `chinawomen.csv`, contains the variables shown in table 7.4, with each observation representing a particular Chinese county in a given year. Note that `post` is an indicator variable that takes the value `1` in a year following the policy change and `0` in a year before the policy change.

1. We begin by examining sex ratios in the postreform period (i.e., the period after 1979) according to whether or not tea crops were sown in the region.

---

[4] This exercise is based on Nancy Qian (2008) "Missing women and the price of tea in China: The effect of sex-specific earnings on sex imbalance." *Quarterly Journal of Economics*, vol. 123, no. 3, pp. 1251–1285.

Table 7.4. Chinese Births and Crops Data.

Variable	Description
admin	unique county identifier
birpop	birth population in a given year
biryr	year of cohort (birth year)
cashcrop	quantity of cash crops planted in the county
orch	quantity of orchard-type crops planted in the county
teasown	quantity of tea sown in the county
sex	proportion of males in the birth cohort
post	indicator variable for the introduction of price reforms

Estimate the mean sex ratio in 1985, which we define as the proportion of male births, separately for tea-producing and non-tea-producing regions. Compute the 95% confidence interval for each estimate by assuming independence across counties within a year. Note that we will maintain this assumption throughout this exercise. Furthermore, compute the difference-in-means between the two regions and its 95% confidence interval. Are sex ratios different across these regions? What assumption is required in order for us to interpret this difference as causal?

2. Repeat the analysis in the previous question for subsequent years, i.e., 1980, 1981, 1982, ..., 1990. Create a graph which plots the difference-in-means estimates and their 95% confidence intervals against years. Give a substantive interpretation of the plot.

3. Next, we compare tea-producing and orchard-producing regions before the policy enactment. Specifically, we examine the sex ratio and the proportion of Han Chinese in 1978. Estimate the mean difference, its standard error, and 95% confidence intervals for each of these measures between the two regions. What do the results imply about the interpretation of the results given in question 1?

4. Repeat the analysis for the sex ratio in the previous question for each year before the reform, i.e., from 1962 until 1978. Create a graph which plots the difference-in-means estimates between the two regions and their 95% confidence intervals against years. Give a substantive interpretation of the plot.

5. We will adopt the difference-in-differences design by comparing the sex ratio in 1978 (right before the reform) with that in 1980 (right after the reform). Focus on a subset of counties that do not have missing observations in these two years. Compute the difference-in-differences estimate and its 95% confidence interval. Note that we assume independence across counties but account for possible dependence across years within each county. Then, the variance of the

difference-in-differences estimate is given by

$$\mathbb{V}\{(\overline{Y}_{\text{tea,after}} - \overline{Y}_{\text{tea,before}}) - (\overline{Y}_{\text{orchard,after}} - \overline{Y}_{\text{orchard,before}})\}$$
$$= \mathbb{V}(\overline{Y}_{\text{tea,after}} - \overline{Y}_{\text{tea,before}}) + \mathbb{V}(\overline{Y}_{\text{orchard,after}} - \overline{Y}_{\text{orchard,before}}),$$

where dependence across years is given by

$$\mathbb{V}(\overline{Y}_{\text{tea,after}} - \overline{Y}_{\text{tea,before}})$$

$$= \mathbb{V}(\overline{Y}_{\text{tea,after}}) - 2\,\text{Cov}(\overline{Y}_{\text{tea,after}}, \overline{Y}_{\text{tea,before}}) + \mathbb{V}(\overline{Y}_{\text{tea,before}})$$

$$= \frac{1}{n}\left\{\mathbb{V}(Y_{\text{tea,after}}) - 2\,\text{Cov}(Y_{\text{tea,after}}, Y_{\text{tea,before}}) + \mathbb{V}(Y_{\text{tea,before}})\right\}.$$

A similar formula can be given for orchard-producing regions. What substantive assumptions does the difference-in-differences design require? Give a substantive interpretation of the results.

7.5.2   FILE DRAWER AND PUBLICATION BIAS IN ACADEMIC RESEARCH

The peer review process is the main mechanism through which scientific communities decide whether a research paper should be published in academic journals.[5] By having other scientists evaluate research findings, academic journals hope to maintain the quality of their published articles. However, some have warned that the peer review process may yield undesirable consequences. In particular, the process may result in *publication bias* wherein research papers with statistically significant results are more likely to be published. To make matters worse, by being aware of such a bias in the publication process, researchers may be more likely to report findings that are statistically significant and ignore others. This is called *file drawer bias*.

In this exercise, we will explore these potential problems using data on a subset of experimental studies that were funded by the Time-Sharing Experiments in the Social Sciences (TESS) program. This program is sponsored by the National Science Foundation (NSF). The data set necessary for this exercise can be found in the CSV files `filedrawer.csv` and `published.csv`. The `filedrawer.csv` file contains information about 221 research projects funded by the TESS program. However, not all of those projects produced a published article. The `published.csv` file contains information about 53 published journal articles based on TESS projects. This data set records the number of experimental conditions and outcomes and how many of them are actually reported in the published article. Tables 7.5 and 7.6 present the names and descriptions of the variables from these data sets.

1. We begin by analyzing the data contained in the `filedrawer.csv` file. Create a contingency table for the publication status of papers and the statistical

---

[5] This exercise is based on the following studies: Annie Franco, Neil Malhotra, and Gabor Simonovits (2014) "Publication bias in the social sciences: Unlocking the file drawer." *Science*, vol. 345, no. 6203, pp. 1502–1505 and Annie Franco, Neil Malhotra, and Gabor Simonovits (2015) "Underreporting in political science survey experiments: Comparing questionnaires to published results." *Political Analysis*, vol. 23, pp. 206–312.

Table 7.5. File Drawer and Publication Bias Data I.

Variable	Description
id	study identifier
DV	publication status
IV	statistical significance of the main findings
max.h	H-index (highest among authors)
journal	discipline of the journal for published articles

Table 7.6. File Drawer and Publication Bias Data II.

Variable	Description
id.p	paper identifier
cond.s	number of conditions in the study
cond.p	number of conditions presented in the paper
out.s	number of outcome variables in the study
out.p	number of outcome variables used in the paper

significance of their main findings. Do we observe any distinguishable trend towards the publication of strong results? Provide a substantive discussion.

2. We next examine whether there exists any difference in the publication rate of projects with strong versus weak results as well as with strong versus null results. To do so, first create a variable that takes the value of 1 if a paper was published and 0 if it was not published. Then, perform two-tailed tests of the difference in the publication rates for the aforementioned comparisons of groups, using 95% as the significance level. Briefly comment on your findings.

3. Using Monte Carlo simulations, derive the distribution of the test statistic under the null hypothesis of no difference for each of the two comparisons you made in the previous question. Do you attain similar p-values (for a two-tailed test) to those obtained in the previous question?

4. Conduct the following power analysis for a one-sided hypothesis test where the null hypothesis is that there is no difference in the publication rate between the studies with strong results and those with weak results. The alternative hypothesis is that the studies with strong results are less likely to be published than those with weak results. Use 95% as the significance level and assume that the publication rate for the studies with weak results is the same as the observed publication rate for those studies in the data. How many studies do we need in order to detect a 5 percentage point difference in the publication rate and for the test to attain

a power of 95%? For the number of observations in the data, what is the power of the test of differences in the publication rates?

5. The H-index is a measure of the productivity and citation impact of each researcher in terms of publications. More capable researchers may produce stronger results. To shed more light on this issue, conduct a one-sided test for the null hypothesis that the mean H-index is lower or equal for projects with strong results than those with null results. What about the comparison between strong versus weak results? Do your findings threaten those presented for question 2? Briefly explain.

6. Next, we examine the possibility of file drawer bias. To do so, we will use two scatter plots, one that plots the total number of conditions in a study (horizontal axis) against the total number of conditions included in the paper (vertical axis). Make the size of each dot proportional to the number of corresponding studies, via the `cex` argument. The second scatter plot will focus on the number of outcomes in the study (horizontal axis) and the number of outcomes presented in the published paper (vertical axis). As in the previous plot, make sure each circle is weighted by the number of cases in each category. Based on these plots, do you observe problems in terms of underreporting?

7. Create a variable that represents the total number of possible hypotheses to be tested in a paper by multiplying the total number of conditions and outcomes presented in the questionnaires. Suppose that these conditions yield no difference in the outcome. What is the average (per paper) probability that at the 95% significance level we reject at least one null hypothesis? What about the average (per paper) probability that we reject at least two or three null hypotheses? Briefly comment on the results.

7.5.3 THE 1932 GERMAN ELECTION IN THE WEIMAR REPUBLIC

Who voted for the Nazis? Researchers attempted to answer this question by analyzing aggregate election data from the 1932 German election during the Weimar Republic.[6] We analyze a simplified version of the election outcome data, which records, for each precinct, the number of eligible voters as well as the number of votes for the Nazi party. In addition, the data set contains the aggregate occupation statistics for each precinct. Table 7.7 presents the variable names and descriptions of the CSV data file `nazis.csv`. Each observation represents a German precinct.

The goal of the analysis is to investigate which types of voters (based on their occupation category) cast ballots for the Nazi party in 1932. One hypothesis says that the Nazis received much support from blue-collar workers. Since the data do not directly tell us how many blue-collar workers voted for the Nazis, we must infer this

---

[6] This exercise is based on the following article: G. King, O. Rosen, M. Tanner, A.F. Wagner (2008) "Ordinary economic voting behavior in the extraordinary election of Adolf Hitler." *Journal of Economic History*, vol. 68, pp. 951–996.

Table 7.7. 1932 German Election Data.

Variable	Description
shareself	proportion of self-employed potential voters
shareblue	proportion of blue-collar potential voters
sharewhite	proportion of white-collar potential voters
sharedomestic	proportion of domestically employed potential voters
shareunemployed	proportion of unemployed potential voters
nvoter	number of eligible voters
nazivote	number of votes for Nazis

information using a statistical analysis with certain assumptions. Such an analysis, where researchers try to infer individual behaviors from aggregate data, is called *ecological inference*.

To think about ecological inference more carefully in this context, consider the following simplified table for each precinct i.

	Occupation		
	Blue-collar	Non-blue-collar	
Vote choice			
Nazis	W_{i1}	W_{i2}	Y_i
Other parties or abstention	$1 - W_{i1}$	$1 - W_{i2}$	$1 - Y_i$
	X_i	$1 - X_i$	

The data at hand tells us only the proportion of blue-collar voters X_i and the vote share for the Nazis Y_i in each precinct, but we would like to know the Nazi vote share among the blue-collar voters W_{i1} and among the non-blue-collar voters W_{i2}. Then, there is a deterministic relationship between X, Y, and $\{W_1, W_2\}$. Indeed, for each precinct i, we can express the overall Nazi vote share as the weighted average of the Nazi vote share of each occupation:

$$Y_i = X_i W_{i1} + (1 - X_i) W_{i2}. \tag{7.35}$$

1. We exploit the linear relationship between the Nazi vote share Y_i and the proportion of blue-collar voters X_i given in equation (7.35) by regressing the former on the latter. That is, fit the following linear regression model:

$$\mathbb{E}(Y_i \mid X_i) = \alpha + \beta X_i. \tag{7.36}$$

Compute the estimated slope coefficient, its standard error, and the 95% confidence interval. Give a substantive interpretation of each quantity.

2. Based on the fitted regression model from the previous question, predict the average Nazi vote share Y_i given various proportions of blue-collar voters X_i. Specifically, plot the predicted value of Y_i (the vertical axis) against various values

of X_i within its observed range (the horizontal axis) as a solid line. Add 95% confidence intervals as dashed lines. Give a substantive interpretation of the plot.

3. Fit the following alternative linear regression model:

$$\mathbb{E}(Y_i \mid X_i) = \alpha^* X_i + (1 - X_i)\beta^*. \tag{7.37}$$

Note that this model does not have an intercept. How should one interpret α^* and β^*? How are these parameters related to the linear regression model given in equation (7.36)?

4. Fit a linear regression model where the overall Nazi vote share is regressed on the proportion of each occupation. The model should contain no intercept and 5 predictors, each representing the proportion of a certain occupation type. Interpret the estimate of each coefficient and its 95% confidence interval. What assumption is necessary to permit your interpretation?

5. Finally, we consider a model-free approach to ecological inference. That is, we ask how much we can learn from the data alone without making an additional modeling assumption. Given the relationship in equation (7.35), for each precinct, obtain the smallest value that is logically possible for W_{i1} by considering the scenario in which all non-blue-collar voters in precinct i vote for the Nazis. Express this value as a function of X_i and Y_i. Similarly, what is the largest possible value for W_{i1}? Calculate these bounds, keeping in mind that the value for W_{i1} cannot be negative or greater than 1. Finally, compute the bounds for the nationwide proportion of blue-collar voters who voted for the Nazis (i.e., combining the blue-collar voters from all precincts by computing their weighted average based on the number of blue-collar voters). Give a brief substantive interpretation of the results.

## Chapter 8

Next

Statistics are no substitute for judgment.
— Henry Clay

What comes next? There are several directions one could take in order to further improve data analysis skills. The current book is a first course in applied data analysis and introduces only a tiny fraction of useful data analytic methods. There is much more to learn. An obvious next step is to learn more about data analysis and statistics. For example, one might enroll in a second course in data analysis and statistics (or read a relevant textbook) that covers regression modeling techniques, which are essential tools for quantitative social science. Another possibility is to take a course on specific topics of interest, such as causal inference, social network analysis, and survey methodology.

As an introduction to quantitative social science, this book does not take a mathematical approach to data analysis. Instead, the focus of the book is to give readers a sense of how data analysis is used in quantitative social science research, while teaching elementary concepts and methods. But since all of data analysis and statistical methods have a mathematical foundation, a deeper understanding of them requires a good command of mathematics. A better grasp of methods will, in turn, enable one to become a more sophisticated user of data analysis and statistics who can critically assess the advantages and limitations of various methodologies in applied research. Furthermore, if one is interested in becoming a methodologist who develops new methods, a solid foundation in mathematics is critical. In particular, it is essential to learn multivariate calculus and linear algebra, followed by probability theory. After these foundations, students can learn statistical theory and various modeling strategies in a rigorous fashion.

Since the main focus of this book is data analysis, we did not discuss how to collect data—yet without data collection, there would be no data analysis. Although we analyzed the data from several randomized controlled trials in this book, little attention was given to experimental designs. How should we recruit subjects when conducting an experiment? What are the experimental design strategies one could use in order to obtain precise estimates of causal effects? These and other questions arise when designing experiments in the laboratory and field. A pioneer statistician,

Ronald A. Fisher, once stated, "To call in the statistician after the experiment is done may be no more than asking him to perform a postmortem examination: he may be able to say what the experiment died of."[1] We must learn how to design randomized experiments in order to take advantage of this powerful tool for causal inference. Even for observational studies, careful planning is required in order to identify the instances in which researchers can draw causal inference in a credible manner. Research design forms a fundamental component of quantitative social science research.

Similarly, while we analyze survey data in this book, we do not examine survey sampling strategy and questionnaire design. In many cases, the simple random sampling we discussed is not feasible, because we do not have a sampling frame that contains a complete list of all individuals of a target population. For example, when studying a population that is difficult to reach (e.g., homeless people, seasonal migrants), other strategies, such as respondent-driven sampling, have been used. Another important question is how to correct for the lack of representativeness in survey data. In particular, Internet surveys are now commonly used, but an online panel is often far from being representative of a target population. Questionnaire design also plays an essential role in obtaining accurate measurements. In chapter 3, we saw examples of a special technique for eliciting truthful answers to sensitive questions. The exercise in section 3.9.2 introduced a survey methodology that reduces measurement error due to the possibility that respondents may interpret the same questions differently. These examples suggest that studying a variety of data collection strategies is as important for quantitative social scientists as learning about data analysis.

While different interests may take people in various directions after completing this book, everyone should continue to practice data analysis. In the words of John W. Tukey,[2] "If data analysis is to be helpful and useful, it must be practiced." Now that users of this book have learned the basic methodology and programming necessary for data analysis, they should begin to conduct quantitative social science research by analyzing data sets of their choice. Just as with data analysis, one learns how to conduct research only by doing, not by reading the research of other people. With the massive amount of data available online, anyone from undergraduate to graduate students and from practitioners to academic researchers should be able to start making their own data-driven discoveries.

This book highlights the power of data analysis. However, it is also important to be aware of its fundamental limitations when analyzing data. In particular, data analysis is far from objective. Good data analysis must be accompanied by sound judgment, which is in turn built upon one's knowledge and experience. Without substantive theories, data analysis can easily be misguided. In quantitative social science research, we analyze data for the purpose of better understanding society and human behavior. This goal is unattainable unless we use social science theories to determine how data should be analyzed. Stronger theoretical guidance is required for the analysis of "big data" because without it we will not know where to look for interesting patterns.

---

[1] Ronald A. Fisher (1938) "Presidential address: The first session of the Indian Statistical Conference, Calcutta, 1938." *Sankhyā*, vol. 4, pp. 14–17.

[2] John W. Tukey (1962) "The future of data analysis." *Annals of Mathematical Statistics*, vol. 33, no. 1, pp. 1–67.

Although a solid grasp of the mathematics that underlie statistical theories and methods is important, we should not underestimate the value of contextual knowledge about the data sets to be analyzed. For example, to competently design and analyze the survey of Afghan civilians introduced in chapter 3, researchers had to understand the cultural, political, and economic environment of local communities in Afghanistan where the respondents live. Interviewing individuals who have little education, during a civil war, is a challenging task. The researchers worked with a local survey firm in order to gain access to rural villages through negotiation with local leaders and militants. For cultural reasons, they were unable to interview female respondents, and interviews had to take place in a public sphere where village elders were able to listen to survey questions and answers. Randomized response methodology is a classic survey method for asking sensitive questions while protecting the secrecy of individual responses. However, this method was seen as inappropriate in the study because the required randomization using coins or dice was considered to be against Islamic law. Other challenges in this study included how to ask respondents' tribal affiliation, how to measure the level of wealth when the economy is largely informal, and what policy questions to ask when measuring respondents' political ideology.

These examples illustrate the importance of contextual knowledge in designing and implementing quantitative social science research. Therefore, data analysts should learn about the relevant substance and background of their study, either on their own or by partnering with experts, well before starting to analyze data. They should also be aware of the danger that mechanical applications of statistical methods to data may lead to unreliable empirical findings. Indeed, this is the reason why applied statistics has developed separately in a variety of fields of the natural and social sciences. While statistical methods rest on universal mathematical theory and are widely applicable, their application requires specific substantive knowledge. The goal of this book has been to illustrate this unique feature of data analysis and statistics by showing how general methods can be used to answer interesting social science questions.

With rapid advancements in technology and data availability, the world needs those who can creatively combine substantive knowledge with data analysis skills in all fields, from academia to journalism. This book opens the door to this exciting world of data analysis.

General Index

R Index